THE SOCIOLOGY OF SOUTHEAST ASIA

THE SOCIOLOGY OF SOUTHEAST ASIA

Transformations in a Developing Region

Victor T. King

University of Hawai'i Press
Honolulu

Published in North America by
University of Hawai'i Press
2840 Kolowalu Street
Honolulu, Hawai'i 96822

First published in Europe by
NIAS Press
Leifsgade 33
2300 Copenhagen S, DENMARK

Printed in the USA

Library of Congress Cataloging-in-Publication Data
King, Victor T.
   The sociology of southeast Asia : transformations in a developing
region / Victor T. King.
        p. cm.
   Includes bibliographical references and index.
   ISBN 978-0-8248-3228-5 (hardcover : alk. paper)—
   ISBN 978-0-8248-3229-2 (pbk. : alk. paper)
   1. Sociology—Southeast Asia. 2. Social problems—Southeast
Asia. 3. Southeast Asia—Social conditions. I. Title.
   HM477.S643K56 2007
   301.0959'091724—dc22
                        2007022074

Contents

Preface: Setting the Scene   *vii*

Acknowledgements   *xv*

1. Introduction: The Sociology of a Diverse Region   1

2. The Sociological Context   20

3. Modernization and Post-War Social Change   37

4. Underdevelopment and Dependency   56

5. Social Class, the State and Political Economy   91

6. Ethnicity and Society   129

7. Patronage and Corruption   155

8. Asian Values and Social Action   178

9. Transformations in the World of Work: Gender Issues   197

10. Transformations in Urban Worlds   225

11. Conclusions: Modernity, Globalization and the Future   246

Images of Southeast Asia   *257*

References   *270*

Index   *317*

Map

Southeast Asia   xvi–xvii

Illustrations

Novice cameraman near Yangon, Myanmar   256

Wat Thaalaat, Yasothon Province, northeast Thailand   257

Transplanting rice, Yasothon Province, northeast Thailand   257

Reflections: Buddhist monks in Siem Reap, Cambodia   258

Reflections: cyclists in Kunming, China   258

Mosque and boat, Padang, Sumatra, Indonesia   259

Carrying offerings, Bali, Indonesia   260

Offering devotions, Bali, Indonesia   260

Akha girls, Chiang Rai, northern Thailand   261

Boat women, Hoi-An, Vietnam   261

Klong slum, Bangkok   262

Democracy monument, Bangkok   262

Singapore skyline   263

Boat people, Hue   263

Tanjung Pagar shophouses, Singapore   264

HDB housing, Singapore   264

Chinatown, Bangkok   265

Chinatown, Singapore   265

Slum housing in Smokey Mountain, Manila   266

Round the bend: street vendor in Hanoi   266

Air pollution, Hanoi   267

Stevedore, Padang, Sumatra, Indonesia   267

Hanoi street vendors   267

Water collectors, Makassar, Sulawesi, Indonesia   268

Child ice cream vendor, Bac Ha market, northern Vietnam   268

Globalization, Indonesia   269

Cool dude, Phnom Penh   269

Taxi rank, Bangkok   269

Table

Southeast Asia: key statistics   xviii

Preface: Setting the Scene

Rather than provide an impersonal introduction I thought it more appropriate to preface the volume with an indication of how and why I came to write this book. A major problem faced by teachers and students with a scholarly interest in Southeast Asia is the lack of user-friendly social science texts. The absence of an introduction to the sociology of Southeast Asia is unfortunate, although my colleagues in politics, economics, history, geography and anthropology fare rather better in the provision of introductory volumes. For over thirty years I have taught courses in Southeast Asian sociology at the University of Hull, and now at Leeds, and I have been acutely conscious of the lack of sociological introductions combining an interest in conceptual issues with the comparative analysis of social life and its transformation.

A general sociology of Southeast Asia is long overdue, and, following the completion of other projects, I decided that I should attempt to provide one. I regret that I have not found the time to produce such a book sooner. Yet I am much comforted when reading Wim Wertheim's 'foreword' to his compilation *East–West Parallels* that 'to find time to write a book is difficult enough for a university professor, who has the privilege of being responsible for guiding the studies of quite a number of students'(1964a: v). Perhaps I cannot use this as an excuse for my tardiness, but had an integrated sociological text on Southeast Asia been available it would have made the academic life of my students much easier, given that we have had to canvas diverse social-science and historical materials, both theoretical and empirical, to help us understand the processes and consequences of social transformation in this complex and diverse region.

vii

Nevertheless, I must emphasize, perhaps unsurprisingly, that had I written this book in the 1970s it would have been very different. What must strike any interested observer of Southeast Asia over the last thirty years are the rapid pace, depth and breadth of change. In comparison with the late 1960s, when I first encountered Southeast Asia as a student, the region in the early years of the new millennium is a very different place. Thirty years ago its economies were still predominantly rural-based with an overdependence on the production or extraction and export of primary products. The manufacturing base and urban population were modest in size; infrastructure, welfare and educational facilities in many parts of the region were rather rudimentary. These characteristics were to a significant extent the legacy of the colonial period and the uneven development which it occasioned. But, although Western colonialism opened the region to a capitalist world and transformed what some social scientists refer to as 'traditional' societies, it was only after 1945 that the pace of modernization quickened. Moreover, during the period of decolonization Southeast Asia saw serious military conflicts and widespread political instability as these newly-independent countries struggled to forge a national identity from ethnically and culturally diverse constituencies and address problems of economic underdevelopment. Rural insurrection, often closely linked with communist political organizations or ethnic-based separatist movements, continued to preoccupy several of the governments of the region.

Southeast Asia was also the focus of superpower engagement following decolonization and the vacuum which this left, particularly in the Indochinese countries of Laos, Cambodia and Vietnam. The preoccupations of academic books published in the late 1960s and 1970s express those years of turmoil, uncertainty and instability: 'region of revolt', 'dimensions of conflict', 'war and revolution', 'preludes to tragedy', 'the search for survival'. In the economic sphere the prognosis for the region was equally pessimistic: 'modernization without development', 'the development of underdevelopment', and 'poverty and inequality' were the main themes of the day. Even in the second half of the 1970s and the 1980s the communist victories in Indochina paved the way for further conflict, tragedy and bloodshed – the Cambodian 'killing fields' and the merciless regime of Pol Pot, the exodus of the Vietnamese 'boat-people', the Sino–Vietnamese conflict, the invasion and occupation of Cambodia by Vietnamese forces, and the continuing military struggles and civil war between the Vietnamese-backed government and the ousted Khmer Rouge.

Nevertheless, despite these continuing political problems, from the mid-1970s we began to witness a period of sustained economic growth in those countries comprising the Association of Southeast Asian Nations (ASEAN) and – notwithstanding the Asian economic crisis of 1997–98 and its aftermath, which in turn severely dented the progress of such countries as Thailand, Indonesia and Malaysia – standards of living are significantly higher now than they were in the 1960s. Economies are more broad-based, and industrialization and urbanization have continued apace. More recently social-science students have turned their attention to the effects of globalization, including, in popular discourse, 'McDonaldization' and 'Disneyization'; the emergence of a consumerist-, status- and education-oriented middle class and the lifestyles of the 'new rich' are now on research agendas; images of post-modern shopping malls and young Asians with mobile phones and luxury cars abound. Several Southeast Asian countries have enjoyed a measure of political stability and the emergence of a civil society. ASEAN has not only survived but indeed expanded its membership, created a 'political region', and entered into dialogue with global political and economic players. Expressions of modernity and post-modernity are seen everywhere, none more so than in the high-rise, efficient and ultra-clean 'world city' of Singapore.

This is not to say that all the problems of the past have disappeared or that 'traditional' Southeast Asia is no more. There are still considerable social and economic inequalities, indeed a widening gap between rich and poor, economic dependency, inter-ethnic tensions, widespread corruption and political repression. Witness the continuing excesses of the military regime in Myanmar with large numbers of refugees from ethnic minorities forced to reside in neighbouring countries and hundreds of thousands of displaced persons in the minority upland areas; the inter-ethnic conflicts and lawlessness in Indonesia after the economic crash of 1997–98, the chaotic collapse of Suharto's New Order, and the Bali bombings of 2002 and 2005; recent violence and kidnappings in southern Thailand in the context of Muslim secessionist activities and inter-ethnic strife with an estimated 1,000 people killed in the hostilities since 2003; and the widespread armed insurgency problems in the Philippines, and the bombings and kidnappings perpetrated by secessionists in Mindanao during the past three decades. Although a cease-fire was negotiated in the southern Philippines, further hostilities were reported in October 2006 between government troops and the Moro Islamic Liberation Front.

In spite of a more general sense of social and economic well-being and a degree of political maturation in the region, there has been a recent resurgence of academic interest in 'violence', and in paramilitary organizations, civilian militias, vigilantes, special forces and criminal networks. These have specifically focused on post-1998 Indonesia, but also during the past five years in the 'Thai South' (Anderson, 2001; Bouvier, de Jonge and Smith, 2006; Davidson, 2003; McCargo, 2006a, 2006b; Schiller and Bambang Garang, 2002; Wilson, 2006). The violence perpetrated by the state and by superpower involvement in the region has been replaced increasingly by a decentralized violence and local ethnic and religious conflict (Chou and Houben, 2006: 17; Fox, 2006: 993–1052). For those who assumed a relatively smooth passage to democracy and the flourishing of civil society in the fast modernizing societies of Southeast Asia, the recent military intervention in Thailand, the continued dominance of the generals in Myanmar, authoritarianism in Singapore and Malaysia, and one-party rule in Laos and Vietnam suggest that nothing is straightforward in our attempts to understand and predict the trajectories of change.

Indeed, within the space of a decade between the publication of the first and third editions of *The Political Economy of South-East Asia* (1997 and 2006a), Rodan, Hewison and Robison have remarked, in their recent preface, on '[h]ow rapidly things changed' (2006b: ix). Some of their vocabulary recalls the turbulence of the 1950s, '60s and '70s – 'turmoil', 'conflict', 'crisis', 'bankruptcy', 'disarray', 'siege', 'volatility' and 'contestation'. At the heart of their interest is 'the continuing conflict over the complexion of economic and political regimes', and the 'forces' and 'interests' which drive this conflict (ibid.: x). In addition, rapid industrialization and urbanization are having serious impacts on the environment, and on cultural values, family life and gender relations. Whilst celebrating the successes of modernity and the benefits of technology, political leaders in the region issue dire warnings of the pernicious effects of globalization on local communities, and call for a strengthening of Asian values against what is called 'westoxification'.

Therefore, these relatively recent transformations require us to reassess the ways in which we study and understand the region, as well as sociology's contribution to that understanding. The present text, in addition to examining key contributions to the post-war sociological literature on Southeast Asia, considers recent studies of the processes and character of modernization and globalization and local responses to these wider forces of change. Of course, I recognize that a general book of this kind might be organized in a variety of ways and address different ranges of topics. My choice of structure and content is guided by my own research interests. It is, for example, somewhat different from the more popular recent text on 'modernization trends' in Southeast Asia by Terence Chong, who examines concepts of modernization and modernity, education, citizenship and ethnicity, religion, the middle class, and mass consumption (2005). However, there is a good deal of overlap between his interests and mine, and there would certainly be a broad measure of agreement among scholars of the region about those issues which should be given priority. My approach is also very explicitly historical and draws inspiration from the Dutch historical-sociological school of Wertheim. It is much less 'culturalist' and post-modern in orientation.

Contents

In the introductory chapter I consider the problems of defining the sociology of Southeast Asia, what I understand as sociological enquiry and how I define the region within which the enquiry will take place. This enables me to provide a brief introduction to the countries of Southeast Asia, focusing on those features of sociological interest. I then contextualize Southeast Asian sociology in Chapter 2 by considering the reasons for the rather slow pace and patchiness of sociological research up to the 1990s. This requires me to consider the contribution of American social science to post-war research in Chapter 3 and the dominance of modernization perspectives. The critical reaction to these perspectives in neo-Marxist underdevelopment/dependency theories is examined in Chapter 4. In both chapters the theories are illustrated with case studies and, in Chapter 4, more detailed consideration is given to historical materials. I then take our story forward from the 1980s to the present and in Chapter 5 consider political economy perspectives and the relationships between state, society and social class. I demonstrate how political economists and development sociologists attempted to address the problems left unresolved by the two dominant paradigms of modernization and underdevelopment/dependency.

From general theories and perspectives we move to substantive issues in Chapters 6–11: first, the significant organizational principle of ethnicity, given Southeast Asia's pluralism, and its interaction with class; second, patron–client relations and their relationship to political and bureaucratic corruption – an issue of crucial importance debated in the context of the recent Asian economic crisis; third, cultural, and particularly religious values, with reference to the high-profile debates surrounding the locally generated concept of 'Asian values' and Samuel Huntington's 'clash of civilizations' thesis; fourth, the increasing importance of women's roles in processes of development in Southeast Asia and their contribution to the commercialization of agriculture and small-scale production; fifth, I examine some of the transformations in urban communities and the connections between town and countryside, given that one of the major changes in Southeast Asia has been the decline in the importance of agriculture and rural industries and the movement of people into urban areas. Finally, in Chapter 11, I consider briefly some recent studies of globalization, cultural change and the politics of identity and give some thought to the likely directions of sociological research in Southeast Asia in the next decade.

I have dispensed with a conventional review of the sociological literature. The contributions which I consider especially important are referred to in the relevant chapters. My Chapter 2 is a kind of review, but for those who want a fuller summary of what had been achieved up to the mid-1990s, then it might be useful consulting my chapter on 'Sociology' in the edited book by Mohamed Halib and Tim Huxley (1996: 148–188; see also King, 1981). To get a flavour of what kinds of sociology were being produced within the region it is worthwhile glancing through *Explorations in Asian Sociology* (1991), edited by Chan Kwok Bun and Ho Kong Chong. As a guide to, and as the 100th issue of, the *Working Papers Series* of the Department of Sociology at the National University of Singapore, it provides an insight into what had excited the attention of locally-based scholars in the sociological study of Southeast Asia. Issues of social class, urbanization, ethnic relations and the family, guided by the preoccupations of Singapore since its independence, absorbed much of the sociological energy in the early years (see also Khondker, 2000). Other very worthy compilations, though now rather dated, have also emerged from the Department and provide important general reference material, among them Peter Chen's and Hans-Dieter Evers's *Studies in ASEAN Sociology* (1978b), Evers's *Sociology of South-East Asia* (1980b), and, though devoted to Singapore, Ong Jin Hui's, Tong Chee Kiong's and Tan Ern Ser's *Understanding Singapore Society* (1997a, 1997b).

In a general book one cannot cover every topic. Just when I thought that I concluded a chapter or brought a particular debate to a reasonably satisfactory conclusion, I then chanced on another publication which served to send my argument and narrative into disarray. Whenever one dares to write a general book on the region, there will always be committed Indonesianists, Thaiologists, Malaysian experts, Singapore specialists, Burma hands and scholars of Philippine studies who will say that I have got it wrong for a particular country, or that I do not address country-based issues in sufficient detail. Those interested in other parts of Southeast Asia will lament that I have not devoted sufficient attention to Vietnam, Cambodia, Laos and Brunei. Weberians, Marxist sociologists, political economists, globalization theorists, and post-modernists will demand that I become more proficient in their particular theoretical perspective. Sociologists of religion, the family, youth, deviance, language, literature and the arts, and migration will despair that I have not focused on these areas of social life to any extent. I have also not said much about rural societies because I think that I have probably said enough in two previous books (King, 1999; and King and Wilder, 2003), and I confess that I cannot do better than Jonathan Rigg's *More than the Soil. Rural Change in Southeast Asia* (2001). Perhaps there is nothing more to say about the 'moral economy of the peasant', 'weapons of the weak' and 'everyday forms of peasant resistance', although I refer briefly to these debates in Chapters 5 and 10 (Scott, 1976, 1985; Popkin, 1979; Evans, 1986). Debates about peasantries and their responses to change were all the rage in the 1960s, '70s and '80s, but the dramatic social and economic transformations in Southeast Asia since then have tended to remove them, at least to some extent, from the sociological consciousness (Rigg, 2001: 62–82). For my obvious failure to address a wide range of sociological issues, I plead guilty. This book is a start; it attempts to say something more generally about social change in Southeast Asia. Others can build on it or discard it.

What I have done is to consider some of the most important principles of social organization which students should address in understanding the structures and transformations of Southeast Asian societies. I have expended much energy in exploring Southeast Asian history from a sociological perspective, and examined some theoretical work in the sociology of development and political economy. This has required me to return to some classic texts, which to others may now seem dated. It will take another substantial volume to examine all the issues raised in this book in any acceptably sufficient detail and to address those matters that have not excited my immediate attention. In having read and assigned an enormous amount of material to my 'pending' tray, there is already sufficient material for a second volume. Indeed, I am conscious of a substantial body of materials in the sociology of knowledge and in the fields of literature, the arts, culture and identity, frequently, but not exclusively within post-colonial debates, which would merit separate treatment in a companion volume to this one. At least my first foray into the subject, which I had wished someone better qualified than me would have attempted before now, gives students, who are starting on the great road of discovery on which I embarked over thirty years ago, a relatively coherent treatment of some of the major issues in Southeast Asian sociology. I have tried, in modest fashion, to follow James Scott's advice to the Malaysian Social Science Association, when he warned against 'narrow scholasticism'. I have therefore spent the past two years, in relatively irregular engagement with a vast array of materials, writing a book 'for an audience larger than a handful of specialists' (Scott, 2001: 101).

Style

As in my other general books on Southeast Asia, I have tried to concentrate on the fluency of the narrative. Therefore, I have dispensed, once again, with footnotes or endnotes. In not using them, of course, one tends to sacrifice the nuances of academic debate, the qualification of a bold statement and the presentation of the alternative view, an additional teasing or fascinating piece of information, and the density of evidence required to support the analysis. I do not expect the academic world to do without these devices, but I am continuing steadfastly to resist the temptation to pepper my text with notes.

Acknowledgements

This book could not have been written without the inspiration of my undergraduate and postgraduate students at the University of Hull over the past thirty years in our encounters in lectures, seminars and supervision sessions, and now at the University of Leeds. It has been my privilege, and an enormous personal and scholarly benefit to advise research students on a range of social-science and humanities subjects in Malaysia, Singapore, Brunei, Indonesia, the Philippines, Thailand, Vietnam and Laos. I have used some of those insights in this book, and I trust that those with whom I have worked also gained something from the experience. In addition, there have been important influences on what I have taught and written from senior scholars of Southeast Asia; three individuals whose work has been of value in my teaching and research deserve special mention – Professors Wim Wertheim, Hans-Dieter Evers and Richard Robison. My sincere thanks to them for making the study of social change in Southeast Asia rather more stimulating and lively than it otherwise would have been. There are many others from whose work I have benefited, but it is the scope of their contribution and the comparative range of my chosen three which I wish to acknowledge. I also pay tribute to my supervisor during my student days, the late Professor Mervyn Jaspan, who introduced me to the emerging literature in Indonesian sociology and convinced me of the importance of combining sociological analysis with anthropological and historical insight. He advised early on in my career that I read Thomas Stamford Raffles's *History of Java* (1965 [1817]), Wertheim's *Indonesian Society in Transition* (1959), Leslie Palmier's *Social Status and Power in Java* (1960), and Clifford Geertz's *Agricultural Involution* (1963a), *Peddlers and Princes*

Acknowledgements

(1963b) and *The Social History of an Indonesian Town* (1965), in quick succession – an interesting juxtaposition for a young student.

I also recognize the contribution, perhaps unwittingly, which my colleagues in the Centre for South-East Asian Studies at Hull have made to this book. Working in a multidisciplinary programme enables you to see problems and issues from others' perspectives, though I have also journeyed through several disciplines myself. I started my university career as a geographer, moved into sociology in the late 1960s and early 1970s, and then embraced anthropology and rural development studies. I have also flirted with environmental and tourism issues. In this cross-disciplinary connection I should draw attention again to the Hull University-Universiti Malaya text edited by Mohamed Halib and Tim Huxley (1996b), which was designed to take stock of the achievements of the main social science and humanities disciplines in their attempts to understand the complexities of Southeast Asia. My present book draws on material from my earlier overview of sociological literature contained in that book, though it has been heavily revised and updated. In my introductory discussion of Southeast Asian sociology I have adapted material from Chapter 1 of my and William Wilder's *The Modern Anthropology of South-East Asia* (2003: 1–24), where it has particular relevance to sociological issues. In my chapters on ethnicity, gender and urbanization I also make reference to some observations in my *Anthropology and Development in South-East Asia* (1999). I must also offer my heartfelt thanks to my colleague, Dr Michael Parnwell, for permission to use some of his excellent photographs as illustrative material, and to Dr AVM Horton for yet another carefully compiled index.

Very finally, I acknowledge the insightful and encouraging observations of the two reviewers of the book manuscript. I have endeavoured to address some of their remarks, but, given the already substantial length of the volume, it has proved impossible to include everything which they would have wished to see. The need for a companion volume now seems pressing.

VTK
Leeds University
June 2007

© NIAS Press 2007

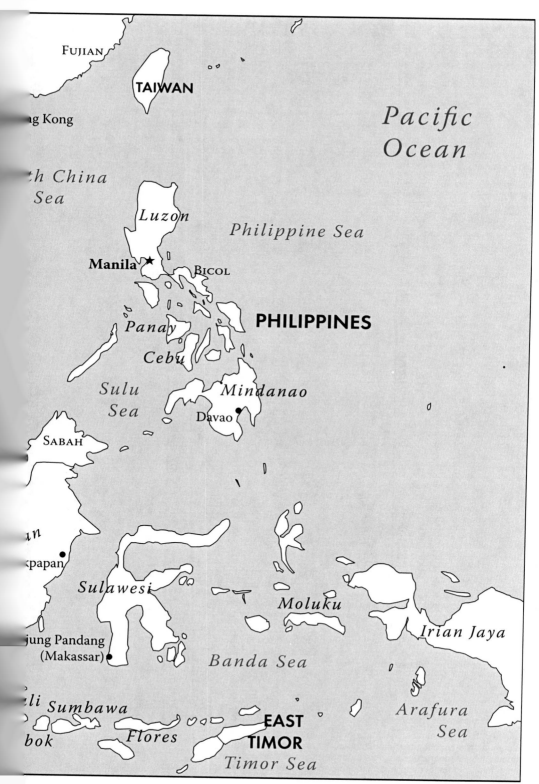

FUJIAN

TAIWAN

g Kong

Pacific
Ocean

th China
Sea

Luzon

Philippine Sea

Manila ★

Bɪᴄᴏʟ

PHILIPPINES

*Pana*y

Cebu

*Sulu
Sea*

Mindanao

Davao

Sᴀʙᴀʜ

n

kpapan

Sulawesi

Moluku

Irian Jaya

jung Pandang
(Makassar)

Banda Sea

li *Sumbawa*

**EAST
TIMOR**

*Arafura
Sea*

bok *Flores*

Timor Sea

Southeast Asia

Southeast Asia: key statistics

	Population 2005		% Urban	% Urban Pop., 2030	GNI US$, 2004		Life expect. years, 2004	Literacy rate %, 2004
	Millions	Density km²	% Urban		Total bn	Per capita		
Brunei	0.374	65	77.6	87.0	NA	NA	76.8	92.7
Cambodia	14.071	78	19.7	36.9	4.8	350	56.6	73.6
Indonesia	222.781	117	47.9	62.7	246.3	1,130	67.4	90.4
Laos	5.924	25	21.6	38.2	2.3	400	55.3	68.7
Malaysia	25.347	83	65.1	77.6	112.6	4,520	73.5	88.7
Myanmar	50.519	75	30.6	49.1	NA	NA	60.8	89.9
Philippines	83.054	277	62.6	76.1	98.3	1,200	70.8	92.6
Singapore	4.326	6,333	100.0	100.0	104.9	24,740	79.3	92.5
Thailand	64.233	125	32.5	47.0	158.4	2,490	70.5	92.6
Timor Leste	1	64	7.8	15.2	0.5	540	NA	NA
Vietnam	84.238	254	26.7	43.2	44.6	540	70.3	90.3

Sources: Population figures, UNDESA, 2003 revision; other data, The World Bank, 2006.

1

Introduction: The Sociology of a Diverse Region

> *We need to probe the past, noting what has been forgotten, what remains unaltered, and what has been transformed, striving to understand the discontinuities and new events, to understand how the different peoples of the region – now increasingly called "Southeast Asians" – have managed to sustain their unique values, traditions, customs, and priorities while adapting to new realities, ideas, institutions and lifestyles (Owen et al.: 2005: 14–15).*

> *[W]e may need to think in terms of not one but many Southeast Asias. On some planes of investigation the region may have one set of dimensions, for others a very different shape (McVey, 2005: 315).*

The Academic Discipline

An introductory sociology of Southeast Asia poses a problem which is by no means peculiar to the theories and practices of this discipline in relation to one particular part of Asia. My difficulty lies in distinguishing sociology from cognate disciplines and fields of study. This is unsurprising in a discipline concerned with the description and analysis of social organization, relations and processes – a field of study to which others have contributed. Therefore, I move freely between the ideas and materials of anthropologists, historians and political economists, and I present approximate discriminations between sociology and related subject areas in examining modern Southeast Asian societies and their recent transformations. I offer a 'sociological perspective' which addresses the social dimensions of such important issues as inequality, urbanization, modernization and globalization, and relationships based on the social organizational principles of ethnicity, gender, class, power, status, and patronage (Evers, 1980a, 1980b). I also examine the global processes acting on the region and the ways in which Southeast Asians are responding to them (Wertheim, 1964a, 1973a, 1974, 1993). This exercise requires attention to the colonial and post-colonial history of the region.

1

The inspiration for the sociological approach to the understanding of the human condition derives principally from three major European social philosophers – Karl Marx, Max Weber and Emile Durkheim. As Hirschman has said they 'addressed big questions such as the development of capitalism, the rise of complex bureaucracies, class conflict, and how a moral order was possible in modern urban societies' (2001: 115). They used comparative and historical methods, examining a range of societies rather than focusing narrowly on one country, culture or case (ibid.: 115–116).

In the post-war period a sociologist who has addressed many of their concerns, theoretically, historically and comparatively in an Asian context, is Wim Wertheim. I refer to his wide-ranging work and that of his colleagues, and his founding of 'non-Western sociology' in later chapters. Wertheim in turn acknowledges his debt to his predecessors, Bertram Schrieke (1955–57) and Jacob van Leur (1955), both of whom analysed and reconstructed Indonesian history using Weberian perspectives and insights (Wertheim, 1993: 2). Several of Wertheim's earlier publications (1959 [1956], 1964a, 1973a, 1974) represent major contributions to the sociological understanding of Asia generally and Southeast Asia specifically. It was a tradition that was carried forward within the region by his distinguished student Syed Hussein Alatas (1972, 1977). In Germany at the University of Bielefeld and through his long periods of teaching and research in the region, particularly in Singapore, Thailand and Indonesia, Hans-Dieter Evers and his colleagues modified, developed and deepened this European tradition and gave it an additional comparative dimension (1973a, 1978a, 1978b, 1978c, 1980a; Mulder, 1983, 1989, 1990).

Overall then, I address the work of sociologists and those in related disciplines who wish to understand the organization and transformation of human societies. Even using this broad sociological perspective the literature on Southeast Asia has been neither substantial nor distinguished when compared with studies of other regions such as South Asia, Africa, Latin America and the Middle East. In 1980 Evers remarked, in his introduction to the then-pioneering book, *Sociology of South-East Asia* (1980b), that, up to that time, 'relatively little progress has been made in furthering the understanding of changing South-East Asian societies' (1980a: ix). The need for a general text on the sociology of the region has not diminished since, although scholarly research on social change and development has increased considerably.

Sociology and Southeast Asia

The problem of defining the sociological enterprise is replicated in delimiting Southeast Asia. Does it make sense to locate and isolate this Asian sub-region for sociological analysis? Several eminent scholars have addressed issues of social organization and change in a Southeast Asian context (Evers, 1980b; Hewison, Robison and Rodan, 1993; Higgott and Robison, 1985b; Robison, Hewison and Higgott, 1987a; Rodan et al., 1997, 2001a, 2006a; Schmidt, Hersh and Fold, 1998a; Taylor and Turton, 1988a), and I could argue that to examine that literature I should adopt the same regional parameters. After all, Southeast Asia has now gained some acceptance as a region in its own right. For the sake of expediency and to keep this introductory volume within manageable proportions I present Southeast Asia as a regional unit distinct from neighbouring regions (Map 1).

Yet readers must be aware of the problematical nature of an area perspective. In both conceptual and empirical terms this premise must be scrutinized critically in the context of a modernizing and globalizing world. For Asia there are increasingly close cultural, economic and political relations between the states of the western Pacific Rim and the strengthening of links to the Indian subcontinent. Indeed, the popular terminology used in the sociological study of change in non-Western regions suggests that we consider Southeast Asia as part of what has been called variously the 'Third World', 'the South', the 'underdeveloped' or 'less developed' regions, or the 'developing world'. In the last decade various Southeast Asian states, including Singapore, Malaysia and Thailand, have joined the ranks of the 'newly industrializing countries'. Moreover as recently as the late 1980s a volume on Southeast Asia appeared in a general series on the sociology of 'developing societies', in the company of such regions as South Asia, the Middle East and Latin America, suggesting that, although it was a separate entity, it shared social, economic and political characteristics with these regions, distinguishing them from the industrialized or developed world (Taylor and Turton, 1988a).

Let me consider the reasons which have been presented, on the one hand, for denying Southeast Asia an identity and, on the other, for endowing it a regional status equivalent to the neighbouring continental land-masses of China (and the wider East Asia) and India (and the South Asian sub-continent) (King, 2001; King and Wilder, 2003: 1–24).

Southeast Asia as a Region? Arguments For and Against

Since the end of the Second World War Southeast Asia's regional status has been accepted despite continued debate about the bases of its delimitation. It is generally agreed that the constituent countries of the region comprise: the mainland states of Myanmar Naingngan (State of Myanmar, or the Union of Myanmar [Myanma Pye], formerly the [Socialist Republic of the] Union of Burma)(I use the term 'Burma' in much of this book and 'Myanmar' occasionally for the very recent period); the Kingdom of Thailand (Siam); the Lao People's Democratic Republic (formerly the Kingdom of Laos); the Kingdom of Cambodia (formerly the Khmer Republic, then Democratic Kampuchea, then the People's Republic of Kampuchea, then the State of Cambodia); and the Socialist Republic of Vietnam/Viet Nam (formerly Nam Viet and then Annam); and the island or maritime countries of the Federation of Malaysia (formerly British Malaya, then the Federation of Malaya, with Sarawak and Sabah [formerly British North Borneo], along with Penang [Pinang] and Malacca [Melaka]); the Republic of Singapore; Negara Brunei Darussalam (the Sultanate or State of Brunei); the Republic of Indonesia (formerly the Netherlands [East] Indies); and the Republic of the Philippines (Owen et al., 2005: xvii–xxiii).

East Timor (Timor Lorosa'e or Timor Leste) was from 1976 until 1999 incorporated into Indonesia; it is now a separate state in the region. The concept of a unified Southeast Asia, comprising a 'community of nation-states', was given greater salience following the formation of the Association of Southeast Asian Nations (ASEAN) from 1967. This regional grouping comprised initially Thailand, the Philippines, Indonesia, Singapore and Malaysia and was created primarily to promote economic cooperation among its member states, encourage peaceful modes of conflict resolution between neighbours and present a stronger regional presence and voice in the context of Cold War confrontations. Brunei joined in 1984, Vietnam in 1995, Laos and Myanmar in 1997, and, finally Cambodia in 1998. The current ASEAN leaders are firmly convinced that there is strength in numbers and an organization comprising all ten Southeast Asian countries (with the exception for the moment of East Timor) makes sense for a variety of economic, cultural, political and strategic reasons. Yet why has it taken so long for the region to gain this recognition?

Diversity and External Influences: the Lack of Definition

In the introduction to *South-East Asia. An Introductory History*, Osborne discusses the status of the region (2004 [1979]: 1–17), noting that up until the time of the Japanese occupation the term 'Southeast Asia' was rarely used. He says: 'For the most part ... neither the foreigners who worked in Southeast Asia before the Second World War, whether as scholars or otherwise, nor the indigenous inhabitants of the countries of Southeast Asia, thought about the region in general terms' (ibid.: 4). Anderson reinforces this point more strongly by stating that the naming of Southeast Asia – for him 'a meaningful imaginary' – 'came from outside, and even today very few among the almost 500 million souls inhabiting its roughly 1,750,000 square miles of land (to say nothing of water), ever think of themselves as "Southeast Asians"' (1998: 3). Rather the major preoccupation has been its cultural diversity, its political and geographical fragmentation, the extraordinary capacity of its populations to absorb and adapt to a variety of external influences over a long period of time, its location as a marchland and meeting place of different cultures, and the divisions established between colonial territories (Fisher, 1962, 1964). From the early first millennium CE the main external influences had come from India and China; then from the sixteenth century Western Europe, and more recently the United States and Japan. The long-established commercial and cultural contacts with the Middle East also resulted in the spread of Islam through the Indian subcontinent to the Malay-Indonesian islands from the early centuries of the second millennium.

Western Colonial Perceptions

Until the 1940s Western observers usually employed the term 'Further India', or 'Greater India' or the 'East Indies' for those territories to the east of the Bay of Bengal; they were seen as an eastward extension of the Indian cultural area (Osborne,

2004: 4–6; Kratoska et al., 2005a: 2). Others saw the countries of Southeast Asia as the southern margins of China and as the tropical appendage of 'East Asia', or as the 'Far Eastern Tropics'. In earlier texts there is a strong emphasis on the Indian and Chinese character of Southeast Asia. The absorption from India and China, and particularly Hindu-Buddhist India, of religions, modes of statecraft, material culture and literature also resulted in Southeast Asia's designation as 'Indochina'. However, eventually this term came to be applied to the French colonial dependencies of Vietnam, Cambodia and Laos, for in central Vietnam the fault-line between the Indianized state of the Chams in the south and the Sinicized state of the Vietnamese to the north was most clearly delineated. Finally, geographers often preferred the term 'Monsoon Asia' because the monsoonal wind cycle dominates the Southeast Asian region, although it is not exclusive to it and affects parts of the Indian sub-continent and southern China as well.

Therefore, until relatively recently Western observers usually viewed Southeast Asia from the perspective of either India or China or both. Moreover, the involvement of most of the major European mercantile powers (and later the United States) in the region and the subsequent division of territories between the competing imperial powers hindered the study and understanding of Southeast Asia as a whole. Anderson notes that '[o]nly the Belgians and Italians were missing' (1998: 4). British writers focused on their own Southeast Asian dependencies – Burma (Myanmar), Malaya, the Straits Settlements (Singapore, Penang and Malacca) and the Borneo territories (Sarawak, North Borneo and Brunei); they saw these as an eastern adjunct of their Indian Empire. Until 1937 Burma had been incorporated as a province of British India and received substantial migrations of Indian citizens, particularly to the Burmese capital, Rangoon (Yangon), and the Irrawaddy Delta; the Straits Settlements had been administered by the British Indian government until 1867, and these and the Malay States and northern Borneo were also a destination for Indian immigration.

On the other hand, the Dutch focused almost exclusively on the Netherlands East Indies or Indonesia – a vast territory stretching some 2,500 miles along the Equator from Sumatra in the west to western New Guinea (Irian Jaya or West Papua) in the east. Like the British, the Dutch viewed their dependencies from an Indian Ocean perspective. Early on in their mercantile histories both these northern European colonial powers had established East India companies which conducted trade with, and for a time at least, administered Southeast Asia from their Indian bases.

The French governed their colonial empire as a direct extension of France overseas ('la France d'outremer'). Vietnam, Laos and Cambodia were linked ever closer to the metropolitan country in the context of the French policy of assimilation and then association. Again, as with the British- and Dutch-governed territories, Southeast Asian connections with France were primarily westwards across the Indian Ocean. Furthermore, as a consequence of Anglo-French rivalry in mainland Southeast Asia in the nineteenth century and the successful diplomatic manoeuvres of two astute and outward-looking Siamese kings, Mongkut and Chulalongkorn, the Kingdom of Siam was left as a politically independent buffer zone between British India and Burma to the west and French Indochina to the east. Nevertheless, Siam was progressively drawn into a global economy dominated by Britain from the second half of the nineteenth century and, in its process of modernization, relied heavily on Western expertise from Britain, France and Germany.

The Philippines is a rather different case. Governed by the Spanish from the latter part of the sixteenth until the end of the nineteenth century, its links were mainly eastwards across the Pacific Ocean to the Spanish American Empire. Following the loss to Spain of its American colonies from the early part of the nineteenth century, the connections between the Philippines and the metropolitan power were re-routed via the Indian Ocean. The status of the Philippines as an outlier of the Americas was reconfirmed when the USA took control of the islands from Spain at the turn of the twentieth century following the Spanish-American War. Given this trans-Pacific identity, the conversion of large numbers of Filipinos to Roman Catholicism, and the Americanization of considerable areas of Philippine economic, political and cultural life, 'the question of whether or not the Philippines formed part of Southeast Asia was to remain a matter of scholarly uncertainty as late as the 1960s' (Osborne, 2004: 5).

Another European mercantile colonial power – Portugal – retained a vestige of its former sea-borne empire until the mid-1970s in the eastern part of Timor. East Timor was invaded by Indonesian military forces and incorporated into the Republic of Indonesia in 1976, only to be released from Indonesian control in 1999 when its people voted on the territory's future status under the auspices of the United Nations. Prior to British and Dutch intervention in the region from the seventeenth century, Portugal had been the major commercial force in the Malay-Indonesian islands, with its base at Malacca. Like the Spanish the Portuguese had also set about converting the local population to Christianity, although it faced formidable opposition from the expanding power and appeal of Islam in these maritime regions.

Therefore, different parts of the Southeast Asian region became part of the histories and identities of particular colonial powers, and their indigenous elites were educated in the metropolitan language – English, French, Dutch, Spanish or Portuguese. Different territories and populations were incorporated into different politico-administrative and economic structures according to different colonial styles and philosophies at different periods of time. From the early twentieth century Southeast Asian worldviews and values were to some extent shaped by European concepts and interests, and privileged members of native societies had the opportunity to study at institutions of higher education in Europe and the USA or in local, European-founded academies. It was Western education and the accompanying exposure to social and political philosophies (from liberalism to socialism and Marxism) which provided the rationale and impetus for the creation of indigenous political movements and the intellectual ammunition to question the morality of foreign domination and the absence of basic human rights. These anti-colonial movements ultimately demanded their political independence and their right to social, cultural and economic autonomy. However, the horizons of the emerging, politically conscious native elites were still usually confined within the 'national' boundaries created for them by competition, conflict and accommodation between rival colonial powers.

It was during the late colonial period that we find the first evidence of reflection and debate about the effects of Western contact on Southeast Asian societies in the writings of Western observers and indigenous scholars and political leaders. However, there is considerable continuity in Western perspectives on Asia which go back to the late eighteenth and early nineteenth centuries in the work of such astute British observers as William Marsden on Sumatra (1975 [1783]), Thomas Stamford Raffles on Java (1965 [1817]) and John Crawfurd more generally on the 'Indian Archipelago' (1967 [1820]). This was not a monolithic Orientalist discourse, contra Edward Said (1985 [1978]), but it marked the beginnings of the 'scientific' study of society and the impulse to order and classify other societies and cultures. Based on the natural science model, social types were arranged on a scale of evolution and were assumed to pass through fixed, 'progressive' stages. Quilty says of the assumptions of such writers as Marsden, Raffles and Crawfurd that 'traits from Europe's past and Southeast Asia's present are seen as being fundamentally the same because they belong to the same stage of development through which all peoples must pass' (1998: 48). It was this evolutionary framework which resurfaced in post-war modernization theory (see Chapter 3).

The writings of Western observers during the late colonial period also considered the character and effects of the encounter between West and East, and the nature and future direction of indigenous identities and organizations. A theme which emerged was the possible negative consequences of colonialism on local societies. Few of these earlier ideas have enjoyed lasting influence on post-independence sociological debate. One such was the concept of socio-economic dualism formulated by the Dutch scholar-administrator, J.H. Boeke, in his doctoral dissertation (1910; 1953, 1980). He observed that the Euro-American-dominated world economy had brought great material benefit to the West but at the expense of the subjugation and impoverishment of rural communities in the East Indies (Evers, 1980c: 2–3). He therefore saw colonial capitalism as socially and economically 'destructive' and 'divisive', though in his view there were also internal 'traditional' socio-cultural and psychological reasons why Asian peasant communities found it difficult to respond to Western capitalism (see Chapter 3).

Another influential paradigm was that of the 'plural society' presented by J.S. Furnivall, a British scholar-administrator, who undertook detailed comparative political-economic studies of British Burma and the Netherlands East Indies (1939, 1942, 1956 [1948], 1957, 1980). He emphasized the importance of the overseas Chinese and Indian trading populations in Southeast Asian colonial society as economic intermediaries between the European and indigenous communities. In particular, developing urban areas such as Singapore, Batavia (Jakarta), Rangoon and Saigon-Cholon (Ho Chi Minh City) were increasingly dominated by Asian immigrants and Europeans. Furnivall's conception of a distinctive type of colonial system in which different ethnic groups constitute 'economic castes' and keep to their own socio-cultural worlds, meeting only in the market-place, has been subject to detailed criticism and refinement in later studies of ethnicity. He, like Boeke, saw colonial society as sharply divided, although for Furnivall 'the conflict between rival economic interests tends to be exacerbated by racial diversity' (1980: 88; see Chapters 4 and 6).

Therefore, prior to the 1940s the impact of European colonialism on native communities began to generate scholarly interest in the social transformations which had occurred in the region and their consequences for local welfare. Wertheim provides a sociological-historical overview of these processes, focusing on the utility of Marxian and Weberian concepts in understanding the complexity of change in the region. He notes that the 'impact of nineteenth-century and early twentieth-century Western capitalism on South-east Asian societies was profound and lasting', but it was not until Europeans introduced large-scale commercial agriculture from the later eighteenth century that fundamental socio-economic changes were set in motion (1980a: 14). Thereafter, the commercialization of land and labour, provision of capital, expansion of the market, accompanied by increased European political and administrative control, and the dissemination of a different set of values transformed indigenous societies (Geertz, 1963a; see Chapters 3 and 4).

India, China and Southeast Asia

The colonial experience and the division of Southeast Asia into separate European-dominated political and cultural areas, was the later phase of a long period of external contact and influence. At the maritime crossroads between the Indian and Pacific Oceans and between the relatively heavily populated continental landmasses of India and China, Southeast Asia has served as a vacuum which has been filled by outside cultures and populations. Southeast Asia had long been a focus of Indian and Chinese maritime trade as a source of precious metals and exotic tropical produce. Reflecting these commercial and maritime interests, the Indians referred to the regions to the east as 'the lands of gold and silver' and the Chinese as the Nan-Yang, the 'southern' region reached by sea (literally 'southern foreign') or the Nan-Hai (Southern Sea) (Wang, 2005: 62). The Japanese derivation *nanyo* or *nampo* had a broadly similar meaning (Hajime, 2005: 85–87; Anderson, 1998: 3). These commercial relations stretching across the sea routes between India and China increased in intensity and scale during the early part of the first millennium CE. Furthermore, aside from China's maritime trade and tributary relations with its southern neighbours, which waxed and waned according to its domestic fortunes, China also had close land contacts with northern Vietnam. The Sino-Vietnamese state of Nam Viet or Nan Yueh, located in the Red River (Songkoi) Delta, had been incorporated as a province of the Han Chinese Empire from 111 BCE and remained as such until 939 CE. During that time the Vietnamese were subject to relatively intense processes of Sinicization, including the introduction of the Chinese script, architecture, material culture, Confucianism and Mahayana Buddhism.

The Vietnamese succeeded in securing their self-determination in 939 CE, although they adopted the Chinese politico-administrative system and continued a tributary-trade relationship with China. The Vietnamese emperor, as the 'Son of Heaven', mediated between the earthly and spiritual worlds. As Osborne has said:

> The bureaucracy was a pyramid with the ruler at the apex and with clearly defined links established between the apex and the lowest officials in the provinces who formed the base of this administration. The law was a written code, detailed in form and complete with learned commentaries. Strict rules covered the amount of authority possessed by each grade of official and the qualifications for each grade ... the Vietnamese believed in the necessity of clearly defined borders [with their neighbours]. (2004: 44)

In much of the rest of Southeast Asia the influence of Indian culture was apparent, although India never dominated the region politically nor occupied territories. During the first millennium CE several kingdoms in both the mainland and islands adopted Hindu-Buddhist precepts and Indian court culture. The political elites of already established Southeast Asian states brought Indian Brahmins, knowledgeable in sacred lore, ritual, and legal and administrative procedures, to their courts as priests and advisors. Indian culture was used to legitimize and symbolize the position, status and genealogy of local rulers, presenting them as divine and as the mediators between heaven and earth (Wertheim, 1993: 18). Osborne contrasts the Vietnamese political system with the Indianized states. In the latter the 'pattern of official relationships was in many ways much more complex, in part because it lacked the clearly defined lines of authority that were so much part of the Vietnamese system' (2004: 45). Rather than a pyramid of authority, Osborne characterized the Indianized systems in terms of a series of concentric circles; 'it was only at the centre, where the smallest of these concentric circles is located, that the king's power was truly absolute. Beyond the central circle ... it was frequently the case that the king's power diminished in clear proportion to the distance one moved away from the capital' (ibid.). The border regions were 'uncertain and porous' and the officials who secured positions of power and authority did so not through qualifications and formal appointment but through family links and personal favour (ibid.: 45–46).

In the first millennium CE and the early second millennium, major Hindu and Mahayana Buddhist kingdoms emerged in Southeast Asia such as Srivijaya in Sumatra, Mataram in Java, Angkor in Cambodia, Pagan in Burma and Champa in central and south Vietnam. Most of the states of island Southeast Asia depended primarily on sea-borne trade, with the partial exception of certain of the Javanese states, whilst the majority of the mainland polities relied significantly, though not exclusively, on irrigated rice cultivation on the extensive plains and river deltas.

Subsequently these states were replaced by new dynasties and kingdoms, which had also taken religious and political structures from India, and, for much of the island world of Southeast Asia, from the Middle East via India. Theravada or Hinayana Buddhism spread from Sri Lanka (Ceylon) and was adopted by the lowland populations of Burma, particularly from the eleventh century. Theravada Buddhist states became established in central and southern Burma, and later in Thailand, Laos and Cambodia. In island Southeast Asia and southern Vietnam Islam expanded along the India–China trade routes and through the Malay-Indonesian islands. However, it was the founding of the Muslim sultanate of Malacca in the southern Malayan peninsula in the early fifteenth century, and its importance as a spice emporium, which led to the rapid dissemination and consolidation of Islam throughout the Malay-Indonesian world and into the southern Philippines. Both Theravada Buddhism and Islam expressed more egalitarian socio-religious principles. Rural communities embraced these religions more decisively, in contrast to the more socially restrictive codes of the hierarchical, court-based political systems of earlier Hindu-Mahayana Buddhist states (Benda, 1972: 135–138). However, even in adopting Theravada Buddhism and Islam, the local populations brought their own genius, and some of their pre-existing beliefs and practices to these new religions, and these latter, in turn, despite their egalitarian impulse, 'gave new life to the old urban hierarchy' (O'Connor, 1983: 41).

Various socio-historical studies have described and analysed the social and political structures of these pre-colonial indigenous states. The work of van Leur on Asian states and trade has had a lasting influence (1955). His studies, undertaken during the 1930s, inspired a generation of students who sought to combine historical and sociological perspectives. Using a concept first developed by Weber, van Leur conceived of the empires founded on irrigated rice cultivation and the organization and management of hydraulic works as 'patrimonial bureaucracies' (ibid.: 56–57). He argued that political control, exercised through a bureaucracy, and expressed in the divine, semi-divine or sacred ruler, depended principally on the mobilization of village labour and the extraction of surplus agricultural products. However, these Indianized states were not highly centralized, stable units; rulers and their retinues depended on political, administrative, legal and cultural practices to counter ever-present centrifugal tendencies (Wertheim, 1980a: 9). Schrieke also examined, with reference to Java, the character of patrimonialism and demonstrated how rulers in decentralized polities overcame opposition and bids for power from other members of the royal family and from provincial nobles (1957).

Another sociological concept, widely used to understand traditional Asian state structures, is that of Marx's notion of an 'Asiatic mode of production' and 'Oriental despotism' (1964). Wittfogel's subsequent treatise on 'Oriental despotism', as a highly centralized polity in which the ruler exercised 'total power', served to popularize this concept in post-Second World War social science (1957). Marx's characterization of pre-colonial Asian states, based primarily on his reading of ma-terials on India and China, as structurally stable, unchanging and politically central-ized, comprising 'closed', self-sustaining village communities, and based on 'a lack of private ownership of land and the complete subjection of the individual peasant to village authority' is now untenable, given our increased knowledge of the flex-ibility, openness and complexity of these systems (Wertheim, 1980a: 9). However, superficially Marx's model has more relevance to the Sinicized Vietnamese state than to Indianized polities. In contrast to his unitary Asiatic model, it is now ac-cepted that there were variations in these state structures; they were subject to changes generated by both internal contradictions and conflicts as well as external forces; finally, they were not highly centralized, the ruler had constantly to ad-dress opposition and attempts at secession among the royal family, nobility and aristocrats, and the matter of rights to land was more complex than Marx or others conceived (Wisseman Christie, 1985; Wertheim, 1993: 18–21).

This was even more so for the so-called 'harbour principalities', described and analysed in Weberian terms by van Leur (1955). These were not based on irrigated agriculture but on 'sea trade and international traffic'. The external commercial ori-entation of these riparian states 'generated a more cosmopolitan atmosphere and a greater receptivity to foreign cultural influences' (Wertheim, 1980a: 11). The power and wealth of the ruling elite was considerable, but these mercantile states were neither centralized nor 'despotic'. They comprised a relatively footloose, ethnically heterogeneous population of merchants, small traders and artisans 'living in sepa-rate quarters according to their ethnic group' (Wertheim, 1993: 22; Benda, 1962). The maritime states such as Srivijaya and subsequently Malacca depended on the control of port-centres and sea routes, and their ability to attract trade to their shores. They also had an important role in hinterland trade, serving as centres for the exchange of upriver commodities such as forest products, obtained from interior tribal peoples, for imported and coastally produced pottery, cloth and metal-ware.

When the Spanish and Portuguese arrived in Southeast Asia in the early six-teenth century, followed soon afterwards by the Dutch, British and French, they encountered representatives of these indigenous states. Some were relatively powerful and extensive, incorporating other states as their clients. However, the fortunes of a polity waxed and waned considerably over time and states and dynas-ties rose and fell. With the exception of the Hindu Balinese and the Filipinos of the northern two-thirds of the Philippines, Muslim communities and sultanates held sway over significant parts of the archipelago; Theravada Buddhist polities domi-nated mainland Southeast Asia, apart from the Mahayana Buddhist kingdom of northern Vietnam. Away from the main trade routes and rice-bowl areas, animist hill peoples practised small-scale agriculture and horticulture and hunted and col-lected in the surrounding forests. In some cases these marginal communities had relations with the large states through trade and tribute. But, as Wertheim notes, the 'most striking feature of these tribal peoples ... is that they were generally not integrated into larger political units' (1980a: 10). It is therefore unsurprising that

Western observers were impressed by the diversity of Southeast Asian peoples, their cultural debt to India and China, and the lack of regional political unity.

Wertheim, in arguing that pre-colonial Southeast Asian societies were more dynamic than writers such as Schrieke, van Leur and Marx maintained, draws attention to the diversity of social and political structures in the region, which provided alternative models with which to organize communities and polities (1993: 24). With reference to his theory of 'societies as a composite of conflicting value systems' (1974; see Chapter 2), he emphasizes, in patrimonial bureaucracies, the importance of the tensions between the 'centre' and 'periphery', 'the basic contradiction between the peasantry and the bureaucracy', between Hindu-Buddhist 'royalty' and 'clergy', between the Vietnamese Confucian scholar-gentry and Buddhist monks, and subsequently between the hierarchical value systems of Hinduism and Mahayana Buddhism and the more egalitarian creeds of Theravada Buddhism and Islam (Wertheim, 1993: 24–25).

Western Influence: Increasing Ethnic Diversity

The European encounter with Southeast Asia began in earnest with the Portuguese conquest of the Muslim spice emporium of Malacca in 1511, situated at a key strategic point on the Straits of Malacca. However, it was to be well into the nineteenth century before the European powers began significantly to administer territories and populations. Their main concern until then had been to control ports and trade routes like the native harbour principalities before them, though from the seventeenth century the Spanish in the Philippines and the Dutch in Java and the eastern Indonesian spice islands established a more substantial territorial and administrative presence. With these exceptions '[t]he first centuries of Western intrusion into the world of Southeast Asia were not accompanied by profound structural changes within the fabric of the affected societies' (ibid.: 26). However, with the introduction of large-scale cultivation of tropical cash crops for export and the expansion of plantation agriculture (coffee, tobacco, sugar, tea and spices) from the eighteenth century, and changes in the social class structure and concepts of property ownership, the Western presence was to have an increasingly significant influence on indigenous societies (ibid.: 28–29, 31–32; see Chapter 4).

Europeans gradually introduced various cultural elements such as language, religion and political philosophies and practices, evidenced most dramatically in the Philippines in the conversion of the majority of lowland Filipinos outside the Muslim south to Roman Catholicism, the administrative reorganization of relatively autonomous local communities (*barangay*) into a larger state structure dominated by conquistadores, and the introduction of privately owned estates (ibid.: 26–27). Subsequently, the Western presence contributed to another element of regional cultural diversity. The Europeans encouraged Chinese and Indian immigration (ibid.: 36, 1980b). Even prior to the European presence, Southeast Asia had received visits from Indian, Chinese, Arab, Persian and other Middle Eastern traders, adventurers, scholars and religious travellers; some had settled in the region in small numbers, often marrying locally and giving rise to culturally hybrid communities. As the Western powers established a favourable environment for trade, commerce and production, migration from the southern Chinese provinces especially, but also from India, increased. From the nineteenth century, when colonial administrations came to exercise an increasingly firm grip on the dependent territories, immigration to the main centres of economic activity became a flood. The Chinese settled in coastal ports, in the tin- and gold-mining areas from southern Burma through the western Malayan Peninsula and the northern Indonesian islands to western Borneo, and in centres of commercial crop production such as the large rice-growing areas around Bangkok, Phnom Penh, Hanoi and Saigon-Cholon. The Indians concentrated mainly in the British-administered territories, as traders, shopkeepers and money-lenders in the urban areas, and labourers in the rice-bowl of lowland Burma and the rubber plantation belt of western Malaya.

Southeast Asia's cultural and ethnic complexity continues to this day; in addition to the rich mix of indigenous ethnic groups, there are significant populations of Chinese and Indians. Some immigrant groups, particularly the early settlers, assimilated more than others through intermarriage and cultural exchange. In Thailand and the Philippines where political, economic and cultural circumstances were more favourable to assimilation, there emerged politically and economically important communities of Sino-Thais and Sino-Filipinos. However, in Malaysia and Singapore, given the scale of immigration and the British approach to the administration of the different ethnic groups, most Chinese retained their separate identities, as did the Indian populations; these are classic illustrations of Furnivall's 'plural society'.

Overall Southeast Asia's geographical openness and political fragmentation, its character as a commercial crossroads between the Indian and Pacific Oceans, its cultural and ethnic diversity, the range of economic activities undertaken there, the variety of external influences to which the region had been subject, and the presence of several of the major Western powers which served to divide rather than unite neighbouring states, resulted in Southeast Asia being perceived by both outside observers and local residents, as a loose bundle of territories and peoples with neither defining features nor regional unity. In this connection, Fisher has referred appropriately to Southeast Asia as 'the Balkans of the Orient' (1962; King, 2005, 2006).

The Creation of Southeast Asia

Political and Strategic Issues

The watershed in perceptions about Southeast Asia was the Pacific War and the Japanese occupation of the region; the Japanese saw Southeast Asia as the 'southern resources area' of their Greater East Asia Co-Prosperity Sphere. From both Japanese and Western military-strategic perspectives it became increasingly apparent that the territories surrounding the South China Sea and at the meeting point between the Indian and Pacific Oceans constituted a unit separate from India and China. The creation of Lord Louis Mountbatten's Southeast Asia Command, which was based in Ceylon during the Second World War, served to raise the profile of the area in official circles, though Mountbatten's remit excluded the Philippines, as well as the Dutch East Indies until July 1945, but included Ceylon and the Northeast Indian frontier (Smith, 1986; Anderson, 1998: 3). After the war various Western governments and the USA in particular, recognized the need to study and understand the region in its own right. Further impetus was given to this emerging regionalization with the foundation in Europe, America, Australia, Japan, Singapore and Malay(si)a of university departments, programmes and centres specializing in Southeast Asian Studies (Mohammed Halib and Huxley, 1996a: 1–9; Kratoska et al., 2005a; 2005b; Chou and Houben, 2006a: 1–22, 2006b; Taufik Abdullah, nd; Wang, 2005: 70–74). From 1941 through to the early 1950s, several general books were written carrying the regional designation 'Southeast Asia' in their titles (Anderson, 1998: 4; Wang, 2005: 70–74, 80–81).

In a reflective paper on the development of Southeast Asian Studies, McVey emphasizes the American role in the conceptual construction of Southeast Asia and the promotion of post-war regional scholarship (1995; 2005: 311–313; Chou and Houben, 2006a: 4–6). She argues that for the Americans the defeat of the Japanese signalled 'the liberation of the Southeast Asia peoples' and the beginning of their journey to 'national self-realization' and 'progress to modernity' (1995: 2). Interestingly it was these central concepts of nation-building and modernization which provided the basic elements of modernization theory – the dominant social science paradigm in the analysis of Southeast Asia and the wider developing world in the 1950s and the 1960s (see Chapters 2 and 3).

Post-war decolonization, the creation of independent states and the need to develop them (Wertheim's 'emancipation period' [1993: 39]), and to counter the perceived threat posed by Third World socialism and communism, resulted in the development in the West of a regional view of Southeast Asia. For Britain the need to sustain its economic presence in Malaya, Singapore, northern Borneo and Hong Kong, following the granting of independence to the Indian sub-continent soon after 1945, meant that it had to think more in terms of a Southeast Asian region; Southeast Asia was no longer an adjunct of India. Similarly for the Americans, Southeast Asia assumed greater strategic importance during the Cold War, after the emergence of a mainland Chinese communist government in 1949; the Korean War; active communist insurrections in Burma in 1949; the French defeat at the hands of the Vietnamese communists in 1954 and the subsequent extension of communism into neighbouring Laos and Cambodia; the anti-government communist insurrection in the Philippines between 1948 and 1954; the British struggle against communist insurgency in the 'Malayan Emergency' in the 1950s; the increasing importance of the Indonesian Communist Party (Partai Komunis Indonesia [PKI]) under Sukarno in the 1950s and early 1960s; and the increasingly active involvement of the USA in the Vietnam War and the wider Indochinese conflict from the 1960s. Anderson puts these events into a wider perspective when he says 'No other region of the world – not Latin America, not the Near East, not Africa, and not South Asia – had this kind of alarming profile' (1998: 7).

The USA, in its attempts to contain the expansion of Asian communism and its preoccupation with the so-called 'domino theory', saw the destinies of the Southeast Asian countries as interlinked. An important preoccupation in American foreign policy circles was that the loss of mainland Southeast Asian states such as Vietnam, Cambodia and Laos to communism might well result, if not checked, in the domino-like fall of other states in the region. Moreover, Southeast Asia was a vitally important producer of oil, tin, timber and rubber for the West. It was this promise of profit and the desire to control the sources of wealth which had first attracted the Western powers and then Japan to the region.

Southeast Asia as a Socio-Cultural Area?

In the post-war 'search for Southeast Asia', increasingly dominated by American-based scholarship, and even more so from the 1960s, attention was directed to those socio-cultural elements which appeared to be widespread in the region and served to distinguish it from China and India. There was a desire to put cultural flesh on the politico-strategic bones of Southeast Asia. What was emphasized was the capacity of Southeast Asians, within their own cultural traditions, to absorb and adapt to outside influences so that the region, it was argued, should not be seen as a pale imitation of its larger neighbours. Even from the turn of the twentieth century there had been a small number of scholars, mainly German and Austrian ethnologists including Robert von Heine-Geldern and Karl Pelzer, who had already coined the term 'Southeast Asia' (Südostasien) and had identified regional social and cultural 'commonalities' (Reid, 1999; Kratoska et al., 2005a: 3).Von Heine-Geldern and Pelzer were subsequently to play influential roles in the post-war development of Southeast Asian scholarship in America (Bowen, 2000: 12). In Japan too the concept of a Southeast Asian region had emerged from around the end of the First World War, though this was 'based entirely on Japan's own interests, and almost no attempt was made to understand the region on its own terms' (Hajime, 2005: 105).

From the late 1940s the socio-cultural similarities, identified earlier by mainly European ethnologists, were then elaborated. The American anthropologist Robbins Burling discovered 'common threads' in folk religions and symbolism, material culture and technology, bilateral family organization and relatively equal gender relations, as well as the 'unifying theme' of the contrast and complementarity between hill and plains people (1992 [1965]: 2–4; Bowen, 1995, 2000). Others, particularly historians, expanded on these similarities and unities across the region in terms of language, indigenous leadership patterns, status arrangements, commercial interconnections, and political and economic organization (Reid, 1988, 1993, 1999; Wolters, 1999 [1982]).

However, the search for 'cultural continuities', 'commonalities', or a 'cultural matrix' has proved more problematical (King, 2001: 13–18; 2005; 2006). Quite rightly our attention has been drawn to the role of Southeast Asians as active agents in shaping their own histories. Their dynamic response to the opportunities and constraints generated in their encounter with the outside world is an important theme in this book. However, in my view, the notion of unifying socio-cultural threads requires qualification. These commonalities are usually framed in such broad terms that they present formidable problems for the social scientist when applied to particular cases. Not all communities in Southeast Asia possess all these traits and, even for those that possess many of them, they are far from having identical characteristics. There are further problems in disentangling what are presented in the historical records as indigenous concepts and practices from those derived from India and China (Reynolds, 1995: 427–428). Moreover, the identification of the character of Southeast Asians as open and outward-looking, and the importance which Burling attaches to his unifying theme of 'hill farms' and '*padi*' fields' could more decisively be used to argue for regional diversity rather than unity. The problematical character of Southeast Asia has been emphasized even more strongly by Kratoska et al. who propose that attempts 'to define an entity to match the term "Southeast Asia" have been inconclusive, and the term persists as little more than a way to identify a certain portion of the earth's surface' (2005a: 14).

Another complication is that definitions of Southeast Asia as a social and cultural space do not coincide with the regional delimitation of nation-states (King, 2006: 33–34). Osborne argues for a 'broad linguistic unity' across Southeast Asia (2004: 7–9). However, students of Southeast Asian languages usually delineate four major language families: Austronesian, Tai-Kadai, Austroasiatic and Sino-Tibetan (Amara, 1993; Bellwood, 1985, 1995). Austronesian (or 'Malayo-Polynesian') found mainly in the island world, and in Taiwan, distant Madagascar and most of the Pacific islands, provides the basis for the national languages of Malaysia, Brunei, Singapore and Indonesia (Malay/Indonesian) and the Philippines (Tagalog); it is also spoken by minorities in southern Thailand, Vietnam and Cambodia. The three remaining language families are primarily located in mainland Southeast Asia. Tai-Kadai is spoken widely in Thailand, the Shan States of Burma, lowland Laos, southern China and the northern fringes of Cambodia, Vietnam and Malaysia. The Austroasiatic languages are spoken by the Vietnamese, Khmers (Cambodians), the Mons of Burma, most of the aboriginal groups of the Malayan Peninsula and the Nicobar Islands. Finally Sino-Tibetan, of which Chinese is a member, is found among the lowland Burmese (Burmans), and among hill peoples in Burma, neighbouring mainland countries, northeast India and Bangladesh.

Although a subject of much dispute amongst linguists, it has been suggested that there might be remote connections between these four Asian language families, particularly between Tai-Kadai and Austronesian. Bellwood proposes that the ancestors of these four families, who were of Mongoloid physical stock, might have inhabited contiguous areas of southern and central China from the early period of agricultural development about 8,000 years ago (1995). He further suggests that the Neolithic revolution then led to the expansion of settlement, and, over a long period of time, the complex movements of populations and cultural traits into other parts of Asia, including the regions to the south. In other words, his theory seems to suggest a movement from some degree of linguistic unity to increasing differentiation over time.

These linguistic and other socio-cultural characteristics, although employed to provide substance to the politico-strategic definition of Southeast Asia, do not set clear boundaries to it, nor do they unify it. Depending on the criterion chosen, the region expands, contracts or shifts accordingly. In Sutherland's terms it is a 'contingent device'; its definition and use depends on the 'sets of relationships' being examined (2005: 20–21; McVey, 2005: 317). Linguistic similarities serve to unite large sub-regions of Southeast Asia, but they connect communities within the region to populations outside it. Mainland languages spill over into southern China and northeastern India; Austronesian languages are found in Taiwan, Madagascar and most of the Pacific Islands. Cultural traits link Southeast Asia with regions beyond, and, although western New Guinea is part of the region politically, in cultural terms it belongs to the Australo-Melanesian area and its populations are of Australoid and not Mongoloid racial stock (Bellwood, 1985). In addition, Southeast Asia is home to significant numbers of ethnic Chinese and Indians, and, despite their having undergone some changes in their interactions with indigenous peoples, they retain cultural and other connections with their ancestral lands. Students of comparative religion also draw attention to the linkages between the Theravada Buddhist cultures of Southeast Asia and Sri Lanka, similarities between Vietnamese and Chinese Mahayana Buddhism, the shared features of Malay/Indonesian Islam and that of northern India and the Middle East, parallels between Hinduism in Bali and India, and between Philippine Catholicism and that of the Christian world of the Americas and Europe. Thus, the socio-cultural, linguistic and racial boundaries of Southeast Asia are permeable, blurred, and shifting.

Concluding Comments

It is by no means clear that sociological analysis of the developing societies of Southeast Asia should be confined within a regional perspective (King, 2006: 30–34). In recent years the countries of this region have been seen increasingly as part of a wider western Pacific Asian economic community, a global economy and a globalizing world (Abdul Rahman Embong, 2004). The social effects of modernization, urbanization, industrialization, labour migration, and consumerism have encouraged some social scientists to examine more general patterns of change in Asia rather than restrict their attention to Southeast Asia (Robison and Goodman, 1996b). These transformations include the development of the 'new rich' and the middle class, adaptation to urban lifestyles, the growth in factory employment, international migration, and changing gender and kinship relations.

Moreover, the earlier post-war perspectives deployed to understand processes of development in newly-independent countries were not necessarily, nor even usually contained within regional parameters. Social scientists were concerned to formulate general theories of modernization, or of underdevelopment and dependency, which would apply to the whole developing world, though their case studies were often selected from a particular part of that world. For example, most empirical material used in the early formulation of the general theories of underdevelopment and dependency was taken from the Latin American experience (Frank, 1967, 1969, 1972). These were only subsequently applied to Southeast Asia (Catley, 1976 [1980]).

Even the politico-strategic definition of Southeast Asia is not as clear-cut as it once seemed. Some students of international relations and security issues have become increasingly interested in the developing connections between Southeast and East Asia. Strategic specialists now talk more in terms of a Pacific Asian or East Asian strategic theatre embracing Southeast Asia, China, Korea and Japan (Huxley, 1996). There is also developing interest in the emerging strategic importance of the Indian Ocean theatre. In a recent edited book on 'locating' Southeast Asia, several contributors refer to the blurring of the boundaries between Southeast Asia and southern China, given Vietnam's cultural and historical links with China and the importance of the South China Sea as a maritime thoroughfare uniting East and Southeast Asia (Kratoska et al., 2005b).

Processes of political liberalization and democratization, and commercial interaction between the countries of western Pacific Asia have also resulted in the realization among political economists that various Asian countries share similar experiences and problems and should be studied comparatively. The phenomenon of the 'Asian tiger economies', for example, links Singapore with Taiwan, Hong Kong and South Korea, and their shared Confucian heritage has led some observers to suggest the importance of a set of cultural factors in promoting Asian economic development (see Chapter 8).

Where does this leave me in writing a regional sociology? I intend to keep cross-regional perspectives in mind, and I have firmly acknowledged that social transformations there are to be found elsewhere and are in part generated by general forces beyond the region. However, we have now arrived at a period of history, characterized by processes of globalization, in which, paradoxically, regional economic and trading blocs such as ASEAN have taken on increasing importance and have a role to play in the global economic and political system (Chou and Houben, 2006: 7–8, 11). Thus, in my view, the ten ASEAN countries will continue to have an identity and a rationale separate from the rest of Asia. There is certainly a political commitment within Southeast Asia to develop and strengthen a specifically Southeast Asian perspective on international affairs (Reid, 1999). In addition, at the level of the nation-state, global processes are adapted and reshaped in local and regional socio-cultural and political contexts (Nas, 1998).

It is also true that an understanding of Southeast Asia requires specialist expertise. The cultural complexity of the region and its rich and varied history set it apart from East and South Asia. The region has never been a pale reflection of India and China. Moreover, the concepts and debates on which I shall focus have emerged from analyses of Southeast Asian empirical material, either country-specific or region-wide, and, although I shall not lose sight of the more general social transformations at work there, it is sensible to locate them in the real-life experiences of one area of the world. Despite the difficulties in defining Southeast Asia as a region, the fuzziness and cross-cutting character of its boundaries, and the need to address local diversities, it is clear that since 1945 it has acquired an identity separate from its larger northern and western neighbours. This identity, or in Anderson's terms an 'imagined reality' (1998: 6), continues to be recognized as valuable in scholarly discourse, and is increasingly, though patchily and sporadically, expressed by Southeast Asian themselves.

2

The Sociological Context

We hold that sociology and history should be viewed not as completely separate, but as disciplines with an identical object; that though their methods and techniques may differ, the 'fundamental preoccupations are the same' (van den Muijzenberg and Wolters, 1988: 2).

Both [sociology and history] seek to understand the puzzle of human agency and both seek to do so in terms of the process of social structuring ... Sociology must be concerned with eventuation, because that is how structuring happens. History must be theoretical, because that is how structuring is apprehended (Abrams: 1982: x–xi).

Instead of searching exclusively for integrative expedients, we should with equal intellectual force try to detect strains and conflicts in society, as possible agents in future change (Wertheim, 1964a: 35).

Introduction

This chapter discusses the reasons for the relative lack of progress, or the 'underdevelopment' of the post-war sociological study of Southeast Asia. It provides a context for the consideration of theories of modernization, underdevelopment and dependency, and political economy perspectives discussed in Chapters 3, 4 and 5. In anticipating the issues to be addressed in the study of Southeast Asia in the immediate future, McVey, in a paper published in the mid-1990s, referred to the 'urban sector', 'labour as well as industry', and 'the media and modern culture'. She suggested that this research agenda 'implies a larger place for sociology', although she doubted the ability of its practitioners 'to assume a leading intellectual role' (1995: 8). She was also doubtful whether other social science disciplines, including politics and economics, could take up the challenge. For her they were too wedded to the old paradigms – particularly modernization theory – and she suggested that economics is 'too mathematical and abstract to have much immediacy' (ibid.: 9). Instead she referred approvingly to cross-disciplinary perspectives and the insights which have emerged from the fragmentation of disciplines into particular specialisms; thus, she commended gender studies, ecology, political economy, agricultural economics, business history, musicology, popular literature, and the visual and performing arts.

In contrast to McVey I believe that a sociological perspective should embrace precisely this multidisciplinary, eclectic spirit. It is in the spirit of Wertheim's approach to the study of Asian societies 'on the move', a spirit which enfolds the social sciences as 'a unity' (1993: 4–5). I have referred to three of the major sources of sociological inspiration: Marx, Weber and Durkheim. What is striking in their approaches and theories is a commitment to the integration of social-science perspectives and methods within a historical framework. They were interested in the 'totality of society', not just in its social or political institutions, its economic structure, nor its cultural values and practices (Martinussen, 1997: 22, 25–30). Sociology then is closely entwined with political economy, history and anthropology, and these areas of expertise have, during the past three decades, drawn on and been embraced by the more recognizably cross-disciplinary studies of gender, culture, the media, the environment and development (Batan, 2006: 2; Bautista, 1994: 12). Therefore, I am casting my net relatively widely in this book.

The Underdevelopment of Southeast Asian Sociology

Even when we adopt this broader sociological perspective, an examination of the post-war sociology of Southeast Asia suggests that it has been an under-achiever in comparison with the study of other developing areas (King, 1981: 391). Evers has already referred to this lack of achievement (1980a; see Chapter 1). Two years before, in a co-edited volume, Evers also stated with Chen that 'One common problem faced by all sociology lecturers in Southeast Asia is the lack of local teaching materials' (Chen and Evers, 1978a: xiii). The editors placed some blame for this lack of progress on imported Euro-American social science materials. With regard to the development of sociology teaching in Singapore they noted, rather depressingly:

> Nearly all university text-books are imported from Britain and the United States. Theoretical frameworks, empirical examples and conceptual illustrations, which may be familiar to most academics who were trained in these countries but in most cases are strange to the students, are taught in the classes and transmitted to the students. (Ibid.; see also Bauzon-Bautista, 1987: 8).

More recently there have been some positive changes. In a survey of the production of social science knowledge in Southeast Asia by local and foreign scholars published in international journals, Gerke and Evers suggest that there is room for optimism, with evidence of an increase in locally produced knowledge between 1970–2000, especially in Singapore (2006: 11; Evers, 2000: 13–22). However, 'knowledge dependency ... is still visible' and, although '[t]he contribution of local social scientists may seem important in many respects, ... from a global perspective the ideas on how Southeast Asian societies work have been outlined and described mainly by foreigners' (ibid.: 2). Clearly the health of sociological studies has improved during the past decade, but the empirical materials are still patchy and we have not seen the robust emergence of distinctive schools of study or internationally recognized academic programmes. Some new developments have shown signs of promise (Anderson, 1984; Doner, 1991; Rodan et al., 1997, 2001a, 2006a) but, despite Chen's and Evers's strictures about the generally unhelpful influence of imported paradigms, we continue to look primarily outside Southeast Asia for insights into such processes as modernization rather than to locally generated sociologies. I recognize, however, that in other disciplinary fields, including politics, anthropology and history, scholars working on Southeast Asia have developed some key social science concepts (Chou and Houben, 2006a: 1; King and Wilder, 2003; Taufik, n.d.).

Wertheim too drew upon the traditions of European sociology to investigate whether or not 'we could establish similarities between developments in earlier European history and developments in contemporary Asian societies' (1993: 2). He did this with considerable skill and historical sensitivity and, in his *Indonesian Society in Transition* (1959 [1956]) and *East-West Parallels* (1964a), adapted concepts which had been devised in the encounter with Western experiences to enable scholarly engagement with the fast-changing societies of Asia. His overall conclusion was that 'such parallel developments could certainly be revealed; but ... in each instance they only hold to some extent', and, in Asia in general contrast to the West, he draws attention to the considerably enhanced role of the state in economic affairs, and the relatively recent emergence of an urban bourgeoisie, which has not had the opportunity 'to play a dynamic, innovative role similar to that played by a parallel group in the West' (1993: 3).

A subsequent set of readings on Southeast Asia in the Macmillan 'Sociology of "Developing Societies"' series reveals the persistence of the problems highlighted by Evers a decade before (Taylor and Turton, 1988a). The editors capture the dilemma in a paradox; they demonstrate that, from any point of view, this socially and culturally complex region is of crucial global political and economic importance. 'Yet the degree and quality of much of the research on the region often does not enable one to address the most important aspects of its current and future development' (Taylor and Turton, 1988b: 1). In this regard the authors contrast sociological research on Southeast Asia with the work of Latin American and other scholars on dependency and world systems analysis, East African studies on 'the role of the state and its relation to indigenous classes', and the analyses of capitalist relations of production in agriculture and agrarian differentiation in South Asia. Taylor and Turton, like Evers, lament that Southeast Asian academics have adopted ideas from outside the area to examine processes of change 'rather than generating indigenous explanations of the region and its place in the world economy' (ibid.: 1). Prior to Taylor's and Turton's remarks, Neher had already contrasted the 'innovative perspectives of Latin American-oriented writers with the poor performance of students of Southeast Asian societies' (1984: 130). Then Doner drew attention to the 'relative weakness' of studies of Southeast Asian political economy (1991: 819), although the situation has steadily improved during the past decade or so since he made this remark (Rodan et al., 1997, 2001a, 2006a).

Comments along very similar lines were made by Preston (1987). Among other things he criticized the writings of the European observers, Boeke and Furnivall, and attempted to counter the claims of Evers, who reproduced key extracts from Boeke and Furnivall in his 'reader' of 1980, that these two colonial writers represent the beginnings of a distinctively Southeast Asian sociology. Preston maintained that the work of colonial administrator-scholars cannot make a contribution to an independent Southeast Asian sociological perspective because their analyses have been shaped by colonial interests. Instead, he argued that any 'indigenous' Southeast Asian sociology 'will only be discovered (if it's there) in the work of local scholars, commentators and activists' (ibid.: 99). He was also critical of local sociologists who were concerned with development policy and planning issues (see Chen, 1983). Preston's view was that this kind of sociology provided a convenient defence of government development strategies and served to maintain the socio-political status quo.

I agree with Preston's criticisms to a point. There are shortcomings in the early studies of Boeke and Furnivall, but their work has intellectual value. Furthermore, although we can be critical of both foreign and local sociological research on the region, we should not underestimate what has been accomplished and we have to be aware of the constraints on sociological enquiry (Neher, 1984: 131). For example, in their review of sociological research in Singapore, Ong et al. remark, with regard to the policies of Lee Kuan Yew's People's Action Party (PAP), that from 1965 when a Department of Sociology was founded in the local university, it had to establish 'its credentials in a difficult arena because it was the domain of a government that was very pragmatic and all-encompassing in its sense of mission' (1997a: viii). Heryanto (2005: 57–89) and Samuel (1999), too, have remarked on the strong relationships of dependency between the social sciences and government in post-independence Indonesia (see also Hadiz and Dhakidae, 2005a: 1–29), as has Shamsul for Malaysia (1995), Bautista during the martial law period under Marcos (1994; Carino, 1980), and Schulte Nordholt and Visser more generally for Southeast Asia (1995). In Thailand, Reynolds and Hong, in their examination of Marxist influences on local historical and political economy studies of Thailand, identify periods of political constraint on scholarship as well as of intellectual ferment (1983: 78). For example, the 1958–73 period of military dictatorship was 'a restrictive one', but in the liberal period of 1973–76 there was a local outpouring of Marxist-inspired analyses of Thailand's underdevelopment (ibid.: 79–98).

Returning to Preston's contribution, there are two points. First, Boeke's and Furnivall's insights have stimulated considerable debate and further studies of Southeast Asian societies, nor is it the case that the provision of imaginative responses to the complexities of social change there should necessarily be the preserve of local scholars. Second, there should be a greater recognition of the value of applied social science research. The practical involvement of local academics in addressing such social issues as poverty and inequality has been an important aspect of Southeast Asian sociology since the 1970s. Batan reinforces this point in his comments on Philippine sociology and the role of local sociologists in examining concrete issues and problems; these concerns are exemplified admirably in the pages of the *Philippine Sociological Review* (2006: 7; Bautista, 1994). I must emphasize that the domain of policy and practice is not my concern here, although previously I have addressed these issues in applied anthropological research (King, 1999).

The Post-War Constraints on Research: Access and American Paradigms

I now turn to the reasons for the relatively lack-lustre performance of sociological research on Southeast Asia. In the mid-1980s a group of Australian-based political economists provided us with clues. Higgott and Robison argued that scholarship had not responded to the dramatic social, economic and political changes which had been taking place in the region since the mid-1970s (1985b). They and their colleagues were critical of the generally conservative approach in Southeast Asian social science, which was 'largely the consequence … of the extraordinary influence of positivist and empiricist traditions … which … have been constituted by an amalgam of orientalist history, behaviouralism and structural-functional social science' (1985b: 3). In other words, they charged that scholars of Southeast Asia had tended to employ Western-derived evolutionary, functionalist models of modernization and change, to describe overt patterns of political and economic behaviour rather than the underlying structural conditions of underdevelopment, and to neglect Southeast Asia's location in a global economy dominated by capitalism. Moreover, historical research had been unduly preoccupied with the Euro-American contribution to Southeast Asian history and its interpretation in terms of Western categories and perspectives. Higgott and Robison also argued that much previous Southeast Asian social science had given insufficient attention to such issues as class formation, conflicting economic and political interests, and the complexity of post-war socio-economic and political transformations. More recently, Schmidt, Hersh and Fold have pressed the case for the importance of understanding 'emerging structures of economic and social inequality' in Southeast Asia (1998a: 1).

However, Higgott and Robison did not consider in detail the context of this preoccupation with concepts of modernization, the generally conservative analysis of socio-economic change, and the relatively modest progress of sociological research. The explanations are relatively straightforward. First, at the time that Higgott and Robison were writing large parts of Southeast Asia were closed to social-science research (Neher, 1984: 131–132). Much of mainland Southeast Asia had been embroiled in war and conflict, and, following the communist victories in Indochina in the mid-1970s, access to data and field-sites was made virtually impossible. There has been little primary sociological research on Indochina during the past 50 years and a lack of research in the political economy tradition. Part of the reason for this was located in the 'divisiveness of the Vietnam War in the U.S. academic community' (Doner, 1991: 821), and the fact that many activists and radical scholars 'either never secured any academic position, voluntarily left, or were forced out of Asian studies' (Allen, 1989: 117; Doner, 1991: 822). On the other hand, various American academics 'of a particular value persuasion' were linked closely to the U.S. government during its political and military involvement in the region. Marr has noted that 'the typical American dissertation', written in the 1960s, 'deals with the people of the area [Indochina] as objects of the post-World War II political policies of France and, later, the United States' (1973: 97).

Moreover, Myanmar had severed its ties with the outside world from the early 1960s, and its government has continued to exclude most foreign scholars from the country and to restrain severely local research. We have had a few sociological studies which can be undertaken from a distance and some patchy recent work undertaken by Burmese scholars (Tin Maung Maung Than, 2004, 2005). But we have survived mainly with the materials collected there by American cultural anthropologists prior to military rule in 1962. As one might expect, these latter used paradigms taken from the American anthropology of the time, employing such concepts as 'culture' and 'modernization' to examine the relationships between 'traditional' village Buddhism and 'popular religion' and the 'adaptation' of small-scale peasant and tribal communities to the wider political and economic systems of independent Myanmar (Nash, 1965).

The difficulties posed for social science researchers in gaining access to Laos, Cambodia, Vietnam and Myanmar have eased slightly in recent years, but broadly the situation persists. Even Brunei, though ostensibly more open to academic inquiry, places controls on local and foreign researchers. Interestingly, the general sociological and comparative political economy text on social change in Southeast Asia edited by Schmidt et al. as recently as the late 1990s focused on Indonesia, Malaysia, the Philippines, Thailand and Singapore, with one chapter on Vietnam (1998a). The editors state that 'the increasing importance of the rest of geographically and politically defined Southeast Asia – Brunei, Myanmar, Laos and Cambodia – to the rest of the region might well have been an argument for including these countries' (1998b: 18). However, the editors chose not to do so, and one of the reasons seems to be a lack of reliable sociological data. Similarly the excellent political economy text on Southeast Asia edited by Rodan et al. continues to exclude Myanmar, Cambodia, Laos and Brunei; these countries do not even merit a comparative reference, though Vietnam appears in one chapter (1997/2001a). Even in their recently published third edition (2006a), the absence of the mainland countries of Myanmar, Cambodia, and Laos, and the sultanate of Brunei continues, although the presence of Vietnam is now firmly established (Beresford, 2006: 197–220).

The sociological neglect of most of mainland Southeast Asia (and Brunei) is then partly a consequence of the obstacles researchers face in gaining access to research sites and data. Yet it is also noticeable that, in general, the more recent political-economy literature on Southeast Asia, perhaps partly because of theoretical and ideological emphases and the fact that capitalism is the scholarly object of scrutiny and criticism, have tended to pay less attention to the socialist countries, either as components of a world order in interrelationship with the capitalist economies, or as providing different models of social and economic development (Warren, 1985: 145; King, 1986). Of course, processes of market liberalization in Indochina since the late 1980s have acted to shift the grounds of the debate about the appropriateness of socialism and centralized control and allocation of economic resources in promoting national growth and development. The gradual opening of these countries to capitalism and their recent membership of ASEAN have also been accompanied by greater access to sources of information for social scientists.

With reference to the market-based economies of the then ASEAN countries in the mid-1980s, Higgott and Robison are correct in stating that critical sociological commentary had been virtually excluded by the pre-eminent position of structural-functionalist and modernization approaches. These paradigms conceive societies as a set of closely interrelated social elements or parts which function to maintain the integrity and identity of the whole, and they concentrate on the ways in which societies sustain an equilibrium, manage conflict, overcome contradictions and tensions, and progress at a measured pace from one social form to another with minimum disruption. The transition from 'traditional' forms to 'modern' ones is generally depicted as a gradual movement from one kind of integrated society to another. Examples of these approaches can be seen in some of the chapters in Evers's edited book (1973b), even though the volume is presented as an attempt to re-evaluate the modernization approach, and in Tham's earlier publications (1972, 1977). The importance of evolutionist assumptions about change and the concern to identify those social elements which either facilitate or retard 'progress' towards modern institutions are also exemplified, in part at least, in some of Geertz's early work (1963b).

The origins of much of this writing can be traced to the post-war political, economic and academic connections between the USA and the Philippines, Thailand and Indonesia, as well as the USA's political and military involvement in Indochina and its more general strategic interest in the region (King and Wilder, 2003: 68–73; Anderson, 1982; Anderson and Kahin, 1982). America had emerged as a world power with strong interests in the developing world, not least in the regions to the south of Communist China, North Korea and North Vietnam. It supported various regimes in the region, which were mainly authoritarian in persuasion, after early experiments with democracy; but, in a contradictory fashion, through academic writings, the media, and political opposition in the USA itself, the Americans also provided space to liberate, educate and radicalize some segments of the population in Southeast Asia (Trocki, 1981: 72). Although certain paradigms were dominant in social science and reflected the concerns of American scholarship, there was still evidence of counter-trends and critical thinking, particularly among local scholars when the political climate permitted (Heryanto, 2005: 85–86; Reynolds and Hong, 1983: 77–104). More recently there has also been an upsurge of contributions from local researchers attempting to counter what they see as 'intellectual imperialism' in their exploration of 'alternative discourses' in the social sciences ([Syed Farid] Alatas, 2000: 1–12; [Syed Hussein] Alatas, 2000: 23–45; Sinha, 2000: 67–104).Taufik Abdullah has pointed to the early post-war impulse in Indonesia, Malaysia and Thailand to 'decolonize knowledge', an impulse which was also witnessed in the Philippines during the 1970s when scholars there were part of the 'intellectual disturbances' and political ferment occasioned by continuing evidence of neo-colonial power and post-independence underdevelopment (nd: 2–3). A similar situation was evident in Thailand from the 1970s when local 'revisionist' and radical scholars used Marxist political-economy perspectives to examine Thailand's 'semicolonial', 'semifeudal' and 'dependent capitalist and underdeveloped' status (Reynolds and Hong, 1983: 97). But despite the calls to decolonize, nationalize, indigenize, universalize, and globalize the social sciences in Southeast Asia, there still seems to be a lack of locally generated theorizing and a continued dependence on Euro-American discourses, although I recognize that there have been important local contributions in such fields as gender, cultural studies and political economy ([Syed Farid] Alatas, 2000: 3–4; Clammer, 2000: 47–65; Reynolds and Hong, 1983; Samuel, 1999; Bautista, 1994).

The dominance of American-based scholarship in major parts of Southeast Asia, particularly during the 1950s through to the 1970s and at the height of the Cold War, is exemplified in the Cornell studies of Thailand from 1948 under the direction of Lauriston Sharp (Skinner and Kirsch, 1975; Bell, 1982), the Modern Indonesia Project under George McT. Kahin (Koentjaraningrat, 1975: 192) and the Cornell Southeast Asia Program. One of the best-known coordinated research programmes was that of the Center for International Studies, Massachusetts Institute of Technology, in Java from 1952, out of which the writings of Clifford and Hildred Geertz and Robert Jay emerged (Higgins, 1963; Koentjaraningrat, 1975: 198–207). Yale University's Southeast Asia Program focused on Indonesia, whilst the University of Chicago continued its pre-war, colonial research interests in the Philippines in close cooperation with American scholars working in academies in Manila (King and Wilder, 2003: 70–71). Moreover, American modernization perspectives and structural-functional analyses are seen not only in the work of the main American exponents, but also in the writings of many Thai, Indonesian and Filipino scholars trained in the United States (ibid.: 112–115).

In comparison with other parts of Southeast Asia, the Philippines, with its close academic connections to the USA, enjoyed a long history of teaching and research in sociology (Lynch and Hollnsteiner, 1961; Bautista, 1994). American academic interest in the Philippines and the desire for close and amicable relations with its former colony also continue to find expression among leading American scholars who have undertaken research on Philippine society (Landé, 2001). Sociology teaching was introduced into the University of the Philippines over 90 years ago during American administration; and, although in the Dutch East

Indies Schrieke was appointed as a Professor of Ethnology and Sociology at the Law School in Batavia in 1924, Indonesia's first full Professor of Sociology, T.S.G. Moelia, did not take up office until after independence in 1950, at the University of Indonesia. In 1938 a local scholar from the Philippines, Sarafin Macaraig, had already published the first general sociological text, *Introduction to Sociology*. In 1953 the Philippine Sociological Society was founded together with its journal, *The Philippine Sociological Review*. During the past 50 years the Society and its journal have disseminated a substantial amount of research material on the Philippines, which reflects the shifting external influences on and internal responses to the study of Philippine society and culture. In 1954 the well known teaching text *Sociology in the Philippine Setting* was published, written by Chester Hunt, in collaboration with two other American and two Filipino scholars. It appeared in second edition in 1963, and was revised and published again in 1976, and more recently in a fourth edition (1987). Another volume in the same tradition was that by Cordero and Panopio (1969), reissued subsequently, and then as an abridged edition (Panopio et al., 1995). Hunt's book has had a significant influence in Philippine sociology; it demonstrates the importance that American sociology and research funding had in the Philippines during the formative years of the discipline. In addition to the contribution of such American Professors of Sociology as Hunt, there was the important presence of Frank Lynch at the Institute of Philippine Culture, Ateneo de Manila (Yengoyan and Makil, 1984). Although Lynch was an anthropologist by training, he played a significant role in the development of Philippine sociology, and the Institute with which he was associated came under considerable criticism from local scholars in relation to its positivist and functionalist preoccupations with traditional values and modernization (Bautista, 1994: 4–6).

A dominant paradigm of American scholarship of the 1950s and 1960s, which can, in part, be traced back to such writers as Durkheim, was behaviourist, positivist and structural-functionalist. There was an interest in social norms, social roles and role expectations; the processes and mechanisms of social integration and institutionalization, and cultural patterns, personality formation and values. For example, early sociological studies of social class in the Philippines generally employed integrationist social stratification models, rather than dynamic concepts of class formation and conflict (Turner, 1978). Social inequality or hierarchy was also translated into analyses of personal, cross-cutting links between powerful patrons and dependent clients (Hollnsteiner, 1963). More general analyses of social change in the Philippines relied heavily on modernization paradigms (Carroll, 1968; Zamora, Baxter and Lawless, 1982; see Chapter 3).

Hunt and Dizon, in a survey of Philippine sociology in the late 1970s, attempted to provide an explanation for the importance of functionalism, and the 'pragmatic and relatively conservative' stance of scholarship (1978: 107). They argued that at the time it was important to understand 'local customs' and address practical social problems and policy issues. On the other hand, in a critical rejoinder to Hunt's and Dizon's overview, Weightman argued that Philippine sociology was dominated by a few senior American scholars, who were well connected to US funding agencies and dictated the content and direction of the research agenda (1978: 178–179; Weightman, 1975: 43–58). In the late 1970s, Weightman proposed that 'Philippine sociology still finds itself trying to escape from the intellectual strait jacket which sees an idealized American modern urban society as the sole model toward which the Philippines is perceived as approaching, departing, or deviating' (1978: 179). Even though Hunt and Dizon put up a robust defence of the American position, they too had to admit that, since the Second World War, in Philippine sociology 'the general trend of the discipline can best be explained as a delayed response to developments in the United States' (1978: 100). In this regard, the Philippine sociologist, Clarence Batan, in an admirable piece of self-reflection, argues recently that 'the world is in need of more non-Western sociologists to come up with descriptions and explanations of our societies and the relevant social problems we encounter' (2006: 8).

Much the same can be said for Indonesian sociology (Samuel, 1999). From the 1950s many young Indonesian scholars were trained in American academies. There was a heavy concentration on studies of community, religion and identity, and problems of agricultural development and national integration, such as in the work of Sunardi Sudarmadi, Tan Giok-Lan (Mely G Tan), Umar Khayam and Harsja Bachtiar (Koentjaraningrat, 1975: 225–226). As one might expect there was a need for basic data collection and therefore a focus on empirical investigations and regional socio-economic surveys (Hadiz and Dhakidae, 2005a: 11–18). There are many examples of sociological research on Indonesia employing modernization perspectives, one of the best known being Selosoemardjan's *Social Changes in Jogjakarta* (1962), arising from his work at Cornell. One of Selosoemardjan's main findings in this court town in east Java is that 'change from a closed to an open class system tends to turn people's orientation away from tradition and makes them more receptive to other changes', in particular, 'the desire for progress has replaced the security of tradition' (ibid.: 411, 412). Hadiz and Dhakidae refer to the formative period in much post-independence Indonesian scholarship when the first students went to the USA in the 1950s and 1960s and returned to shape Indonesian social sciences and focus on the examination of 'processes of social change, nation-building, economic development and political institutionalization' (2005: 11). Selosoemardjan was a central figure in this process and the founder of the Faculty of Social Sciences at the University of Indonesia.

In Thailand, too, American academic influence, particularly up to the early 1970s, was significant. There was an emphasis on culture and personality studies, the harmony- and stability-inducing influence of Buddhism, interpersonal patron–client dyads, social networks and clusters focused on hierarchy and status, the benevolent autocracy, and a preoccupation with the 'looseness' and informality of Thai society (Hewison, 1989a: 7–14; Trocki, 1981: 64–73). The roots and processes of tension, class conflict and exploitation played little part in this early literature, although several Thai scholars increasingly employed radical, neo-Marxist and underdevelopment perspectives in their analysis of Thai society; these emerged especially during the turbulent times of the 1970s in mainland Southeast Asia (Phillips, 1973; Juree and Vicharat, 1973; Morell and Chai-anan, 1981; Reynolds and Hong, 1983; Wedel, 1981, 1982). Interestingly the American modernization paradigm, in its application to Thailand, demonstrated a subtle shift in emphasis, linked to the circumstances of the country's status as a politically independent state which had not been subject to colonialism. American observers generally viewed Thailand in a positive light. However, as McVey indicates, with the American need to support anti-communist regimes and secure their alliance, the early post-war preoccupation with the twin goals of democratic nation-statehood and the progress to modernity gave way to the concern to bolster pro-Western governments and encourage social stability. Thus, 'what was emphasized in American analyses of Thailand was its ruralness, its perduring institutions, the lack of a colonial disruption that elsewhere had destroyed traditions without creating the institutions necessary for a smooth transition to modernity. Studies about Thailand thus tended to praise what elsewhere might be seen as obstacles to the struggle for modernity – the coherence of its culture and hierarchy, its unsullied rurality, its lack of intellectual dissent and social conflict' (McVey,1995: 3–4; Cohen, 1991).

For obvious reasons the American involvement in the Vietnam War created its own problems for American academics involved in Asian Studies and in disciplinary studies related to Asia. An academic counter-movement resulted in the foundation of the Committee of Concerned Asian Scholars, and its associated *Bulletin*. The Committee, among other things, challenged the perspectives and approaches to the study of Vietnam, promoted by the Center for Vietnamese Studies at Southern Illinois University and its journal *Southeast Asia*, in the context of Richard Nixon's 'Vietnamization' policy. The Center broadly accommodated the general American view of a more backward society in need of modernization with an emphasis on economic and social development and post-conflict construction (Allen, 1976: 2–16). Its close relationship with government and its activities in support of American policy provoked a strong reaction both within and beyond the USA and resulted in an international boycott and the final demise of the Center.

Finally, there are the remaining areas of Southeast Asia; the former British possessions of Malaya, Sarawak, North Borneo, Brunei and Singapore. In contrast to the early granting of political independence to the Philippines by the USA and, after a bloody revolutionary struggle, which culminated in the Dutch withdrawal from Indonesia in 1949 (with the exception of West New Guinea), the scatter of British-administered territories around the South China Sea achieved independence later: Malaya in 1957; Singapore, Sarawak and North Borneo (Sabah) in 1963, and Brunei in 1984. Aside from the conflict occasioned by the Malayan Emergency, political autonomy came relatively peacefully, and there was continuity in colonial scholarly perspectives in the early post-colonial era, dominated by colonial historians, linguists, scholars of literature, geographers and functionalist anthropologists, many of whom worked at the University of Malaya in Singapore and

Kuala Lumpur. Orientalism – the Western construction of particular images and knowledge of Eastern societies – provided an enduring legacy for the understanding of the cultures, histories and geographies of the Malay world within the British sphere of influence. We might note in passing that there have been virtually no sociological analyses of Brunei, with the partial exception of Brown's historical and sociological-anthropological study of the Brunei Sultanate (1970), and subsequent analyses of the concept of 'Muslim Malay Monarchy' and the nature of a rentier state (Braighlinn, 1992; Gunn, 1993). Sociological research is difficult to conduct in the Sultanate, although there were early, mainly American anthropological studies of Brunei Malays and non-Muslim minorities.

The formation of the Federation of Malaysia in 1963 and the establishment of the Republic of Singapore in 1965 were followed by major attempts by the respective political elites to promote economic growth, whilst maintaining political stability, particularly in the plural society of Malaysia. There was little room for a critical sociology in this environment, and it is of no surprise that local sociologists (and there were not many of them) should be concerned with basic data collection, descriptive studies, and practical issues of development. With regard to Singapore, Ong et al., in their overview of sociological research, refer to the political context within which it was conducted, the social and political control exercised, and the role of sociologists in policy research (1997a: viii). Khondker confirms, with regard to Singapore sociology, that in spite of recent evidence of academic autonomy and a more general openness in debate, 'the agenda for sociological research is still set in response to the concerns of social development. Sociologists exercising a good deal of pragmatism often choose topics of research on their own that somehow fit into the agenda of national development' (2000: 119).

The contexts within which sociologists worked in the first three post-war decades are seen clearly in the studies presented in Chen's and Evers's book on ASEAN sociology (1978a). Apart from general chapters, the book is mainly concerned with Singapore, and to a lesser extent Malaysia, Thailand and Indonesia. There is considerable attention to the characteristics and roles of elites, especially in the context of modernization and nation-building. There are empirical studies of different ethnic groups, inter-ethnic relations and ethnic-based institutions, and chapters on the consequences of urbanization, especially high-rise living in Singapore. The research on Singapore is obviously closely associated with the need for the government to collect data on and form conclusions about its public housing policies (Tai, 1988; see Chapter 10). In Malaysia, there has been much empirical work on describing and explaining the relatively disadvantaged and constructed status of the Malays as against the economic achievements of the immigrant Chinese (Husin Ali,1981), mainly in terms of explanatory frameworks which perceive religion and tradition as obstacles to economic development (see Chapters 6 and 8).

The 'regnant paradigm' or 'vision', in McVey's words (1995: 1), of early post-war American-dominated social science, preoccupied with nation-building and modernity, and Western perspectives which created 'the Oriental other', therefore provide the environment in which we must consider the early post-war socio-logical enterprise in Southeast Asia. Moreover, the priority accorded the national project and the achievement of modernity, principally through the mechanisms of economic growth and industrialization, coincided precisely with the interests and policies of indigenous elites, which were closely entwined with Western in-volvement in the region; the pathways to these goals might be varied and tortuous, the ideological expressions of them diverse, but the vital importance of national resilience underpinned by economic growth and development remained constant (Cohen, 1991: 36–46, 128–149). Studies of social change in the 'Third World' therefore focused on development; indeed the two became almost synonymous in post-war social science, and development in turn was primarily envisaged as a 'progressive' economic process, although it clearly had social, cultural, psychologi-cal and political dimensions as well. As Hulme and Turner state, '[t]he concept of development is essentially concerned with social change and human progress in a group of countries, mostly former colonies, which are lumped together under convenient but increasingly misleading collective titles such as the Third World or the South' (1990: 33).

An Alternative Tradition?

Before considering in more detail McVey's 'regnant paradigm' and the counter-paradigm of underdevelopment and dependency in Chapters 3 and 4, it is worth examining briefly a rather different sociological tradition. This was critical of American-led modernization theory and, to some extent, ran in parallel with radical scholarship, although, in important respects, it also pre-dated it (van den Muijzenberg and Wolters, 1988). This tradition, established by Dutch scholars from the early post-war period, had only modest influence on the modernization paradigm, and it did not receive much attention from neo-Marxists and political economists whose work began to take on a higher profile in the study of Southeast Asia from the late 1970s (King, 1996: 168–173). I am referring to the historical-sociological school of Wertheim and his successor at the University of Amsterdam, Otto van den Muijzenberg. In important respects, these carried the same messages as the underdevelopment and dependency writers, but they provided an intriguing bridge between neo-Marxist concerns, certain neo-evolutionary ideas, and Weber's sociology. I have already remarked on the unfortunate neglect of Wertheim's and his colleagues' work in the general sociology of Southeast Asia (ibid.: 169). Their specifically theoretical contribution to the analysis of social change did not receive much attention in Evers's sociology reader, although Evers did feature Wertheim's historical overview of Southeast Asia (1980a: 8–23), his early descriptive work on 'trading minorities' (1980b: 104–120; 1964a: 38–82), and van den Muijzenberg's piece on 'involution or evolution in the Philippines'(1980: 209–219). Nothing from the Dutch school appeared in the compendium of Taylor and Turton (1988a). The Dutch contribution was mentioned in passing in Higgott's and Robison's book, to the effect that the socio-historical approach 'sought to integrate political, social and economic approaches' but had been overtaken by other Western writings influenced by 'Orientalist' and 'empiricist' preoccupations (1985b: 5). This very cursory observation serves to assign Wertheim's work to the margins of the study of social change in Asia. However, we must recognize that the Dutch contribution is substantial, but its disadvantage in international scholarship is that much of it has been published in the Dutch language (van den Muijzenberg and Wolters, 1988: 31).

The distinctive contribution of the Dutch school, and its major preoccupation with transformations in Indonesian society, also demonstrate, although I am oversimplifying the complexities of academic debate, a broad distinction between American and European scholarship on Southeast Asia, which is replicated in other areas of research (King, 2006b: 23–25, 36–37). In the field of anthropology, for example, I have already drawn attention to the differences between the American cultural anthropological tradition, especially prominent in the first three decades of post-war decolonization, which focused on nation-building, modernization and the peasant heartlands of Southeast Asia, and the European tendencies towards structuralism, neo-Marxism, political economy and the marginal, tribal populations of the region (King, 2001: 19–23). In sociology, we can discern another diverging pathway, between, again in post-war American social science, a preoccupation with modernization, democratization and economic growth, and the ways in which these can be achieved or obstructed, and, in my view, a mainly Dutch-led European concern with the problematical relations between colonial powers and the colonized, and an interest in conflict and dynamic change.

Van den Muijzenberg and Wolters note the Dutch encounter with the modernization paradigm as comprising 'a mixture of acceptance and scepticism'; there was a positive move to replace the schematic modern-traditional dichotomy with a more nuanced and detailed historical-sociological understanding of social change and conflict (1988: 20–24).There was also a recognition of the value of ideas drawn from Weber and Marx, although Weber's perspectives were more sympathetically received. It was Wertheim who translated these European interests into a grand theoretical project in his notion of society 'as a composite of conflicting value systems' and his focus on the principle of emancipation in human history (from 'the forces of nature'and from 'human domination') as a major driving force in the dynamics of social change (1964a: 22–37; 1974,1993). Van den Muijzenberg and Wolters refer to this perspective as 'dialectical evolutionism', which also drew on the ideas of the Dutch historian, Jan Romein (1962), and his concept of the 'dialectics of progress' and 'common human patterns' with reference to the achievements of Asia in the twentieth century (1988: 23; Wertheim,1964a: 3–20).

The context of this harmonious marriage between history and sociology was Wertheim's appointment in December 1946 to a Chair in the Modern History and Sociology of Indonesia at the University of Amsterdam, subsequently to become a professorship covering the whole of Southeast Asia. It was both his predecessor Schrieke's concept and Wertheim's task in his academic career to understand how Indonesian society, and later the wider Southeast Asian region had undergone change and reacted to external forces (Wertheim, 1993: 1). But, as Wertheim notes, his mentors, Schrieke and van Leur, though they had adopted a Weberian approach to the analysis of Indonesian society, using, in particular, the concept of an 'ideal type', were silent on the colonial relationship (ibid.: 2). Wertheim was to address this blind-spot in the Dutch historical-sociological project.

Although I have been critical elsewhere of Wertheim's concept of society and social change, there are elements of it which have considerable analytical value and they have some resonance with the approach of the political economists (see Chapter 5; King, 1996: 170–171). The area of Wertheim's theory which seems problematical is his attempt to reformulate and use evolutionary theory, including the notion of certain societies 'skipping stages' and others being overtaken and even regressing, and to develop a grand theory of human history. In my view, his approach to an understanding of the dynamics of social change does not need to be cluttered with a generalizing view of evolution, which then organizes societies on a scale or trajectory of sequence or progression. His concept of evolution is rescued to some extent by his notion of rapid revolutionary change, but it is still unnecessary. On the other hand, and dispensing with the distraction of evolution, what is important in Wertheim's work is his focus on points of strain, tension, contradiction, opposition, antagonism, protest, discontent and struggle in societies. He conceptualizes this dissonance in terms of 'conflicting values' and he counters those social scientists preoccupied with notions of societal harmony and integration, with the apt reminder that 'no human society is a completely integrated entity' (1993: 8). He notes that, although one can usually discern a dominant set of values in any given society, which is espoused and supported by those in power, there are always undercurrents of protest and different, deviant or competing sets of values (ibid.: 11). Scott also comes close to this position, according to Evans, in his 'motto' that 'wherever there is domination there is bound to be resistance' (Evans, 1986: 30). In similar vein, Evers and his colleagues at the University of Bielefeld have been finely tuned to processes of conflict and contradiction, seen most notably in Evers's illuminating concept of 'strategic groups' (1973a, 1978c, 1980d; see Chapter 5).

These undercurrents of protest can be controlled, channelled, and institutionalized so that the appearance of integration and harmony is reinforced, but the 'counterpoints' do not disappear. They can resurface and become 'rallying points for 'opposition to the official hierarchy' (Wertheim, 1993: 11). An interesting and contentious position that Wertheim promotes is that value systems are 'psychical realities', and 'subjective interpretations of society by different social layers'; they are 'accepted in different shades of intensity among definite segments of society' (ibid.: 13, 14). Wertheim argues against the concept of an objectively existing, generally accepted hierarchical social system and against the structural-functionalist position that social structures are 'rigid realities' (ibid.: 16). For him societies are about 'thinking' and 'feeling' and '[t]his conceptualization enabled him to describe and analyse developments in a less deterministic and reified way' (van den Muijzenberg and Wolters, 1988: 23).

I am content with Wertheim's emphasis on conflict, struggle and opposition as a social dynamic and on the dialectical interaction between contending forces and processes, but his focus on ideas and 'mentalities' in human history and his claim that social institutions are only 'images' in the minds of real people, need some qualification. This seems a too 'idealistic', indeed a Hegelian view of social organization, which sees society as far too 'unreal'. After all there are institutions which we simply cannot 'un-think'; they have a presence and a reality above and beyond what we imagine; they direct and constrain us to act and behave in certain ways. It is not merely that they are a product of the value system of those in power. They are supported and enforced by something more than a value system. There are clues to the ways in which those in power defend their position, and which Wertheim does not really address, in Evans's remark that 'hegemony is not simply a matter of high ideals it must have some material reality' (1986: 27).

We should also note the close interconnection, in their mutual concerns with conflict, struggle and opposition, between the Dutch historical-sociological perspective and that of the later Australian-based political economists. Take, for example, the comments of Rodan et al. that not only institutions, but also markets are defined 'within wider and system-level processes of social and political conflict' (2006c: 6). The focus, as with Wertheim, is on competing and conflicting interests, but for these political economists, power is much more 'powerful'. The transitory nature of social formations in Wertheim's theory is translated into something far more 'real' in the political economy framework; '[e]xisting regimes, therefore, cannot be dismantled at will because they embody a specific arrangement of economic, social, and political power' (ibid.: 7). What is also apparent is that wealth and the control of economic resources (money politics and capitalist accumulation) 'provide mechanisms by which powerful corporate interests directly capture and appropriate state power' (ibid.: 25).

Concluding Remarks

I have discussed the problems of defining sociology and locating it within a regional framework, and explained the context and constraints within which early post-war sociological research was undertaken, with its emphasis on nation-building and modernization. I have highlighted the importance of addressing social conflict, competing interests and values, protest and opposition, with reference to Wertheim's work. In the next two chapters we shall move to a more detailed consideration of the two major competing paradigms in the sociology of change and development – modernization and underdevelopment/dependency theory – which dominated sociology and development studies into the 1970s and 1980s. Modernization theory, given both its practical and theoretical shortcomings, began to provoke a reaction even in the late 1950s from those theorists who took their inspiration from Marx and writers on imperialism such as Lenin, Luxemburg and Bukharin. The neo-Marxist critique gathered pace in the 1960s and the 1970s, and, in response, modernization theorists revised their framework to account for the complexities of socio-economic change, the variable responses to it, and the ways in which continuing problems of poverty and inequality could be addressed in the developing world.

3

Modernization and Post-War Social Change

What is involved in modernization is a 'total' transformation of a traditional or pre-modern society into the types of technology and associated social organization that characterize the 'advanced', economically prosperous, and relatively politically stable nations of the western world (Moore, 1963: 89).

If industrialization describes the physical change of society, then modernity describes the intellectual and cultural features of this society. Modernity conventionally denotes the modern age and the ideas and styles associated with this age … [It is] associated with a strong belief in rationality and the triumph of science over religion as an explanation of the world (Chong, 2005: 7, 8).

Introduction

The social transformations set in motion in Southeast Asia after the Japanese occupation and the processes of decolonization which gathered pace following Ho Chi Minh's declaration of Vietnamese independence on 2 September 1945 and Sukarno's proclamation of the Indonesian Republic on 17 August 1945 defy simple generalization. We must recognize that during the period of decolonization significant parts of the region were embroiled in political and military conflict, there were serious internal ethnic conflicts between majority lowland populations and minorities, and the problems of former colonial economies, given the imbalances in resource exploitation and the dominance of external groups, were formidable. New socio-economic groupings were emerging as these economies became increasingly integrated into a global system and as local people began to fill the political and administrative spaces left by the departing colonial powers.

Yet in the 1950s and 1960s many senior social scientists attempted to understand this complexity, in retrospect rather surprisingly, by recourse to a general theory of social change, which, it was thought, would assist them in anticipating the future character and direction of these newly-independent societies. Although 'modernization theory' has been frequently talked about as if it were a coherent and all-encompassing explanation of dynamic processes, it embraced a range of different emphases and interests and was concerned above all to understand how stability and structure could be sustained in periods of transition; some observers focused on economic organization, others on political institutions, others on social structures, and still others on personalities, values and attitudes; some were concerned with theory, others with policy. Some concentrated on a particular country or case, others were more general in orientation. Nevertheless, there were common principles or ideas which enabled supporters and critics to talk about it as if it was a unified theoretical system (Hoogvelt, 1982: chs 3–4). Modernization theory has also continued in modified form since then, resurfacing in another guise in the more recent 'Asian values' debates. These focus on the compatibility or otherwise of 'traditional Asian values' and modernization, and were, in part at least, attempts by senior politicians in such places as Singapore and Malaysia to argue for the capacity of Asian societies to accept Western technology, science and capitalism without the need to absorb undesirable, or 'polluting' cultural values (Clammer, 1985: 22–30; 1996; see Chapter 8).

A major problem faced by those who attempted to analyse processes of modernization was the vagueness and elasticity of the concept. Even in the late 1970s a prominent Singaporean sociologist, who had worked within a modernization paradigm, indicated that '[t]here is no common definition of modernization which is acceptable to all social scientists, or even to social scientists of any particular discipline' (Chen, 1980: 236). Other concepts jostled with modernization for priority – Westernization, industrialization, urbanization, development, economic growth, progress; sometimes modernization was used as an umbrella to embrace all of these, and at other times was distinguished from them so that some observers argued that, for example, there could be modernization without industrialization, without development (Jacobs, 1971), or without Westernization (Alatas, 1972; Cohen, 1991: 39–41). Chen, in his study of Singapore, prefers to distinguish three key concepts – modernization, industrialization and development – and he follows the approach of Bendix (1964) and Apter (1965) in defining modernization in socio-cultural and political rather than in techno-economic terms (Chen, 1980: 237–238). In other words, modernization refers to differentiated and flexible social structures which can cope with and adjust to change, values which can, without disintegrating, address and encourage innovation, and to 'a social framework to provide the skills and knowledge necessary for living in a technologically advanced world' (Apter,1965, cited by Chen, 1980: 238). In similar vein Alatas, in his study of Singapore, distinguishes modernization from Westernization in that 'Westernization means the adoption of Western values and cultural elements of the type that have nothing to do with the process of application of modern scientific developments in society' (1972: 72). As we shall see the main focus of modernization theorists was precisely the relationships between social structures, cultural values and behaviour, and techno-economic development.

Why was modernization theory such a powerful paradigm? First, its very simplicity and apparent ability to organize a range of diverse 'social facts' held great appeal. It seemed to provide an ideal blueprint for the explanation of general processes of change. Second, it presented an optimistic and positive view of the developing world, which placed enormous faith in the power of capitalism to bring blessings and good wherever it put down its roots (Hulme and Turner, 1990: 37). In other words, in practical and policy terms (because modernization theory was both a way of seeing the world and a means to encourage it to move in the desired direction), the transfer of capital through aid and investment, as well as the diffusion of scientific knowledge and Western values would serve to promote the modernization process (Roxborough, 1979: chs 1–2). It was also closely associated with the struggle and competition on a global scale between the ideology and practice of liberal democracy and that of communism and socialism. Some contributions such as that of Rostow's 'stages of economic growth' were explicitly anti-communist (1960). Some social scientists, particularly development economists, also worked for development agencies responsible for engineering economic growth and social change in the developing world. Of course, these Western observers were not blind to economic backwardness, poverty, inequality and political and military conflicts in such places as Latin America and Southeast Asia, but there was a firm belief that the American dream was within the grasp of everyone provided those factors which underpinned Western modernity were properly disseminated or diffused to other parts of the world.

Third, modernization theory stemmed directly from a major preoccupation of Western thought from the late eighteenth century. This was the description and analysis of the transition in Europe from feudal, mainly agrarian-based societies to capitalist, urban-based ones. Underlying this focus was a strong dependence on the concept of evolution, influenced from the mid-nineteenth century by Darwin's theory. It was a short step to transfer the paradigms used in explaining modernization processes in Europe to other parts of the world. Modernization theory attempted to capture what were thought to be the crucial elements in the transition from 'traditional' relatively static social forms to 'modern', dynamic, 'democratic' ones. The assumption was that the processes which had been at work in eighteenth- and nineteenth-century Europe and had led to the transplantation of capitalism in North America and other white settler areas would be broadly the same, if delayed, in the former colonial territories. Clear differences (which *in extremis* was seen as a confrontation) were discerned between the social structures, economies and cultures of the small-scale, slow moving, relatively undifferentiated agrarian societies which had been written about by colonial observers and anthropologists and the large-scale, fast changing, complex, industrialized societies of the West. Even informed observers like Hugh Tinker were seduced by this paradigm and tried to incorporate the analysis of change in Southeast Asia into a framework of evolution and continuity (1969: 97–116).

In this exercise of comparing different 'ideal types' of society, key ideas from classical sociology, especially from Durkheim and Weber, were deployed and re-formulated in the creation of modernization theory. The critical views of Marx on the exploitative, conflict-ridden dimensions of capitalism were left to one side. Durkheim's thesis expounded in *The Division of Labour in Society* (1984 [1893]) was particularly compelling. In his major study of social change, Durkheim traced the movement from traditional societies which, for him, were held together by 'mechanical solidarity', to modern societies organized in terms of 'organic solidarity'. He argued that these changes were primarily the result of increases in population and demographic density. From small-scale, self-contained, village communities which replicated one another in segmental or 'mechanical' fashion, where social and economic roles were personalized, undifferentiated and multiplex and the division of labour rudimentary, there was an evolutionary movement to a complex, differentiated society in which roles became specialized, individualized and impersonal. The result was increasing 'organic' interdependence in the division of labour (Webster, 1990: 44–46). The attraction for modernization theorists was Durkheim's emphasis on the problems of social order and the importance of moral values and norms in securing cohesion.

It was the American sociologist Talcott Parsons, in his grand post-war socio-logical synthesis *The Social System* (1951; also 1960), who combined Durkheim's insights with those of Weber. Weber saw the transition to capitalism as both a cultural and economic process. In *The Protestant Ethic and the Spirit of Capitalism* (1971 [1905]) he identified 'rationalization' and a certain religious-inspired attitude to this-worldly economic activity as key elements in the emergence of capitalism. Capitalism, unlike other economic systems, was characterized by the preoccupation with profit, the efficient use of capital, control of quality and costs, effective organization of production, the need for diligence, competition, discipline, and moderation, and above all the rational re-investment and accumulation of capital rather than conspicuous consumption. According to Weber this frame of mind and lifestyle, which was opposed to a traditional outlook, emerged in the Protestant Reformation in Europe and was especially associated with the Calvinist doctrine of predestination. He did not discover the motivational conditions for the development of capitalism in either Chinese worldviews, specifically Confucianism and Taoism (1951), or Indian Hinduism and Buddhism (1958), or subsequently in Islam (Turner, 1974). Weber's comparative sociology was directed, in part at least, to explaining the unique history of Western capitalism (1963). For example, for Weber, 'China's economic backwardness was fostered by the values inculcated by Confucianism' (McVey, 1992b: 9; 1992a).

Returning to Parsons, he saw traditional society as characterized by an orientation to the past, stability, fatalism, superstition, and ascribed roles and responsibilities; for him, it would be replaced by modern organization and values oriented to

the future, innovation and achievement. Parsons's grand theory focused on the formulation of what he termed 'pattern variables', and he discerned two all-embracing
and contrasting sets of value orientations and role expectations: 'the traditional'
and 'the modern'. His model provided modernization theorists, like Hoselitz (1960),
Lerner (1958), Moore (1963) and Rostow (1960), with an analytical framework and
a mode of explanation for the social and cultural issues posed by development in
the non-Western world and how these might be overcome in order that successful
'take-off' to sustained economic growth and modernity might be achieved (Chew
and Denemark, 1996a: 2).

A final consideration in explaining the seductiveness of modernization ideas
was that the post-war transfer of capital and resources from the United States to
Japan and Western Europe to rebuild the war-torn economies there had had a
positive developmental effect. It was thought that a similar transfer or 'diffusion'
of capital and aid, as well as the appropriate knowledge, values and attitudes to
underpin the use of those resources would have a similar effect in the developing world. Therefore, the study of modernization became synonymous with the
study of post-war development, and orientations to innovation, achievement and
entrepreneurship had to be cultivated. One of the major interests of modernization
theorists was the identification of those values, attitudes and social forms which
would facilitate or hinder modernization. In other words, it was necessary to delineate its pre-conditions and the obstacles to its achievement. One also needed to
identify those social groups which would assist in the development process and the
best ways in which 'the modern' could be disseminated to those who were seen to
be encapsulated in a backward-looking, risk-averse world.

In an influential statement on these problems, Soedjatmoko, who provided the
impetus and inspiration for a conference on *Cultural Motivations to Progress in
South and Southeast Asia*, held in June 1963 in Manila, stated that 'it will be necessary for the modernizers to increase their manipulative capacity with regard to the
traditional sectors of their society' (1965: 2). In a direct reference to the growing
appeal of socialist and communist ideologies in nationalist solutions to Asian economic development, he proposed an alternative, which resonates with the concerns
of modernization theorists. 'Modernizers', and by this he means national political
elites, must seek to activate 'more basic and more specific motivations for the acceleration of economic development'; these motivations lie not in secular ideologies
but are 'undoubtedly embedded in the cultural religious matrix' (ibid.: 6).

Boeke and Dualism

Although modernization theory was predominantly an American preserve, an
early statement sharing many of its defining characteristics came from the Dutch
administrator-scholar, J.H.Boeke, who based his ideas on the Netherlands East
Indies' experience. His original theory of social and economic dualism (1910) was
elaborated in a series of important publications, some of them in English (1953);
these appeared at the time that concepts of modernization were being formulated.

However, Boeke's conclusions on the impact of European colonialism on tropical dependencies differed markedly from those which were to be drawn by post-war American social scientists. Boeke pointed to the great benefits which colonialism had brought to the West, but argued that this was achieved by the impoverishment of colonial peasantries. He also indicated that there were social and cultural reasons ('the force of tradition') internal to peasant society which helped explain their plight because 'Western capitalism did not find in Eastern society the institutions ready to take charge of propagating its principles and achievements' (1980: 28). Nevertheless, his conceptual framework, like that of modernization theory, was based on a dualistic model. For him Indonesian society demonstrated 'a sharp, deep, broad cleavage' between a modern European-dominated capitalist sector which obeyed the laws of market-based economic theory and a traditional Asian subsistence sector which did not.

According to Boeke the traditional peasantry did not respond to capitalist-generated stimuli because their economic needs were limited whilst their social needs in terms of status and reciprocity were more important. He says that 'economic needs and their strictly economic gratification are of no more than secondary importance' (ibid.: 35). Local farmers were averse to risk-taking, capital accumulation and continuous profit-seeking, and lacked discipline and organizational abilities. These latter were the characteristics which Weber had identified as crucial in the emergence and development of the 'spirit of capitalism'. Instead village society was characterized by social harmony and the overriding importance of religion, customs and traditions. Yet Boeke waivers between an explanation for these circumstances in the conditions of colonial exploitation and one which stems from the persistence of 'traditional culture', 'mentality', 'spirit' and 'personality' (Koentjaraningrat,1980: 42). Furthermore, unlike modernization theorists who assumed that an evolution from tradition to modernity was achievable, Boeke seemed more pessimistic (Hulme and Turner, 1990: 40). The occurrence of two different kinds of society and economy side-by-side in the East Indies seemed set to persist, and peasant society to deteriorate further.

Some of the criticisms of Boeke's conception of Indonesian society can be made of modernization theory. The characterization of non-Western, especially rural societies is misleading because peasant economic needs are not necessarily limited, nor are rural dwellers necessarily unresponsive to market opportunities, lacking organizational abilities; and religion and tradition are not necessarily obstacles to economic growth. Van der Kroef, for example, in his examination of the Indonesian entrepreneur, argues that Boeke's concept of dualism ignores the dynamism in Indonesian socio-economic life and wrongly assumes that Indonesian culture is 'entirely at odds with western capitalist processes' (1953: 302). Higgins, a Canadian economist, was also critical of Boeke's pessimism and argued for the possibility of economic progress in such countries as Indonesia (1980). But in line with modernization thinking, Higgins searched for sociological obstacles to economic development in such factors as the extended family, the limited scope of entrepreneurial spirit, the backward-sloping supply curve of effort and risk-taking, and unrestricted population growth (ibid.: 53–54).

I shall return to the criticisms of modernization theory in Chapter 4 but what is needed is a detailed examination of the historical contexts in which particular kinds of response to change were generated. In the case of Java, on which Boeke focused, the explanations for the plight of rural dwellers are to be found primarily in the character of Dutch colonialism rather than in any innate predispositions of the peasantry. A similar argument can be presented to understand the problems of rural impoverishment in British Burma. Furthermore, if one wishes to use a dual sector model, and with appropriate modifications it has some explanatory value, we should at least be more sensitive to the interconnections between the sectors, to the variations within each sector and to the dynamic processes of change and response.

Some Southeast Asian Examples

One of the most important channels of scholarly communication for those who were attempting to apply concepts of change and modernization to development issues was the journal *Economic Development and Cultural Change* of the University of Chicago's Research Center in Economic Development and Cultural Change. The first issue appeared in 1952. The introductory editorial by Alexander J. Morin set out its main objectives and character, and the very first article to appear was by Bert Hoselitz, who worked at the Center, entitled 'Non-Economic Barriers to Economic Development'. In outlining the main concerns of the journal, Morin refers to 'the possibility of relating (in both directions) particular sets of ideologies and their constituent values to particular social and economic structures, and of determining those values of particular cultures, of various degrees of malleability, which aid or hinder the development process' (1952: 7). As the title of the journal suggests, and Hoselitz's and Morin's initial statements confirm, a major preoccupation was the relationship between economic processes and 'non-economic' values and ideas. This also involved the identification of individuals and social groups who 'perform the main innovating function' (ibid.: 5). Morin places the journal's concerns in an international context characterized by the diffusion or transfer of resources, expertise and values from the West to the developing world. He says 'the development of the West has created an environment in which local progress will inevitably consist in large part of selective imitation and adaptation from this environment. The problem of economic growth in presently underdeveloped areas therefore can be viewed as one involving the transmittal of culture rather than simply one of local innovation' (ibid.: 4).

Hoselitz too refers to the relationships between economic change, behavioural patterns and cultural norms and states boldly that 'there is no doubt that the obstinacy with which people hold to traditional values, even in the face of a rapidly changing technology and economic organization may impose obstacles of formidable proportions' (1952: 9). In this general article he does not make many specific references to Southeast Asia, but at one point evaluates the prospects for economic improvement in Burma arguing that in 'present-day Burma independence is not only accompanied by a resumption of traditional names and dress, but a strengthening of Buddhism, a religion which reflects an ideology totally opposed to efficient, progressive economic activity. The realization of economic advancement meets thus with numerous obstacles and impediments' (ibid.: 10). He is not enamoured of Theravada Buddhism's other-worldly orientation which 'calls forth a philosophy of life which is not conducive to economic advancement' (ibid.: 14; Ayal, 1963; Kirsch, 1975; Tambiah, 1973, 1976; see also Chapter 8). For Hoselitz, like Morin, one of the crucial conditions for economic development is the presence of social groups committed to innovation, usually what has been termed 'a middle class', with 'a spirit of venturesomeness' (ibid.). Hoselitz also discerns other related conditions such as a high degree of social mobility, a fluid class structure without a wide gulf between rulers and ruled, realistic and rational development plans, and, very importantly, appropriate aspirations, value orientations, skills and modes of work.

Articles in the journal in the 1950s and 1960s therefore tended to be preoccupied with the identification and analysis of the social, cultural and institutional factors which, on the one hand, appeared to encourage and, on the other, hinder economic development. There were also contributions on the kinds of social and cultural arrangements in developing countries which differed from those in the West and which seemed to have some influence, potential or actual, on economic activity. There were, for example, papers by the noted scholar of early post-war Indonesia, Justus van der Kroef, on the entrepreneur and the middle class (1953). Van der Kroef reinforces the observations of Boeke on Indonesian attitudes towards economic activity. He points to the inadequate deployment of capital in business and the lack of knowledge of its function, economic conservatism, lack of specialization, 'irrationality' in business operations, and lack of re-investment in production. For him this outlook should be understood in terms of Indonesian perceptions of needs which are primarily social and 'welfarist' rather than economic (the importance of leisure, harmony, self-control and prestige).

Another important contribution in this genre was Manning Nash's comparative study of the social prerequisites to economic growth in one country in Latin America and one in Southeast Asia (1964). Nash was to go on to publish his major contribution to Southeast Asian anthropology *The Golden Road to Modernity* (1965), which explored the constraints and opportunities, particularly in the realm of religion, on the modernization process in Burma. His earlier comparative article, though it did not mention Burma by name, was clearly based on his field research there prior to the military takeover in 1962. For Nash a central motor of modernization was 'the application of a growing science to all branches of production' (1964: 226). However, modernization was much broader than this because economic growth is but one dimension of 'the larger and more general process of social and cultural change'. For him 'Modernity is the social, cultural, and psychological framework which facilitates the application of science to the processes of production' (ibid.).

Nash was well aware that the notion of the 'traditional' embraced a diversity of social and cultural forms, hence his comparison of two different non-industrial societies. He coins the term 'multiple society', which embraces a diversity of cultural traditions and ethnic groups, to draw attention to the horizontal and vertical divisions within a given country and the different levels of access to resources, control over people and symbols, 'impulses to change' and differential possession of political skills, among different segments of society. He suggests that, within the 'multiple society', it is only the 'nation-bearing segment' (alternatively the 'modern elite', or 'political class'), which 'can organize for purposeful political action' (ibid.: 228; 1980: 76–84). This segment is poorly articulated with other segments or 'smaller-scale societies' within the nation (including the peasantry, minority groups and tribal populations). Nash addresses what he sees as Burma's failure to modernize ('its developmental woes') and he does so in a manner which improves on the preoccupations of earlier modernization writings with low achievement motivation, lack of entrepreneurship, particularism and so on (1964: 234, 242). He attempts to combine macro- with micro-sociological analysis and identifies the responses of different groups to change, explaining the choices they make and their consequences. He is also aware of the problems posed by a colonial legacy. However, he still seems to be tied to the dichotomy between the socio-cultural factors which facilitate and hinder economic development. For him it is the nation-bearing segment in Burma which lacks the 'organizational norms' necessary for action in a country in which the government plays a crucial developmental role. These norms are largely seen in Western terms (functional authority, standards of performance, feedback and communication, attitudes towards failure and success in government action). These are in turn compounded by conflict and power struggle within the national segment. Ultimately Nash falls back on tautology to explain economic failure. Burma has not modernized because its social structure is only partially modern, its national segment is not organized in modern terms to do modern things, and rural farmers 'rarely create economic opportunities or devise new forms or means of production' (ibid.: 236, 241).

The developmental problems posed by resource-rich Burma clearly exercised American social scientists. One of the most important studies in the modernization genre was Lucian Pye's examination of the relationships between Burmese (or rather lowland Burman) psychological characteristics and the failure to achieve political and economic advancement (1962). In his study of political culture, he concentrates on what he terms 'transitional politics' as well as the problem of nation-building and the search for a meaningful identity in a post-colonial world. He is also preoccupied with the ways in which 'representative' or democratic political institutions can be developed, and the reconciliation or fusion of the demands of 'parochialism' on 'traditional' societies and those of 'universalism' in modern nation-hood (Sloan, 1967: 17–18). It is Pye's contention that the Burmese failure to modernize can be explained with reference to their psychological reactions to change. He combines insights from political science, anthropology and psychology to analyse Burmese personality structure, socialization processes, and social attitudes and values (as does Spiro, 1967, 1970). He does this empirically by interviewing politicians, bureaucrats and intellectuals about Burmese modernization and the problems of achieving it.

As Geertz suggests in his penetrating review of the book, Pye fails to conceptualize the concepts of 'culture' and 'identity' with sufficient precision so that in his hands they become a vague, undifferentiated set of values, emotions, attitudes, feelings, images, patterns of action, reflections and views (1964: 205–209). However, overall, for Pye, culture is a psychological concept; it is about personality, or more grandly 'national personality or character', and processes of socialization, and it does not address the relationships between psychology and such issues as the distribution of wealth and power, the evaluation of status and prestige, the recognition of sets of obligations and expectations, and the realities of national and international politics in the historical contexts in which they are embedded. Pye's thesis is that Burmese psychological traits are obstacles to progress seen in Western political and economic terms. More generally he argues that in the 1950s 'the new countries of Asia have had more difficulties with the psychological than with the objective economic problems basic to nation building' (1962: xv). For Pye the search for both individual and collective identities 'can be successful only with the achievement of a psychologically satisfying and organizationally effective fusion of traditional and rational attitudes' (ibid.: 291). With this conclusion he argues that American aid programmes should not overemphasize technical and economic assistance at the expense of imparting Western democratic values because it is 'the democratic ideal ... which illuminates the links between politics, personality, and nation building' (ibid.: 301). We should note here that Pye has continued to interpret the Burmese economic and political malaise in terms of cultural factors and processes of socialization. The Burmese, according to this view, have a basic distrust of those in power, and they have loyalties to personal patrons rather than to national political institutions (2001: 386–387). Although I am persuaded that patronage has something to do with the dynamics of social change and authoritarianism in Burma and Southeast Asia more generally, I am more sceptical of the cultural-psychological explanations for the Burmese predicament, as is Callahan (2003). In her recent analysis of the Burmese military, she argues that their character and perspectives are primarily borne out of the historical, political, economic and ethnic context of Myanmar, and the military's continuous involvement in conflict and 'war-making' since independence (ibid.; Selth, 2002). Yet a recent analysis of Burmese politics continues to rely on a rather outdated perspective based on cultural explanations, and eschews political-economic analysis (McCarthy, 2006; see also Chapters 4 and 6).

In his critical commentary on Pye, Geertz poses the crucial question 'Even if he [Pye] is right, and the Burmans are hyper-individualistic, distrustful, liable to violence, fond of empty social form, and prefer uncertainty to determinism, is it so clear, especially in the absence of an explicit analysis of the Burmese polity and economy as such, that these could not turn out to be very valuable traits in supporting modernization?' (1964: 209). Geertz prefers a sociological interpretation of modernization, although in some of his work he too operates within the framework of a transition from tradition to modernity, and associated notions of economic rationalization and take-off into sustained economic growth. As we shall see later, his concept of 'agricultural involution' in Indonesia moves closer to a more historically informed and contextualized analysis of change, akin to Wertheim (1959 [1956]), and shares some of the same perspectives as underdevelopment and dependency theory (Geertz,1963a). However, in a more locally focused study of economic modernization, Geertz searches for socio-economic groups which might serve as potential modernizers. In *Peddlers and Princes* (1963b), he compares the commercial activities of a group of Muslim (*santri*) small businessmen or 'peddlers' in the eastern Javanese town of Modjokuto with an entrepreneurial group of 'displaced aristocrats' in the court town of Tabanan in southern Bali. Much of the analysis of Muslim traders and shopkeepers is reminiscent of Weber's study of Protestant capitalists and 'burgesses' (see also Peacock, 1978). Like their Western European counterparts, these ascetic Javanese entrepreneurs are imbued with the desire to promote their economic activities, expand their enterprises and avoid unnecessary consumption. However, for Geertz, they are constrained by the difficulties of developing larger-scale organizational forms in order to realize increasing profit and accumulate sufficient capital to move into 'modern' forms of economic activity. Instead these small-scale operators spread their risks, conducting a large number of small face-to-face commercial transactions. We should note that there are many examples in the literature of the search for modernizing social groups, including professionals, intellectuals, politicians and entrepreneurs (see, for example, Evers, 1978a; Evers and Regan, 1978; Chen, 1978a, 1978b).

The advantage of Geertz's approach to the study of modernization is that he avoids the temptation to indulge in generalization and instead analyses concrete cases in an attempt to understand the diverse and subtle responses to modernity. His conclusion on the Indonesian situation in the early years of its independence was that it was in 'permanent transition'. Modernity was still a long way off, but one could hardly categorize Indonesia, or at least the local communities which Geertz observed in detail, as traditional. Geertz talks about the social situation as 'confused', 'vague', 'contradictory', and 'incomplete'. What we might propose here is that if the problem is posed in terms of clearly defined categories of tradition and modernity and it is assumed that the ideal goal for developing societies is to achieve modernity, then it is likely that the conclusion we reach is that, in the newly independent, politically and economically unstable state of Indonesia in the 1950s, social groups and relations were contradictory and confused and the transition incomplete.

Similar excursions into the analysis of society and politics in terms of modernization concepts can also be found in an important body of work undertaken by American social scientists on post-war Thailand (Hanks, 1975; Riggs, 1961, 1964, 1966; Wilson, 1962). Wilson's study of Thai politics, though he recognizes that Thailand does not fit a Western analytical model, nevertheless attributes the dominance of a small, powerful military and civilian bureaucratic elite over an apolitical citizenry to cultural factors. According to this view Thais were individualistic and loosely organized, preoccupied, as Buddhists, with the accumulation of merit (1962: 45–97). Therefore, 'political behaviour can be best understood as representing particular, shared patterns of values, attitudes and beliefs. Ignoring conflict, the emphasis is on stability, individuality, deference and social cohesion' (Hewison, 1989a: 9). In his criticism of this work, Hewison argues that the adoption of what is essentially an ethnocentric, neo-evolutionary, structural-functionalist framework, the end-point of which is 'modern' society, does not successfully address questions of social change, nor does it satisfactorily consider issues of class formation and conflict, and their historical development, and the nature of the state within a political economy framework. Change is seen as 'disturbance' within processes of differentiation and evolution, rather than as an integral process within social systems (ibid.: 11–14). Evaluation in terms of Western industrial democracies therefore posits non-Western systems in terms of notions of 'deviance' or 'residual' status (ibid.).

Even later adjustments to the modernization paradigm, including the work of Girling (1981) and Morell and Chai-anan (1981), do not satisfactorily address these shortcomings, according to Hewison (1989a: 21–27) and Ockey (2004: 143–144); nor for that matter does Cohen's emphasis on the 'fundamentally incongruent basic cultural codes of Thai society' (1991: 46). Hewison's conclusion, and his assessment in particular of Riggs's concept of the 'bureaucratic polity', is that the political culture approach marginalizes economic interests and the importance of class struggle (ibid.: 26). Also, according to McVey, for Riggs in the 1960s the dominant Thai military and civilian bureaucracy was uninterested 'in any kind of economic development that would free business from bureaucratic control or recognize entrepreneurial activity as of equal social value to office holding' (1992b: 16). Thailand had become 'bogged down halfway on the path of modernization' (ibid.: 15); indeed, in phrasing transformations in Thailand in terms of the categories of 'tradition' and 'modernity' and 'continuity' and 'change' within the modernization paradigm, Cohen argues that it merely produces 'ambiguous or profoundly contrasting images of culture and society' and 'contrary motifs' (1991: 38).

On the other hand, McVey notes that in the Philippines in the 1960s there was not an 'overwhelming bureaucracy', industrialization was proceeding, members of the Chinese mestizo and landed class were investing in industry, Filipinos enjoyed a relatively high level of education and 'had imbibed much American entrepreneurial ideology' (1992b: 16–17). Yet two decades later with the Thai military-dominated bureaucracy continuing to play a central role in the economy (and with the state occupying centre stage in other neighbouring countries including Malaysia, Singapore and Indonesia), Thailand 'had become the widely praised model of Southeast Asian capitalist transformation', whilst the Philippines had fallen far behind in economic terms (ibid.: 17). We shall take these issues up again in Chapters 4, 5, 6 and 7.

Before moving on to examine some early attempts to overcome the short-comings of modernization perspectives in Southeast Asia, it is worth referring to the extraordinary persistence of concepts of political culture in explaining socio-political change. This is best illustrated in the context of more recent transitions from centralized socialist political systems to more open, democratic ones in such countries as Laos, Cambodia and Vietnam, and the problems accompanying the attempts to establish successful representative institutions. In her political economy analysis of Cambodia's transition in the 1990s, Hughes refers to those who view the Cambodian case as 'unpromising' for democracy (2003: 7; see also Bit, 1991; Diamond, 1994; Roberts, 2001). According to her, these pessimists explain this predicament in terms of Cambodian or specifically Khmer culture, which 'is regarded as antagonistic to democracy, because innate tendencies towards hierarchy, deference and intolerance of difference [or dissent] preclude the Cambodian people from either seeking or being able to sustain, meaningful participation in the peaceful debate and formulation of national policy agendas' (Hughes, 2003: 214–215). This recent emphasis on an unchanging 'passivity' and the resilient 'reactionary' character of Cambodian culture is reminiscent of the debates of the late 1950s and early 1960s, including Pye's influential contribution, on the psycho-cultural obstacles in Burma to the achievement of modernity and democracy.

Partially Rethinking Modernization

The failure of the predictions of modernization theorists to materialize, the persistence of poverty and extreme inequality in the developing world, the problems experienced in development projects, the emergence of political authoritarianism, the increasing strength and popularity of socialist and communist movements, and the growing criticisms of modernization theory led to attempts to reformulate and rethink it (Higgott and Robison, 1985c: 18). With reference to Southeast Asia an important volume edited by Evers began to state the case for an alternative approach (1973b). However, it should not be forgotten that Wertheim, using Romein's concept of 'dialectical evolution', had long been critical of the unilinear evolutionism of such modernization proponents as Rostow (Wertheim, 1964a: 19–20). For Wertheim, 'modernization and industrialization in Asia need not necessarily follow the course taken in the West, via private capitalistic enterprise' (ibid.: 18).

Evers's book was organized around a conference held in Singapore in 1971 with S.N. Eisenstadt, one of the leading figures in studies of modernization in the developing world (1964, 1966, 1970), providing a keynote address. Interestingly, Evers, in his introductory editorial remarks, presented a set of trenchant criticisms of Eisenstadt's own attempt to rethink the earlier position of modernization theorists (Evers, 1973a: xii–xix). Overall the volume comprises what one might see as a compromise between earlier modernization ideas and later underdevelopment and dependency positions, the latter illustrated most directly in a chapter by Wertheim (ibid.: 97–107).

There are various matters on which agreement with Eisenstadt was reached (Eisenstadt, 1973a: 3–18; see also Cohen, 1991: 36–41). Rather than a unilinear evolutionary path to modernity, Eisenstadt subsequently argued that the paths to development and change and the character of 'post-traditional social and political orders' are diverse (ibid.: 3; Cohen, 1991). In other words there is no necessary convergence towards modernity, and Eisenstadt has continued this theme of 'multiple modernities' in his most recent work, though, for him, the Western model continues to enjoy historical precedence and is the basic reference point (Eisenstadt, 2002: 2–3; Dore, 1973). This lack of convergence is because there are differences among traditional societies and elites, as Nash among others had already suggested (1964), as well as between the ways in which and the degree to which modern forces 'impinge' on traditional societies, between the different historical contexts in which these encounters occur, and between those societies which were subject to colonial rule and those which were not. Eisenstadt had also already argued a decade earlier that, from a modernization perspective, various countries were experiencing 'breakdowns' of modernization (1964). These were precipitated by continuing severe social conflicts, the emergence of protest movements, periodic economic crises, and the demands made by different constituents as a result of the modernization process which could not be met, regulated or addressed by the government. Thus, the military takeover in Burma in 1962 was interpreted by Eisenstadt as a disruption, even a partial reversal of the modernization process (ibid.: 345).

His critics pointed to the fact that Eisenstadt's interpretation of modernity at that time was based on a Western model of the nation-state, democracy, and a highly differentiated political structure, and therefore the introduction of authoritarian and autocratic governments, including military regimes and one-party states, was evaluated by him in negative, pathological terms. In other words, for Eisenstadt, various governments in the developing world had failed to formulate common symbols of identity to which the nation could subscribe, to establish stable institutional frameworks and introduce and uphold normative injunctions. In his later keynote address he continued to hold to the notion that, in the 'political sphere', such countries as Burma and Indonesia 'are among the most pertinent examples of the possibility of breakdown after some initial – or even sometimes relatively advanced – stages of modernization have been reached' (Eisenstadt, 1973a: 6). He therefore appears to continue to subscribe to 'an older, rather narrow and culturally biased concept of modernization' (Evers, 1973a: xiv). However, Eisenstadt later concedes that this collapse does not necessarily mean a return to tradition nor does it signal an inability to reorganize and ensure some degree of social and political continuity (Eisenstadt, 1973a: 7; 1973b; 1973c).

Interestingly some modernization theorists, notably Huntington (1968) and Riggs (1966), had already begun to address some of the conceptual difficulties

so that 'political development came to be viewed as a process of creating political institutions able to solve specific problems pertaining to stability and regime
maintenance rather than the reproduction of democracy' (Higgott and Robison,
1985c: 19). In addition, the emphasis placed on replicating some form of Western
industrial capitalist system shifted subsequently to a focus on achieving economic
growth by applying technocratic, 'rational', 'scientific' economic policies and the
triumph of economics over politics (Myint, 1972). It also draws inspiration from
neo-classical political economy and the emphasis on the concept of the 'market', its
'inherently efficient' and rational character, and the ways in which the 'state' should
interact with the market to ensure its effective operation (Rodan et al., 2001b: 2–4).
However, the preoccupation with the tradition-modernity dichotomy remains in
the emphasis on the contradictions between modern political organization and
traditional political culture, and the need to accommodate a modernizing society
in the face of the personal interests of political patrons and senior bureaucrats
involved in factional and clique-based conflicts (see Chapter 7).

Eisenstadt notes too that the relationship between traditional and modern
elements are much more complex than had hitherto been realized so that, for example, so-called traditional symbols, social groups and relations, or cultural forms,
can persist, reassert themselves or be used in novel ways to encourage modernity
(1973c: 268–269). He refers, for example, to 'modern patrimonialism', which combines modern and traditional elements. He had also argued a decade earlier that
rarely was there 'a complete reversal to truly traditional types of central social institutions' (1964: 347). Although in the early 1970s he still phrases the process in terms
of 'traditional' and 'modern' at least he moves away from the concept of a unilinear
transition or progression from one to the other (1973c). He also argues that 'we
have to distinguish between several aspects of what has been usually designated as
"modernity" or "modernization"' (1973a: 7). However, he continues to propose that
modernity is achieved from the political centre in changes in symbols, values and
institutions and it spreads out from there. The mark of this modernity continues to
be movement towards 'a mass consensual' socio-political order, one which is differentiated and diverse, and with 'propensities to continuous change and to system
transformation' (ibid.: 10).

Evers, in his introductory statements, makes three main critical points
(1973a: xii–xiii). First, he states that the broad structural-functionalist categories
of tradition and modernity have generally been phrased by Western observers
in ethnocentric terms. In addition, he proposes that the assumption of Western
cultural and political superiority at the apex of the evolutionary process was 'only
too easily translated into economic imperialism through the attempt of foreign
advisers and foreign aid to push development in modernizing societies into the
anticipated direction, if necessary by outright intervention, force and war, as in the
American involvement in Indochina' (ibid.: xii). Second, he suggests that the focus
on nation-building and political order in modernizing societies overemphasizes
the integrative function of government at the expense of the exercise and main-

tenance of power and political repression. Indeed, the later emphasis on political order served, wittingly or unwittingly, to lend justification to authoritarian forms of rule, from Suharto's New Order regime in Indonesia to Marcos's martial law in the Philippines. In this connection, for example, it has been suggested that 'two of the leading political scientists of Indonesia', Emmerson (1976, 1978) and Liddle (1973, 1989), had argued for Suharto's New Order government as 'a modernizing force'; it was 'the only alternative to chaos and disorder', and for Huntington (1968), Suharto's regime 'provided the strong institutional cement for a disintegrating society and performed the historical role of the middle class – it was its "advance guard", its "spearhead into modern politics"'(Robison and Hadiz, 2006: 115). Third, in a similar vein to underdevelopment theorists, Evers argues that the relationships between dominant Western societies and dependent developing societies may retard development rather than encourage it, that bureaucracies may serve as instruments of oppression, exploitation and corruption, and that foreign aid and investment may act to bolster conservative political elites who in turn block rather than promote progress (1973a: xiii).

Evers also makes several specific criticisms of Eisenstadt's address: first, that Eisenstadt concentrates on political symbols rather than economic and social processes (ibid.: xiii). Second, the emphasis on innovations at the political centre neglects the fact that the political elite may constitute a reactionary force, that revolutionary changes may emerge in the periphery, and that a political 'breakdown' at the centre may be necessary to achieve this. In other words, modernization may not be achieved by a differentiation of structures at the centre. Wertheim, in his contribution to the volume, argues that this view tends to assume that rural dwellers (the peasantry) are passive traditionalists who are 'resistant to change' when their past experiences of repression and exploitation often account for distrust and a reluctance to participate in development projects framed in terms of Western modernity (Wertheim, 1973b: 99–102). Third, Evers proposes that Eisenstadt does not provide us with a view of what kinds of post-traditional order have emerged in the Southeast Asian region (1973a: xii–xiii). With regard to the importance of analysing economic and social processes, Evers's own contribution to the edited volume is an exploration of the formation of social classes and group conflict in Southeast Asia (1973c). He formulates the concept of strategic groups to embrace such groupings as civil servants, the military, teachers, professionals and Chinese businessmen; these are forged in conflict situations, and in their competition over resources, positions and services, they increasingly become aware of their shared 'class' identity and solidarity (ibid.: 114–117; see Chapter 5).

What is apparent from Evers's and his colleagues' attempts to rethink the concept of modernization is the importance of placing developing countries in a global context and examining the consequences of colonial rule and continuing economic dependence to help explain the problems they face. Dore, in his contribution to the volume, examines the dilemma in terms of 'the late development effect' (1973). He says that developing countries ('the late starters') 'have to operate under the domination of those who started earlier. The late-starters cannot seize and exploit colonies' (ibid.: 68). He warns against assuming, as some underdevelopment theorists tend to, that domination and subordination is the only relevant element of late development because it denies 'any possibilities even of national autonomy' (ibid.; see also Chapter 4). However, the relationship between the advanced and the less developed countries is certainly an important factor.

In this regard it is interesting that Evers's volume, although it refers to some of Geertz's work, does not address his important historical study of change in Indonesia in *Agricultural Involution* (1963a), and the related volumes *The Development of the Javanese Economy* (1956) and *The Social History of an Indonesian Town* (1965). Evers later devotes considerable attention to the concept of 'involution' in his 1980 sociology reader. However, in my view, Geertz's study of involution provides an important bridge between the two opposing schools of thought – modernization and underdevelopment – and is helpful in any rethinking exercise. I shall explore his ideas briefly here before examining underdevelopment perspectives and processes of change in nineteenth century Java and Indonesia in more detail in Chapter 4.

Geertz defines involution as the 'overdriving of an established form in such a way that it becomes rigid through an inward over elaboration of detail' (1963a: 82). In other words, the transformations in Indonesia from the early nineteenth century cannot be characterized as evolutionary let alone revolutionary; they have not led to the emergence and development of very different socio-cultural and economic forms. Instead they have become increasingly 'involuted', intricate and involved, confined within an existing social framework. Geertz relates this process of internal over elaboration to three other notions – the transition from tradition to modernity, dualism and ecosystem. He poses the question why Japan was able to modernize from the nineteenth century while Indonesia failed to do so, and, in the 1950s newly-independent Indonesia seemed stranded between tradition and modernity, exhibiting, in Boeke's terms, a dualistic society and economy. As van Niel notes, at the time when Geertz was conducting his research in the 1950s, the Javanese agricultural situation (from 1950 to 1965) was seen 'as one of rural stagnation when landless laborers and marginal farmers were competing for employment and land' (van Niel, 1992: 182; Collier et. al, 1982). For Geertz the major difference between Japan and Indonesia was that one had avoided colonial occupation and the other had succumbed to it. '[W]here Japanese peasant agriculture came to be complementarily related to an expanding manufacturing system in indigenous hands, Javanese peasant agriculture came to be complementarily related to an expanding agro-industrial structure under foreign management' (1963a: 135).

Geertz searches for factors and processes which, on the one hand, act to facilitate and on the other obstruct modernization. However, unlike modernization theorists who tended to restrict their search to social, cultural and psychological explanations internal to a particular society, Geertz, in similar vein to underdevelopment theorists, looked for part of the answer in external forces and processes. Yet his perspective also differs from that of underdevelopment theory. He does not refer to the Marxist literature on, for example, imperialism, inequality and class conflict, for analytical insights and inspiration; rather he turns to the anthropological literature on cultural ecology, which, in turn, was preoccupied with evolutionary change. Rather than the political economy of Paul Baran and Andre Gunder Frank, Geertz turns to the cultural ecology of Julian Steward (ibid.: 6–11). For Geertz what happened to the Javanese farmer during the nineteenth and the first part of the twentieth century was also predicated on ecological relationships, on the interaction between human actors and their environment, either as irrigated rice cultivators or shifting agriculturalists. Geertz therefore focuses on the ways in which Indonesian and particularly Javanese culture (human motivations, values, behaviour and social action) shaped and was shaped by Dutch intervention and by a particular kind of adaptation to environmental opportunities and constraints.

There have been numerous criticisms of Geertz's study (Alexander and Alexander, 1978, 1979, 1982; Collier, 1981; Elson, 1978, 1984; Hüsken, 1979; Koentjaraningrat, 1975; van Schaik, 1986; White, 1983a, 1983b), some to which Geertz subsequently responded (1984), and I do not have the space to consider them in detail. One major oversight, however, was that Geertz did not take account of the fact that 'traditional' Javanese village society of the nineteenth century was not 'traditional' at all, but had already been subject to change during a long period of Dutch contact (Gordon, 1992: 506). Geertz also attempts to present a general theory of involutionary change in Java rather than a specific historical analysis of particular elements of society, culture and economy (van Niel, 1992: 183–184). In other words, he tends to sacrifice empirical and historical detail for the construction of Weberian ideal types. In this connection some critics have also pointed to his dependence on a narrow range of source material, including Furnivall's study of the Netherlands Indies (1939), and the work of the Dutch writers Burger and Reinsma (van Niel, 1992: 185–190). Nevertheless, the importance of Geertz's work lies in his exploration of some of the effects of colonialism on indigenous societies, and the consequences of unequal relations between a dominant colonial power and the subordinate native population. One of his main failings was not to take his analysis of colonialism far enough nor indeed to present an overall concept of colonialism and imperialism in examining the varied impacts which Dutch rule had on the Javanese and others, and the effects of a range of colonial policies and practices on local communities rather than those directed to agriculture and land use. Nor did he offer a concept of evolution against which to assess involution and the divergence from what presumably he considered as 'normal' patterns of change (Gordon, 1992: 495–499).

Concluding Remarks

In the next chapter we shall see how different kinds of colonial experience and the incorporation of differently organized communities at different times in different places into wider politico-economic systems generated a variety of responses. It is this concern with historical investigation and the location of social and economic forms in a global context which distinguishes underdevelopment and dependency theorists from modernization theorists. Yet the influence of modernization theory persisted and concerns about the values and institutions which aid or hinder the realization of modernity have continued to surface. More recently the Asian financial crisis has served to revive interest in the relations between values, behaviour and economic activity (see, for example, Unger 1998). Moreover, modernization theory did draw attention to the possibility of positive change under capitalism, and this optimism, with qualifications, was to gain some justification with the emergence of the newly-industrializing countries of Singapore, Malaysia and Thailand, and the increasing importance of Export Oriented Industrialization (EOI) strategies from the 1970s.

4

Underdevelopment and Dependency

[T]he worldwide expansion of capitalism and the concomitant relationships of exchange and domination between the capitalist metropole and its colonies in Asia, Africa and Latin America exerted a determinant influence on the historical development or rather underdevelopment of these regions (Frank, 1978a: 20).

[I]mperialism, whatever the motive, is expensive, and it is inevitable that the price will fall upon the conquered themselves (Phelan, 1959: 94).

Introduction

The response to the inadequacies of modernization theory drew its inspiration from Marxist work on colonialism and imperialism and the ways in which capitalism as a mode of production generated economic benefits for some and poverty and hardship for others. This response focused on the importance of 'the economic' rather than values and ideas ('the cultural') in Parsonian- and Weberian-derived modernization theory. It also shifted attention from the experiences of particular states or territories to the world economic system as the unit of analysis (Wallerstein, 1974, 1979). However, in the early studies of processes of underdevelopment by Baran (1957) and Frank (1969a, 1969b, 1972, 1981) some of the classic Marxian concepts used to understand social change and the nature of capitalism and feudalism either did not figure prominently or were radically revised. Underdevelopment and dependency theorists were by no means working within a unified theory; there were disagreements and differences in emphasis between different strands within the Marxist tradition (Bernstein, 1979; Booth, 1985, 1993). There is also a burgeoning neo-Marxist literature on development and it is impossible to cover the detailed nuances of the debates, although Brewer usefully surveys the field (1980), as do Apter, (1987), Hettne (1990),

Hoogvelt (1978, 1982, 2001), Roxborough (1979), Taylor (1979) and Webster (1990), among many others, and Reynolds and Hong give us insights into the vigorous discussions among Marxist-influenced Thai scholars of the political economy of Thailand (1983). Nevertheless, as with modernization theory, there were certain common elements.

One characteristic of underdevelopment theory which it shared with its competitor theory was that it attempted to provide an all-embracing framework to address major processes of change in the post-colonial world. However, one of the significant differences was the critical view it took of the reasons for and consequences of the unequal relationships between the West and the developing world, or, as it came to be known during the Cold War era, the Third World (Frank, 1969a, 1969b, 1971). In other words, while modernization theory tended to view colonialism as unproblematic, underdevelopment theory emphasized the historical and global character of the problems which faced the developing world (Amin, 1974, 1990). Rather than searching for social and cultural factors internal to developing societies to explain economic backwardness, writers such as Frank saw colonialism and neo-colonialism as the very cause of underdevelopment (Frank, 1969a, 1969b, 1996; Chew and Denemark, 1996b; Hoogvelt, 1978; Schuurman, 1993a). Moreover, in contrast to the modernization approach, which, in its earlier manifestations, posited an evolutionary sequence from a state of 'undevelopment' or tradition to one of modernity, Frank and his followers focused on the process of underdevelopment generated by the exploitative relationships between the West (the 'metropolis') and the Third World (the 'satellites') (Frank, 1969a, 1969b, 1971, 1972, 1975, 1978a, 1978b; Emmanuel, 1972; Schuurman, 1993b). Therefore, the obstacles to economic growth were not the persistence of tradition and the absence of modernizers and an entrepreneurial spirit, but the very relationships between dominant countries and their subordinate territories (Frank, 1971; Hoogvelt, 1978). By the logic of this argument, underdevelopment theorists proposed that these relationships, which modernization theorists saw as essential for development, must be severed, and the path taken to autonomous development (Frank, 1996: 28; Amin, 1990). In addition, while modernization theorists wished to identify those who could invest surplus productively, Marxist theorists focused on those who produced surplus and how and by whom it was extracted (Laclau, 1971).

Karl Marx and Colonialism

As with other nineteenth-century social philosophers, Marx tended to arrange societies or 'social formations' in evolutionary terms on the assumption that change in world history has been generally progressive. His major categories were primitive communism, Asiatic society, ancient society, feudalism, capitalism and socialism, although it is disputed whether Marx saw these categories in terms of a unilinear sequence (1964; Reynolds and Hong, 1983: 79–95). For Marx processes of change were located primarily in economic production, and particularly in the contradictions between the forces of production (including raw materials, technology, and human labour) and relations of production (the social relations of economic production, distribution and exchange) (Mandel, 1971). Changes in the division of labour and the mode of production generate changes in the social order, specifically in the social classes which occupy different positions in the socio-economic order and are involved in struggles either to maintain the economic and political status quo or transform it (ibid.). In abstract terms each mode of production is characterized by two major opposed social classes, one which produces and an exploitative non-producing class (Brewer, 1980: 11). Marx was primarily concerned with the analysis of the transition from feudalism to capitalism in Europe and the processes by which peasant cultivators were separated from land and their means of subsistence and became wage labourers (the 'proletariat') working for capitalists (the 'bourgeoisie') in a competitive market environment.

He also turned his attention briefly to the global expansion of European capitalism which he saw generally as progressive. He concentrated on British relations with Ireland, India and China. For Marx the progressive character of capitalism was evident in Asia where, as we have seen, he characterized the Asian socio-political order as static, self-sustaining and despotic (1964). It was Western capitalism, based on the exploitation of 'free' wage labour, which, once it had set down its roots in fresh ground in the East, would sweep away pre-capitalist Asia, and open up the self-contained village, by integrating it into the world market and the capitalist division of labour, promoting economic productivity and enabling capital accumulation. Asiatic societies were unable to achieve these changes by themselves (Marx 1964, 1972). To this extent, Marx's general evaluation of capitalism as a positive force followed that of the classical political economists such as Adam Smith and David Ricardo and was in line with the later modernization theorists, though for Marx this progression to capitalism was a necessary step to the ultimate realization of a socialist society. This position was also to be re-invigorated by such writers as Warren, who, contra Frank, took a more positive view about the post-war prospects for successful industrialization and capitalist development in developing countries (1980).

However, in his consideration of British colonialism in Ireland Marx draws a rather different conclusion which comes close to the later position of Baran and Frank in that external domination stunts and undermines economic development rather than promoting it; 'every time Ireland was about to develop industrially, she was crushed and reconverted into a purely agricultural land' (Marx and Engels, 1971: 132; 1978). Overall Marx emphasized the exploitative character of capitalism, processes of surplus extraction, inequality and uneven development. But his writings on the international expansion of capitalism were relatively limited and he did not develop an extended theoretical appreciation of imperialism.

Theories of Imperialism

It was the work on imperialism by Lenin (1950 [1917]), Luxemburg (1951 [1913]), Hilferding (1981 [1910]) and Bukharin (1972 [1917]) which took this perspective a stage further, although, with the partial exception of Luxemburg, they were more concerned to explain the reasons for the global expansion of capitalism and its effects on capitalism as a system rather than the impacts on dependent economies (Luxemburg and Bukharin, 1972; Hobsbawm, 1987). Again there were considerable differences between the main strands of thinking on imperialism but all assumed that it 'was the product of factors within Europe and that colonies were acquired to save capitalism from a moribund condition in which the further accumulation of capital within Europe was becoming impossible' (Fieldhouse, 1967: 187–188). More generally, all writers assigned 'a central role to the evolution of the economic system' and assumed that imperialism 'must be explained in terms of the development of "capitalism"' (Brewer, 1980: 10).

It was Lenin who brought the various strands together into a comprehensive and popular treatment of imperialism, for him 'the highest stage of capitalism' and 'the monopoly stage of capitalism' (1950 [1917]). The basis of the explanation for the expansion of capitalism overseas rests on competition between companies or individual capitalists; the concentration of capital in fewer hands leading to monopoly (and the creation of the multinational corporation); the fall in the rate of profits (a very contentious issue in Marxism); expansion in the scale of production; the need to find markets, cheap labour and sources of raw materials; the increase in the importance of finance, banks and shareholding, and the separation of the ownership of capital from its application to production; the need to find outlets for investment and to export capital, particularly for infrastructural projects; and the increasing clash between competitive capitalist nations as they search out and secure exclusive fields for investment, exports and raw materials to secure their own national economic interests. In other words, capital is at one and the same time internationalized and nationalized (Brewer, 1980: 103).

Various writers have pointed to defects in perspectives on imperialism: the issue of whether or not capital was forced out of Europe because of some internal evolutionary necessity of the capitalist system or whether investment overseas was more voluntary and eclectic; the problem of the lack of historical and geographical coincidence between territorial acquisition, crises in capitalism, the scale of capital export, and the flourishing of monopoly and finance capital; and the importance of non-economic and case-specific factors such as political ambitions, individual fortune-seeking and adventuring, the urge to religious conversion, age-old historical rivalries between the European powers, and the strategic need to protect territories already conquered (Fieldhouse, 1967: 187–194; Hobsbawm, 1987). Clearly no one theory will explain all the facts, but there is reason to claim that economic motives, operating in particular political contexts, were of primary importance in the surge of European expansion overseas (Magdoff, 1978: 4–5). As Osborne says of the early European encounter with Southeast Asia, '[t]hey wanted to gain a part, the largest part indeed, in an existing spice trade that promised great riches … . They [the Spanish and Portuguese also] wanted converts to Christianity, it is true. But this hope never excluded the possibility of gaining wealth through trade …'

(2004: 96). Nevertheless, this observation does not entail the assumption that capitalism required the acquisition of colonies to survive. In summarizing Marx's work on colonialism, Brewer confirms that '[c]apitalism does not need a subordinated hinterland or periphery, though it will use it and profit from it if it exists' (1980: 60). This is for the simple reason that individuals and social groups have purposes and needs, but capitalism as a system does not. In the competitive struggle for profits individual capitalists can and do work against the system and trigger problems of oversupply and economic crisis.

Baran and Frank

Paul Baran established the foundations of the theory of underdevelopment in the immediate post-war period, shifting the emphasis to the developing world and to the negative rather than progressive effects of foreign capital on the prospects for non-Western development. Basing his ideas primarily on America's overseas involvement, Baran divides the world economy into the advanced capitalist nations and the underdeveloped ones (1957); others use such terms as 'metropolis-satellite' (Frank, 1969a, 1969b), 'core', 'semi-periphery' and 'periphery' (Wallerstein, 1974, 1979), and 'centre' and 'periphery' (Amin, 1974 [1970], 1976 [1973]). Put simply, Baran argues that the international division of labour serves to provide the advanced countries with cheap sources of primary products and labour; that economic surplus is extracted from the underdeveloped countries in the form of profits and dividends at the expense of the development of those who produce the surplus; and that the advanced countries use their political and military leverage, and their greater economic strength to sustain governments in power in underdeveloped countries which are supportive of foreign investment. Baran's conclusions are therefore that underdeveloped countries 'are dominated by foreign capital with its local hangers-on, and by mercantile and landlord interests' (Brewer, 1980: 157).

Frank then carried forward Baran's work and provided a sustained criticism of the empirical and theoretical inadequacies of modernization theory. In his earlier studies he focused on the experiences of Latin America (1969a, 1969b; Oxaal, Barnett and Booth, 1975). However, later he extended his analyses to the global system, and began to embrace historical developments in such regions as Asia (1978a, 1978b, 1981, 1998). His early work comprises four important elements: that Western contact (primarily through the medium of mercantilism and capitalism) with other areas of the world served to develop some at the expense of others; that surplus is expropriated along chains uniting the capitalist 'metropolis' with the subordinate 'satellites' in a 'world (capitalist) system'; that the problems of development lie in the relationships between metropolis and satellites and not in the nature of 'traditional' societies, which, in any case, cannot be characterized as traditional following their contact with the West; and that a dependent domestic ruling class, which Frank refers to as a 'lumpenbourgeoisie', works to sustain this system because it depends on foreign capital for its survival (1972). Although Frank uses the term 'dependence', primarily to refer to the position of satellites in a chain of exploitation, he also uses it, like the 'dependency theorists', to refer to a situation in which an underdeveloped economy is conditioned by and subject to the expansion and development of a dominant economy (Brewer, 1980: 177–180).

Frank's Critics

Frank's earlier work provoked a massive outpouring of debate (Oxaal et al., 1975; Laclau, 1971; Roxborough, 1979; Schuurman, 1993a; Hoogvelt, 2001). Three major areas of contention were addressed subsequently by Frank himself in his historical treatment of the process of capital accumulation from 1500 to 1930 (1978a; 1978b). Firstly, he was charged with overemphasizing external relations of unequal exchange within the world economic system at the expense of internal relations of domination within particular modes of production. In other words, the internal structures of a given society will exert a strong influence on the ways in which external forces penetrate, use and change them. For Marxist writers these structures comprise social classes and the conflicts between them (Laclau, 1971). This position also requires us to examine the different phases of capitalist development rather than assuming, as Frank does in earlier work, that capitalism, defined as a system of exchange, developed from the earliest stages of Iberian contact with and conquest of Latin America from the sixteenth century. It also requires us to examine the interrelationships (or in Marxian terms 'articulation') between different forms of production, specifically between capitalist and non-capitalist ones in a colonial context, and how economic surpluses are used. For writers such as Laclau, capitalism should not be defined as a global system of exchange but as a mode of production characterized primarily by wage labour and commodity production. However, it coexists with, draws on and sometimes strengthens pre- or non-capitalist forms of production.

Second, it was argued that Frank took insufficient account of the socio-economic, cultural, political and geographical variations between different parts of Latin America and beyond, the different phases of European contact with other parts of the world and the different stages of capitalist development. Put simply, the different conditions in different parts of the world provided economic opportunities at different times. And third, it was proposed that Frank did not provide a sufficiently detailed and dynamic analysis of the differentiated process of capital accumulation on a world scale in which the development of some and underdevelopment of others are seen as part of a single interrelated process which should be examined simultaneously and serially (Wallerstein, 1974, 1979; Amin, 1974). This in turn involves the study of 'the differential contributions of each of the major world regions to the process of capital accumulation during each of its major stages of development' as well as 'the underdeveloping consequences of this participation in world accumulation for each of the major regions of the now underdeveloped "third world"' (Frank, 1978a: xiii). In response to his critics Frank attempted to remedy these shortcomings. To do this he returned to the classical political economy of Smith and Ricardo and to Marx's historical materialism (ibid.: 1).

Another major criticism, which led to several revisions in recent political economy research on Southeast Asia and elsewhere, is the failure, at least in the earlier work, to anticipate the kinds of adaptive changes in capitalism which occurred from the 1970s onwards, and, for example, 'the materialization of the Southeast Asian entrepreneur' (Warren, 1980; McVey, 1992a, 1992b; Aseniero, 1996: 171–199). In this connection, the most important changes have been: the transfer of manufacturing and other operations from the increasingly 'post-industrial' West to various parts of the developing world within the 'new international division of labour' (NIDL) (Frobel, Heinrichs and Kreye, 1980; Higgott and Robison, 1985a: 4–6); the increasing importance of export-led economic growth in the newly-industrializing economies of Southeast Asia, and more widely in Asia, driven by the economic engine of Japan and the USA, and then Korea, Taiwan and Hong Kong, and more recently China, and the positive developmental effects on the 'underdeveloped' world (Leaver, 1985: 149–171; Aseniero, 1996: 172–173, 189–184, 191–193); the failure of various socialist experiments in economic development; and the opening up of these economies to the capitalist market-place. These processes have resulted in a re-evaluation of the pessimistic prognosis for development in underdevelopment theory and the recommendation that it was necessary to sever links with the capitalist economies and embark on autonomous development (Kiely, 1995: 6–7; Schuurman, 1993a). Indeed, Leaver argues that reformist capitalist strategies in 'peripheral' countries require greater integration into the world economy in order to realize the benefits of further growth (1985: 162–168). There was the need then to consider in more detail the ways in which political leaders and senior bureaucrats deploy state power and resources in the context of a global economic system characterized by uneven development and 'unequal specialization' (Amin, 1974, 1976; Aseniero, 1996: 175–184). Another complementary field of investigation has been devoted to the examination of Southeast Asian capitalists, not at the level of the small-scale trader, or even 'middling entrepreneurs', but instead at the level of big business and national government (McVey, 1992a; 1992b: 9; see also Hawes, 1992; Heng, 1992; Robison, 1992; Sieh, 1992). In the case of Thailand, for example, domestic entrepreneurs in finance and industry formed relationships with local power-holders and foreign capital. However, Suehiro argues that this 'dependence' does not mean that Thailand is 'simply a "dependent" capitalist society of the sort posited by dependency theory' (1992: 61). Rather, at a stage of the development of the Thai economy, local business groups have used practical ways to raise and accumulate capital, and this 'does not reflect the nature of the whole economic system at the level of the nation-state' (ibid.). Indeed, subsequently, some business groups changed their modes of operation, and became less dependent on patronage and foreign capital (ibid.: 62–63).

European Mercantilism, Colonialism and Imperialism: Case Studies

The European and later American interaction with Southeast Asia must be seen as part of a global encounter within which this region played particular roles. Later work in the underdevelopment tradition periodized history in terms of the different kinds of encounter with subject populations determined by the level and nature of economic development of the different European economies (Amin, 1976; Wallerstein, 1974, 1979). These periods may differ in extent, their commencement and termination, and in nomenclature but broadly they conform to Frank's later three-fold categorization: (1) mercantilism, roughly from 1500 to 1770; (2) industrial capitalism, 1770 to 1870 (some writers argue for 1880 or even 1900); and (3) monopoly or finance capitalism, 1870 to 1930 (some writers take this period to 1940; see Catley,1976: 54–74). Magdoff divides Frank's first period into two: from the end of the fifteenth to the mid-seventeenth centuries, which saw 'the rise of commercial capital and the rapid growth of world commerce', and from then to the late eighteenth century when 'commercial capital ripens into a dominant economic force'. He then divides the last period into two: from roughly 1880 to 1918, which saw 'the rise and victory of monopoly capital', and since 1918 'the beginning of socialism as a rival social system, eventual decolonization, and the rise of the multinational corporation' (Magdoff, 1978: 99–100). We should note that Frank's recent work has sought to extend the world system 'as far back as it will go' and he finds it 'five thousand years ago in Asia instead of five hundred years ago in Europe'; he plots the extended shift of power from the East (specifically India and China) to the West during this long historical period and the triumph of the West from the turn of the nineteenth century (1996: 43; Frank and Gills, 1993; Aseniero, 1996: 173). The examination of cycles of expansion and decline in the world system does have considerable merit, but, for my purposes with regard to Southeast Asia, I focus on the last five hundred years.

Mercantilism

In Frank's first stage of the development of European hegemony, embracing the sixteenth and seventeenth centuries and much of the eighteenth, the impact of Europe on indigenous societies in Southeast Asia was relatively insignificant (Osborne, 2004). However, particular parts of the region such as the spice-growing areas of eastern Indonesia where the Portuguese and then the Dutch attempted to control and reorganize the sources of supply, parts of west Java which were used by the Dutch East India Company as an administrative centre, and the north and central Philippines which were the focus of Spanish missionary activities and administrative and political changes, were affected more dramatically (Wertheim, 1980a: 13). European traders were content to establish trading stations and factories along the India–China sea-routes, and conclude commercial treaties with local rulers to secure marketable products. For a considerable period of time they were one set of traders among many others. In Java where the Dutch gradually became dominant, the East India Company, 'hitherto a powerful harbour principality, constituted itself as a patrimonial bureaucracy ruling over the inland state of Java and, thus, attained a position similar to that possibly achieved by Srivijaya in earlier times in relation to the inland state of early Mataram' (ibid.: 13). However, superior military and maritime technology enabled the Europeans, often through force, coercion and plunder, to establish a pre-eminent position in Southeast Asia.

Catley characterizes this period, which for him extends for a further century, as one in which Europeans 'sought the products which the existing mode of production already provided' and, therefore, 'the effect of imperial penetration on the social structure of South-East Asia was limited' (1976: 56). Frank too argues that the consequences of the trade in Asian spices and textiles, paid for primarily by European bullion and then Latin American silver and gold, 'for changes in the mode of production in Asia were for a long time relatively moderate' (1978a: 15; Wertheim, 1980a: 13). The exchange of American precious metals for Asian agricultural and manufactured products brought considerable financial benefit to Europeans (Frank, 1978a: 18–19). Nevertheless, up to about 1800, '[they had] spent three centuries and tons of American silver trying to buy their way into the flourishing Asian markets' (Aseniero, 1996: 173).

For Frank, the main European focus during the period up to 1770 (or 1800), and the main source of capital accumulation was the Atlantic triangular trade between northern Europe (manufactures), West Africa (slaves), and the Americas (plantation crops of sugar, cotton and tobacco) (1978a: 13–24). The Europeans increasingly exerted control by force, supported by the power of the state, and trade was accompanied by plunder, although once an advantage had been established, it helped generate changes in the structure of the European economies. It was a period characterized by the increasing organization and scale of European mercantile activity on the one hand, and the increase in production for export in the colonies on the other (ibid.: 13). However, prior to the second half of the eighteenth century Frank has argued that the global economic system had not been focused on the West; its hegemony only really began to be established with the beginnings of industrial capitalism (1998).

Industrial Capitalism

The enormous increase in capital accumulation during the mercantile period helped lay the foundations of the industrial revolution which gathered pace from the late eighteenth century. The availability of overseas markets also provided an impetus for increased production and technological development. During this period Asia, particularly India, began to assume greater importance for Western Europe, marked by the British defeat of the Indians at the Battle of Plassey in 1757 and the British displacement of the French from the 1760s. This was the period when one of the major preoccupations of the Europeans, particularly the British, was to secure and open markets for their rapidly expanding domestic manufactures, initially textiles, primarily in exchange for colonial plantation crops and other raw materials (Magdoff, 1978: 106). Among other things, this resulted in the destruction of indigenous industries where these competed with European goods; the rapid decline of the Indian textile industry and the import of British cotton manufactures into India during the nineteenth century is a case in point; Frank refers to this process as the 'de-industrialization' and 'de-urbanization' of India (1978a: 87–91). By imposing tariffs and duties on those goods in competition with British products and relaxing or removing them from British goods and the raw materials necessary for British production the balance was altered in Britain's favour. Systems of 'unequal exchange' were progressively introduced and developed, which witnessed 'the breakup of the noncapitalist societies' (Magdoff, 1978: 106; Emmanuel, 1972 [1969]).

Among the major changes were the transformation of land and labour into a commodity; the production of goods for the market; private property in land was progressively established; local populations became increasingly involved in wage labour; the colonial state introduced various forms of taxation, duties and tariffs, usually to be paid in currency, and, as the state apparatus expanded, a range of tasks from the administration of taxes, to census-taking and statistics gathering, to the maintenance of law and order, to the provision and operation of public services needed to be performed by local people on behalf of the foreign rulers; the colonial state rationalized and simplified the complex realities of everyday life to achieve social and political control (Scott, 1998). These changes resulted, in turn, in major alterations in the indigenous class structure and racial or ethnic factors increased in importance in defining populations for the purposes of administration. Cheap immigrant or 'coolie' labour from India and China was introduced adding complexity to this changing plural society. Two of the key features of the colonial landscape were the 'plantation' and the 'mine' to supply the raw materials for industrial production. A crucial change was 'the expansion of commercial crop cultivation [which] stimulated more direct forms of internal administration and the colonial government and its civil service penetrated more deeply into the rural areas' (Wertheim, 1980a: 14). The main characteristics of capitalism were therefore a 'free market', 'free labour' where individuals were 'economically compelled to sell their labour power on the market', and 'private ownership of the means of production' (Bottomore, 1965: 12).

Monopoly Capitalism

This period is marked by rapid territorial expansion which began in the earlier part of the nineteenth century. The 'new vigor in the pursuit of colonies is reflected in the fact that the rate of new territorial acquisitions of the new imperialism was almost three times that of the earlier period' (Magdoff, 1978: 34). It was also marked in Europe by 'the second Industrial Revolution' characterized by the importance of steel, oil, electricity, synthetic chemistry and the internal combustion engine, as well as the steamship and worldwide communication (ibid.: 108–09). The European powers began to penetrate the interior of mainland Southeast Asia and the major islands of the maritime world. Territories and their populations were interconnected by an expanding railway, road, river and sea transport system and by a network of communications and, where competing colonial powers confronted each other on the margins of their expanding possessions, treaties and boundary agreements were concluded and lines drawn on maps. What had previously been a relatively fluid indigenous political situation in which control over populations was of key importance, territorial control within fixed borders became the basis of political systems. Urban areas expanded and the colonial capitals became the head-links between the metropolitan economies and the colonial suppliers of raw materials. As Wertheim says, '[i]ndustrialization was deliberately retarded by the colonial powers, and the cities were developed as sea ports for the export of commercial crops and minerals and the import of ready-made industrial goods from the West' (1980a: 18).

From the 1870s we witness the British forward movement in the Malayan Peninsula and into the interior and hill regions of Burma, the completion of the French colonization of Indochina, the expansion of Dutch power from its main base in Java to the outer islands; the transfer of sovereignty over the Philippines from Spain to the United States and the latter's intervention in the unadministered parts of the interior and the Muslim south; and the economic incorporation of Thailand, though it was not formally part of any colonial empire, into the British imperial enterprise as a supplier of a limited range of primary commodities (rice, teak, rubber and tin) and the inclusion of Thailand's marginal territories into the British and French mainland dependencies (Hewison, 1989a: 30–33).

However, just at a time when European power was at its zenith processes were set in train which led to decolonization. A watershed was the catastrophe of the First World War, but what followed was the increasing strength of socialism and communism as alternative ideologies to liberal democracy and capitalism, and the stirrings of nationalism and anti-colonial liberation movements. The growing might of Japan in Asia was also to play an increasing role in more general national awakening. It was not simply that local people began to organize themselves to protest against foreign domination, but changes which had been wrought in the social, economic and political structures of the colonies gave rise to social groups, including urban-based, educated white-collar workers, small-scale traders, and wage-labourers in the plantations, railways, docks, and mines, which were increasingly able to mobilize. Wertheim says, 'The impossibility of attaining their ends by individual achievement in the face of institutional barriers and other frustrations compelled the South-East Asians, whose main asset via-à-vis the colonial powers was their number, to discover the meaning of collective action' (1980a: 20).

Country Case Studies

It is important to indicate some of the main differences in the character and effects of the encounter between dominant and dependent societies in different Southeast Asian cases. It illustrates the inadequacy of lumping Southeast Asian societies together as either 'traditional' or as 'underdeveloped'. In some cases, local agrarian populations were incorporated into large, foreign-owned landed estates, as in parts of French Indochina; or a powerful native landowning class was created as in the Philippines; or small farmers were rapidly integrated into the world market through money-lending and merchant capital to specialize in the production of cash crops for export as in the Burma Delta; or plantations were established growing export crops, often using cheap imported labour as in British Malaya; or forced taxation systems were introduced using local land and labour to grow cash crops on behalf of the colonial state as in Dutch Java during the 'Cultivation System'; or established farmers were encouraged to grow subsistence crops to meet their own needs whilst diverting part of their resources to market-based activities such as small-scale rubber cultivation, which was very widespread in Southeast Asia; or, as in Thailand, primary producers, particularly rice farmers, were brought into relationship with the world market through a social class which comprised elements of the established ruling elite (the 'sakdina ruling class') and 'Chinese merchant-functionaries and compradors' (Hewison, 1989a: 33).

Let us now move to the case studies of British Burma, the Netherlands East Indies and the Spanish and American Philippines (for comparative material on Thailand, see Bell 1978; Chatthip, Suthy and Montri, 1978, 1981; Hewison, 1989a, 1989b; Reynolds and Hong, 1983). Ideally I would like to have included material on French Indochina, but space does not permit this. I chose three contrasting cases, illustrating rather different experiences under three different colonial regimes. From a different perspective with different emphases and with a greater interest in the political and cultural dimensions of change under colonialism, Cohen also presents a valuable comparative study of Burma, Thailand and Laos (1991: 128–149). But though using different case studies, he comes to the same conclusions as I do when he proposes that 'global and geo-political factors, ... the pattern of Western penetration, and the nature of Western interests are the principal factors which explain the divergent fates of the three countries' (ibid.: 146). Importantly he also emphasizes that the difference in local responses to the colonial encounter help explain the 'different paths of development' which these countries took, and these differences were also 'conditioned' by 'important differences in the configuration of ... internal sociocultural and socio-political factors' (ibid.).

British Burma

The British forward movement in Burma from 1824 provides an excellent illustration of the ways in which a relatively closed, primarily self-sufficient economy was transformed into an export-oriented enterprise producing rice for the world market (Adas, 1974: 3–11). The British annexed Burma in three stages following the three Anglo-Burmese Wars of 1824–26 (the coastal strips of Arakan and Tenasserim), 1852–53 (Pegu and the whole of Lower Burma) and 1885 (Upper Burma). British colonial administration continued until 1948, excluding the Japanese interregnum. Prior to colonial intervention, the central core of Burmese settlement was the interior dry zone along the upper Irrawaddy River in the vicinity of Mandalay, Ava and Pagan where the environment was ideally suited to rice agriculture, using a complex irrigation system of drainage and feeder channels, canals, weirs and tanks. Aung-Thwin says, '[f]or much of the monarchical period, the most stable component of the pre-colonial economy of Burma was the production of padi in the irrigated plains of Upper Burma in what is commonly known as the dry zone' (1990: 1). It was 'the most dependable and stable economic area of Burma', and whilst trade was also significant in the coastal areas, revenues were much more risky (ibid.: 4, 62–63). The kingdom also imported rice from Lower Burma and the control of the market was essential to ensure that sufficient supplies were available in the interior at low prices (Myint, 1966: 42). In the nineteenth century, the Konbaung kings had imposed restrictions on the export of rice and a range of other activities (Khwin Win, 1991: 6; Cheng, 1968).

It was not until the second half of the nineteenth century that the frontier regions of the lower Irrawaddy began to surpass Upper Burma in rice production and the political centre moved to the colonial coastal capital of Rangoon. The key factors in this shift were the removal of restrictions on rice production and trade by the British, the rapid increase in demand for rice on the world market, improvements in international transport (with the opening of the Suez Canal in 1869 and technical improvements in steam navigation in 1870–1880), and the movement of large numbers of Burmese peasants from the interior to the frontier in search of improved economic opportunities. Exports of rice began to increase significantly from the 1860s and the area under rice increased from 993,000 acres in 1855 to 9.855 million acres in 1936 (Myint, 1966: 50–51). In the Burma Delta region alone the acreage of cultivation expanded from about 700,000 to 800,000 acres in the mid-1850s to 8.7 million acres by the mid-1930s (Adas, 1974: 22). The increase in rice production was achieved not by innovation in rice technology or reorganization of production but by the expansion of the cultivated area, an increase in labour supply and the application of established agricultural methods to pioneer lands. This was later to store up problems when the availability of cultivable land diminished and population growth exceeded the supply (ibid.: 128–153). In addition, it was exacerbated by dependence on one commodity and the decline of other economic activities, particularly small-scale rural industry (Resnick, 1970).

The British realized the potential for large-scale rice cultivation in the Delta by developing flood control and drainage using British technology, migrant Burmese farmers and cheap labour from India. The large areas of land available needed population to farm it and peasant farmers had to be drawn mainly from the interior dry zone. To attract Burmese labour the British remitted the capitation tax on peasant families for two years and made land available on easy terms. Farmers could open unoccupied land as in effect 'squatters', and after paying land revenue on it continuously for 12 years could secure ownership of it (Myint, 1966: 52, 75). The British wished to create a class of prosperous owner-cultivators and they experimented with various arrangements to achieve this including leasing and land grants. As Burmese farmers became established Indians were imported as cheap seasonal labour and employed in rice-milling and on the docks as rice exports increased towards the end of the nineteenth century. From an annual figure of Indian immigration of 15,000 in 1876, there was a substantial increase to over 300,000 per annum by the late 1920s

(Furnivall, 1957: 72–73). Overall population in Lower Burma increased from 2.59 million in 1872 to 8.918 million in 1941 (Myint, 1966: 55).

Sources of capital in the form of short- and long-term credit were available to the Burmese farmer, based on land mortgage arrangements, to enable land to be cleared and reclaimed and annual production costs covered. Most of the loans in the later colonial period were provided by Indian Chettiars (a caste of hereditary moneylenders), familiar with British financial systems in India; they began to send their agents to the countryside from about 1880 (Furnivall, 1948/1956: 86). By the 1930s there were some 1,300 Chettiar firms in the country, the majority based in rural districts (Myint, 1966: 58).

For a time the development of commodity production provided a rising standard of living and enhanced economic opportunities for peasant farmers (Adas, 1974: 122–123). However, the small cultivator was increasingly exposed to the vagaries of the world market, compounded by the heavy reliance on single-crop agriculture. The Depression years of the late 1920s and early 1930s in particular had a devastating effect on Burmese households. Following defaults on the repayment of loans and interest, land increasingly fell into the hands of money-lenders and larger landlords, and the small land-owners became tenants and labourers on others' land. However, the size of Burmese farms remained small at between 10 to 20 acres. When more land fell into the hands of absentee money-lenders, these usually comprised a scatter of farms rather than consolidated blocks which were then rented out to individual farming families, or sold on.

The British expanded rice production and created political instability. 'The relationship between landlords and tenants deteriorated to such an extent that the country experienced ethnic conflict and political uprisings resulting from the agrarian crisis. The impact of higher rice production ended in the frustration of farmers as a result of land alienation' (Khwin Win, 1991: 8). The colonial government only passed a Land Alienation Act in 1941 by which time it was too late to redress the problem of large areas of land passing into the hands of non-agriculturalists. Myint argues that the failure of British agrarian policies was the result of the preference for laissez-faire practices and sustained opposition to government regulation by the European and Indian business communities (1966: 80–81).

In contrast to Western modernization perspectives on the dual economy and native traditionalism, Furnivall draws attention to the importance of Burmese entrepreneurship and initiative in developing the Burma Delta (1956 [1948]: 82). Myint, too, says 'the transformation of millions of acres of cultivable wastes into fertile rice fields is mainly a Burmese achievement' (1966: 62–63, 87–88). Interestingly, in the Delta region '[m]ost of the persons listed as moneylenders in the first decades after 1852 were Burmese' and during 'the first phase of development, a large majority of the paddy brokers and rice merchants in Lower Burma were Burmese' (Adas, 1974: 65, 111, 210). Not only did Burmese peasants embrace production for the market with alacrity, but they did so in response to the availability of imported foreign manufactures and luxuries. 'The imports, consisting of cotton piece goods,

European provisions (biscuits, sardines, condensed milk), cigarettes, boots and shoes, household wares, etc., found their way to the humblest hamlet through the medium of the Chinese and Indian trader' (Myint, 1966: 66; Andrus, 1948: 197–98). Taylor also draws attention to 'the Burmese peasants' clear and ready grasp of the profit motive and of the advantages of trade for the social advancement of himself and his family' (1987: 189). These dynamic changes required an appropriate administrative, commercial and fiscal regime, which the British introduced, to encourage the Burmese farmer to develop land and cultivate rice for sale. Indian immigrants also made their contribution as field hands and seasonal labourers, urban manual workers, money-lenders, and import–export agents. Nevertheless, only gradually did Indian Chettiars edge out Burmese entrepreneurs in agriculture (ibid.: 110–120). Chinese merchants also helped service urban-based commerce.

The major problem for the Burmese, which demonstrates the relevance of an underdevelopment perspective, was that major areas of the economy were controlled by non-Burmese, and the majority of Burmese were confined to rice agriculture. There was negligible industrialization and manufactured goods were imported, not made locally. As Fenichel and Huff state 'Capitalism in colonial Burma meant that few of the skills necessary to run a modern economy were transferred to or developed by the indigenous population' (1975: 321–322; Taylor, 1995: 45–63). Myint also points to the 'colonial drain'; for much of the colonial period Burma enjoyed a substantial surplus of exports over imports, which included 'remittances abroad of incomes and profits by immigrants and foreign companies' and which in turn were not available for re-investment in the country (1966: 118). Overall the Burmese benefited less than others, a situation compounded by the fact that from the establishment of the colonial state in 1825 until independence in 1948, 'Burma was in the eyes of the imperial government merely a distant appendage of the Indian empire' (Taylor, 1995: 69).

Although rather more complex than Furnivall depicted, the actions of the British served ultimately to transform the social class structure of Burma, creating new groupings of primarily Burmese landless labourers and tenants; wealthy, primarily non-Burmese landlords and middlemen; urban labourers who were mainly Indian, but increasingly joined by Burmese in the 1920s and 1930s; and a class of mainly Burmese white-collar bureaucrats and professionals. A relatively small Burmese middle class emerged as a result of the availability of educational and career opportunities in the lower levels of the colonial bureaucracy, and it was this class which provided the political leaders for the modern Burmese nationalist movement. Many of the small Burmese entrepreneurs who had been active in the rice industry were progressively squeezed out by competition from Indians and the pressures of the 1930s economic depression. But although economically marginalized, the Burmese were relatively well placed in administrative and political terms with the departure of the British in 1948 (Fenichel and Huff, 1975: 326–327).

The class system was complicated by its interrelationship with ethnic divisions (Adas, 1974: 109–123). There were class-based conflicts during the late colonial period, particularly peasant protest, but during times of acute economic crisis such as when rice prices more than halved between 1928 and 1931, discontent tended to express itself in 'racial' or ethnic terms. Serious rioting broke out in Rangoon in May 1930 between Indian dock-workers and Burmese labourers, with 120 killed and 900 wounded, and spread to neighbouring districts where Indian landowners and tenants were concentrated (Taylor, 1987: 198; Adas, 1974: 197–199). The Saya San rebellion, led by a former Buddhist Burman monk, erupted in December 1930 and continued sporadically until mid-1932, and, although, it was not communal in character, there was associated inter-ethnic violence (Adas, 1974: 201–205). Rangoon witnessed anti-Chinese riots in January 1931 whilst the most serious Indian–Burmese conflicts occurred in July–August 1938, stretching from Rangoon to Mandalay, with over 200 killed and 1,000 injured (Taylor, 1987: 199–201; Adas, 1974: 206–207).

Therefore, Burma was far from being a cohesive state, and certainly not one that could realize democracy. It was a radically plural society and not a nation, held together primarily but not exclusively by alien political, administrative and military means (Furnivall, 1942; Adas, 1974: 107; Pham, 2005). For Furnivall Burma had been subject to 'the economic force of unbridled capitalism' (Taylor, 1995: 51). Moreover, for administrative purposes, the British had divided the territory into two major areas: 'Burma proper', essentially the lowland, rice-growing areas occupied by the majority of Buddhist Burmans, and where, with the dismantling of the Burmese monarchical structure, direct rule was instituted and administration reorganized through British and Burmese-appointed salaried officials; and the 'excluded' or 'frontier areas', primarily the northern, western and eastern upland areas bordering India, China and Thailand, where indirect rule through native leaders was implemented and such minority groups as the Karen, Karenni, Chin, Kachin and Shan resided. Other minorities including the Mon and Arakanese lived intermingled with the Burmans in lower Burma (see Chapter 6). In other words, the British destroyed the previous authority structure and its Buddhist foundations as well as radically changing the nature of the relationships between the king, the ruling class and their Burman and non-Burman subjects.

These processes of administrative demarcation led to the definition of the populations in Burma in ethnic terms and the demarcation of boundaries between ethnic groups, which had previously been fluid (Brown, 1994: 33–36). It was also in these surrounding areas that Christian missions were active, and from which the British recruited troops for the regular Burma Army. At the outbreak of the Pacific War, the majority of troops, aside from the British and Indians, comprised Karens, Chins and Kachins (Taylor, 1987: 100). With the Japanese invasion in 1942 there was a massive exodus of the British to India, and nearly half of the Indian, Anglo-Indian and Anglo-Burmese population departed, leaving a large vacuum in the economy. The war experience gave the Burmese the opportunity to acquire military skills and, prior to the war, the Japanese had trained leaders of the Burma Independence Army (Fenichel and Huff, 1975: 327).

Post-war Burma has grappled with this colonial legacy, the problem that an indigenous middle class had little control over economic resources and that the development of a national identity was compromised by pluralism. The Constitution of the Union of Burma in 1948 recognized ethnic diversity by establishing a federal state to accommodate the main minority populations, although, in reality, a relatively centralized government structure was instituted with power in the hands of Buddhist Burmans (Brown, 1994: 43–47; Taylor, 1987: 227). Tensions between the central government and the minorities were expressed in secessionist rebellions and military conflicts, which further destabilized the post-colonial state, and undermined the economy. Major and prolonged insurrections were waged in the hill areas with the Karen rebellion of 1949 and the Shan and Kachin conflicts from the 1950s. However, the earliest signs of post-war unrest came from the Arakanese in the western Irrawaddy region (Brown, 1994: 33–35).

It was to be anticipated that, after independence in 1948, the government would play an increasing role in controlling and regulating the economy, and the ideology employed for doing so would be broadly socialist (Steinberg, 1990: 56–58). With the departure of the British and the uncertain future of the Indian population, the Burmese were faced with a major dilemma. Their relative inexperience in managing economic affairs, given that major sectors of the colonial economy had been largely in foreign hands, meant not only that Burma would in all likelihood experience severe economic difficulties in the immediate post-war period, but that the solution to these problems was state control, central planning and nationalization of economic assets (including inland water transport, timber extraction and export, rice trading, and, rather fitfully, land, with joint state-private ventures in technologically-based industries such as oil). The Indian population had already been much reduced from 1942, and, though some returned to Burma after the war, the Burma Immigration Act of 1947 further restricted numbers. Nationalization of land in 1948 and 1954, although only partly implemented, and increased political instability in the late 1940s and 1950s, led to a further Indian exodus (Taylor, 1987: 270–272). Given their colonial experience, it was unsurprising that the Burmese leadership adopted an anti-capitalist, anti-colonial, anti-Indian stance.

Political and economic instability in Burma and the failure of civilian government under Prime Minister U Nu resulted in a military coup on 2 March 1962, the establishment of a Revolutionary Council, with its political party arm, the Burma Socialist Programme Party (BSPP) under General Ne Win, and the renaming of the state as the Socialist Republic of the Union of Burma. The military has been in control in Burma ever since, with the elimination of opposition (all political parties, other than the BSPP, were declared illegal from March 1964), the further expansion of state power and the political socialization and cultural indoctrination of the populace according to Burman priorities. From the 1960s Ne Win's government pursued policies of assimilation and incorporation with regard to the ethnic minorities and under the new Constitution of 1974 Burma's federal state was replaced with a unitary one (Brown, 1994: 48–51: Steinberg, 1990: 14).

During the 1960s, 1970s and 1980s the one-party military-socialist state promoted the disengagement of Burma from the world economy, increasing state intervention in the economy, and an emphasis on self-sufficiency and peasant agriculture. 'They sought not to please an entrepreneurial class of manufacturers or traders. No significant bourgeoisie existed in Burma' (Taylor, 1987: 300). The nationalization of external and internal trade and substantial sectors of manufacturing resulted in a further Indian exodus in the 1960s. The two major consequences of these policies are succinctly expressed by Taylor: 'one was to concentrate economic control and management in the hands of the state; the other was to decrease the involvement of Burma's economy in the world economy' (1987: 341). The consequence of this policy was the slow economic growth of Burma, though it did serve to restrict the development of alternative sources of non-state power based on private wealth. The political elite chose bankruptcy in the 1980s in order to overcome the extreme problems of pluralism (Taylor, 1995; 2001a; 2001b: 3–14).

The more recent history of Burma (or the Union of Myanmar as the country was renamed in 1989), following the violent demonstrations and riots of 1988, Ne Win's resignation, and the establishment of the State Law and Order Restoration Council (SLORC) under General Saw Maung, has been marked by some economic liberalization. The underlying reasons for the crisis and violence of 1988 are obvious; 'gross economic mismanagement by the ruling BSPP and Ne Win's whimsical *Burmese Way to Socialism*. An idiosyncratic blend of Marxist, Buddhist and nationalist ideology, it had seen Burma decline from a country once regarded as amongst the most fertile and mineral rich in Asia to one of the world's ten poorest nations' (Smith, 1991; 24; Taylor, 2001b: 5–6). The transformation of the SLORC into the State Peace and Development Council (SPDC) in November 1997 has also not augured any real change in the military government's policy (Callahan, 2003; McCarthy, 2006: 418). Economic malaise, suspicion of foreign economic domination, autarkic economic policies, and the strong centrist tendencies of the government continue (Steinberg, 1990: 4). It seems clear that the military government (Tatmadaw) intends to pursue its emphasis on the 'preservation of order and the status quo' (McCarthy, 2006: 418; Taylor, 2001b: 14). It is also indisputable that the events of 1988 were a response to Burma's 'underlying systemic economic and structural weaknesses' (Taylor, 1995: 46). The government, with little inclination to manage a capitalist economy, and with its ill-conceived restructuring policies of the late 1980s, further eroded the capacity of the private sector, including the illegal trading sector, and its links with local state officials, to generate economic growth (Kyaw Yin Hlaing, 2003: 49–53). The state and the 'official economy' were bankrupt, and this national disaster demonstrated the inability of Burma to industrialize and grow on the basis of state socialism (ibid.: 47). The malaise continues; there is excessive expenditure on the military and security; an inadequate trickle of foreign inward investment, and a lack of pluralist politics and power-sharing with technocrats and private entrepreneurs (Booth, 2003: 166–167). Recent evaluations of the political economy of Burma suggest that this authoritarian paralysis will continue (ibid.: 131–171; McCarthy, 2006).

Overall the case of Burma suggests that rather than explanations for the Burmese predicament which emphasize traditional religious motivations, Buddhist doctrines and broader cultural and psychological predispositions (Mya Maung, 1962; Sarkisyanz, 1965), our analysis should focus on historical processes and the consequences of colonial rule. As Adas indicates, prior to colonization the Burma Delta was 'a sparsely populated frontier region' and in the rapidly expanding export economy, largely driven by the Burmese cultivator, 'the traditional or precapitalist institutions and ties that have often proved barriers to social and economic change were not major obstacles' (1974: 211). Moreover, the Burmese owner-cultivator became so attuned to profit that 'he completely lost the sentimental attachment to his land that was characteristic of agriculturalists in traditional Burman society' (ibid.: 212). Nevertheless, the Burmese experience remained largely rural, and after the departure of the British and the exodus of large sections of the Indian population, 'there was no [indigenous] force, other than the bureaucratic/military structure, available to mobilize the economy' (Fenichel and Huff, 1975: 333). Taylor has the sense of it when he says that 'the Burmese had been denied access to modernity, but they had been bequeathed at independence both the ideas and institutions of modern society' (including concepts of nationalism and the modern state, 'reified ethnicity', impersonal rules, citizenship and human rights, a national army, and integration into a world economy (1995: 62). The Burmese destroyed the colonial legacy of the plural society by removing those who controlled the economy; the cost was bankruptcy.

Netherlands East Indies (Indonesia)

As we have seen the changes in Javanese society and economy were appropriately expressed in Boeke's concept of dualism, but the concept, far from being a general theoretical formulation which helps us capture local experiences under colonialism, tells us more about the historical particularities of Dutch colonial policies. The Dutch attempted to address their own level of economic development in the nineteenth century and devise the most appropriate way to exploit a dependent territory. They were handicapped in opening up Java to market-based commercial agriculture, given the lack of a free labour force, the circulation of money, and 'Dutch private capital and entrepreneurial skill'; this suggested that the development of the colonial economy would require a degree of coercion from above (Fasseur, 1992: 23). 'The Netherlands was never able ... to develop a manufacture export economy even remotely comparable to that of Britain, and so the interest of the Dutch in Indonesia remained overwhelmingly mercantilist to the end. The stimulation in Indonesia of extensive markets for industrial goods, it was feared, would lead only to increased British (or, later, Japanese) influence' (Geertz, 1963a: 47–48, 63).

The Dutch approach to the exploitation of their colonial territories, characterized by 'state capitalism' and subsequently 'bureaucratic capitalism' (ibid.: 50), was therefore rather different from that of the British in Burma, though there is debate about the significance of the changes which the Dutch introduced and the degree of continuity in Javanese society before and after the introduction of the 'Cultivation System' (Cultuurstelsel) (van Niel, 1992: 204, 224–227). Nevertheless, the Dutch progressively integrated Javanese peasant agriculture into a commercial system producing coffee, sugar, tea, indigo and tobacco for the world market. From the 1850s there was increasing emphasis on sugar and coffee; sugar, and for a time indigo, was grown on a proportion of village land (in theory about one-fifth of the land, though this was variable), whilst coffee was cultivated on 'wastelands', usually in foothills and hedgerows and on the margins of villages. The framework for these arrangements was provided primarily by the Cultivation System, introduced by Governor-General Johannes van den Bosch in 1830; it 'was a form of government agriculture in which the colonial government forced the peasant population to grow tropical export products that were subsequently sold at the auctions of the Netherlands Trading Company (Nederlandsche Handel-Maatschappij [NHM]) for the benefit of the Dutch Treasury' (Fasseur, 1992: 7). In this 'state plantation' system, crops were delivered at a fixed price. Ricklefs says: 'Local officials, both Dutch and Indonesian, set both the land tax assessment and the level of export crop production for each village, then compelled the village to produce' (1981: 115). The officials were paid a percentage of the crops delivered, but the payments were variable from district to district and they generated considerable corruption (van Niel, 1992: 67: Fasseur, 1992: 46–55; Elson, 1984: 10–12). Therefore, a contract was agreed between the local administration and the neighbouring villages to cultivate cane on areas of village land; then a contract was established between the local sugar-mill owner and the villagers to deliver the cane to the mill and then to the government at a fixed price (van Niel, 1992: 33). These 'productive arrangements … operated quite apart from the self-regulating principles of the world market. In short, Java became in a sense a self-contained production area with some features of modern socialist societies' (ibid.: 48–49). Peasants were also subject to corvée services, unpaid or poorly paid, to develop and maintain a communication infrastructure including roads and bridges (Fasseur, 1992: 58–59, 241).

The arrangements were implemented partly as a consequence of the colonial government's inability to sustain the land rent system introduced by Thomas Stamford Raffles during the British interregnum in Java from 1811 to 1816 and to realize a profit from the East Indies (ibid.: 90–94; Elson, 1984: 7). The Dutch government badly needed revenue, following the collapse of the Dutch United East India Company (Vereenigde Oost-Indische Compagnie [VOC]) at the end of the eighteenth century, the drain on resources caused by Anglo-Dutch conflict, the French occupation of the Netherlands from 1795, the Java War of 1825 to 1830, the Dutch–Belgian conflict of the 1830s, and the eventual recognition of Belgian independence from the Netherlands in 1839; all these placed great strain on the Dutch budget (Ricklefs, 1981: 105–114; Fasseur, 1992: 22–25; Geertz, 1963a: 63; van Niel, 1992: 123–153).

Peasants were required to cultivate cash crops, in part to pay their land rent, but the emphasis was on taxation in the form of labour rather than in money; if, however, the value of the crops grown by a given village did not meet the land rent requirement, then the villagers would have to make up the shortfall; if they grew crops in excess of the land rent then they received money payments (van Niel, 1992: 15–17). In contrast to Burma, where peasants were 'voluntarily' incorporated into the world market, in Java the process was involuntary, and, in principle at least, represented a partial return to the forced delivery system of the former VOC based on the monopoly supply of tropical products like nutmeg, mace and cloves in the Moluccas and pepper in West Java (Ricklefs, 1981: 59–66: Elson, 1984: 34–35).

In implementing the 'Cultivation System', which, despite its name, was not monolithic and was subject to considerable local variation (Fasseur, 1992: 26), the Dutch worked through relationships between Javanese regents (*bupati*) and their subjects, and between village chiefs and villagers. Local rulers therefore became officials in the service of the colonial government, an arrangement established by Governor-General Herman Willem Daendels from 1808 and reinforced by Raffles from 1811 when territories previously governed by the Javanese were annexed and their independence ended (Ricklefs, 1981: 105–110). However, there were relatively few Dutch supervisors, 'controleurs' and contractors to monitor the system, and very little direct intervention in Javanese society. The Dutch therefore knew 'very little about the burdens the system placed on the people', nor, until the mid-nineteenth century, were the Dutch parliament and the Department of Colonies very well informed of the situation (Fasseur, 1992: 240; and 13–25). The principle was to preserve the Javanese social order as far as possible, but inevitably changes occurred; for example, payments for crops introduced cash into the rural areas which were progressively opened to the market (ibid.: 41; Elson, 1984: 80–83).

The interconnections between cash crop and subsistence agriculture continued after 1870 when the Cultivation System was replaced by Dutch private enterprise and commercial plantation agriculture, particularly in the sugar industry, which Geertz styles 'the corporate plantation system' (1963a: 83). A watershed was the introduction of the Agrarian Law and the Sugar Law in 1870, coupled with 'the rapid mechanization of sugar-milling' and the increasing generation of capital in the predominantly Dutch-owned milling sector. This so-called 'Liberal Period' from about 1870 to 1900 ushered in the dominance of Dutch private capital, and the perception of the East Indies as a site for investment and a market for Dutch goods. Henceforth, the exploitation of Javanese labour and land was left in the hands of the private sector operating a leasing arrangement with Javanese villages to use the land for sugar cultivation (ibid.: 83–123). These changes had been prefigured in increasing demands from the Dutch middle class, 'grown wealthy on the profits which the Dutch economy had derived from Java', to liberalize the colonial economy and encourage free wage labour (ibid.: 118; Fasseur, 1992: 135–184; Elson, 1984: 103–123). The forced cultivation of tropical cash crops was progressively dismantled from the early 1860s, first with the least profitable crops of pepper, cloves, nutmeg, indigo, tea, cinnamon and tobacco, and then sugar and coffee from the 1870s; other compulsory services were also progressively removed (Elson,

1984: 115). 'By around 1870, practically all the labourers used in the government sugar industry, apart from those employed in planting and tending the cane, were contracted wage labourers' (ibid.: 120). However, the land rent system remained, requiring cultivators to find revenue to pay their taxes, and, overall '[m]ost peasants remained trapped in a subtle web of dependence, obligation and economic need which nurtured them and at the same time enfeebled them' (ibid.: 123). It was the sugar manufacturers who became powerful patrons and stepped into the shoes of government agents.

From the mid-nineteenth century a significant body of Dutch capitalists had emerged, backed by financial institutions, and there was also an increasing trend towards takeovers and the creation of 'multi-enterprise, limited-liability corporations rooted firmly in the motherland, or, in some cases, in other European countries' (Geertz, 1963a: 84). These private interests moved into plantation and other activities, but agrarian legislation prohibited them from owning land and therefore they leased it from villagers from between 5 to 20 years; if land was categorized as wasteland or 'unused' it could be leased from the government for a period of up to 75 years (ibid.). But increasingly market mechanisms came into play, and impoverished peasants borrowed money from wealthy rural money-lenders, native, Arab and Chinese; native usurers could foreclose on mortgages and take over land; non-native lenders had to work through indigenous middlemen and agents. In consequence, rural debt and landlessness increased.

The benefits of the Cultivation System for the Dutch were enormous. Fasseur indicates that between 1832 and 1850 'the colonial contribution to the Dutch treasury amounted to about 19 per cent of total Dutch public revenue' (1992: 242). This increased to almost 32 per cent between 1851 and 1860; of the profits from the Indies more than 85 per cent came from sugar and coffee sales. Ricklefs states that '[t]hese revenues kept the domestic Dutch economy afloat: debts were redeemed, taxes reduced, fortifications, waterways and the Dutch state railway built, all on the profits forced out of the villages of Java … . Amsterdam again became a major world market-place for tropical produce, especially coffee and sugar' (1981: 117). Between 1831 and 1877 the Dutch treasury received 832 million guilders from the East Indies (ibid.). So the exploitation of Javanese land and labour underpinned the Dutch domestic economy; it supported the colonial administration and the Dutch forward movement into the outer islands from the second half of the nineteenth century. Van Niel concludes that the Cultivation System 'was, in the main, brutally exploitative, and was managed by greedy, power-hungry persons' (1992: 223); and Elson refers to 'coerced drudgery on a massive and relentless scale' (1984: 77).

Dutch intervention transformed the Javanese social structure; the upper aristocratic stratum of Javanese society generally benefited from the forced delivery of crops in the form of crop percentages; their positions were also secured, given their role in the operation of the Cultivation System. But their status depended increasingly on Dutch support; they became detached from their own society, and 'frozen' in bureaucratic roles as dependent administrators rather than as agricultural modernizers. They became integrated into an indigenous administrative structure which included the assistants of the regents (*patih*) and district heads (*wedana*). The Dutch began to work more through these officials, and the regents were progressively bypassed, and their traditional prerogatives of office such as labour services abolished. The sons of the higher elite were also sent to Dutch educational establishments, but increasingly the administration was staffed by the sons of lower officials or by personnel recruited from outside the aristocracy, who had completed the European lower school and then attended Training Schools for Native Officials or Native Doctors. However, new officials, brought in from better-off non-aristocratic families were lumped together with the 'traditional' administrative class as *priyayi* (Ricklefs, 1981: 123).

The Cultivation System was based on the principle, which Boeke later identified as 'dualism', of separating the peasants' production of cash crops from the subsistence cultivation of rice. Javanese labour then was reproduced in the 'traditional' rice sector while surplus was generated, mainly for the benefit of the Dutch, in the 'modern' sector (Geertz, 1963a). The Cultivation System, according to Geertz, 'brought Indonesia's crops into the modern world but not her people'; it also served to give 'a final form to the extreme contrast between Inner and Outer Indonesia' (see Fasseur, 1992: 9). For Geertz, the consequences of this dualistic development for the Javanese was 'involution' or 'stultification' and 'ossification', a high level of socio-economic homogeneity at the village level, and 'shared poverty', based principally on the capacity of irrigated rice cultivation to respond to intensification and enable more peasants to be supported on the same or reduced areas of land. Moreover, agricultural modernization was precluded because the peasantry became increasingly impoverished either on small-holdings or as landless labourers, tenants and sharecroppers, and were prevented from moving into the 'modern' sector by the Dutch; they became, in Geertz's words 'post-traditional' (1963a: 99; van Niel, 1992: 58).

Some well-placed villagers did prosper, particularly the 'village chiefs and their lieutenants', and those who owned land and administered the system on behalf of the Dutch (Elson, 1984: 41). The Dutch land rent system also resulted in these core villagers regularizing rights in land and taking over 'fixed portions of land' (van Niel, 1992: 39). The middle peasant who had sufficient land to meet subsistence needs also exhibited a degree of resilience in the face of intense economic pressures (Elson, 1984: 255). In some areas, the effects on which Geertz focused were in evidence, that is the widening of land ownership to spread burdens and give others a share in the work; however, overall 'land ownership appears to have become increasingly concentrated in the hands of a prosperous village elite' (Ricklefs, 1981: 117; see also Elson, 1984: 12–19, 90–97, 222–224). Many Javanese became impoverished; some drifted into the urban and coastal areas looking for work, others became 'transport workers, tradesmen, traders and permanent factory employees'; landless labourers also began to form 'coolie' settlements in the vicinity of coffee plantations (Geertz, 1963a: 58–59; Elson, 1984: 254). Nevertheless, many farmers stayed on the land and eked out a living on small-holdings or by renting or working for others. Rice shortages and famines occurred because of the pressures placed on village land from sugar growing and population increase, rather than the irrigated fields responding progressively to these demands, as Geertz's thesis suggested (Ricklefs, 1981: 117; Geertz, 1963a: 28–37, 74–82, 94–95; Elson, 1984: 85–90).

One major consequence of the concentration of the Dutch on Java was to accentuate the contrasts – demographic, economic, social, political, cultural – between the major part of Java (excluding some south-western areas), Madura, south and central Bali, and western Lombok (or 'inner' Indonesia) and the vast, remaining area of the outer islands ('outer Indonesia'). Sugar remained the most important Indies export crop until the 1930s, and continued to use Javanese peasant land on a rotational basis. However, the Depression years dealt a major blow to the industry from which it did not recover, compounded by the destruction wrought during the Japanese Occupation and the post-war Indonesian revolution from 1945 to 1950. But there remained a large, densely-populated rural Java, and a lower density population in the outer islands, many of the villagers there growing such crops as rubber, tobacco, coffee, tea, coconut, pepper and kapok on a small-holding basis; there was also enclave plantation agriculture in such places as the Sumatran east coast around Deli, growing tobacco, rubber, tea and oil palm, and using imported coolie labour from China and Java.

The outer islands also became the source for oil production and other minerals using wage-labour in southeast Sumatra around Palembang-Jambi and in eastern Borneo at Balikpapan, and tin on the islands off the Sumatran east coast (Geertz, 1963a: 103–106). Royal Dutch Shell was created in 1907 with the merger of 'De Koninklijke' (Koninklijk Nederlandsche Maatschappij tot Exploitatie van Petroleum-bronnen in Nederlandsch-Indie [Royal Dutch Company for Exploitation of Petroleum Sources in the Netherlands Indies]) and the London-based Shell Transport and Trading Company. From the 1840s through to about 1910, most of the remaining areas of what was to become Indonesia were brought under Dutch control (Ricklefs, 1981: 125). The outer islands eventually overtook Java as the main source of East Indies exports. As Ricklefs says:

> The outer islands were the areas of deeper Islamic commitment, greater entrepreneurial activity, more valuable export products, greater foreign investment, more recent Dutch subjugation and lesser population pressure. Java was the land of less profound Islamisation, less entrepreneurship, declining value as a source of exports, lesser new economic development, longer and more fundamental colonial interference, and overpopulation'. (ibid.: 146)

Thus the Javanese sugar industry was built not on privately-owned landed estates, nor on slave labour, nor on a fully proletarianized, landless working class, nor on local small-holding cultivators channelling products into the market. Rather the Javanese cane-worker 'remained a peasant at the same time that he became a coolie, persisted as a community-oriented household farmer at the same time that he became an industrial wage laborer. He had one foot in the rice terrace and the other in the mill' (Geertz, 1963a: 89). However, Geertz's rather pessimistic view of nineteenth century Java did tend to understate the dynamism, flexibility, openness, and stratified nature of Javanese socio-economic organization as well as the growing tide of Javanese protest and anti-government activity from the unionization of sugar factory labourers to the popular, village-level, religious appeal of Sarekat Islam (Islamic Association) (van Niel, 1992: 190; Elson, 1984: 195–227).

Various social elements in the story of post-war Indonesia will be told in more detail in subsequent chapters, but I draw attention here to the legacy of the colonial period and some of the issues faced by the newly-independent Indonesian government. Although Indonesia had to address some of the same effects of European colonialism as Burma there were clearly significant differences in the form and content of post-colonial society. Geertz's vivid summary of 1950s Java captures some of the problems, although his characterization had particular relevance for Sukarno's post-war 'Old Order' Indonesia rather than Suharto's 'New Order'; for Geertz, Java was 'crowded with post-traditional, wet-rice peasant villages: large, dense, vague, dispirited communities – the raw material of a rural, nonindustrialized mass society' (1963a: 129). The sea of small-holding cultivators and landless labourers and tenants and the general economic deprivation in Java prompted Sukarno to embark on an ill-fated land reform programme from 1959–60 to 1965 which so generated social conflict that it contributed to his downfall, the massacre of large numbers of Communist and suspected Communist supporters, and the ushering in of the military dictatorship of General Suharto.

The move towards a more centralized, socialist style of government under Sukarno, and the bitterness evoked by the Dutch colonial experience, the issue of western New Guinea (Irian Jaya) and the Dutch attempts to retain their empire in the East after the Second World War resulted in the Indonesian nationalization of Dutch-owned companies, particularly the plantation sector in 1957. Much plantation land was taken over by peasant squatters and turned over to subsistence agriculture. The imbalances in the contribution of 'inner' and 'outer Indonesia' to Indonesian exports, the location of political power in Java, and the problems occasioned by the need to support the burgeoning population of Java on some of the proceeds of outer island production contributed to the outbreak of regional rebellions in the 1950s and the demand for autonomy from central government in Jakarta. The demographic problems of Java and the availability of land in the outer islands also meant that one major plank of Indonesian development planning was 'transmigration' or inter-island resettlement. It comprised an ambitious programme to move large numbers of impoverished peasants from Java and Madura to the assumed open spaces of Sumatra, Kalimantan, Sulawesi and, following its incorporation into the Republic in 1963, western New Guinea.

Finally, as with Burma, much of the entrepreneurial expertise in Indonesia and particularly Java, resided with foreign Asians, in the Indonesian case the overseas

Chinese. There was a relatively small native middle class, with a not insignificant group of Muslim small businessmen. Most Indonesians were therefore economically dependent, and most local politicians and senior military leaders were from the lower administrative class with few if any business connections and no resources in land. In his analysis of sugar cultivation in Java, van Niel, in a modernization mode of analysis and with reference to the Dutch policy in Java of using 'traditional' mechanisms to operate the Cultivation System, suggests that the 'continuance of the traditional cultural forces within this [Javanese] society into the present day [up to the 1960s] operates as a brake upon development now as in the past' (1992: 59).

Economic contradictions in post-independent Indonesia, the imbalances between inner and outside Indonesia, and the continuing dependence of the Indonesian economy on non-Indonesian actors were major factors in generating a period of extreme political instability during Sukarno's 'Guided Democracy' from 1957, until the fateful coup of September 1965 and the emasculation of the Indonesian Communist Party (PKI). Indonesia under Suharto's 'New Order' then embarked on a long period of economic modernization from 1967, opening its doors to foreign investment, exploiting the country's natural resources, including oil and timber, and strengthening centralized, political control and state involvement in the economy. What is more studies of rural society in the 1960s and the 1970s, rather than demonstrating 'agricultural involution', 'were showing a very lively and flexible Javanese (Indonesian) society to be in existence' and one which was 'tough, flexible, and enduring' (van Niel, 1992: 190).

Spain and America in the Philippines

There were considerable differences between the experiences of Philippine communities under European colonialism and those of the Burmese and Indonesians. Early on in the process of European interaction with Southeast Asia, large sections of lowland Philippine society were drawn into Hispanic culture through religious conversion, although, as Larkin observes, there was continuity with, or at least slow evolution from pre-Spanish patterns and local selective adaptation and adjustment to external influences (1972: 16). Therefore, Philippine populations or at least a significant proportion of them, and with the exception of the Muslim south and many of the interior hill tribes, were incorporated into a Western cultural environment over a long period of time (Phelan, 1959: viii–ix). The islands were also seen as a stepping-stone for the religious conversion of and economic engagement with the larger populations of China and Japan.

What is more, Spanish colonialism, though culturally important, was conducted primarily through native intermediaries, as well as Catholic priestly orders. Unlike other parts of Southeast Asia, a politically and economically strong native class which had subsequently intermarried with Chinese merchants and financiers, and with Spanish colonialists, emerged as a local mestizo class and was consolidated further under American patronage. Following their failure to secure a stake in the spice trade in competition with the Portuguese, and subsequently the Dutch, or to realize any success in the cultivation of spices in the Philippines, the Spanish concentrated on the China–Mexico galleon trade which, from 1571, used the Spanish-Philippine capital of Manila as an entrepot. Manila enjoyed a monopoly in foreign trade, and the majority of the Spanish population resided there, leaving oversight of the local population to Spanish friars and a scatter of provincial administrators. The connection with China also resulted in Chinese immigration to Manila and, by the early 1580s, there was a Chinese commercial quarter there. This urban population also enjoyed the advantage of close proximity to the 'rice basket' of the central Luzon plain for its food supplies.

Given the distances between Spain and the Philippines, the debilitating climate, and the fact that the local population was scattered across numerous islands, many of which had inaccessible hinterlands, Spain struggled to attract personnel to this remote outpost. By the seventeenth century there were only a few thousand Spaniards there, including some 300 priests (Cushner, 1971: 4; Phelan, 1959: 11, 33). Up until the nineteenth century, Spain's colony in the East was a financial liability ('a fiscal nightmare'), but the threat of Dutch ambitions in the seventeenth century and British and French activities in the eighteenth century served to provide Spain with a reason for its continued presence. The Mexican treasury covered the Philippine deficit, although many Spanish and Chinese merchants in Manila realized handsome profits from the galleon trade (Phelan, 1959: 93).

In addition to the China–Americas trade, involving the exchange of high value/low bulk Chinese fabrics and luxury goods from other parts of Asia mainly for Mexican silver, Spain saw the Philippines as a field for religious conversion to counter the expansion of Islam (Cushner, 1971: 129–130). Roman Catholic missionaries were early arrivals, and within 50–60 years of the establishment of a Spanish settlement in 1565 by Miguel Lopez de Legazpi, large numbers of Filipinos in the northern two-thirds of the islands had embraced the new religion, though many of them did so only nominally whilst continuing to hold to local folk religions. The main orders in the Philippines were the Augustinians, Jesuits, Dominicans, Discalced Franciscans and Augustinian Recollects, and parishes in a demarcated contiguous area were usually assigned to one order. Cushner says that '[a]lthough great progress was made during the first fifty years of evangelization, an estimated five hundred thousand had been baptized by 1622, the question of how deeply Christianity had penetrated was legitimately asked' (ibid.: 97). The Filipinos were skilled in adapting their existing beliefs and practices to the new religion, and they tended to embrace the overtly ritualistic and ceremonial (fiesta) elements of Catholicism. Nevertheless, one of the main points of contact between the Spanish and the provincial population was through parish priests who learned the native languages and conducted their teaching in this medium (Larkin, 1972: 31–32). The previously scattered Philippine population increasingly focused on the church, the centre of the parish (*cabecera*) and the outlying chapels, visited periodically by non-resident clergy (*visita*); it was these that provided a focus for the later development of the small town (*población*), the municipal township (*pueblo*) and the rural settlement (*barrio*, or previously *barangay*) (Phelan, 1959: 47–48, 122–129).

The Spanish administered the Philippines indirectly, using rural leaders. Parish priests assumed a range of secular duties, including tax collection, arbitration and the maintenance of law and order. In any case Spanish colonialism was based on the principle of 'the inseparable union of the Church and the state' (Phelan, 1959: 6). Pre-Hispanic Philippine society (outside the Muslim south) comprised a de-centralized village- and kinship-based social order. In much of the Philippines, the Spanish, unlike the British in Burma and the Dutch in Java, were not confronted by powerful states, and subjugation was achieved primarily by cultural assimilation.

The Spanish incorporated a pre-Hispanic, dispersed and hierarchical socio-political order to help administer their colony. At the top of the native social ladder was a chiefly class (*datu*), one of whose number served as the local ruler (also referred to as *datu*) of the rural community or *barangay* (Cushner, 1971: 71). In certain cases, there may have been an embryonic supra-village political organi-zation in which a chief had nominal authority over a confederation of *barangay* (Phelan, 1959: 16–17). The chiefly class did not owe tribute to the ruler, but there were apparently some lower *datu* who delivered labour services to higher chiefs. The chief oversaw the agricultural calendar and was custodian of the village lands; he served as military leader and administered local justice. Below the *datu* were freemen (*timagua* or *timawa*), and slaves (*alipin*) (Larkin, 1972: 20–22). Freemen provided services to the *datu* during the busy period of farming and delivered trib-ute, but they were mainly left to their own devices; they had rights in property and owned their own houses. The designation 'slaves' is misleading in that these were debt peons rather than chattel slaves, though some were the result of capture in inter-village raids, or had been convicted of particularly serious crimes; indebted or convicted freemen could become slaves, and a slave could be redeemed by debt repayment. Slaves and freemen could intermarry. However, '[a] slave was bound to full service to his or her master and was subject to severe penalties for violation of the law' (ibid.: 21). Phelan suggests that the term 'dependent' might be more appropriate than 'slave' (1959: 20). Class divisions were neither rigid nor fixed; there was considerable social mobility, and individuals and families straddled class boundaries. Following the abolition of slavery towards the end of the seventeenth century the freeman and slave classes increasingly merged (Larkin, 1972: 38).

The Spanish incorporated the chiefly class into their administration as lower level officials. They, or at least their children, were also the first target for reli-gious indoctrination in the catechism, baptism and the receipt of certain of the sacraments. Once they had converted usually ordinary villagers and dependents followed (Phelan, 1959: 55–71). The local chief was transformed into an official (*ca-beza de barangay* [later *barrio teniente*]) and his village became the basic unit of lo-cal government, although the Spanish standardized and increased the size of these units to enhance administrative efficiency. The *cabeza* collected taxes and tribute and helped organize the delivery of labour services, administered local justice and served as an intermediary between the village and the Spanish state (Mulder, 1998: 103). The next unit down was the municipal township (*pueblo*), an extensive territory which comprised a number of *barangay*, and was presided over by a native petty governor or chief magistrate (*gobernadorcillo*, later *capitán municipal*). The candidate was nominated by the senior constituent *cabezas* and selected by the Governor in Manila for those communities near the capital and by the Spanish *alcaldes mayores* or provincial governors in the outlying provinces. There were 12 provinces with some of the more extensive subdivided into *corregimientos* administered by a *corregidor*. The leading native families, office-holders and retired officials came to be known as the *principalia*, and it was they who became wealthy at the expense of their villagers and dependents. As Phelan notes 'the Filipinos had had extensive experience on the level of local government since the late sixteenth century' but the system was 'oligarchical' and not democratic, controlled by a small group of 'bosses', and referred to in Spanish terms as 'caciquism' (1959: 126–127).

One of the most important changes introduced by the Spanish was in land-ownership. They gradually replaced the concept of access rights to and use of land, usually organized and coordinated at the village level and presided over by the *datu*, with that of individual ownership and the concept of land as a commodity and subject to mortgage. This enabled the privileged *datu* class to accumulate land under their ownership over which previously they had only a custodial right. This trend increased during the seventeenth century with 'more and more chieftains acquiring the actual title to the land that their dependents cultivated' (ibid.: 117). Rather than the development of large, privately-owned estates, there was therefore the accumulation of scattered small land-holdings owned by a native ruling class and acquired through an administrative rather than an entrepreneurial function.

The native population had to deliver labour services and tribute to the Spanish colonial government which defrayed the cost of administration. The right to collect tribute or head tax was farmed out to Spanish individuals or colonists and to representatives of the Spanish crown in a system of *encomiendas* (Cushner, 1971: 102–112). Priestly orders were also given rights over land and people and much of the burden of their support fell on the local population. From the early colonial period onwards these orders acquired estates (the so-called 'friar estates') around Manila. Absentee *encomenderos* received an annual tribute, usually in kind, and sometimes in labour services. Native chieftains served as agents of the *encomenderos* in collecting tribute and assisting the government in operating such systems as the *polo* and *vandala*. The Spanish introduced a more general system of draft labour (*polo*), principally to support the Spanish naval enterprise as woodcutters, shipbuilders, crewmen and munitions makers (Phelan, 1959: 99; Larkin, 1972: 26). In return labourers would receive a modest monthly stipend of rice from village treasuries, which were in turn supported by an annual levy on local farmers. Chiefs and their sons and office-holders were exempt, as, indirectly, were wealthy villagers who could buy substitutes to meet their labour obligations. More onerous was the *vandala* which was 'the compulsory sale of products to the government' based on an annual quota and comprising such items as rice and timber (Phelan, 1959: 99–100). Often the government would make token payments or no payment at all so that the *vandala* became 'an extralegal form of taxation' (ibid.: 100). In this system the *cabezas* as agents of the Spanish 'acquired new and lucrative sources of enrichment, and the tendencies towards debt peonage increased' (ibid.: 115). In addition, in the eighteenth century landowners increasingly entered into arrangements with landless natives in which land was rented on a sharecropping basis (*casamajan*), and loans provided to tenants.

British intervention in the Philippines in 1762–64 marked a turning point. The Spanish found it difficult to resist the expansion of foreign trade and commercial interest in its islands. Manila was opened to foreign merchants and capital, particularly British and American, after 1790, and it was given *de facto* free port status from 1820. The nineteenth century saw the rapid expansion of commercial agriculture and the influx of foreign commercial houses (ibid.: 189–190; Larkin, 1972: 43–44, 63–65). But 'Spain ... lacked the entrepreneurial, administrative, and financial resources to capitalize on the rapidly growing Philippine economy' and it was left to the British, Americans and others to 'reap the benefits' (Stauffer, 1985: 244; Fast and Richardson, 1979: 10).

Therefore, up to the first part of the nineteenth century, Philippine society remained primarily subsistence- and rural-oriented, with a focus on the cultivation of rice and root vegetables, fishing and animal husbandry, and with no class of agricultural wage-earners, no plantation sector and no mining industry. Increasing commercialization in the countryside during the nineteenth century resulted in the expansion of such cash-crops as sugar, abaca, tobacco, coffee and indigo, the increase in the size of land-holdings in certain favoured areas, and more intense interaction, and then intermarriage, between the native elite and Chinese traders, money-lenders and sugar-dealers and processors who progressively extended their operations outside Manila in search of profits in agriculture (Larkin, 1972: 41, 46). This interaction led to the emergence of a Sino-Filipino mestizo class which was to play a crucial political and economic role during the American colonial period, and which increasingly took over the land-holdings of some of the members of the former native upper class through a loan and land mortgage system known as *pacto de retrovendendo*, as well as colonizing and opening up new lands, and purchasing available estates (ibid.: 49–51, 53–55, 73–74). They continued the personal patronage and dependency relationships with their tenants and sharecroppers, but increasingly they became entrepreneurs and speculators in real estate (ibid.: 63, 74).

The *principalia* also took advantage of educational opportunities provided by the Spanish, both in Spain and Manila, which enabled them to take up professional occupations in administration, the church, education and the law (ibid.: 59). The leading families, with extensive inter-provincial networks and with links to Manila, came to be known as *ilustrados* and it was members of these families, based mainly in Manila and the surrounding main provincial towns, who confronted their Spanish masters in the late nineteenth century with demands for colonial reform (ibid.: 103–105). Larkin says 'Land wealth, education, and broad social contacts differentiated the nineteenth century *ilustrado* from the rest of the *principalia*'; 'they represented the pinnacle of native society' (ibid.: 97).

However, there were two groups of anti-colonial protesters: first, members of the upper class who wanted improvements for the local population, the removal of Spanish 'exclusionist policies', and the retention of their own privileged position to be secured by legal and constitutional means; and, second, discontented lower-class peasant farmers and urban workers who wanted to end the inequalities generated by Spanish rule, by force if necessary. From 1882 to 1896 protests were primarily urban-based, intellectual and reformist, dominated by the upper class, and given expression by Jose Rizal and Marcelo H. del Pilar. One of the main targets of criticism was the Spanish priesthood because of its visibility, conservativeness, landed wealth and exclusiveness (Steinberg et al., 1971: 259–260). A second phase from 1896 was driven by the lower classes and triggered by an armed attack against the Spanish led by Andrés Bonifacio; from early 1897 this movement then passed into the hands of the landed class of central Luzon led by Emilio Aguinaldo, a Chinese-mestizo *gobernadorcillo* (Larkin, 1972: 106–107; Steinberg et al., 1971: 262). From May 1898, the Filipinos controlled most of the lowland areas of the Philippines, except Manila; they declared an independent Republic under Aguinaldo on 12 June 1898 and promulgated the Constitution on 21 January 1899 in the provincial city of Malolos (Larkin, 1972: 107). In the third phase of the Revolution from early 1899, the Republic subsequently lost its newly gained status in its struggle with the invading Americans, following the decision of the United States Senate to retain possession of the islands (Steinberg et al., 1971: 265). The United States had begun to intervene in the Philippines in 1898 as a result of their intervention in the Cuban revolution and their decision to destroy the Spanish Pacific fleet in the Philippines. The Philippine–American conflict was brought to a close by mid-1901 with the annexation of the Spanish colony.

The American period was marked by considerable continuity in the position of the native/mestizo upper class. Although there were senior American political figures who advocated the importance of 'new economic and military bases in the Orient' the overriding American orientation to their new colony was one of progressive religious proselytizing, a civilizing, reformist spirit, a concern for native welfare, health and education, a desire to promote 'native participation at all levels of government' and a commitment to withdraw from its colony as soon as this was practicable (Larkin, 1972: 134, 241). However, 'policy-makers realized that improved conditions in the native sector would undoubtedly produce a more stable environment in which American commercial interests could thrive [and] the money for this development all came from local Philippine taxes' (ibid.: 131–132). As in the Spanish period, much was left to the discretion of prominent members of the Filipino educated upper class who had begun to collaborate with the Americans from mid-1899 (Owen, 1971a: 4; Mulder, 1998: 105). It was they who implemented American policy, whilst 'the basic fabric of Philippine society was left intact' (Larkin, 1972: 135). Soon after the Americans established themselves in Manila native political parties (the Nationalist Union, the Federal Party [later the National Progress Party], and the Independent Party) began to be formed. Electoral politics were introduced from 1907 with elections to the First Philippine Assembly, comparable to the American House of Representatives (Jenista, 1971: 77). These were accompanied by a progressive Filipinization of public life. The Americans also governed through the Philippine Commission whose membership comprised senior American administrators and prominent Filipinos.

The commercialization of agriculture, the acceleration of processes of modernization, the pull of Manila and the financial attractions of non-agricultural pursuits led to the growing phenomenon of absentee landlordism and the weakening of the social bonds between landlord and tenant. There was a gradual transformation of labour relations in the countryside in that the customary rights of tenants were weakened and the emphasis on the efficiency of production rather than personal reward and insurance for long service led to the replacement of tenants by seasonal wage labour, increasing specialization of functions and technological advances. The remaining tenants were also subject to more intense pressures from their landlords to deliver crops at lower cost.

Given that the Americans came to depend on the *ilustrados* and *principalia* in their progressive introduction of self-government, and their reliance, as with the Spanish, on a system of indirect rule, they 'found from an early date that they were never in complete command of events' (Owen, 1971a: 5). Theirs was a policy of 'conciliation' which served 'to continue to satisfy the political aspirations of the Filipino elite' in return for their cooperation and the need to put an end to nationalist resistance; this in turn undermined American attempts to introduce a fully democratic political system (Cullinane, 1971: 14). The Americans were faced with several problems in managing the increasingly Filipinized political and bureaucratic system including 'neglect of duty and abuse of authority, protested elections and violations of the election laws, and the misuse of public funds' (ibid.: 31). The American administration did not address the rapidly polarizing agrarian problems; rather they 'legitimized the elite's *de facto* power at the local level by supplying it with a strong political identity through the holding of public office' (ibid.: 38). Moreover the wealthy Filipino Assemblymen 'had been raised and educated under Spanish rule and seem to have accepted the traditional Spanish view of public office as a mandate for monetary and social aggrandizement' (Jenista, 1971: 85).

However, what the Americans did was 'resolutely to rationalize' the colonial economy bequeathed them by the Spanish and 'deepen the integration of the Philippines into the capitalist world economy via the United States on the basis of colonial specialization in producing primary products' (Stauffer, 1985: 244). In particular, they introduced a subsidized import quota for Philippine sugar to the metropolitan market 'thereby guaranteeing a continuation of the Philippine political economy with its heavy reliance on the sugar plantation landowning class' (ibid.). It also encouraged the production of a range of other export crops and the export of minerals and other raw materials, without laying the foundations for an industrialized economy.

Many of the features of the post-colonial Philippines demonstrate the legacy of the Spanish and American periods. Owen characterizes American rule as one of 'passivity or ineffectiveness' (1971b: 103). The problems of landlessness, tenancy and poverty remained unresolved, although the American administration had demonstrated 'a growing rhetorical commitment to land reform' (ibid.: 105). The failure to address the deteriorating situation of tenants helps explain the frequent outbreaks of both spontaneous and organized rural unrest, expressed in such organizations as the Hukbalahap (the 'Huks'), which, though an anti-Japanese people's army, was also born of peasant disaffection (Kerkvliet, 1977). When the Philippines gained its independence on 4 July 1946 the country faced extreme problems of physical, social and economic dislocation and destruction caused by the Japanese occupation. The Communist-led Hukbalahap had waged a series of guerrilla campaigns against the Japanese in south and central Luzon, but the powerful and wealthy *principalia* had always looked with suspicion at their left-wing allies, particularly as the Huks advocated a land reform programme. If carried through, this would strike at the very heart of the economic dominance of the upper-class Filipinos and the ability to provide primary commodities like sugar for the export economy. In the elections of 1946, the Huks also won a small number of parliamentary seats but were forbidden to take them up by the controlling conservative politicians. Instead, they raised arms in rebellion against the government, and a struggle ensued for the hearts and minds of the Philippine peasantry. The Huks attempted, with some success, to mobilize the landless and impoverished; the landowners evoked relationships of patronage to gain support for their cause. The Filipino upper class ultimately defeated those who advocated radical reform, including the Congress of the Labor Organization which had links with the Huks, and they were aided by the government's capture of most of the senior leaders of the Huks in Manila in October 1950, by the ability of many of the landowners to secure sufficient support from their clients, and by the skilful and inspired leadership of the then Secretary of Defence, Ramón Magsaysay, who was to become President of the country in 1953, at the time when the Huks were largely a spent force (Osborne, 2004: 195–197).

The extremes of inequality which were a product of the consolidation of a Filipino upper class, the domination of caciquism and the crucial role of this class as an intermediary between the external power and the local population, have remained a dominant feature of Philippine society. American tariff and import–export policies also had the effect of discouraging investment in local manufacturing and allowed the 'free entry of American goods into the Philippine market, which, after the Second World War, left the Philippines as a primarily agrarian country' (ibid.: 107). Owen says that the country was 'in 1938, almost as "agrarian" as it had been in 1902' (ibid.: 108), primarily dependent on agricultural exports of sugar, abaca, tobacco and coconuts, which in turn gave enormous power and influence to the landowning class. However, a relatively modest-sized domestic but dependent commercial and manufacturing sector developed, again mainly owned and run by members of the mestizo upper class.

The legacy of the American period, which built on and consolidated rather than changed what the Spanish had bequeathed was '[o]verdependence on a few exports, tenantry, indebtedness, low productivity, corruption and inefficiency, under-capitalization, miserable working conditions – all the symptoms of economic backwardness were present at the end of the American period as they had been at the beginning' (ibid.: 112). In the post-war period the land issue and social inequality continued to dominate political debate, and, although the government made frequent promises to ameliorate the position of the poor and landless, these were only fitfully fulfilled. Moreover, 'the export-crop landlord class, the bourgeoisie in commerce and manufacturing, and their closely allied professionals, many of whom were elected politicians or high civil servants, remained united and firmly committed to capitalism, to a conservative nationalism ... and to "special relations" with the United States that amounted to acceptance of neo-colonialism' (Stauffer, 1985: 245–246). In cultural terms, in the early decades of independence Filipino leaders 'saw themselves as part of Western civilization; the third largest English-speaking country in the world; the only Christian nation in Asia; the showcase of democracy in a region ruled by strongmen; the bridge between East and West' (Mulder, 1998: 107). As we shall see in Chapter 5, all this was to change dramatically with the advent of Ferdinand Marcos's dictatorship in the 1960s.

Conclusion

Our case studies demonstrate the importance of historical-sociological analysis in understanding the changes wrought by the colonial powers. It is vital to emphasize that these processes and their consequences were not everywhere the same. Given that countries such as Britain, the Netherlands and Spain incorporated different peoples and territories at different times then the opportunities and constraints on Southeast Asians also differed depending on the level of development of the metropolitan power, the different and changing economic and other interests and capacities of the different European (and American) powers, and the variations in local social, economic and political structures and circumstances (Higgott and Robison, 1985c: 32; Hewison, 1989a: 14–15). In Burma there was the growth of socio-economic inequality and a landowning class in the countryside, but this process was complicated by the involvement of immigrant Indian merchants, moneylenders and labourers and the exclusion of the majority of Burmese from controlling positions in the colonial economy. The Dutch focus on Java exacerbated the differences between it and the outer islands and led to burgeoning population in Java and the proliferation of small-holdings and a landless peasantry; the Chinese played an important role as intermediaries in the colonial economy, but, unlike the Indians in Burma, they could not establish rights in land, and therefore did not become alien landowners. While state capitalism developed in Java the outer islands were incorporated into a more thorough-going colonial economy. The land question was much less important in the outer islands than in Java, and one of the solutions to Java's problems was seen to be the resettlement of the landless to the apparently empty spaces of Sumatra, Kalimantan and Sulawesi. In the Philippines a wealthy, powerful mestizo class emerged as a product of Spanish and American indirect rule and the dependence of the colonial powers on local politico-administrative intermediaries in governing the scattered population. Here leading native families, intermarried with Chinese compradors, took over the reins of power on independence, but they were tied to a colonial, agricultural-based export economy.

However, in all cases, pre-colonial social, economic and political organizations were transformed and new social classes emerged, which were in turn complicated by the migration into Southeast Asia of Indians and Chinese. In Chapter 5, I shall focus on the socio-economic groupings brought into being by these changes, and examine transformations in the post-colonial economies of the region, as well as the relationships between the state and social class.

5

Social Class, the State and Political Economy

South-East Asian societies have already developed or are in the process of developing a rather specific type of class structure and ... this class structure and its inherent conflicts provide the framework within which political activities and economic efforts will have to take place (Evers, 1980d: 248).

The division of society into classes or strata, which are ranged in a hierarchy of wealth, prestige and power, is a prominent and almost universal feature of social structure which has always attracted the attention of social theorists and philosophers (Bottomore, 1965: 11).

[T]he ruling ideas in society are those of the dominant class, but this does not lead to a value consensus of society because there is always a subordinate value system whose social source or generating milieu is the local community (Evans, 1986: 33).

Introduction

In the previous chapters we have referred to pre-colonial forms of social hierarchy and the transformations occasioned by European intervention. Frequently the concept of social class is deployed to capture these changing relationships of dependence, modes of exploitation, differences in wealth and access to material goods, social evaluation, and the bases of political power and authority. Social class is one of the central concepts in the sociological literature, and its crucial importance helps explain the degree of dispute and debate that surrounds it.

Observers of societies in the developing world have argued variously that, in comparison with Western societies, the former are more complex and diverse in social class terms, or that it is inappropriate to transfer a concept developed in the analysis of industrialized societies to very different socio-cultural systems which have been subject to colonialism and underdevelopment. Others have argued that social classes are less developed or 'weaker' in newly-independent countries, given the emphasis on relationships between patron and clients, factions and cliques, ethnic groups and gender which cut across class relations and inhibit the formation of class consciousness (Abdul Rahman Embong, 2001b: 359–365; Evers, 1980d: 248; Hanks, 1962: 1252; Hulme and Turner, 1990: 69–70; O'Brien, 1982: 1–12; Webster, 1990: 11–13). In such countries as Indonesia under the New Order, where political leaders constrained debate about issues perceived to be nationally sensitive, the concept of class, which was considered to be part of 'radical political jargon', was all but eliminated from academic discourse (Farid, 2005: 167–195). The concepts of 'workers', 'proletarians' and 'peasants', for example, were replaced by such terms as 'the poor' or 'low income groups', and in any case, Indonesian society was presented as broadly egalitarian; where inequalities existed these were explained as part of the traditional order and based on ascribed status (ibid.: 169–172).

The concept of class does not only apply to a modern industrialized society; in its classical definitions which stem primarily from the writings of Marx, Weber and Durkheim, it serves generally to arrange people in social strata or in a hierarchy of domination and subordination, and it does so principally on the basis of economic criteria. One of the interesting questions for students of social class is the ways in which class structures change from one type to another. As Evers says, 'any firmly established social order contains already the seeds of a new social structure in the form of individuals or groups who might under certain conditions at certain times grow and develop into larger units, groups or classes' (1980d: 249). However, in the cases which we examined in the previous chapter, the class structure has been transformed by the incorporation of Southeast Asian societies into a capitalist world economy, as well as into a foreign-controlled, rational-bureaucratic administrative system. Colonialism brought into being new social groupings such as landowners, wage labourers (both urban and rural), a commercial or comprador bourgeoisie, and those who were provided with education to serve in the lower levels of the colonial administration as clerks, technicians and native officers. Even in Thailand, which was not subject to colonial domination, a 'modernized administration' emerged following the revolution of 1932, and, according to Evers, a bureaucratic elite has gradually been consolidating itself into a new social class (1978b: 83–95).

A Brief Political and Economic Overview

Before examining the concepts of class, status and power and their relationship to the state and political action, I shall provide a brief overview of political and economic change in post-colonial Southeast Asia up to about 1970 to provide a context for considering changing class structures in the region. Following the end of the Japanese Occupation, the Southeast Asian countries (with the exception of Thailand, never colonized) sooner or later secured their political independence; some of them – like Indonesia and, eventually, a united Vietnam – achieved it with substantial conflict and bloodshed, others like Malay(si)a, Singapore and the Philippines relatively peacefully. Yet in all cases the colonial powers bequeathed their former dependencies considerable economic and political problems, and, in some the destruction wrought by the Pacific War only added to these difficulties. The major preoccupation of the newly-independent governments was to create a sense of nationhood, maintain the territorial and political integrity of their fledgling nations and promote development. Native political elites assumed the reins of power in situations in which their economies were largely in the hands of outsiders. In countries like Indonesia, the Philippines and Burma the new political leaders had also to tackle the land question and rural poverty. As Osborne has stated eloquently, 'colonial rule ... was *never* introduced or maintained in the interest of the colonised country or people ... This basic fact meant colonial regimes had different priorities from the newly independent regimes that followed them' and 'the leaders of the newly independent Southeast Asian states found all too often that they and their countrymen had only limited control over their own economies' (2004: 214–215).

There were marked differences in economic policy between different countries in the region, and there continues to be much debate about the precise role of the state in development (Wee, 2002a: 6; Malhotra, 2002). But in all cases, and in the absence of an indigenous entrepreneurial class, economic strategies depended significantly on state-directed and -generated economic planning. Some countries adopted socialist solutions, with central state planning, and the nationalization of the key means of production (North Vietnam was a very early exponent of this approach, and Cambodia and Laos subsequently, and, in a rather different way Burma, with its Buddhist 'road to socialism'); the Philippines and to some extent Thailand, with some government intervention, relied on market-led strategies influenced very much by Anglo-American modernization models of development; the others, Indonesia, Singapore and Malaysia instituted much more state-led capitalism (as did Thailand in certain sectors), though even here there were considerable variations in the nature of state intervention. Brunei, though oriented to the West, developed its own style of Muslim-Malay monarchy buoyed by its oil and gas wealth. Generally, however, economic nationalism and Import Substitution Industrialization (ISI) strategies were favoured in an attempt to overcome balance of payments problems, absorb local labour, and encourage local industries to contribute to national self-sufficiency (McVey, 1992b: 11).

The ISI strategy relied on a relatively high level of state involvement in licensing, regulating and controlling production, markets, local labour and capital; in influencing and directing foreign investment and regulating company ownership (to secure more local ownership and control of production); in formulating and implementing import and export, interest and exchange rates, and taxation policies (to favour locally produced as against imported goods) (Robison et al., 1987b: 3–10). It also required considerable investment in education and training and the provision of infrastructure such as industrial estates and communication networks (Hulme and Turner, 1990: 101–111). The major sectors which benefited from these policies were those which could tap into local, predominantly urban consumer markets, and which were relatively easy to establish – food, drink, tobacco, textiles and clothing industries. However, there was soon pressure to move into more advanced intermediate and capital goods production. In Indonesia the civilian governments of the 1950s and Sukarno's regime of the late 1950s to the mid-1960s directed themselves to the creation of an industrial base and these policies continued into the 1970s under Suharto's New Order. Thailand under Field Marshal Phibun Songkhram in the 1950s invested heavily in the sugar, food, beverages and textile industries, although private investment became more important from the late 1950s onwards (Robison et al., 1987b: 3). The Philippines too adopted ISI policies from the 1950s and protected the growth of home industries in consumer goods, light engineering and agricultural processing, policies which continued throughout the 1970s (ibid.: 4; Bautista, 2001a: 44). Malaysia and Singapore pursued ISI strategies during the 1960s, with the assumption of a larger, unified Malaysian market, but, following Singapore's departure from the Federation in 1965, its government soon had to look for an alternative policy (Tremewan, 1996: 31–33). Singapore embarked on Export Oriented Industrialization (EOI) from the mid-1960s (ibid.: 33–35).

Generally economic development policies during the 1950s and 1960s focused on economic growth and the mechanisms required for its achievement in line with prevailing modernization thinking (Webster, 1990: 30–31). When these policies failed to generate sufficiently rapid growth, solve the problems of widespread poverty and inequality, close the gap in standards of living between rich and poor countries, and promote modernization, such organizations as the World Bank, the International Monetary Fund (IMF), the International Labour Organization (ILO), and international advisers advocated redistribution with growth strategies, targeting poverty, addressing basic needs, supporting self-help schemes and the informal sector, encouraging 'development from below', and improving social welfare (ibid.: 32–38). Some adjustments were therefore made to the modernization paradigm (Higgott and Robison, 1985c: 38). However, these policies were overtaken by the changes taking place in the global economic system and the emergence of the new international division of labour.

I do not have the space to discuss the problems of ISI and the reasons for the switch to EOI strategies from the 1970s, but these included inefficiencies in production, lower quality of commodities, technical inexperience, corruption and misuse of funds, high prices, trade imbalances, and the saturation of often small domestic markets (McVey, 1992b: 11–15). There was a need to find overseas markets based on competitively priced production for export. But the ISI strategy obviously resulted in changes in the class structure with the emergence of local capitalists, and the expansion of an urban-based, wage-earning class as manufacturing industry developed. It confirmed the importance of those who controlled the state apparatus – senior political figures and bureaucrats – because of the increasing role that the state played in economic affairs; it also enabled some state managers to take over the ownership of economic resources in the context of predominantly authoritarian political systems (Schmidt et al., 1998b: 3). Interest in the importance of strong, developmental states and their contribution to economic growth emerged in the 1970s (McVey, 1992b: 12–13). Further social structural changes took place with the increase in production for export but in many countries, including Indonesia, Thailand, Malaysia and the Philippines, the ISI approach continued to be important even into the 1980s, given the vested interests among state managers, officials, and domestic manufacturers.

Definitions and Concepts

The terms 'social class' and' social stratification' are sometimes used interchangeably, but the notion of stratification refers to a system arranged hierarchically into strata on the basis of defined criteria. The strata or constituent elements are sometimes referred to as social classes, but they could also be castes, estates or status groups, or, with reference to the upper stratum, the term 'elite' (or 'power elite') is also used. Often the depiction of a stratification system provides a static picture or a snapshot of a particular social order; it categorizes social characteristics in a vertical or layered fashion. Much of the early literature on social class in Southeast Asia, particularly in countries like the Philippines under the influence of American structural-functionalist social science, was preoccupied with the delimitation of social strata (Turner, 1978). It is also surprising how persistent this preoccupation is within recent studies of Philippine class (Manlove, 2002).

This ranked system is not part of the natural or biological order of things, although it may be justified and explained in these terms (that is, that hierarchy is preordained and based on different physical or racial properties), but rather it is the product of social processes. It is therefore subject to human-generated changes, and, although we might present a stratification system as fixed and static, in practice it is always undergoing transformations, whether internally or externally induced or both, and the fit between the classification and ongoing social processes is imperfect. Economic growth, or population expansion, or military conquest, or changes in state policy, or technological transformations can lead to changes in the structure and character of social strata. It is also worth noting that sociologists often use the term 'social inequality' when referring to the dynamic, distributional qualities of social hierarchy.

So a stratification system is based on inequalities or privileges of various kinds; these usually include wealth, income, education, occupation, knowledge and skills, social honour and political power (Hulme and Turner, 1990: 69; Béteille, 1969a: 13). It is 'a system of differential distribution of desired and scarce things' (Dahrendorf, 1969: 36). However, the concept of social class is primarily based on differential ownership and/or access to economic resources, and is closely associated with the division of labour. In the classic Marxist definition, the ownership and non-ownership of the means of production serve to differentiate classes, and in the industrialized society of nineteenth-century England, which Marx analysed in detail, the two main classes were the wealthy bourgeoisie (property-owners) and the increasingly impoverished proletariat (wage-earners). Of greater importance was that Marx examined social and economic change; he anticipated class polarization and the sharpening of class conflict, with the result that other classes and groups (small producers, craftsmen, artisans, peasants, landowners, self-employed professionals) would decline in numbers and importance and be absorbed by or ally with the two main antagonistic classes. In addition, this implies that the relationship between classes is not only an economic relationship but also a political one, and for Marx, the struggle between the bourgeoisie and the proletariat would end ultimately in the political triumph of the proletariat and the foundation of a classless society, based on socialist principles.

Marx also made a distinction between the 'objective' definition of a class, based on certain shared economic or material criteria, and its 'subjective' dimension in that members of a class may or may not recognize their shared life circumstances and interests and combine to pursue these through class-based action (Ossowski, 1963, 1969: 79–89). In other words 'class consciousness' may or may not develop; if it does then, for example, '[e]ach group uses the resources that each possesses, labour or capital, to pursue their interests, which may lead to conflict' (Webster, 1990: 11). Marx therefore distinguished between 'a class in itself' (politically immature and unconscious of its shared interests) and 'a class for itself' (politically mature and aware of its interests). However, for him, the upper class which owns the principal means of production is 'necessarily the ruling class; that is, it also controls the means of political domination – legislation, the courts, the administration, military force, and the agencies of intellectual persuasion' (Bottomore, 1965: 61).

Since Marx's time changes in the class structure of industrialized societies have not occurred in the ways in which he anticipated, and in non-Western countries newly-emerging classes generated by Western intervention, and established, indigenous classes which have emerged from local circumstances are interrelated in complex ways. In the West there has been a burgeoning rather than the disappearance of the so-called 'middle classes' – salaried workers who range from upper-level managers, administrators, technicians, and educated professionals down to lower-level clerks, secretaries and office-workers, with increasing numbers employed in the service industries (in leisure and recreation, information technology, education, health and welfare provision, administration and government). It is often problematical to discern the boundaries and establish the membership of these intermediate strata which shade into one another, and are relatively fluid, with considerable social mobility between them (ibid.: 17).

Moreover, the several criteria used to differentiate strata may not coincide to demarcate clearly defined ranks or classes. Level of education or type of occupation might not relate directly with levels of wealth, for example. Other forms of identity also compete for people's allegiance – nationalism, ethnicity, patronage, gender – and the extension of the benefits of economic growth, rising standards of living, universal suffrage, educational opportunities, the emphasis on human rights, social welfare provision, and the separation of the ownership of the means of production from its control have worked to undermine the impetus which Marx had discerned in the mid-nineteenth century for increasing class conflict and eventual proletarian revolution. In any case the character and composition of the bourgeoisie have changed significantly since Marx's day; it does not constitute a clearly defined ruling class and is much less significant in economic and political terms than it was. The working class too has become more heterogeneous; manual occupations have declined in importance; the proletariat is less significant politically; and certain sections of it are generally more prosperous and aspire to middle class life-styles. Having said this it is easy to exaggerate the effects of social mobility, educational provision and redistribution policies in decreasing class conflict and inequalities. In the West and elsewhere there is still a strong tendency for those who were born with advantaged life circumstances to retain them.

In an attempt to address this complexity and to move away from Marx's dialectical model, Weber distinguished between different co-existing dimensions of social inequality – class and the economic dimension of production, distribution and exchange; status and the dimension of social honour, prestige and estimation; and finally the differential distribution of power and authority and the political dimension. Although these are interrelated, they are conceptually distinct (Runciman, 1969: 45–63; Roberts et al., 1977). The matter of social status, for example, is particularly germane to the differential evaluation of occupations, life-styles, cultural characteristics such as dress and speech, and educational attainment, and it provides a mode of ranking different from one based on economic criteria. The concept of prestige is more relevant to situations where one finds a social continuum of difference, particularly with regard to the middle class. Moreover, in cases of authoritarian rule (one-party states, personal dictatorships and military regimes) where a political elite or those who control the apparatus of the state and the formulation of national ideology have the ability to deploy economic resources and make decisions across the range of socio-cultural, economic and political life, then politics can have a direct bearing on the class structure (Ossowski, 1963). In highly centralized, non-democratic political systems, those who wield power can order or re-order society in various ways, and, as Bottomore says with regard to state-dominated socialist systems, 'classes no longer arise spontaneously from the economic activities of individuals; instead a political elite imposes upon society the type of stratification to be found in a bureaucratic hierarchy' (1965: 51–52; see Taylor on Vietnam, 2004b).

These considerations are especially pertinent to Southeast Asia where Western-derived democratic forms of governance have been fragile and easily overturned by powerful and well-organized groups like the military in Indonesia and Myanmar and by politically skilful dictators like Marcos in the Philippines. It has also been argued that colonial rule with its overthrow of traditional authoritarian Buddhist kingdoms and Muslim sultanates, hardly provided fertile ground for parliamentary democracy and a counter-balancing civil society in the new post-war nation-states. The experience of electoral politics and formal education had been limited, and freedom of expression and association severely curtailed (Pye, 1967: 42–76). The kinds of class structures which had developed in the West were only partially transplanted in Southeast Asia, given that on independence:

- The major part of the population was still located in the rural sector.

- The wage-labouring class was relatively small and concentrated in such sectors as transport, port industries, urban services and plantations, and tended to be divided ethnically.

- The native entrepreneurial class, characterized mainly by small-scale commercial activity, was very weak (in effect closer to Marx's notion of a 'petty bourgeoisie'), and suffered from competition from a larger-scale alien Asian bourgeoisie with close comprador ties to Western capital.

- A small indigenous intelligentsia, which had mainly been recruited into the lower ranks of the colonial bureaucracy and usually formed the new political elite, had little experience of running a complex society and polity and had no direct experience of economic affairs.

- Associated with the intelligentsia, there was what has been referred to as an emerging 'urban-based middle class'.

Approaches to Social Class and the State in Southeast Asia

Strategic Groups and Classes

Evers was one of the first sociologists to address the particularities of social inequality across Southeast Asia in the context of the rapid post-war transformations (1980d: 247–261). He examines social change and the creation of new social classes by using the pre-class concepts of 'quasi-group' and 'strategic group'. He also utilizes the Marxist distinction between objective and subjective dimensions of class. In other words, changing economic and political circumstances have given rise to new groupings of people in the bureaucracy and the economy whose members are still divided by ethnic, kinship or community loyalties (a quasi-group) and in which there are still previously established groupings vying for prominence. A growing sense of common interest and purpose, usually associated with an increase in numbers, leads to a degree of political mobilization and organization and these quasi-groups are consolidated into strategic groups. These latter identify with political leaders and form political pressure groups to secure an increasing share of societal resources. They are formed in situations of political struggle and conflict, and as Mulder suggests they are 'the very loci of new consciousness and embody the dynamics of social change' (1983: 14; 1979: 11–17). Examples which Evers gives of these new strategic groups are civil servants, teachers, independent professionals and Chinese businessmen; note that one of them is defined in occupational/economic and ethnic terms while the others are occupational groupings with particular educational levels and skills and comprise parts of what is usually referred to as a middle class (1980d: 250). Elsewhere Evers mentions other groups including a landed gentry or feudal nobility, the clergy, the peasantry, military officers, government administrators, students, intellectuals, religious specialists and village headmen (in traditional occupations), and an urban bourgeoisie (ibid.: 250, 251, 252, 256; Mulder, 1979: 12–17, 1983: 14–18).

Clearly, for those who adopt a more thorough-going class model, some of these strategic groups would be designated as classes or class-fractions and Higgott and Robison et al. suggest that 'many fractionalised classes exist in societies where pre-capitalist relations of production have not been entirely eliminated, and where capitalism might be at only an immature stage of development' (1985c: 49). Brennan too refers to class fractions in his analysis of Malaysian society and identifies within the 'dominant ruling class', the Malay aristocracy, rural landlords, senior state functionaries or bureaucrats, and comprador, mainly Chinese capitalists (1985: 98–105). He then identifies a middle class (or a 'petty bourgeoisie') comprising 'middle-ranking bureaucrats, teachers, workers in the social agencies, professionals and small-scale capitalists mainly in retailing and shop-keeping' (ibid.: 105). Finally, the 'dominated classes' comprise three main fractions: the peasantry, plantation and mineworkers, and the urban proletariat (ibid.: 106–111).

In developing countries dominated by and dependent on powerful external forces, these processes of group formation may regress, stall or be redirected creating 'a situation of confusion and long-term conflict' (Evers, 1980d: 251). Evers argues that classes emerge from strategic groups – which ally or ultimately merge to control material resources and power, and perhaps become a dominant or ruling class – or from dominated groups, which combine to become a revolutionary class to overthrow the rich and powerful. Dominant strategic groups appear to be equivalent to the several elements of a 'power elite', which Wright Mills analysed in the USA in the 1950s (Mills, 1967; Bottomore, 1965; Thomson, 1978). Indeed, on occasion, Evers refers to influential strategic groups as elites, as I do later in this book (1980d: 257, 258), and those which he examines coincide broadly with what Chen refers to as a 'power elite' in Singapore (1978a). However, in his examination of specific groups, at least in the 1960s and 1970s, he casts doubt on their political effectiveness, and, in the case of professionals, suggests that their incorporation into bureaucracies and their transformation into technocrats have resulted in their adopting a conservative political stance (1978a: 10–11). Evers's and others' studies of professionals such as doctors in Malaysia and Indonesia demonstrate their 'low degree of involvement ... in community affairs, their minimal contribution to general social development and their low modernization efficacy outside the confines of their professional specialization' (Evers and Regan, 1978: 24; Chen, 1978b; Lee, 1978).

The obvious examples which lend themselves to Evers's analysis, though they can be characterized as class fractions in political economy perspectives, are the alliances between politically powerful and economically well placed strategic groups, such as military officers, senior bureaucrats and Chinese businessmen in Thailand, and Malay politicians (and the remnants of the Malay aristocracy) and Chinese business interests in Malaysia (1980d: 257–258; Sieh, 1992: 110–112). Indeed, Evers suggests that the modernization process is consolidating 'a new upper class' which is in conflict with the 'peasant or urban masses' (1980d: 258–259). Heng, with reference to Malaysia, draws attention to the class consolidation of the 'Chinese business and Malay power elites', but does not detect similar class formations at the lower levels of society (1992: 143); and, although anti-Chinese politics in Indonesia under Suharto led to 'a decline of small Chinese business', there is substantial evidence of military-bureaucratic and Chinese big business alliances in the late Suharto period (ibid.: 257–258; Robison, 1992; 1978: 37–39). These alliances have also changed in character during the past two decades, so that some politicians and bureaucrats have become more deeply involved in business and have moved out of the politico-bureaucratic arena, whilst retaining links with it. Also 'some sons of high officials take MBAs instead of attending military or civil service academies' (McVey, 1992b: 24). Therefore, McVey notes that, even in the late 1980s, the division between political and economic power was decreasing, as well as the ethnic distinction between the indigenous politician-bureaucrat and Chinese entrepreneur (ibid.: 23–27).

The New Middle Class

Much interest has recently been expressed in the 'new urban middle class' in Southeast Asia, and as an important component of 'the new rich' (Robison and Goodman, 1996a: 1; 1996b; see also Abdul Rahman Embong, 2001a, 2002, 2006a: 159, 2006b; Earl, 2004: 351–379; Hsiao, 1993, 1999, 2001, 2006; Mulder, 1979, 1983, 1989, 1990). Defined primarily by the acquisition and use of an advanced level of education and specialist knowledge, the emergence of a new middle class is the product of changes in the economic organization of developing societies ('the capitalist revolution' and the internationalization of capital) and the demand for people with new skills and expertise (Hewison, 1996: 142–145). With reference to the Philippines, Java and Thailand, Mulder notes since the 1970s the emergence of 'a quantitatively impressive, new middle stratum ... whose members are the product of novel conditions that shape their lives and outlook, their culture and political demands' (1998: 99). He draws attention to the important difference between this new stratum and earlier educated generations who went to university and college 'as a matter of privilege'. More recently, those who acquire higher education do so primarily for 'professional and career considerations' and they are consumers par excellence in pursuit of new lifestyles; they 'consume' media products, fashion, cuisine, entertainment, tourism and educational services (ibid.: 100–101; Robison and Goodman, 1996a: 1; Abdul Rahman Embong, 2006a: 160; 2001a). As Robison and Goodman say, 'It is as consumers that the new rich of Asia have attracted an interest of almost cargo-cult proportions in the West. They constitute the new markets for Western products' (1996a: 1). The emergence of the middle class is also a profoundly gendered process, and in the construction of lifestyles, family life and consumption, women, with their role in the household, in deciding what is consumed, and as socialization agents, are crucial actors (Stivens, 1998a: 2–9,13–17; Earl, 2004; see Chapter 9).

Defining the middle class is no easy matter, and is complicated by attempts to translate Western-derived concepts of social structure to non-Western contexts (Stivens, 1998a: 15–17). Hewison refers to the middle class as a 'residual class category' (1996: 143); there are those who prefer the plural form 'middle classes' to reflect the considerable diversity in the middle orders of society (Kahn, 1996: 71–72); others talk of 'fractions' of the middle class in relation to differences in consumption and leisure practices (Paritta, 2002: 237). Dhakidae has concluded that, in the Indonesian context, the issue of the conceptualization of the middle class is 'confusing' and 'complex' (2001: 476–485; see also Dick, 1985). Hsiao and Wang also see the Southeast Asian middle class as 'a class in the making', comprising three main segments: the 'new middle class' (salary-earning professionals and administrators), the 'old middle class' (small proprietors, the self-employed), and the 'marginal middle class' (lower grade white collar workers and small proprietors who deal with more routine tasks) (2001: 5–8, 35–36; Hewison, 1996: 143; Robison and Goodman, 1996a: 9). Problems of definition loom large in the Singapore case where studies have indicated, despite claims that it is a relatively homogeneous 'middle class society', that it is divided in a much more complex fashion. Tan, for example, discerns at least four classes, which he refers to as 'upper', 'middle', 'working' and 'lower' or 'poor', though he accepts that the majority of Singaporeans, both objectively and subjectively can be categorized as 'middle class', given low unemployment rates, and high rates of literacy and social mobility (2004: 1–19). On the basis of income, Chua also differentiates the Singaporean population into a 'techno-bureaucratic elite', 'middle management' and 'independent operators in the private sector', 'production and labouring workers' and 'those who continue to live in poverty' (1995: 95). There is a further complication in cases like the Philippines where large numbers of middle class Filipinos are working in manual jobs overseas because of the lack of opportunities at home (Bautista, 2006a: 178–180; 2006b: 192–193).

The problems of delineating the middle class for Robison and Goodman are compounded by lumping them together with the bourgeoisie (or capitalists) in an even more indeterminate category (which is clearly not a class) of 'the new rich' – 'a diverse and fractured social force' (1996a: 3, 5–7). Indeed, they indicate that there is a significant distinction between the bourgeoisie, as owners of capital, and the 'professional middle classes' as 'possessors of managerial and technical skills' (ibid.: 5). Their concept of the middle class is also defined more in terms of Weberian notions of market capacity (and of occupation, housing, lifestyle and education) and not in terms of the ownership and non-ownership of the means of production, though elements of the middle class often own property or have links to it (see Hsiao and Wang, 2001: 5–8; Pinches,1996: 123; Hutchinson, 2001: 54–55). In any case, in the Robison and Goodman collection (1996b), one gets the impression of a relatively high degree of indeterminateness, diversity and fluidity and, in a later publication, Robison refers to the middle class as 'a vast and internally undifferentiated social category with differing sets of interests and relationships with other social and political forces' (1998: 61; Saravanamuttu and Loh, 2004: 355–358; Kahn, 1996). However, in my view, Hsiao and his colleagues provide some precision in their three-fold sub-categorization of the 'new', 'old' and 'marginal' middle class, and Evers's designation of some elements of the middle class as 'strategic groups' also helps us arrive at some level of clarity in what are murky waters.

Furthermore, there are broadly common issues which tend to be of concern to members of the middle class – law and order; political competence and integrity; educational provision and merit; the rights of citizenship; and the existence of private property (Robison and Goodman, 1996a: 2). Specifically in Malaysia, Abdul Rahman Embong found that, on the whole, the second-generation middle class had a strong commitment to family values, a pluralist acceptance of other ethnic communities, and a preference to be less dependent on the state (2006b: 150–153). The middle class has been associated with the emergence of civil society (of 'new social forces') and with demands for more representative institutions (Girling, 1988; Hewison, 1996: 137–138; Saravanamuttu, 2001b: 93–111).

In his coordination of wide-ranging comparative research in East and Southeast Asia, Hsiao has drawn attention to broad dimensions of 'middle classness' in the region, though there are clearly variations in detail from country to country (Hsiao and Wang, 2001: 3–38; Hsiao, 2001, 2006). In the first phase of research on East Asia (Taiwan, Korea, Hong Kong and Singapore), Hsiao and his fellow-researchers discovered that the major segment of the middle class which had emerged after the 1970s as a result of rapid economic growth and industrialization had its roots in the agricultural labouring and working classes. Variable results came from the second phase of research on Southeast Asia in 1996–97 (Malaysia, Thailand, Indonesia and the Philippines). It was discovered that a significant proportion of the Malaysian middle class, roughly half, also 'had their origins in relatively humble farmer or working class families'. However, the percentage was much lower in Thailand, with only about a fifth from lower class backgrounds (as with the Philippines, with between 20 to 25 per cent), with the majority from various segments of the middle class itself, particularly the old middle class. In Indonesia, the overwhelming majority of the current middle class are themselves from middle class backgrounds (Hsiao and Wang, 2001: 8–12). One of the reasons for these results was the concentration of the research on major urban centres, Bangkok, Manila and Jakarta, where there would be a greater likelihood of the old middle class reproducing itself in the same or other segments of the middle class. Dhakidae, for example, suggests that because Jakarta has been 'the very center of the process of [Indonesian] industrialization', this 'has given rise to a specific kind of Indonesian middle class' (2001: 509). Finally, there has been considerable variation in the extent of growth of the 'new middle class' which has been at its greatest in Malaysia, with much lower levels in Indonesia and the Philippines. Furthermore, in the Philippines there was an early development of the middle class in the 1950s with the growth of ISI, and even before that with the introduction of a system of mass public education by the Americans, but a much slower rate of growth subsequently (Bautista,

2001a: 44–48; Rivera, 2001: 209–210). The survey, which focused on Metropolitan Manila, revealed that about 70 per cent of the informants had grown up in the capital; a significant number also claimed their origins in middle rather than lower class families (Bautista, 2001b: 110–113).

Hsiao's research programme also discovered that the middle class in East Asia, including Singapore, had benefited in particular from state-generated economic development and the availability of education; they enjoyed advantages and opportunities in the market-place. They were rewarded with higher incomes and were developing particular 'consumer tastes and symbols' (housing, cars, electronic goods, recreational and social activities, including vacations); they were tending to marry with those of their own class background and to draw distinctions between themselves and other classes, particularly the working class; and they were oriented to achievement, careers and success (see also Earl, 2004 on Vietnamese urban women and expressions of status and lifestyle in motorbike ownership, cinema-going, café culture and shopping; Taylor, 2004: 31–32, King, Nguyen and Nguyen, 2007). However, there was ambivalence in middle-class political attitudes in the region; on the one had there was a tendency to support the status quo to maintain their material benefits, but on the other hand members of the middle class saw themselves as supporters of democracy, playing a role in society and in social movements. The interesting issue raised by Ockey with regard to the Thai middle class (but it applies more generally in Southeast Asia) is the strong tendency 'to distrust the masses and to disparage their ability to function democratically' (2001: 330). Thus, the role of the lower classes in pro-democracy movements is erased or marginalized in middle-class representations of these events and democracy becomes 'an elitist middle-class ideology' (ibid.: 332).

These middle-class political views and activities have been examined in Robison's and Goodman's volume (1996b). They, and several of the contributors, draw attention to the participation of 'elements' of the middle class, along with members of other classes, in anti-government movements and protests, sometimes violent, to depose dictators and authoritarian rule. These include Sukarno's demise in Indonesia in 1965–66; the overthrow of Thanom Kittikachorn's military rule in Thailand in 1973 and the experimentation with democracy until 1976; popular protest or 'people power' against Marcos's dictatorship in the Philippines in 1985–86; a resurgence of protest and street rallies against the Thai military regime and Suchinda Krapayoon's attempt to restore military rule in 1992; the 'reformasi' movement in Jakarta and the removal of Suharto in 1998; the demonstrations and protests associated with the 'reformasi' movement against the Mahathir government in Malaysia in the late 1990s and into the 2000s; and the ouster of Joseph Estrada's corrupt regime in the Philippines in 2000. On the other hand, they also point to occasions when middle-class people have sided with or at least acquiesced in political authoritarianism, more in the interest of political competence and stability, or material self-interest than in any firm commitment to democracy, as in the modernizing authoritarian state of Singapore (Robison and Goodman, 1996a:

7–8; Dhakidae, 2001: 505–508; Hedman, 2001: 921–951; Hewison, 1996: 154–155; Pinches, 1996: 123; Prudhisan and Chantana, 2001: 381–396; Rivera, 2001: 251; Rodan, 1993: 52–71; Robison, 1998; Tanter and Young, 1992).

Members of the middle class may also develop interest-group activities, lobbying government on particular issues (the environment, heritage, social welfare), although they may not mount a serious and direct political challenge to an incumbent regime (Rodan,1993; Saravanamuttu and Loh, 2004: 371–373). Saravanamuttu has detected a universalizing tendency in various issues and agendas adopted by civil organizations in Malaysia acting outside mainstream politics in the late 1990s and into the 2000s, though this has not resulted in regime change; the government has broadly delivered economic success and, in the eyes of members of the middle class, a degree of 'performance legitimacy' (2001a: 107–108; Hwang, 2003: 206–230). As Robison and Goodman suggest, there is 'some question about the capacity of Asia's new rich [which includes the bourgeoisie] to carry out a genuine democratic revolution' and they indicate that civil society has emerged in Southeast Asia, with the partial exception of the Philippines (where there was an early introduction of some form of democracy as well as the emergence of a relatively autonomous private economic sector), from political authoritarianism and state intervention (1996a: 2; Jones and Brown, 1994; Rivera, 2001: 210). Hedman has drawn attention to the considerable variations in the strength and character of civil society and political mobilization between Malaysia, Indonesia, Thailand and the Philippines in relation to differences in colonial legacies, class structures, ethnic composition and political and religious institutions (2001: 921–951). Moreover, Robison argues that members of the middle class are frequently not 'conscious and cohesive agents of social and political change' (1998: 63). Hsiao's research tends to confirm these findings. 'On political activity, the middle classes of the four Southeast Asian countries had an extremely high rate of participation in voting, but their participation in other political activities was rather low, and furthermore did not display any clear differences to other classes' (Hsiao and Wang, 2001: 36). With specific reference to Malaysia, it seems that whilst those members of the new middle class which Abdul Rahman Embong surveyed in the Klang Valley in the mid-1990s supported democracy, they were also oriented to the maintenance of law and order and therefore did 'not necessarily oppose state authoritarianism' (2001b: 372). Furthermore, although some of the Malaysian middle class were active in the development of civil society, they were constrained by their lack of autonomy in relation to the state, specifically with regard to the policies to do with fundamental human rights (ibid.).

In sum, the middle class is not really a class at all in a defined economic or political sense; it is, at the moment at least, a differentiated category whose constituents may not and frequently do not identify with one another on particular issues, though they may broadly share certain orientations and interests. Pinches, with reference to the Philippines, refers to 'middle forces' characterized by ambiguity and 'a political orientation that lies somewhere between the right and the left' (1996: 123); Rivera too notes that middle-class involvement in Philippine politics has ranged from 'conservative to moderate and radical projects' (2001: 209–220). The fluidity of class situations in Southeast Asia continues, and the financial crisis of 1997–98 had an uneven effect on middle class households; some survived and subsequently prospered, whilst others lost their livelihoods and properties. Several of those of the marginal middle class also sunk into the lower class (Koo, 2006: 9–10). This suggests a further differentiation of the middle class, and, although it is a too simplistic division, it gives some weight to contrasting images of the middle class as on the one hand 'well-educated, rational, democratically minded and generally liberal' or on the other 'security-oriented, anxiety-laden, state-dependent and generally conservative' (ibid.: 15).

Class Consciousness

Although I do not wish to dwell on the subject of class consciousness, there are issues which have emerged from debates in peasant studies, particularly surrounding the work of James Scott, which have more general consequence for our understanding of class interests and relations, and which connect with Wertheim's notion of 'counterpoint' (Evans, 1986: 5–6). Scott's 'moral economy of the peasant' thesis served to generate a veritable 'moral economy' industry (1976; King and Wilder 2003: 174–178). However, Evans has probably provided the most careful appreciation of Scott's earlier work and, most importantly, emphasizes Scott's preoccupation with class interests and consciousness and the relationships between material conditions, cognitive structures, and notions of justice, legitimacy, rights, and power within a 'phenomenology of everyday experience' (Evans, 1986: 5, 12–13, 22). Indeed, we cannot begin to understand middle-class identities, for example, without addressing the 'perceptions that structure the order of everyday life'; these are precisely the main concerns of Mulder in his wide-ranging comparative ethnographies of the educated middle class in Thailand, Java and the Philippines (1979: ix, 1983, 1989).

Evans draws attention to Scott's examination of 'hidden ... forms of protest' and 'dissonant sub-cultural themes' in peasant relations with elites (these are Wertheim's 'counterpoints') and with issues of domination and hegemony (1986: 17; Scott, 1985). As we have seen, Wertheim presents a view of society comprising conflicting values, and indicates ways in which discontent and protest are channelled and institutionalized (1974). Scott also examines relations between 'ruling elites' or an upper class, and, in his case, peasants, and how the class structure is kept in being. Although there are clearly direct class encounters and interactions between 'winners' and 'losers', Scott identifies vitally important factors in sustaining class differences. These include the distance (geographical, cultural, and economic) or 'indirectness' which those of the lower classes can maintain in relation to the 'superior class' (Evans, 1986: 18–21, 25–26). There are also 'class devices', 'negotiations' and 'dissembling in power laden social situations' used by both dominant and subordinate groups which serve to present a public sense of consensus and conformity (ibid.: 26–28). Representatives of different classes therefore need to be questioned 'offstage' to reveal what they really think and to uncover the 'hidden transcript' (ibid.: 27; Mulder, 1979, 1983, 1989). In understanding class relationships, and for that matter strategic group formation, the lesson from this debate is that, aside from the exercise of raw power and the existence of opposing group interests, there is often class compromise. The Marxian concepts of 'class consciousness' and 'false consciousness' simply do not reveal the complexities of ideological thought in class-structured situations (Evans, 1986: 28). So 'dominant ideologies are [also] products of class compromises, not unmediated impositions by the powerful' (ibid.: 27).

Classes, the State and the International Economy

Evers's references to upper-class alliances comprised of different strategic groups and Scott's and Evans's concerns with class interests lead us neatly to a consideration of an important body of work dating from the 1980s by Australian-based political economists (Higgott and Robison, 1985b; Robison et al., 1987a). Evers does not address the issue of the relationships between social class and the state in any specific way, though he draws attention to some of the important interconnections between class and political action. It was the work of the political economists which explored these interconnections more systematically, with early studies beginning to surface in two radical journals from the early 1970s: the American-based *Bulletin of Concerned Asian Scholars* launched by the supporting Committee in 1968 (after 32 years to become *Critical Asian Studies* in 2001) and the mainly European-based *Journal of Contemporary Asia*, founded in 1971. These journals combined political activism and scholarship, adopting a critical perspective on such issues as American policy in the developing world. The Committee of Concerned Asian Scholars, in particular, had emerged in the context of American involvement in Indochina and US policy in Asia in the Cold War era. In the early years there was still a considerable commitment to Marxist-inspired perspectives and to Frankian underdevelopment theory and its subsequent modifications, but one can also detect a direct influence from this early radical scholarship on later political economy.

Robison, Higgott and their colleagues have adopted a political economy perspective to analyse the interrelationships between economic and political change in post-war Southeast Asia (and, on occasion, the wider Asian region), and particularly the changes occasioned by rapid industrialization, international specialization in production, and the role of the state in this process (Higgott and Robison, 1985a: 3–5). They also expressed dissatisfaction with both the modernization model of development and the underdevelopment/dependency approach in coming to terms with the complexities of a region 'where the penetration of industrial capitalism is having the most decisive impact upon pre-capitalist modes of production and socio-political relationships' (ibid.: 6). Theirs is 'the productionist critique' of dependency theory and the 'social conflict' variant of the political economy perspective (Robison, 1985: 295; Rodan et al., 2001b: 7–9).

Higgott and Robison refer with approval to an important early contribution to our understanding of the relationships between the state and domestic classes in the context of international capitalism in Southeast Asia; this is Rex Mortimer's edited book *Showcase State. The Illusion of Indonesia's 'Accelerated Modernisation'* (1973) (Higgott and Robison, 1985c: 36). Mortimer adopted the underdevelopment/dependency paradigm in his criticism of modernization theory and demonstrated the ways in which 'domestic ruling groups' were in alliance with and dependent on trans-national capital. He argued that rather than these groups being dynamic modernizers (as they were portrayed by those who focused on the importance of political order and strong government to achieve modernization), they had created a corrupt and inefficient politico-economic system. Mortimer draws attention to the alliance between military leaders and Chinese big business, and the role of foreign capital in the formation of this alliance, in New Order Indonesia. As we have seen, Evers too has referred to the alliance between indigenous political leaders and Chinese businessmen in the process of class formation more generally in Southeast Asia.

However, the dependency paradigm does not provide a sufficiently detailed examination of domestic classes and struggles and, as Higgott and Robison et al. indicate, it tends to emphasize the dependent or comprador character of the 'political or ruling classes', their role as 'agents of foreign domination' and the function of the state as 'a mediator between local and international capital' (1985c: 37, 47). Yet from the 1970s it had become 'clear that industrialisation of various sorts and to varying degrees was taking place, that indigenous bourgeoisies were emerging and were both integrating with [and] confronting foreign capital' (ibid.). McVey too emphasizes the role of the state and the changing attitudes of local political leaders and bureaucrats to business and industry (1992b: 27–35). Therefore, one important observation which was made by these political economists was that politically dominant groups were not straightforwardly dependent on foreign capital but actively engaged with it, and they had room for manoeuvre, though some had more flexibility for independent action than others (ibid.). As Webster has said of the newly- industrializing countries of East and Southeast Asia in the 1980s, they 'have demonstrated a remarkable capacity for sustained real growth via a strongly directive central government that has marshalled indigenous labour and capital very effectively' (1990: 88). The response by some dependency theorists to the criticisms of their pessimistic prognosis was to accept that there was some development but that this was still 'dependent' or 'semi-peripheral'. But they could not really account for this 'sustained growth' and 'rapid development', particularly under authoritarian government, nor 'the significant gains in material life, health and welfare' (Rodan et al., 2001b: 11). Export-led growth has also generated a significant level of variation among developing countries; some, like Singapore, have industrialized rapidly and moved on to develop capacity in high technology and knowledge-based industries, and others like Indonesia continue to have a substantial agrarian sector and a dependence on primary industries, though with some industrialization, both of the ISI and the EOI variety.

As I have said the changes in social, economic and political structures accompanied the shift to EOI and associated economic deregulation, and the decline in the importance of ISI. Following the international recession of the 1970s and the rise in oil prices, along with the increasing costs of labour in the West, many large companies restructured their manufacturing operations. This, in turn, was accompanied by technological advances which made it possible to distribute the labour-intensive production of components and their assembly in, for example, electronics, across several states or to relocate whole industries like textiles to take advantage of cheap labour (Higgott and Robison, 1985c: 45). European, Japanese and American-based trans-national corporations increasingly organized production on a global basis to secure cost advantages and to compete more effectively. It also marked a shift in development thinking, from the basic-needs approach to a concentration on economic growth through, in the World Bank's terminology, the use of 'comparative advantage' and making the 'structural adjustments' needed to promote production for export (encouraging privatization and productivity, reducing public sector expenditure, controlling inflation and the money supply, and making 'necessary' exchange rate adjustments). In this regard it also marked a resurgence of modernization theory, in modified form, in its claims that economic growth and capitalist development (through EOI) provide an impetus and a climate for democratization and the expansion of civil society and the middle class (Rodan et al., 2001b: 13). 'Export-led growth or growth through trade is clearly the orthodoxy in development thinking in the first half of the 1980s' (ibid.: 39); and Rodan noted that '[o]ne of the most concise and ominous reaffirmations of free trade and EOI came in the 1981 World Bank Development Report, marking an official dispensing of the Basic Needs approach which had coloured the Bank's thinking in the 1970s' (1985: 172). It marked a reaffirmation of neo-classical economics, and, although the role of the state in the process of economic growth was initially denied or at best played down, in influential reports in the 1990s the World Bank recognized the importance of 'the effective regulatory and coordinating capacities of states' in the increasing internationalization of capital (Rodan et al., 2001b: 12).

With the departure of Singapore from the Federation of Malaysia in 1965 and the loss of most of its domestic market, the demographically and territorially small, though strategically placed port-city was the first in Southeast Asia to move decisively from an ISI to an EOI strategy. In the 1980s such countries as Thailand and the Philippines embarked on structural adjustment strategies with the aid of World Bank loans to enhance export activities (Higgott and Robison, 1985c: 41, 42). With reductions in public sector expenditure, an emphasis on production rather than redistribution and targeting the poor, and a shift to export-led growth rather than protection of local industries and their domestic markets, various socio-economic groupings (the rural poor, domestic manufacturers) were increasingly disadvantaged. The need to remain competitive in international markets also required governments to keep wage rates and other costs low, ensure a plentiful supply of cheap, acquiescent, non-unionized, particularly unskilled and semi-skilled female labour, and incentives such as tax holidays and purpose-built infrastructure such as industrial estates to attract footloose trans-national manufacturing. Structural adjustment usually required strong government and an emphasis on political order. Thus, there emerged a relatively 'strong correlation' between EOI strategies and various forms of political-bureaucratic authoritarianism, military rule administered by technocrats, and 'corporatism' (ibid.: 42; Rodan, 1985: 188).

Higgott, Robison and others point to the complexity and variability of the class structures which emerged in this rapidly changing context. They also reject the simple notion that the interests of senior bureaucrats, military officers and party officials who control the state apparatus and have access to capital and the means to enhance their own economic position have given rise to a unified and homogeneous 'bureaucratic bourgeoisie' (1985c: 47–48). Rather they argue that the 'dominant classes' of many of the developing countries comprise 'significant entrepreneurial and professional sectors as well as bureaucratic and military ones', and these may use the power of the state not just to serve the interests of international capital, but at times to confront it in their own interests and in the interests of domestic capital (ibid.: 48, 49). The important exercise is to identify the socio-economic groups (classes or class fractions, or, for Evers, strategic groups) which embody and/or are associated with the state, to address their power relations and conflicts, and examine the ways in which they deploy economic and political resources. This in turn depends on a historical understanding of the ways in which socio-economic groupings have emerged and been transformed during the colonial and post-colonial periods (see chapter 4). Rather than a preoccupation with the rationality or efficiency of markets or policy-makers, the political economists focus on 'competitions and conflict over production, profits, wealth, and power'; these conflicts are engaged by classes and class fractions (or strategic groups) and are not only waged on a national but also on a trans-national stage (Rodan et al., 2001b: 7–8).

Let us now examine case material within the political economy framework, keeping in mind that, despite its attractiveness as a means of overcoming problems left unresolved by earlier theories, the conceptualization of class remains problematical in some of this work. Rather than the adoption of a broadly Marxist perspective, certain of the social groupings isolated for analysis by political economists, particularly the middle orders of society, seem to be based on Weber's distinction between class, status and power – and, as I have indicated, some of the class fractions coincide more or less with Evers's notion of 'strategic groups'. In other words, the classes and class fractions in political economy analysis are not necessarily based on the control over or ownership of economic resources and the means of production (or capitalist relations of production), but are defined primarily in terms of the differential access to and distribution of power (the terms political and bureaucratic 'elite' are used), as well as differences in occupation and income, in the scale of wealth and economic operations (market opportunities), and in status and lifestyle (in the concept of the middle class). Nevertheless, although there are problems in political economy analysis and some vagueness in the social classes identified, an approach addressing political and economic processes and the conflicts thus engendered has much to commend it.

Some of the problems generated by the political economy approach have also been addressed by another recent perspective which has concentrated more on the cultural dimensions of change: the relations between global cultural flows and the state in its attempts to construct a national identity, and the sub-national identities of social classes and ethnic groups (Kahn, 1995, 1996, 1998a, 1998, 2006; Wee, 2002a, 2002b, 2002c; Yao, 2001a, 2001b, 2001c). Given the interests of observers like Kahn, Wee and Yao in the cultural meanings of 'nation' and 'class', they tend to focus particularly on middle-class values and lifestyles, as well as on such issues as the relationship between Asian values and state practices. For example, Berger proposes that we need to continue to emphasize the importance of class, 'but in an historically and culturally contingent fashion', and 'to problematize the nation as a key site in the wider process of cultural change' (2002: 86). I shall return to some of these issues in Chapters 6, 8 and 11.

In the following case studies of Indonesia and the Philippines, which continue the historical analysis of Chapter 4, and also Thailand, which (because of its success in resisting European political domination) introduces a new element into our consideration of changing social structures, I adopt a relatively informal narrative approach. I am not endeavouring to define and capture neatly delimited social classes, nor am I attempting to present a formal class analysis according to a determined set of definitional criteria. In this regard I am in sympathy with the political economists who attempt to locate changing social relations in a wider historical, economic and political context. My focus on these case studies and the examination of ethnicity and class in Malaysia in Chapter 6 have also profited from the collection of essays, broadly in a political economy frame, edited by McVey, which considered 'business leadership and its relationship to political power holding' in these four countries up to the 1980s (1992a, 1992b: 15).

Country Case Studies

Indonesia

Of all political economy research on Southeast Asia, Robison's detailed examination of New Order Indonesia since 1965 is probably the best known (see especially, 1978, 1980, 1985, 1986, 1987, 1992, 1993, 1997, 2001). It is claimed, for example, that Robison's now classic study *Indonesia: the Rise of Capital* (1986), was 'the first effort to develop a class analysis of Indonesian politics' (Farid, 2005: 182). He traces the colonial origins of the Indonesian state, and, as we saw in Chapter 4, the significance for post-colonial politics of the absence of a strong 'national bourgeoisie'. Instead this position had been occupied by the Dutch and their compradors who were primarily Chinese merchants, tax farmers, money-lenders, operators of state monopolies, and sugar and rice processors. The Chinese also later moved into manufacturing industries such as textiles, food, beverages and cigarette production and gradually squeezed out small-scale indigenous, Muslim entrepreneurs and traders (the petty bourgeoisie) (1985: 300–303). These latter had been one of Geertz's research interests in the 1950s (1963b). Given their position as immigrant Asians, dependent on the colonial, agrarian-based, export economy, and predominantly small-scale, it proved impossible for the Chinese to transform themselves into a genuine national bourgeoisie. As we have also seen in Chapter 4, no large landowning class emerged in Java, nor a prosperous and powerful class of native entrepreneurs; instead local rulers were turned into salaried bureaucrats (an 'agrarian bureaucracy') serving the colonial state (Robison, 1985: 302).

Progressively it was native politicians, senior state officials, and military leaders who took over the reins of power and presided over an ISI strategy in Sukarno's Indonesia, and also took control of Dutch plantations and trading houses in the late 1950s. Government revenue from oil, mineral and agricultural exports, as well as foreign loans, were used to establish a state-led and protected industrial sector. State corporations (involved in banking and finance, utilities, manufacturing industry, transport and distribution) were established. There were no strong social classes to support the process of capital accumulation so it was left to those who controlled the state apparatus. However, after the failure of Sukarno's populist authoritarianism – expressed in Guided Democracy and Guided Economy and the economic chaos and political conflict which ensued, generated in part by the disastrous land reform programme of the early 1960s, but also by the more general failure to contain the increasingly irreconcilable political conflict between the Indonesian military, the Communist Party, and Muslim activists – it was Suharto's military-dominated government assisted by technocrats, planners and economists who directed Indonesia's shift towards a more outwardly-oriented economic strategy (ibid.: 299).

Direct inward investment and international capital were encouraged to promote economic growth, but a crucial basis for economic growth was oil revenue (Robison, 1987: 16). However, from the 1970s foreign capital rather than being given free rein was regulated and often forced into joint ventures, alliances and production-sharing agreements with local partners, while certain strategic national industries established under the continuing ISI strategy were afforded protection and patronage (automobiles, motorcycles, television and electrical products, glass, tyres, a range of metal engineering products, steel, shipbuilding, cement and petrochemicals) (ibid.: 34–35, 41). Large 'national business groups' emerged which were 'partly owned by generals, ministers and other leading political and state officials whose interest in national capital accumulation has become proprietary rather than simply ideological' (Robison, 1985: 313). But Indonesian economic policy has always served national interests and, wherever feasible, restricted the operation of international capital (Robison, 1987: 17).

Chinese entrepreneurs have had to form alliances with indigenous politico-bureaucrats who have a shared identity and 'a coherent set of values and interests' in order to secure licenses, concessions and contracts in an environment increasingly dominated by international capital (Robison, 1993: 46). The exercise of power and the maintenance of strongly authoritarian, increasingly centralized government is also legitimized in terms of the importance of national political order and security and in terms of economic growth and rising prosperity in a period of transition from tradition to modernity. This configuration of state power and its relationship to economic processes are characterized by Robison as 'the technocratic, authoritarian developmentalist path' to capitalism directed by a 'military bureaucratic state' (Robison, 1985: 325; 1978: 37–39).

Another possible force for social change in post-colonial Indonesia up to the 1960s was the Indonesian Communist Party (PKI), representing the interests of significant sections of wage-labour, the peasantry, and the intelligentsia, which was increasingly attempting to organize opposition along class lines during the Indonesian land reforms. However, it was destroyed by a conservative alliance of small-scale Muslim entrepreneurs, landowners and the military. The military, in particular, was anxious to keep its stake in the economy and access to political power. Religious differences between staunch Muslims and secular Communists also fuelled the conflict (Robison, 1985: 305). The PKI's ability to mobilize class interests was compromised by cross-cutting patronage, family and other ties, particularly in rural areas, and the recruitment of members who were not ideologically committed to a communist cause.

Therefore, between 1949 and 1965 a small group of politicians, military leaders and bureaucrats 'appropriated the state apparatus, fusing political power and bureaucratic authority ... [and] dividing amongst themselves government departments, banks, state corporations controlling trade, economic policy, resources, credit and contracts' (ibid.: 302). It was these groups (strategic groups in Evers's terms) which deployed the power of the state to promote economic growth and capital accumulation. But from 1965 it was increasingly military leaders, as senior members of a well organized national force, who became dominant, using their position to access revenue from oil, gas, minerals, timber and other resources, as well as foreign aid and loans, to transform the economy and at the same time enhance their own private wealth. They were also skilful in managing and weakening any potential opposition from 'students and intellectuals, the [M]uslim petty bourgeoisie and the landlords', not simply by the exercise of the repressive power and sanctions of the state and the force which the military had at its disposal, but by sponsoring and controlling state organizations, including the military's own political organization, Golkar, closely controlling and reorganizing other political parties, and creating 'functional groups in business, labour, and the civil service' rather than allowing competing interest groups (ibid.: 306; Robison, 1993: 43–45). Robison's rather vague, catch-all category of the 'urban middle classes' (managers, technicians, civilian bureaucrats, students and intellectuals), which overlaps with some of his classes or categories mentioned above, was also neutralized by the Suharto regime. Nevertheless, the capacity of the Indonesian state to counter potential opposition has depended very much on oil and gas production and prices.

Robison argues that the Indonesian state constitutes the general interests of an alliance of politico-bureaucrats and a bourgeoisie/landowning class (Robison, 1985: 307–308). However, Indonesian 'corporatism is less concerned with interest representation than with state control and social discipline' (Robison, 1993: 45). Landlords, the middle classes, the bourgeoisie and petty bourgeoisie have supported the military or merely acquiesced, given that those who wield state power have enhanced the economic prosperity of these groups; the position and power of the President, his family and close allies have also been secured by the formation of a host of informal links of patronage (ibid.: 49). For Robison the Indonesian national bourgeoisie and petty bourgeoisie, though referred to in class terms and having economic interests and relationships to property, are constructed on the basis of access to state power, resources and privileges (including monopolies, concessions, contracts, licences and public credit), are divided into 'categories', fractions or strategic groups, partly on the basis of ethnic considerations, and are differentiated according to a graded scale or size which does not serve clearly to distinguish one from another. They comprise medium- and large-scale business groups often formed by alliances between politico-bureaucratic power and indigenous and Chinese capital (many have become international conglomerates with interests in manufacturing, banking, property, construction and primary resource exploitation); a small- to medium-scale native bourgeoisie and petty bourgeoisie divided into Muslim capitalists involved in rural trade, and textile, batik, food and beverage manufacture; and newer enterprises in the service sector and manufacture which owe their existence to links forged with state officials and political organizations; and a small- to medium-sized Chinese bourgeoisie and petty bourgeoisie in trade, agricultural processing, workshop manufacture and services (Robison, 1985: 315–316; 1993: 55–56; Farid, 2005: 182–187). Robison further argues that in Suharto's Indonesia indigenous small-scale entrepreneurs increasingly lost out to the large business groups based on alliances between senior military figures, state officials and Chinese businessmen. It is in this environment that corruption, graft and 'rent-seeking' flourish and anti-Chinese sentiments, particularly among Muslim business groups, grow. Robison argues that state power has been used 'to secure large sources of income from non-budgetary sources to finance … political survival, and to distribute largesse or economic opportunities to political clients and family members' (Robison, 1985: 322).

As we have seen, from the early 1970s, the position of the politico-bureaucrats depended significantly on oil and gas revenue, given that ISI was then experiencing difficulties. It allowed the government to prolong ISI for a further decade, propping up uncompetitive industries using state investment and contracts, protection and subsidy, and continuing to operate through patronage (Robison, 1992: 67–69). When income from oil and gas was no longer sufficient and the ISI strategy no longer sustainable, Indonesia sought foreign loans, aid, and investment capital; the leverage of international investors increased and the state's ability to protect national economic interests came under pressure (Robison, 1987: 50–51; 1992: 73–78).

With the decline in oil-prices in the mid-1980s, Indonesia was forced to relax its policies on foreign investment to encourage a more competitive export-oriented sector, which in turn threatened some domestic interest groups, particularly the business interests of the politico-bureaucrats. These reforms were also associated with aspirations on the parts of some liberal reformists for increasing democratization (Robison, 1993: 56–57).

Yet, in the early 1990s, Robison did not detect much support for more open, liberal government because the bourgeoisie 'continues to rely on the military to control organised labour and impose its dominance in industrial relations', and it was still relatively weak and poorly organized (ibid.: 59, 60). The criticisms of authoritarianism came not from the bourgeoisie but from certain 'elitist' elements (intellectual and professional) of the middle classes (academics, lawyers, political and cultural figures, popular entertainers, Muslim preachers, and economic commentators). But like the bourgeoisie there was no strong, united middle class reformist movement. Rather it was 'depoliticised', 'materialist' and 'conservative', dependent on the largesse and protection of the state (ibid.: 60–61). It also comprised a rather fragile alliance of disparate interest groups from a range of socio-economic backgrounds.

Let me now say a brief word about the post-1997 situation in Indonesia following the economic crisis and the fall of Suharto. The increasing involvement of private business interests in the Indonesian economy connected to the President and his family led to an increasing privatization of loan capital; business groups borrowed for investment from domestic banks as well as foreign financial institutions. 'Risky loans' were made to 'well-connected individuals' and, given the power and leverage of the business families and conglomerates, including the President's own family, there was very little that the Indonesian Central Bank and government advisers and planners could do to control the spiralling debt situation and the inefficiencies generated by private monopolies and rent-seeking behaviour (Robison, 2001: 115). Conflicts also intensified between those in favour and those who had been squeezed out of the economic game, and there was increasing resentment and discontent among the middle class.

The economic crisis of 1997, the collapse of the Indonesian currency, capital flight and the dramatic increase in unemployment triggered widespread public protest and rioting, as well as attacks against Chinese and their business operations, particularly in Jakarta (ibid.: 117–119). Suharto was forced to resign in May 1998, but his successors found it difficult to implement reforms necessary to transform the Indonesian economy, given the entrenched position of the politico-bureaucratic business alliances, the absence of any viable alternatives to rescue the economy, the persistence of economic nationalist sympathies and continuing struggles for political power. The Suharto family lost some of their preferential economic position, the reformist process strengthened under subsequent presidents, and now under Susilo Bambang Yudhoyono, a presidential democracy operates with a significant degree of decision-making and financial discretion devolved from Jakarta (Liddle and Mujani, 2006: 132–193). Indonesian public life has been opened more to parliamentary scrutiny and political party democracy, but, in some cases, the old business and family alliances have persisted or been replaced by new ones, and there are continuing high levels of corruption (ibid.: 136–137). Finally, the Indonesian class structure demonstrates considerable continuity from the Suharto period; indeed, his regime 'left a powerful legacy and the complex social and cultural edifice centred on the patrimonial state' (Berger, 2001: 207). It is still a system run by 'money politics and violence' in which earlier power-holders have reinvented themselves and new 'political gangsters', bosses, businesspeople and semi-private militias at the local level have appeared (Hadiz, 2004: 615).

The Philippines

As we saw in Chapter 4, the Philippines gained its independence as an American neo-colony and continued to rely heavily on American capital and expertise, particularly given the considerable destruction occasioned by the Pacific War (Jayasuriya, 1987: 82). However, although the Philippine upper class, which had emerged originally from the commoditization of land, was a relatively cohesive and conservative body, having defeated, with American military and logistic support, the main forces of radical reform in the late 1940s and early 1950s, there were fractions of this class, as well as increasingly a nationalist intelligentsia emerging from the ranks of the educated middle class, who advocated increasing Philippine economic autonomy through state intervention (Pinches, 1996: 109). Some fractions continued to derive benefits from American financial support, particularly the sugar barons, while others did not. The Philippines, therefore, entered a phase of increasing economic nationalism (Stauffer, 1985: 247–248; Jayasuriya, 1987: 83). Expressions of this were legislation passed in 1954 to restrict Chinese and Chinese mestizo activities in retailing and commerce, light industry and the processing and marketing of rice and corn. The Philippines was also one of the first Asian nations to embark on a protectionist phase of ISI to favour domestic production (Jayasuriya, 1987: 83). The proportion of Philippine production, labour and exports in manufacturing increased through the 1950s and early 1960s, and a fraction of the upper class emerged tied to industry and commerce, but originally, in part at least, deriving from and enjoying close links with the rural landlord class (Pinches, 1996: 108; Hutchinson, 2006: 49). The domination of the landed class was undermined to some extent in the 1950s, and with ISI a 'new class segment emerged, bringing into economic and political power people who had been traders, merchants, and bureaucrats, as well as some diversifying landlords' (Hawes, 1992: 159).

By the 1970s the country possessed 'a substantial industrial base', and by 1980 manufacturing constituted 37 per cent of GDP as against 23 per cent in agriculture (Jayasuriya, 1987: 85; Hutchinson, 2006: 43). Nevertheless, the Americans, in cooperation with domestic partners, gained some of the benefits of tax incentives and protection within the ISI strategy, given their deep involvement in the Philippine economy. By the 1960s the country was experiencing severe balance of payments problems, currency overvaluation, mounting external debt, economic inefficiencies, decline in real wages, unemployment and underemployment, and increasing social inequalities. Economic growth stalled, the IMF and the World Bank forced currency devaluation with consequent rising prices of consumer goods, and social and political discontent, directed primarily at the Americans increased (Pinches, 1996: 105–106). In class terms there was therefore 'the emergence of a domestic industrial class dependent upon state protection, and an expanded urban middle and working class' (Hutchinson, 1993: 195).

With these growing economic problems discontent became increasingly radicalized, and although segments of the upper class played a prominent part in pro-nationalist, anti-American protests, it was worker and peasant unions, and intellectuals, students and professionals (from the middle class) who contributed significantly to the organization of opposition to the conservative political leaders and their American supporters (Jayasuriya, 1987: 91). In addition, in 1968 a newly-formed and refreshed Communist Party of the Philippines emerged with its military wing, the New People's Army, to engage in guerrilla activities against the state (Stauffer, 1985: 249). Yet the Philippine nationalist movement remained divided between those who wanted a socialist transformation of society, and those who embraced a reformist agenda within a broadly capitalist framework. By the end of the 1960s, the original compromise between fractions of the upper class (particularly the rural-based landlords and the urban-based industrialists, mercantilists and financiers) was being rapidly undermined (Jayasuriya, 1987: 89).

Ferdinand Marcos was elected President in November 1965 and, to overcome some of the economic problems, embarked (contra the nationalists) on a different strategy to attract foreign investment and re-orient production for export (Hutchinson, 2001: 47–48). This marked the gradual shift to an EOI strategy, particularly from the 1970s, with the establishment of export processing zones, the provision of favourable terms for foreign enterprises, the encouragement of local entrepreneurial activity through such things as joint ventures, reliance on international aid to develop infrastructure, and continued dependence on American, as well as Japanese investment and expertise (Stauffer, 1985: 248–250, 255–256). The 1970s also began to see the increasing export of Philippine manual labour to other parts of Asia and the Middle East (ibid.). Marcos also increasingly centralized state power and strengthened the armed forces and the police (Hutchinson, 1993: 194). To do this he relied on American funding, advice and training, and surrounded himself with civilian and military technocrats closely in tune with IMF and World Bank thinking. There are some similarities with the Indonesian experience from the late 1960s, with the increasing involvement of the state in economic affairs, centralization of power, and the personalization of economic activity through alliances with political leaders within the 'bureaucratic state' and 'state capitalism' (Robison, 1978: 27). However, although Marcos swept aside liberal democracy 'this did not mean that he had smashed political opposition in the manner of a Suharto' (Jayasuriya, 1987: 92).

To contain and neutralize the increasingly vocal nationalist opposition and student and youth militancy, Marcos declared martial law on 21 September 1972 and rounded up and imprisoned many of the opposition leaders (Stauffer, 1985: 250). One of his main arguments for strong government, and the maintenance of law and order, was the need for the state to direct and promote economic development, and move away from an economy dominated by old landed interests. Marcos was able to draw on support from the military and technocrats, and from 'sections of the Filipino capitalist class, in industry, finance and commerce as well as agriculture, and many layers of the middle class' (Jayasuriya, 1987: 92). Indeed, Marcos [and] his advisers [as well as elements of the political opposition] ... had occupied positions as career politicians, professionals, bureaucrats, military officers and academics or students'. They were 'people located in the intermediate layers of Philippine society assuming immediate responsibility for the political affairs of the nation' (Pinches, 1996: 111). They emerged from new middle class elements, and though some had connections with the landed oligarchy, most had secured their opportunities for advancement in the post-war development of those sectors of the economy and polity which spawned a middle class. Some of the old families suffered under Marcos and had their assets seized and their political power constrained, but 'the majority of the elite and bourgeoisie remained relatively unscathed', and the government continued to uphold and protect private property and constrain organized labour (ibid.; Hutchinson, 2006: 50). Marcos was successful in promoting the wealth and well-being of his family and close retainers, and the concept of 'crony capitalism', with its monopolistic and rent-seeking character, was born in Southeast Asia; it replaced notions of 'the traditional oligarchy' and the weak state (De Jesus, 2002: 57–61). The cronies 'were largely "newcomers" to business who derived their wealth and power from personal links with the Palace' (Hutchinson, 1993: 196; 2001: 55, 58; 49–50). However, they 'represented less the tide of change than the president's desire to patronize men whose lesser wealth and position would ensure their loyalty' (Hawes, 1992: 159).

Nevertheless, the Philippines in the 1970s 'presented such a picture of economic crisis and political decay as to trigger fears among foreign investors and their governments of impending political instability' (Stauffer, 1985: 242). Under Marcos's increasing authoritarianism, growth rates were relatively low, inflation increased, general wage levels fell and external debt grew dramatically. The regime continued to borrow heavily on the international markets to avoid economic crisis and social confrontation, prop up failing businesses and underpin the attempts at economic modernization. This was in an environment of a deteriorating balance of payments with oil prices rising and revenue from export crops falling, particularly in sugar and coconut. Many of Marcos's cronies, preoccupied with amassing their private fortunes and with little experience of business, were spectacularly unsuccessful. His circle of supporters were granted state financial support, contracts and licences, tax advantages, monopolies and protection, and they had moved into core activities, particularly 'agribusiness, construction, shipping, banking and real estate' (Pinches, 1996: 111). Indeed, many of the international loans 'were dispensed for entirely political ends, and inadequate controls meant that a large proportion simply went offshore as capital flight' (Hutchinson, 2006: 46). Although Marcos presided over the growth of a relatively affluent 'middle class', this was small, and large numbers of the Philippine population, both urban and rural, were in poverty (ibid.). His bold 'New Society' had emasculated the main political institutions of the pre-martial-law period (particularly Congress), cracked down on freedom of expression, and resorted to various forms of detention, harassment and surveillance.

As Stauffer has said from the vantage point of the 1980s, 'The pattern that emerges ... is of a government that is rapidly expanding its role in the major sectors of the economy in ways to expand and diversify greatly the capitalist economy while simultaneously reproducing past patterns of dependency-creating relationships with nations, foreign corporations and international financial institutions' (Stauffer, 1985: 256). It had led, as it did in Indonesia under Suharto, to the rise of what Stauffer refers to as 'the new oligarchs' and, at the same time, the weakening of certain sectors of the old upper class, including the 'old landlord class', as their assets were plundered by the President and his family and close friends (ibid.: 257; Jayasuriya, 1987: 105). On the other hand, there was an expansion of the working class with the development of manufacturing industry, as well as of rural labourers with the modernization of the countryside, and increasing class polarization. Indeed, the persistence of dramatic socio-economic inequalities in the countryside has been one of the major features of the Philippines. Poverty in rural areas increased with the Marcos regime's emphasis on large-scale commercial and technology-based export-oriented agriculture. A large proportion of tenant farmers, labourers, and even small-holders lost out.

Marcos had never been able to destroy completely those who opposed him, and there were increasingly marginalized fractions of the upper class who continued to counter his policies, as well as a groundswell of mass protest among the working and peasant classes, and among elements of the middle class, including Catholic priests, intellectuals, professionals and opposition politicians. As Jayasuriya says, 'major sections of the capitalist class, which had been badly hurt by crony capitalism, came out into the open to denounce the regime's support for such cronyism' (1987: 109). But importantly, the opposition from the radical left and the Communists, although contained to some extent, had continued and grown under Marcos (Pinches, 1996: 114–115). Marcos was eventually overthrown, even though martial law officially ended in 1981, and he was succeeded by Corazon Aquino in February 1986 'on a wave of popular support' (Hutchinson, 1993: 193). But at the end of 1985, 'the Philippines had the lowest per capita income of all the ASEAN member nations', and was 'in the grip of the biggest political and economic crisis since the Second World War'; Aquino 'inherited an economy in ruins' (Jayasuriya, 1987: 80, 110). '[I]t plummeted, within a generation, from the most advanced capitalist society in Southeast Asia to the most depressed and indigent' (De Jesus, 2002:

57). This sorry state of affairs was precipitated by the international fall in commodity prices from the early 1980s, a decline in the terms of trade from the mid-1970s and 'a profound crisis in the international financial system centred on the global debt problem', as well as political corruption and fraud on a large scale (ibid.: 81, 82). By the time of Marcos's downfall 'crony capitalism was literally bankrupt' and the relations of patronage 'which had long characterized Philippine society hypertrophied, under Marcos, into a grotesque exaggeration' (Hawes, 1992: 160). Indeed, as Hutchinson says, 'If crisis marks the turning point in the political and economic affairs of a nation, the Philippines had its most significant crisis of recent times in the mid-1980s rather than in the late 1990s' (2001: 42). Furthermore, this crisis 'saw the Philippines mostly miss out on the considerable wave of Japanese investment that entered South-East Asia from the mid 1980s' (ibid.: 49).

The post-Marcos political situation saw the rise of 'a more moderate, liberal leadership', comprising middle class elements, and 'the bourgeoisie has widened and become more variegated', although it continues to embrace some of Marcos's cronies who managed to avoid prosecution and the sequestering of funds (Pinches, 1996: 115, 119). The fragile and loose coalition of forces which had opposed Marcos soon fell apart. The old upper class reasserted itself, though its economic base was increasingly in industry, banking and real estate and not in agriculture; socio-economic reform was postponed and radical labour and peasant movements curtailed (Anderson, 1988: 23–25). But, following a period of extreme instability in the country under President Aquino, as various social forces from the left and the right of the political spectrum contended for prominence, a level of stability was achieved and consolidated under Fidel Ramos's Presidency from 1992, and particularly with national elections in that year following the return to electoral politics under Aquino. This stabilization was due in no small part to the return to prominence of some of those who had enjoyed a privileged position during the pre-Marcos years, including those from 'traditional' political backgrounds, mestizo landed interests, patrician families who had diversified from agriculture into business and commerce, and from some of the business community, particularly ethnic Chinese and Filipino-Chinese who had emerged as small manufacturing and finance capitalists during the 1950s and 1960s under ISI policies, and extended their operations away from retailing and commerce (ibid.: 120). Indeed, Ramos was also supported by a substantial segment of the urban business community, elements of the middle class, particularly professionals and managers, as well as senior military personnel (ibid.: 116). Hutchinson points to the return to prominence of 'the wealthy families that dominated electoral processes in the pre-martial law era' (1993: 193). Economically there was considerable improvement with the emphasis on free-market capitalism, private investment, deregulation and privatization, and the undermining of crony capitalism and monopolistic practices (Hutchinson, 2001: 60–63). Nevertheless, the succession of the populist, pro-poor, political leader, Joseph Estrada, to the Presidency in 1998, and despite his government's further attempts to liberalize the economy, he slipped back into the old-style politics of patronage and cronyism.

Estrada was forced out of office in 2001 following another demonstration of people power 'and the withdrawal of military support' (Hutchinson, 2006: 63).

Therefore, despite some continuity with the class structure of the Spanish–American period and the persistence of landed interests, the Philippine upper class 'has become more variegated, ... its oldest leading families have diversified their economic interests to include capitalist enterprise, and ... there is a growing bourgeoisie which includes among its numbers people who have risen from a background in the professional middle classes as well as in the Filipino-Chinese trading and artisanal community' (Pinches, 1996: 124). Nevertheless, following Ramos's Presidency and the election of Joseph Estrada in 1998, another prominent feature of Philippine socio-economic life reasserted itself, 'cronyism', 'rent-seeking' and the use of the state and its assets for private purposes (Hutchinson, 2001: 63–64). The consequence is that, even after a long period of popular protest as well as the development of a middle class and civil society, 'political society in the Philippines continues to feature shifting, short-term, tactical coalitions and alliances' and corruption remains a pervasive element within the country's political life (Hutchinson, 2006: 66).

Thailand

A very interesting case in the development and transformation of social classes is Thailand, as the only country in the region which, formally at least, retained its independence from colonial rule. Nevertheless, from the mid-nineteenth century onwards, and specifically from the signing of the Bowring Treaty in 1855, Thailand was incorporated into a global capitalist system, mainly accomplished through the agency of British capital. Thailand's dependent economy was based on the supply of primary commodities (rice, teak, rubber and tin) to the world market (Hewison, 1985: 268; Hong, 1984). It was this opening up of Thailand which saw the emergence of a local capitalist class, private property in land, more generalized wage labour and a broadening of commodity production (Hewison, 1989a: 32–33). Thailand, like the Philippines, though for different reasons, also demonstrates the alliance and intermarriage between members of a native upper class and Chinese merchant class. In Thailand, a close relationship developed between the traditional ruling (*sakdina*) class, comprising the monarchy and nobility, which held monopolistic control over areas of trade, particularly in the agricultural sector, and which enjoyed the proceeds of taxation, and Chinese merchants (ibid.; Suehiro, 1992: 40–41). Surplus extraction was achieved traditionally through labour control mechanisms such as slavery, corvées, and military service. With the expansion of commodity production it was these traders and middlemen, who had accumulated their wealth from their control and organization of the rice trade, and tax-farming and administration on behalf of the native ruling class, who in turn began to invest in such activities as sugar-, rice- and timber-milling, banking and finance, 'often jointly financed with royal money' (Hewison, 1989a: 33; 1989b; 1985: 270–271; 1996: 140; Suehiro, 1989). Given the native class's privileged position, when the market in land developed, they began to invest in rural as well as urban land. Another source of capital came from association with European business when local entrepreneurs or compradors, particularly the Chinese, served as distributors of foreign imported goods and as collectors and coordinators of local commodities for export (Suehiro, 1992: 41). As Hewison says, 'It was from this group of Chinese merchant-functionaries and compradors, and from the upper ranks of the sakdina class, brought together in a symbiotic relationship, investing in land, industry, commerce and banking, that the Thai bourgeoisie emerged' (1985: 271). By the 1930s there was also a small industrial sector based mainly on the processing of agricultural and primary commodities and on the production of local consumer goods.

Another significant development was the result of the modernization processes set in train by King Chulalongkorn (r. 1868–1910) and his ministers, and sustained fitfully by his successor, King Vajiravudh (r. 1910–1925). The transformation of the Thai administration from a patrimonial bureaucracy to one which was increasingly formalized and depersonalized led to the creation of an influential grouping of commoner, educated, younger civil servants, including with the modernization of the armed forces, military officers, as well as trained professionals (Steinberg et al., 1971: 313–320). However, the monarch and his immediate retinue continued to exercise personal power at the centre of government. It was perhaps inevitable that there would be increasing calls for the modernization of the monarchy from these new men in the Thai bureaucracy, and in June 1932 a bioodless revolution was instigated by the 'People's Party' which ultimately saw the military come to power. Hewison states that:

> The event is usually portrayed as the replacement of one elite by another in a coup. It was far more than this. The People's Party, although not cohesive or ideologically coherent, established the fundamentals of the new political and economic landscape and discourse. It defined a political opposition (royalists), brought the military to political prominence, and raised economic management, modernisation and progress, constitutionalism, representation, and opposition as important issues. (Hewison, 2006: 103)

Discontent had also been fuelled by the world economic depression. A few years later the incumbent King Prajadhipok abdicated to be succeeded, as a constitutional monarch, by the 'boy-king' Ananda (r. 1935–1946). The power of the military was further consolidated with the installation of Luang Phibun Songkhram, an army colonel, as Prime Minister in 1938. It has been said that '[t]he increasing prominence of the military in the Thai elite stemmed primarily from the unique advantages of military organization, which helped the army to maintain strong hierarchical and personal (patron-client) relationships while inculcating cohesive and modern values' (Steinberg et al., 1971: 319). The linkages between this strategic group of senior bureaucrats dominated by the military, and the emerging bourgeoisie are of special importance in any class analysis of Thailand. It is therefore no surprise that, in attempting to characterize the Thai political system, Riggs coined the now-famous term in Thai studies, 'bureaucratic polity' (1966; see Chapter 3). It was a system dominated by a civilian and military bureaucracy, largely self-serving and unresponsive to the interests and demands of the population at large, which, so he claimed, was in any case rather apolitical and quiescent. It was also a system in which, for Riggs when he was studying Thailand (in the 1950s and 1960s), the bureaucracy dominated business and state enterprises and was predatory on them; patron-client links were established between bureaucrats and Chinese and Sino-Thai entrepreneurs (Hewison, 2001: 72, 80: Ockey, 2004: 143–144; Girling, 1981).

After the end of the absolute monarchy, the country entered a phase of economic nationalism and early attempts at ISI to limit the involvement of the Chinese in certain sectors of the economy, support ethnic Thai and Sino-Thai business, and support domestic industries in agricultural processing, paper and textile manufacture (Hewison, 1985: 271). Local industries were given a boost during the Japanese Occupation with the closure or confiscation of European operations, including banks and import–export agencies. Economic nationalism was continued during the second military government of Luang Phibun Songkhram (1947–48 to 1957); the government began to establish monopolies in certain manufacturing operations in a rather haphazard fashion (ibid.: 275–276). Nevertheless, in spite of the anti-Chinese stance, certain powerful Chinese families managed to profit during this period in alliance with senior politicians and bureaucrats (Hewison, 2006: 84).

After 1945 Thailand was drawn into the American orbit as a key bulwark against the expansion of Communism in mainland Southeast Asia. It became increasingly dependent on American financial support through aid, loans, and investment in military resources. After the Americans, came Japanese investment, particularly from the mid-1980s (Hewison, 2001: 86). But it was during the 1960s, when General Sarit Thanarat came to power following two coups in 1957 and 1958 that Thailand embarked on economic modernization under authoritarian rule, with significant 'Americanization' (Anderson, 1977: 14–15). Sarit's regime began to develop an industrial sector on the basis of ISI with trans-national investment attracted by the country's plentiful supply of cheap, non-unionized labour, generous tax concessions and growing markets in Asia (Hewison, 1985: 269; Suehiro, 1992: 50–57). Sarit announced that his government would deliver political stability 'necessary for the expansion and strengthening of the middle class', and attract private and foreign investment (Hewison, 2006: 84). Indeed, a new middle class, which Anderson referred to as a 'new middle bourgeoisie', was spawned from the 1960s with the influx of American capital (Anderson, 1977: 16). From this time the proportional contribution of agriculture to Gross Domestic Product declined relatively rapidly, though there was considerable class transformation in the countryside with the emergence of rural entrepreneurs and landlordism (Hewison, 1987: 52–53; 2001: 80–81). There was also significant state investment in infrastructural development, a gradual withdrawal of the state from its interference in certain economic activities, and encouragement of private enterprise (Hewison, 1985: 278). An important mechanism in this early industrialization was joint-ventures between foreign business and Thai capitalists, initially to serve the domestic market (ibid., 273). It was also the period which saw the rise of some 15 to 20 economically powerful families, in alliance with the military-led governing elite, who controlled the domestic banking sector and established bank-dominated business and industrial conglomerates (Hewison, 2001: 82; Suehiro, 1992: 42–50; Suthy, 1980). Importantly, there was a movement into manufacturing by powerful families that had accumulated capital in the financial, trading and import-export sectors (Suehiro, 1992: 53–55).

Hewison, in his analysis of class formation in Thailand, refers to the post-war period as the 'second phase' in the development of a capitalist class, which demonstrated some discontinuity with the pre-war period. In this later phase, 'a range of Chinese and Sino-Thai tycoons emerge[d] from the ranks of petty traders and labouring classes' [and] ... [i]n a multitude of Chinatown rags-to-riches stories, these people moved into agriculture, trading, finance and then manufacturing, eclipsing the previous generation of capitalists. Much of their initial wealth came from financing trade' (1996: 141). 'Almost all the owners and controllers of Thai big business are descendants of overseas Chinese ... they have mostly been locally born, hold Thai nationality, and use the Thai language; younger business leaders have been educated entirely in Thai schools' (Suehiro, 1992: 39–40).

EOI began to be emphasized from the promulgation of the national development plan of 1972 at about the same time that other countries in the region were embarking or had embarked on this strategy. This move was supported by elements of the Thai capitalist class whose manufacturing and financial strength had outgrown the domestic market and who needed to seek markets internationally; an important export growth area was in agro-industrial products (Hewison, 1987: 57; Suehiro, 1992: 57–61). However, protectionist policies continued during the 1970s and it was not until the mid-1980s that EOI became the dominant philosophy (Hewison, 2001: 83; 2006: 87). Thai economic growth, and with it the domestic bourgeoisie, continued throughout the 1970s, and especially during the governments of Generals Thanin Kraivixien and Kriangsak Chomanan in the late 1970s. However, the economic crisis of the mid-1980s, brought on particularly by mounting foreign debt, currency appreciation, commodity price falls and public sector deficits resulted in the introduction of structural readjustment programmes with a firm emphasis on export growth, the private sector, deregulation and the opening of the Thai market to foreign capital under General Prem Tinsulanond (Hewison, 1987: 61–76; Pasuk and Baker, 1995: 144–145). EOI was also facilitated by the devaluation of the Thai baht (Hewison, 2006: 87). The shift to manufacturing was dramatic; in 1960 agriculture accounted for 40 per cent of GDP, but by the mid-1990s it had dropped to 11 per cent, and manufacturing had increased to just over 28 percent (ibid.: 88).

It was from the late 1970s that the third phase of the development of the capitalist class can be traced, with the emergence of 'a new generation of capitalists.'

These are 'well educated, often from business families, increasingly identifying themselves as Thai, and are national and international in orientation' (Hewison, 1996: 141). It would appear that these capitalists have connections with the previous generation and many have Chinese and Sino-Thai roots, but they have moved into activities involving land and construction, tourism, stock-market dealing and into higher technology and value-added manufacturing (ibid.: 141–142; 2001: 88–89).

Hewison also notes that this Thai bourgeoisie is divided or diversified into particular segments or 'fractions' comprising those involved in finance who progressively lost their dominance from the 1980s, those in industry, 'with groups representing royal capital', joint-venture capital and comprador capital (Hewison, 1985: 275; 2006: 92). Suehiro, focusing on Thai capitalists up to the 1980s, presents a slightly different categorization. This comprises the commercial bankers/financiers who built up their businesses from the 1950s, industrial/manufacturing groups, which had emerged from the ISI period, and the agribusiness/merchant groups which developed principally during the 1970s on the basis of agricultural exports, industrial activity and wholesaling (1992: 36–37). Suehiro also emphasizes the importance of large companies in Thailand's industrialization, and development of a smaller number of conglomerates (ibid.: 36). Although foreign multinational business was significant in the development of an industrial base, Hewison also points to the considerable power which the Thai bourgeoisie can exercise, given that the government supported local capital, that there were close business and family links between large-scale entrepreneurs, and they enjoyed close links with state functionaries, particularly senior military figures who dominated politics for long periods of time up to the early 1990s. Interestingly, the large domestic companies and business groups are 'mostly dominated either by a single family or a group of families' which, in turn, illustrates the importance of understanding and analysing personal relationships and patronage in Thai society and more widely (ibid.: 39; see Chapter 7). It should also be noted that from time to time there have been political tensions between non-business political leaders, particularly senior military figures and powerful businesspeople; the recent events in Thailand and the bloodless military coup is evidence of this continuing tension.

Writing in the early 1990s, Hewison remarked that '[c]apitalists, who make up only a few per cent of the population, are firmly in control of the Thai economy'. They have an important presence as well as influence in government circles, and they are 'the dominant class in contemporary Thai society' (1993: 167, 177–180; 1996: 140; 1989). Moreover, and as in the Philippines, in efforts to promote industrialization, the Thai Government curtailed the attempts of wage labourers to organize themselves, although when Sarit was overthrown in 1972 they had rather more room for manoeuvre, until the military coup in 1976 brought a return to previous policies (Hewison, 1985: 284). Sarit could also not contain the increasing discontent among the middle class, with economic crisis, growing unemployment, unsatisfied demands for political representation, and anxieties about national security with the withdrawal of the Americans (Anderson, 1977: 17–18). Hewison also states that '[r]epression of the working class has been one of the state's essential political and economic tasks in providing a climate conducive to the accumulation of capital' (1985: 286). With the exception of brief periods of relaxation, organized labour has found it difficult to secure a political voice. Therefore, senior political and bureaucratic leaders have usually formulated economic policy to favour the capitalist class and to reflect its increasing economic and political power. As Hewison has stated, during this period of economic growth and industrialization 'income and wealth distribution became increasingly skewed ... [and] ... workers' lives were characterised by low wages and poor working conditions ... In addition there was widespread exploitation of women and children in sweatshops throughout the country' (2006: 93).

Thailand has also witnessed the rapid growth of a middle class or 'new social forces', particularly since the 1960s (Hewison, 1996: 137). Given their increasing spending power they have an important position in the Thai economy and an increasing political voice among students, intellectuals and professionals (Anderson, 1977; Likhit Dhiravegin, 1985; Sungsidh, 1983). Some of these constituents helped to bring Chatichai Choonhavan to power in 1988. Hewison also notes the importance of political alliances between big business and elements of the middle classes, expressed in the defeat of the short-lived military government of General Suchinda Krapayoon in May 1992, when it was discovered that of those who participated in the violent demonstrations two-thirds had academic degrees and the majority enjoyed middle-class salaries (1993: 171–173, 175–177, 183–184; 1996: 138). Suchinda and elements of the military had overthrown the Chatichai government in 1991 (Hewison, 1996: 139). However, as Hewison and others have argued, the middle class or elements of it will not necessarily support moves to democracy. They tend towards political competence and 'clean' government, which in certain cases, could be authoritarian. Nevertheless, with the demise of the military government a democratic process was reinvigorated with the coming to power of the coalition led by Chuan Leekpai, a Sino-Thai and himself a member of the professional middle class (ibid.: 155).

The crisis of 1997, brought on by reductions in investment and exports, the unsustainable level of the Thai currency, over-capacity in various areas of the economy, and the continued influx of hot money into unproductive sectors and those with over-capacity, resulted in the decimation of the domestic capitalist class, with 'bankruptcies, mergers, and acquisitions' (Hewison, 2001: 92, 93). 'The crisis cut a swathe through the domestic business class, destroying or weakening all of the bank-based conglomerates that had long dominated the domestic capitalist class, and crushed many of the new business groups that had mushroomed during the boom' (Hewison, 2006: 97, 99). It led to the increased penetration of the Thai economy by outsiders both from other Asian countries and beyond (ibid.: 98). Hewison has anticipated a strengthening of that fraction of the capitalist class, or at least those who have survived, who are involved in export-oriented and internationalized activities, and a relationship between capitalists and state functionaries which sees a more limited role for government and 'more attention given to regulatory activities' (2001: 96). However, subsequently the surviving domestic capitalists seized control of the state, parliament and ministries, through Thaksin Shinawatra's Thai Rak Thai Party in order to ensure that the state served their interests (Hewison, 2006: 99). Thaksin was himself 'one of the few local tycoons to come through the crisis relatively unscathed' (ibid.). He had built up his telecommunication and related businesses prior to 1996 on the basis of state concessions and close personal and family relations with the military and the police (ibid.: 104). What we see under Thaksin is the creation of 'a capitalist state controlled by capitalists', though corruption and nepotism resulted in protests on the part of middle class elements, students and representatives of NGOs and organized labour (ibid.: 102). This process of industrialization and the relationships between different power blocs in Thai society also illustrate the importance of analysing the conflicts and tensions between 'various classes and class fractions, nationally and internationally' (ibid.: 103).

Relatively recent analyses of the Thai state and society have focused on 'the consolidation of democratic government' and 'stable governance in a highly developed democracy' (Albritton, 2006: 140–147). Yet the bloodless military coup on 19 September 2006 demonstrates that the military is still a force to be reckoned with; the military leadership has instituted a military-appointed Parliament, indicated that elections will not be held for a further year, and placed restrictions on various freedoms. It is worth referring back to Glassman's assessment of Thaksin's election triumph in 2001, on an ostensible 'economic nationalist' and 'populist' ticket with support from rural areas in particular, and the government's actions to resurrect certain sections of the Thai bourgeoisie, with political connections and, at the same time, discourage any domestic opposition (2004: 37–64). Glassman reminds us of 'the always latent capacity of the Thai state for repression' (ibid.: 59; Pasuk and Baker, 2004). Despite the relative decline of the 'bureaucratic polity' in the face of the emergence of other social forces, including capitalists, a middle class, students and intellectuals, Ockey has argued that military and civilian bureaucrats are still powerful and exercise considerable influence, which, in part, explains the Thaksin government's efforts to reform the bureaucracy during the past few years (2004: 143–156; and see Morell and Chai-anan, 1981). The military, with its strong organizational capacity, esprit de corps, access to state resources, resources from its patronage of criminal elements and its weaponry, can intervene in what is considered to be an unfavourable or unstable political and economic situation, and remove civilian politicians (Ockey, 2004: 150, 156). However, Ockey indicates the complexities of the current class structure in Thailand, and by extension in other parts of industrializing and democratizing Southeast Asia (ibid.; for Vietnam see Taylor, 2004a, 2004b: 1–40). To capture this complexity, Ockey draws a distinction between the (bureaucratic) state, with its constituent administrative, legal and coercive/security groupings; the regime, which embraces elected politicians (these in turn comprise different sub-groupings of financiers, provincial notables, retired government officials and technocrats, and professional politicians), and the polity comprising various other political players, including active elements of the middle class, organized labour and other pressure groups and non-governmental organizations (2004: 150–151). There has been a shift in power and influence to business and the capitalist class, and Thailand has become increasingly pluralist in political terms, but, as McCargo indicates, 'old inequalities and contradictions continue to persist' (2002: 84).

Conclusions

In our examination of the importance of social class analysis in understanding the direction and character of social change in Southeast Asia and its underlying processes, we have seen how different populations reacted to different opportunities and constraints. However, it is usually difficult to capture with any precision the social arrangements of a hierarchical kind which have been produced by these processes. The template of social class can only approximate the complexity and variety of unequal social relations which are constantly in a state of flux and transformation. For this reason we have competing concepts which have been deployed to understand social inequality – class, class fraction, status group or category, power elite, caste, and strategic group among others, and the concept of class itself 'carries a plurality of meanings' (Schmidt et al., 1998b: 2). In reading the work of the political economists like Robison I am left with an impression of the vagueness of such categories as 'bourgeoisie', 'middle class' and so on. There is also the issue of the complex divisions within social classes, which are, in any case, 'in a process of embryonic segmentation' (ibid.: 6). These problems are not easily, and perhaps impossible to resolve.

What is clear is that European intervention in the region and the subsequent internationalization of Southeast Asian economies and polities introduced and developed different kinds of hierarchical social forms (and the conflicts which inequalities generate) based on such institutions as private property. Therefore, owners and non-owners of the means of production emerged: a bourgeoisie and wage labourers were created (ibid.: 3–6). However, colonialism also provided the state and its representatives with the power and opportunities to modify and transform the bases of social forms, or indeed to create or re-create class structures. Politicians and senior bureaucrats, civilian and military, have emerged as important elements of class structures in Southeast Asia; social scientists of other persuasions refer to these as 'elites', and Evers talks about 'strategic groups' in trying to understand these social phenomena. And whatever we do in refining and modifying our concept of social class we shall still be faced with the intractable problem of the middle class (or classes) and how to conceptualize and analyse it (or them) as well as the interaction of class with other kinds of social relations, particularly ethnicity and patronage. A very significant feature of Southeast Asian societies is the presence of other Asian communities and the ways in which they, the Chinese in particular, have accommodated to and interacted with the native populations and the representatives of the state. We have seen that Chinese merchants and compradors have contributed to the development of the domestic bourgeoisie in the Philippines and Thailand, and, they have been partially assimilated by the indigenous upper class. Economically powerful Chinese entrepreneurs have also been key players in the Indonesian economy in alliance with senior military leaders, politicians and bureaucrats. We have also raised the issues of state intervention in the economy and the ways in which it has deployed state resources through patronage, cronyism and corruption both to build and support a domestic ruling class, to redirect wealth to the favoured few and to promote economic growth. It remains now to examine the interrelationships between patronage, ethnicity and class in Chapters 6 and 7.

6

Ethnicity and Society

[Ethnicity] constitutes one of several forms of association through which individuals pursue their interests relating to economic and political advantage. But there is more to ethnicity than this, since it appears to offer intrinsic satisfaction as well as instrumental utility. Individuals seem to need to distinguish between 'us' and 'them' communities, and ethnic consciousness arises when such psychological constructs are attached to observable differences of language, religion, lifestyle or physiognomy (Brown, 1994: xii).

At least in modern social scientific jargon the term ethnic refers to two separable phenomena: the existence of more or less objective markers of human difference on the one hand, and the social recognition of these markers on the other (Kahn, 1992: 159).

For better or worse, ethnicity is a widespread – though far from universal – social fact, and it seems to be closely bound up with the institution of the nation state and with the very process of nation building (Benjamin, 1975: 32).

Introduction

I have made frequent reference to the importance of ethnicity in the understanding of social change in Southeast Asia, not least because the region is ethnically diverse and complex, and comprises what have been referred to as 'plural societies'. Southeast Asia has also been a focus of debate about how we can best comprehend ethnicity and ethnic relations. Therefore, I disagree with Gladney's statement that '[t]he general theoretical discussion of ethnicity and cultural identity has largely been absent from Asian nation studies, and from much of Asian studies in general' (1998a: 3). Osborne has tended to address Southeast Asian ethnic diversity in terms of 'minorities' and 'outsiders' – indigenous and immigrant Asian, but even the majority ethnic groups are internally diverse (2004: 61–69). One only has to dissect the category 'Malay' to realize that, what on the surface appears to be a culturally homogeneous unit is, in effect, a composite of differ-

129

ent groupings which have been subject to processes of homogenization, rationalization and construction through time (Kahn, 2006).

Ethnicity and Class

We saw in Chapters 4 and 5 that political economy and neo-Marxist interpretations of society have tended to give prominence, not unexpectedly, to class analysis and to see ethnic tensions and conflict as surface or ideological expressions of more deep-seated economic processes, or in Brown's words 'a derivative manifestation of class' (1994: 206). Ethnic ideologies may also be depicted as 'false consciousness' in that they are seen to disguise the underlying economic structure (Cham, 1975; Kahn, 1992: 170–174). However, ethnic identity and consciousness, although interrelated with economic processes and at times generated by them, can also directly affect or influence economic and political action. In other words, ethnic considerations may be a primary motivational force in generating certain organizational forms, behaviour and activity. As Brown's quotation above suggests, it provides a mode of identity formation through which people come together to pursue their interests (1994: xii). Of course, I recognize that social class difference can be expressed as ethnic difference and that ethnicity can be used as an idiom in discourses about political and historical relationships (Muhammad Ikmal Said, 1992: 256–257). The close relationship between ethnicity and class with regard to Chinese entrepreneurship and the processes of inclusion and exclusion which operate in both ethnic and class terms to delineate a Chinese bourgeoisie have been recognized in Wee's and Chan's concept of 'ethno-class' (2006: 336–337). Identity formation and struggles in which people engage to establish and defend their identities are also bound up with processes of modernization and globalization (Wee, 2002a: 1–27). More specifically in constructing, reworking and debating culture and identity, Southeast Asians are engaged in 'a creative dialogue with modernity' and with 'the West'; and debates about ethnicity also shade into the more general postmodern and postcolonial preoccupation with identity construction and transformation (Kahn, 1992: 174; 2006). Having acknowledged this, I still maintain that ethnicity can directly cut across class and other divisions, and appeals to shared ethnic identity can be a powerful means to mobilize people to take a particular course of action.

Ethnicity and Culture

There is a conceptual or categorical dimension of ethnicity in which individuals and groups construct cultural classifications to which they assign themselves and others, and an organizational and behavioural dimension in which ethnicity comprises a field of social interaction and communication. Given this distinction, one may well find that certain categories only exist in the ideational realm and do not translate into identifiable groupings, whilst others, under certain circumstances, such as increased competition for resources take on the characteristics of active groups (Nagata, 1979). In addition, ethnicity is closely related to the more amorphous concept of culture because, although one element of identity construction may be physical or biological characteristics (usually referred to by the contentious term 'race'), it is primarily a cultural phenomenon. It relates to the realm of values, beliefs and behaviour; it uses for purposes of identification and differentiation such criteria as religion, language and material culture. It also assumes shared or common origins and a shared humanity (King and Wilder, 2003: 198).

In a substantial amount of earlier work on ethnicity, the preoccupation was with what Geertz termed 'primordialism'. In other words, it was assumed that the basic building blocks of society comprised groups formed on the basis of long-established loyalties stemming from kinship, descent, race and locality (1963c). The focus was on origins, 'basic givens' of identity, and on biological self-perpetuation, which, in turn, tended to depict ethnic groups as unchanging, homogeneous, self-reproducing and defined 'culture-bearing units' (Naroll, 1964, 1968). This essentialist position fails to capture the importance of processes of cultural construction and invention, and the role of the state in constructing and transforming identities (Wee, 2002a: 12–13; Kahn, 1992: 160–163). It must be emphasized that it is in social interaction and cultural encounter that identities are created, maintained and transformed because they are part of a system of categories and groupings, and they cannot be formed nor sustained in isolation (Barth, 1969: 9–10). They are created through a process of 'othering'; identity is a product of comparison and contrast with others who are deemed to be different. This is clearly demonstrated in the case of minorities who usually express their identities in relation to a majority population, though, in the same way, majorities are also 'made' or 'created' (Gladney, 1998a).

Ethnicity and Boundaries

In Southeast Asia one has to address the phenomenon of ethnic complexity and a shifting and fluid pattern of differentiation in which it is problematical to draw discrete boundaries, and in which criteria of similarity and difference seldom coincide, different classificatory systems (in simple terms those constructed by 'outsiders' and those deployed by 'insiders') compete with one another, and people change their ethnic affiliation, or claim that they belong to this or that group according to situation (King and Wilder, 2003: 193–230). Boundary-crossing is frequently initiated through such mechanisms as religious conversion, intermarriage, adoption, assimilation, and economic and ecological transformations. Wertheim, for example, refers to processes of 'creolization' and the formation of 'mestizo' cultures in colonial Southeast Asia, as well as 'a partial imposition of one's own value system upon the members of the dominated groups' (1964a: 68–69). However, as we shall see in our case studies below, colonial administrations with their obsession for categorization and naming, tended to draw sharp boundaries around ethnic groups, identify them more precisely for census, tax and administrative purposes, and render them as homogeneous and static entities. Western perceptions of ethnicity also assumed that pre-colonial groupings could be defined in 'racial' and 'national' terms (Lieberman, 1978: 455–456).

Yet our focus must be on the ways in which people construct, maintain and transform their identities and create and sustain cultural boundaries for purposes of social interaction and avoidance. It is a process of incorporating some and excluding others and selecting certain socio-cultural features which are given priority in constructing identities and boundaries. Ethnic interaction requires the adoption of particular roles based on assumptions about similarity and difference. Identity and boundary formation are also generated and sustained in times of inter-ethnic crisis, seen particularly in recent ethnic conflicts in Myanmar, the southern Philippines, southern Thailand and in numerous places in Indonesia. These conflicts are of two major types, exemplified by recent events in Indonesia:

- Those which occur between ethnic groups; increasingly these take on the character of inter-religious strife, particularly between Christians and Muslims in such places as West Kalimantan, Maluku and Sulawesi, and they often occur when members of one group move into the territory and economic niches of others.

- Conflict between the state and a particular ethnic group which assumes the character of a secessionist movement or one which demands greater autonomy from central government as in Aceh and West Papua; they often occur when the state is strongly centralizing, oppressive and promoting a national ideology which concedes little to local identities (Kusuma and Scott Thompson, 2005a, 2005b: ix–x; Rizal, 2005: 1–41).

The increasing intensity of religious conflict in the region, closely entwined with inter-ethnic tensions, is an especially vexing and tragic one. It is generated and sustained by a range of factors, among others political oppression, economic exploitation, inter-ethnic competition, cultural dissonance, and the messages framed and disseminated by the global media. As Cady and Simon state, 'The emotional resonance of religious narrative, symbols, and rituals, their power to shape individual and collective identity, and their transcendental frames qualitatively transform violent religious conflict. When religion enters the mix ... the violent conflict becomes less susceptible to negotiation' (2007b: 16; 2007a; Schober, 2007: 63). Evidence of this intensification of religious violence can be seen not only in the recent events in Indonesia but also those perpetrated in southern Thailand in the encounter between the Muslim minority and state-sponsored Buddhism, and in the Philippines between the marginalized Muslims of the south and a Roman Catholic majority government (Liow, 2007: 154–173; Ferrer, 2005: 109–150).

Pluralism

As we have seen Southeast Asian social science witnessed an early attempt to address ethnic diversity. Furnivall's concept of the plural society focused on some of the socio-economic, political and cultural consequences of economic immigration during the colonial period (1956 [1948]; 1980). We should also take note of the underlying political position which Furnivall adopted in analysing Burmese society, his involvement in the Fabian movement, his qualified criticism of British colonialism, and his hope for the integrating possibilities of Burmese nationalism (Pham, 2005: 321–348; see Chapter 4). Yet in spite of his championing of Burmese nationalism to solve the problems of pluralism, this was tempered by evidence of Furnivall's paternalism and Orientalism, and his desire that Burmese nationalists would remain closely tied to the British Commonwealth and build a polity on the basis of British ideals and principles (Pham, 2004: 237–268).

Furnivall's concept also gave rise to the related notion of the 'ethnic division of labour' and 'economic castes'. In other words, he claimed to have discovered a coincidence of class and ethnicity because members of different ethnic groupings were seen to occupy different positions in systems of production, exchange and distribution. I have also noted that, though there was indeed an interrelationship between ethnicity and labour (anyone with only a superficial acquaintance with Southeast Asia would immediately recognize, for example, the important position of the ethnic Chinese in economic life and in central urban commercial districts), the situation was and is much more complex than this. In class terms, for example, one could discern broadly in overseas Chinese society, an entrepreneurial upper class (or elite), a 'middle class' of shopkeepers, wholesalers, moneylenders and skilled craftsmen, and a substantial working class in both urban and rural areas (Clammer, 1978: 174). It is misleading to categorize the Chinese in simple terms as a class of intermediaries or 'middlemen' linking the indigenous population with Europeans.

National Identity, Imagined Communities and the State

A further complication, which has emerged significantly in the post-war period with decolonization and nation-building, is a concern with the relationships between pluralism, ethnicity and national identity (or 'national communities') (Anderson, 1991 [1983]). National identity requires the construction or creation or 'imagining' of similarity or homogeneity based, among other things, on shared ethnicity or cultural roots. States invent or create these shared identities and construct the clearly defined boundaries between insiders and outsiders by various means. These usually comprise a national language policy and print media; narratives of a shared history (which may include shared struggles against enemies or outside domination); an educational policy which socializes the younger generations into a particular view of the world; often but not always a shared religion; and finally shared national symbols (which include monumental architecture, flags, rituals including national day or independence day celebrations, anthems, institutions, and the creation of a national 'cult' in capital cities, where various of the symbolic forms are condensed and brought into close relationship one with another) (Evans, 1998; see Chapter 10).

A fascinating case of the creation of a national identity from a multi-ethnic environment is Laos. It is all the more interesting because of the complex shifts in political and ideological positions: from French protectorate status and the emergence of a national identity in opposition to the French, to an independent kingdom with its nationalism based on ethnic Lao culture and differentiation between the majority Lao and minorities, then to a poly-ethnic socialist state which incorporated ethnic minorities on socialist principles and attempted to create 'a social homogeneity which would transcend ethnic identity', and finally to a post-socialist nationalism (Pholsena, 2006: 55; Evans, 1998, 1999). In dismantling the monarchy and Buddhism, but, then recently from the late 1980s, retreating from socialism, Lao political leaders have attempted to create national images of cultural homogeneity and historical continuity, with the accompanying resurgence of Buddhism as an important part of Lao identity (Pholsena, 2006: 10–11). This national identity, in turn, depends on working out the relationships between the majority lowland Lao, who dominate national politics and myth-making, and the surrounding ethnic minorities in the upland areas (ibid.: 13). There is then a mix of socialist principles and the struggle for modernity, but harking back to a reconstructed, and partly invented and shared authentic cultural heritage, which combines the majority culture with those of the minorities, in a unity within diversity framework (ibid.: 46–73). Pholsena proposes that a nation is not merely about myths and images, but it has to make sense to the citizens, providing them with or giving them access to resources; as citizens they have rights and obligations (ibid.: 214–215). With the distancing of socialism, the incorporation of Laos into the global market as a 'backward' country, as well as the state promotion of tradition and the search for an 'eternal Lao-ness', Evans detects 'a deep and growing sense of disorientation in Lao society' (1998: 191). A similar situation of uncertainty can be found in Cambodia as it too has moved from socialism to embrace the market and from authoritarianism to democracy. But there the forging of a nation is even more problematical, given the country's recent violent history and the massive social and economic dislocation which it has suffered during the last 30 years (Hughes, 2003).

The problematical nature of nation-building and the encounter with ethnicity are issues which Brown has addressed in his ambitious comparative studies. He argues, in his examination of the state and ethnicity, that the ways in which ethnic relations and ethnic politics work themselves out depend crucially on 'the capacity of the state' and on the strategies for creating a national consciousness and identity (1994: 258–265; Lian, 1997: 1–6). This helps explain why there is 'endemic violence in Burma, fragile but generally non-violent ethnic relations in Malaysia, and generally harmonious ethnic relations in Singapore' (Brown, 1994: 259). In each case we are dealing with plural societies, which the state seeks to portray as 'potentially culturally homogeneous' and as possessing 'a cultural core around which nationhood can develop'. In Malaysia the core has been built around the attributes of the Malay-Muslim indigenous populations, and those claimed to be indigenous (the *bumiputra*, or 'sons of the soil'), in Burma the focus has been lowland Buddhist

5, the complexities of the class structure and the emergence of class fractions, or strategic groups, also have the effect, in certain circumstances, of undermining or softening class identities. In this connection the growth of the middle class across Southeast Asia has introduced all kinds of ambiguities and uncertainties (and 'fragmentation') into the arena of political and cultural identity (Crouch, 1992; Loh and Kahn, 1992).

It should also be borne in mind that ethnic identity can have a powerful influence on the ways in which social hierarchy is perceived. Nagata proposes that Malaysians express 'social differences in an ethnic idiom', and that emerging classes are really not characterized by class consciousness (1974, 1975a, 1975b, 1979). Rather, and as with Evers's concept of strategic groups, they comprise something less than classes; she identifies, for example, businessmen, professionals, civil servants, and workers. She also suggests that ethnic groups take on the character of status groups 'associated with a particular evaluation of honour and ideal style of life' (1975b: 117). She, therefore, incorporates subjective considerations of status to reveal differences in the ways in which Malays, Chinese and Indians perceive stratification. Malays tend not to accord priority to social class, but instead operate with a complex and finely graded status ranking which includes elements of the traditional system of royalty and aristocracy, the grading of religious authority and prestige, and positions in the bureaucracy and the modern economy (1979: 147–150). In contrast, the Chinese accord particular importance to wealth, urban occupations and English education so that businessmen are given higher priority than professionals, politicians and government officers; but they also considered clan affiliation, dialect and region of origin when differentiating people within their own ethnic group (ibid.: 160). Among the Indians the main principle of categorization is religious affiliation followed by regional and linguistic differences, but in status terms wealth, professional position, qualifications and the English language are important. Nagata concludes that these ethnic differences and the 'subjective pluralism' which they generate continue to cut across class and occupational formations. Inequality, therefore, is not perceived primarily in class terms but instead is personalized and individualized within ethnic and patron–client frames of reference. Malaysians of different ethnic identity would also tend to rank different ethnic groups one above the other rather than separate out particular sub-groupings within ethnic groups according to class (ibid.: 127,133–134).

It is clear, therefore, that class-based action is compromised by communal considerations and certainly economic, political and ethnic factors are very closely interrelated in Malaysia. Class interests have been overridden by ethnic ones so that it is difficult to argue for the primacy of class when it has a weaker claim to people's loyalties than ethnic identity and communalism. Even left-wing or left-leaning political organizations, though usually expressing a non-communal perspective 'end up carving mass support along communal lines' (Muhammad Ikmail Said, 1992: 254). Moreover, the Malay rural population and the Malay elements of the upper and middle classes have mainly supported the UMNO-dominated government, though with important exceptions in, for example, certain of the east coast states of Peninsular Malaysia. They have not formed class alliances with those from other ethnic groups, and this is especially noticeable among the middle and lower classes. However, as Crouch has suggested, communal politics though linked to economic concerns also 'involved fundamental perceptions of identity' (1993: 151). These perceptions and the identifications of similarity and difference are based on certain core precepts: that the Malays are native to the area and therefore have a prior and overriding claim to Malaysia as a territorial and political unit, and pre-eminence in formulating what defines the nation. Chinese and Indians, on the other hand, point to the importance of citizenship, place of birth and equality before the law in defining a nation. There are also very clear cultural differences in religion, customs and behaviour between Malays and non-Malays despite some cross-cultural exchanges and interaction.

In a rather more complex treatment of the relationships between class and ethnicity in Malaysia which moves beyond the view that ethnic ideologies are deployed by the dominant class to serve their interests, those of the state and domestic and international capital, Brown proposes that the state does not simply manipulate ethnicity but serves 'as the arena in which the contending ethnic ideologies must be problematically balanced' (1994: 207). In this perspective, the state (or more specifically state bureaucrats and politicians) is seen not as the tool of a dominant class, but as a sufficiently autonomous actor which mediates between contending classes and class fractions and also 'expresses the contradictory relations between the different fractions within the power bloc' (ibid.: 210). In the run up to independence and thereafter the governing alliance which took over from the departing British was organized into ethnic-based class fractions. Their electoral success and strength was based on their claims to protect and promote the interests and welfare of lower-class constituents within their respective ethnic groups. However, what happened from the late 1950s through to the late 1960s was an increase in the economic disparities between the ruling groups within the alliance and the subordinate classes. In explaining the 1969 Malay-Chinese 'race riots' in Kuala Lumpur in which 196 people died, over 9,100 were arrested and over 750 buildings damaged, Brown points to the 'widespread discontent amongst both the Chinese and the Malay subordinate classes that their bourgeois "patrons" had failed to defend their interests, and had instead furthered their own bourgeois interests' (ibid.: 235). Nevertheless, it was not class conflict and consciousness which were the result, but rather the search for alternative 'communal patrons' and the outbreak of ethnic conflict (ibid.: 234).

However, this partial breakdown in intra-ethnic relationships was not a sufficient reason for the open conflict. Brown also points to the increasing contact between members of different ethnic groups, primarily of the labouring class, as a result of modernization, Malay migration to urban areas and competition for employment and resources, combined with the fact that the Malays and non-Malays 'did not interact with each other on an equal basis, so that their interactions tended to promote mutual distrust and resentment rather than integration' (ibid.: 237). There were also changes in the composition of the Malay state bureaucracy from the 1950s, which, up until then, was dominated by the aristocratic-landowning group, with the recruitment of civil servants from mainly rural and lower- or middle-class backgrounds (ibid.: 239).

This change in the composition of the Malay element of the state bureaucracy occasioned a shift in the approach to inter-ethnic relations and the partial undermining of the compromise that had been reached between the fractions of the Malay and Chinese upper class and their agreement on power sharing. The new recruits to the middle ranks of UMNO and to the Malay bureaucracy argued for more direct state intervention in the economy and greater active support for the Malay community in order 'to foster the entry of poor rural Malays into entrepreneurial activities' and to provide 'state help for aspiring Malay businessmen' (ibid.: 241). They gave a particular edge to the claims for the special position of the Malays, emphasized the importance of developing a specifically Malay dimension to national ideology and drew attention persistently to the dangers for the Malay community of being overwhelmed, left behind and economically marginalized within their own country.

Although this change in emphasis on ethnic identity and inter-ethnic relations had something to do with issues of class and power, it also arose from a very firm commitment to one's own group. From Brennan's preoccupation with the deployment of ethnic ideology by a ruling class we move with Brown towards a much greater concern with the interests and needs of one's own ethnic group. There was still the need to sustain some form of dominant class alliance and to respond to the demands of the lower classes, as well as to ensure overall political stability and the health of domestic and international capital, but there was a shift by UMNO towards an emphasis on ethnicity qua ethnicity, and a more vigorous emphasis on the unifying power of Islam and Malay culture, following the riots of 1969. This change in strategy was given substance with the introduction of the NEP in 1970. It marked the emergence of 'bureaucratic entrepreneurs' or a 'bureaucratic bourgeoisie' or 'bureaucratic capitalist class' (ibid.: 245–248). It also marked the emergence and development of various kinds of informal arrangements and cooperation between Malay state bureaucrats and entrepreneurs and Chinese businessmen (Khoo, 2001: 188). Especially during the later Mahathir period, with the privatization of state assets and monopolies, and the award of large infrastructural projects to favoured political clients, '[a] new category of politically connected Malay, non-Malay, or often interethnic conglomerates arose and evolved into privileged oligopolies' (Khoo, 2006: 184).

Overall Brown proposes a class-based analysis of Malaysian society and politics, but one which recognizes the complexities of the relations between class, ethnicity, power and the state. Rather than a straightforward use of ethnicity by the ruling class, we find a more subtle relationship in the ways in which the state's representatives use ethnicity, characterized by a combination of 'reactive, responsive and manipulative elements' (Brown, 1994: 257). In addition, as competition for power, resources and capital intensified following economic restructuring, relations became increasingly strained between the Malay-dominated bureaucracy (administrators, technocrats and professionals), UMNO, as well as 'old-style' senior and 'young Turk' junior politicians within the party, and emerging Malay capitalists (Khoo, 2001: 188). Furthermore, the post-Mahathir government of Abdullah Badawi has sought to rein in some of the excesses of the previous regime and the politics of corruption and patronage by appealing to the interests and sensitivities of 'rural Malay communities, the [Malay] civil service, and the UMNO grassroots' (Khoo, 2006: 192).

Burma

Burma provides us with an excellent example of the differences in the perceptions of boundaries between the British and the Burmese Konbaung monarchs, particularly during the reign of Bodawpaya (1782–1819) and his grandson Bagyidaw (1819–1837), and the ways in which boundary definition became more explicit as the British progressively incorporated Burmese communities into a colonial administration. From the turn of the nineteenth century the main issues at stake between the British East India Company and the Konbaung dynasty 'involved differing concepts of sovereignty and territorial control' as well as trade and respective socio-political statuses (Owen, 2005: 87). Whilst the British held to the importance of clearly delineated borders within which they exercised political and administrative control and which should not be violated by outside powers, the Burmese 'perceived a zone of overlapping influences' with more vaguely defined, shifting boundaries, frontiers and spheres (ibid.; Osborne, 2004: 73–74). These differences in political viewpoint eventually contributed to open military conflict and Bagyidaw's invasion of British Bengal, progressive territorial annexation following the three Anglo-Burmese wars (1824–26; 1852–53; 1885), the fall of the Burmese capital at Mandalay, the deposition of King Thibaw (1878–1885) and the abolition of the monarchy. The British concept of a state with demarcated borders, within which its government at Rangoon exercised sovereignty, prevailed, and it was this concept which had consequences for inter-ethnic relations and ethnicity, given that, prior to British intervention, identities were also relatively fluid and unbounded. So that over time 'the colonized came to perceive the world in much the same terms as the colonizers did' (Owen, 2005: 202).

I have described in Chapter 4 the major transformations in Burma from the second half of the nineteenth century onwards: the rapid increase in commodity production and the integration of the Burmese economy into the global economy and administratively into British India; the influx of Indian merchants, moneylenders, clerks, civil servants and ordinary labourers into the Burma Delta; the imposition of direct rule in the lowland areas of the country dominated by the Burman population where a new indigenous administrative class was created and where traditional supravillage institutions, other than the Buddhist monkhood (*sangha*), were dismantled, and the separate systems of indirect rule through local elites in the upland minority areas. Even the Burman village system was reorganized. The British then set about demarcating people and territories, surveying 'tribal' areas, describing and categorizing customs and local laws, and presenting diverse, exotic cultures in museums and ethnographic narratives. Ethnic groups were established as primordial within a British discourse about origins and shared histories. It is far too simple to capture this process as a deliberate policy of 'divide and rule'; it had elements of that, but it was part of a more complex and subtle encounter with those who were different, whose values, beliefs and behaviours had to be understood at least insofar as this was necessary for administrative and commercial purposes, and who were dependents of regimes which styled themselves enlightened, 'civilizing' and progressive (Taylor, 1982, 1987). Yet the administrative separation between the majority Buddhist Burmans in 'Burma Proper' and the minority hill peoples in the 'Frontier Areas' (many of whom were converted to Christianity and some who served in the colonial army) only served to sow the seeds of conflict after political independence in 1948. As Smith says, British colonialism 'did immense damage to inter-communal relations; the appearance of preferential treatment for different ethnic groups did, without doubt, bring about a widely varying response to British rule' (1991: 46).

Prior to the setting up of separate administrative structures for both the lowland and upland regions, the relationships between the majority Burmans and the minorities, including the Shan, Kachin, Karen (Kayin), Chin, Karenni (Kayah), Palaung and Wa, were relatively fluid and characterized as 'variations on a theme' rather than fixed, contrasting ethnic categories. To be sure there were armed conflicts and tensions, but these were tempered by relations of patronage, accommodation, alliance, intermarriage, cultural exchange, and multiple identities, and disaffected minorities could still switch their allegiance between other contending powers (Leach, 1954; Lehman, 1963, 1967, 1979; Taylor, 1982). Minorities were also divided by territory, clan and kinship, and did not usually react to outsiders in a unified way. The situation in Burma was further complicated by the presence of significant minorities who inhabited the lowland areas intermixed with the Burmans; these included the Mons, the Arakanese and the Karen.

Nevertheless, what the colonial project demanded was 'the maintenance of clear racial and cultural boundaries between colonizers and colonized, between Westerners and Southeast Asians' (Owen, 2005: 246). These preoccupations in situations in which Europeans, natives and other Asians were brought together, especially in the expanding urban areas of Southeast Asia where they usually resided in defined 'quarters', served to enhance the importance of ethnicity and identity, and during the late colonial period, when indigenous, anti-colonial nationalisms emerged, to cement divisions between broad categories of people and emphasize the importance of boundaries. One such broad rallying point for the lowland Burmans was Buddhism, and early on educated Burmese formed the Young Men's Buddhist Association (YMBA) in 1906 to begin to establish a modern and separate identity from the British, the Indians and others (ibid.: 324; Smith, 1991: 49). Some of the more radical members of the YMBA then formed the General Council of Burmese Associations (GCBA) in 1917 (Brown, 1994: 43). Even the Anti-Fascist People's Freedom League (AFPFL) which fought the Japanese on a nationalist platform to embrace all indigenous people, was dominated by the Burmans (ibid.: 45). Moreover, 'it developed as an essentially Burman ethnic-nationalist movement which articulated the goal of Burmese independence in the name of a defence of Burman ethnic language and culture, and of the Buddhist religion, portraying the independent Burmese state as rightful successor to the Burmese dynasties of the past' (ibid.).

The differences between the Burmans and the Indians were further cemented during the Depression years when a considerable amount of land passed into the hands of Indian moneylenders and, with the decrease in the availability of employment, Burmans and Indians competed for jobs in both urban and rural areas. Anti-Indian riots broke out in Rangoon in May 1930 (Owen, 2005: 327). In addition, increasing economic dislocation triggered a rebellion in lower Burma in December 1930, led by a former monk, Saya San. He had been active in the radical wing of the GCBA in the 1920s. The rebellion was an anti-colonial protest, but also directed against the Indians and Chinese, who were seen as beneficiaries of colonialism. Its major symbolic rallying point was Buddhism and Burman identity, and Saya San harked back to the Burmese monarchy as a focus of Burman loyalty and patriotic sentiment.

It was in the first phase of independence that the first Prime Minister, U Nu, a devout Buddhist, amended the constitution of the Union of Burma to establish Buddhism as the state religion, though there were also safeguards for followers of other religions, at least in constitutional terms (Brown, 1994: 46; Owen, 2005: 334). These safeguards were countered by a significant Buddhist missionary push among the minorities. U Nu was at heart a Burman assimilationist. The constitution of the Union of Burma, which had been drafted in 1947, a year before independence, had also included the option for the Shan and Karenni states to secede from the semi-federal 'union' after a period of ten years. Limited administrative discretion was given to these states, along with that of the Kachin; a 'special division' was also established for the Chin. In crucial meetings to draft the constitution, some of the minorities, including the Karen and the Karenni, along with the Arakanese and Mon were not represented (Smith, 1991: 79). The powers of the minorities were therefore limited, and the difficulties faced by the Karen (Kayin) were compounded because they lived intermingled with the Burmans and there was no possibility to carve out a physically distinct regional enclave for them (ibid.: 82). In addition, the Burman language was introduced into government business circles in 1952 and as the medium of instruction in schools, and Burman history was introduced into the school curriculum.

Brown argues that the emasculation of established socio-political structures in lowland Burma and the displacement of traditional elites provided spaces (or a 'power vacuum') within which a more Burman-, Buddhist-oriented identity could ultimately flourish (1994: 41, 46). He refers to Burma as an 'ethnocratic state', which is one dominated by a majority ethnic community. He also includes Thailand and the Philippines within this category (1988). 'Ethnocracy' is characterized as a situation in which 'the state acts as the agency of the dominant ethnic community' in the promotion of its ethnic values, policies and resource distribution as the core of its nationalist ideology and practice (ibid.: 34, 36). The state takes on a 'distinctly centralizing and assimilationist character' (ibid.: 38; Silverstein, 1980: 239), and is the 'key causal agency of ethnic rebellion' (Brown, 1994: 64). Members of the ethnic majority are favoured in appointments to public office and the political institutions of the state are contrived to ensure that the majority continues to monopolize power. Therefore, ethnocratic states direct themselves to the marginalization of minorities, and it is this which generates a response from the minorities, and the solidification of their identity in relation to a dominant and threatening 'other'. The majority also espouses their modernity, advancement and nationalist credentials in comparison with their backward minorities (ibid.: 48). The leaders of the minority groups search for an accommodation and attempt to secure room for manoeuvre with the central politicians, but when they do not succeed in this, they take more overt forms of action, usually expressed in rebellion. 'Each of the peripheral communities has come to see the expanding state as the dominant influence upon them, and to identify themselves in relation to this dominant other' (ibid.: 51). But the realization of identity is a complex process, and in the case of Burma it was generated not only by the confrontation between majority and minority but also by the action of Western agents in creating distinct ethnic groups.

Therefore, Burma, perhaps most markedly of all in Southeast Asia, became an arena for widespread inter-ethnic tensions, ethnic unrest, and armed rebellion; the political and military situation in the country was also complicated by the civil war waged between the governing elite and their former communist allies, and by the influx of defeated Guomindang troops from China into the Shan Hills. With regard to inter-ethnic conflicts, predictably the Karens, who felt themselves under threat and with no safeguard of a state of their own, were the first to confront the Burman-dominated government. '[W]ithin a year of independence the Karen National Union (KNU) took up arms against the government, commencing an insurgency that lasted into the next century' (Owen, 2005: 332). It should also be noted that the forerunner of the KNU, the Karen National Association (KNA), as a firm expression of Karen identity, was established in 1881, and pre-dated the Burman-based Young Men's Buddhist Association by over two decades (Smith, 1991: 45).

It is therefore not surprising that after independence several of the minority groups engaged in rebellions against the central government and began to develop a pan-ethnic consciousness which overrode local, village-based loyalties. They did so because they felt that their own leaders and communities were likely to be bypassed by the central government, although the Chin appear to be an exception to this (Taylor, 1982: 15). Karen armed resistance, which began in 1949, was followed by rebellions among the Karenni, Mon and Pao, then the Shans in 1952, as they came together to recognize a 'Shanness' which was not really identifiable prior to independence. The Shan leaders (*sawbwas*) attempted to reach an accommodation with the Burman politicians during the 1950s, but failed, and the more radical Shan, allied with some young Shan aristocrats, formed the Shan State Independence Army in 1958 in order to secede from the Union. They had become increasingly unhappy about the intervention of the central state in their affairs and the reduction in their already very limited administrative autonomy, and clashes with the Burmese army began to occur in 1959. Open insurrection was triggered following the military coup of April 1962 and the arrest of senior Shan leaders who were attempting to negotiate genuine autonomy for the Shan state. The Karens, led by an educated Christian elite, also experienced this ethnic awakening, though an emerging sense of identity was already evident by the late nineteenth century (Brown, 1994: 60–61). The Karens were also prominent in the colonial army and the lower levels of the administration. Demands for a separate Karen colony and a status distinct from the Burman-dominated post-colonial state went unrealized, and helps explain the founding of the Karen National Defence Organization (KNDO). During the decade after independence some Karen leaders attempted to reach an accommodation with the central government, some even converted to Buddhism, but it became increasingly clear that compromise would not secure what they wanted. The relations between the Burman state and the minorities had become so dire that, by 1961, the Kachin Independence Organisation (KIO) had also raised arms and was involved in an insurrection (Smith, 1991: 93).

Importantly, although some of the rebellions have been associated with communist sympathies and perhaps suggest an economic dimension to the conflicts, the prime-mover in revolt has been ethnic antipathies and issues of self-determination, with, in the most extreme position, demands for complete secession from the Burmese Union. The military takeover of 1962 under General Ne Win, who assumed full executive, judicial and legislative powers, and the establishment of the Revolutionary Council and its political wing, the Burma Socialist Programme Party (BSPP), was aimed at arresting the political and economic chaos, factionalism and corruption generated by the experiments in multi-party democracy (Smith, 1991: 198–218). The central government became even more Burman-centric and xenophobic; it nationalized all foreign and larger domestic businesses in 1963–64, forcing out of the country some 300,000 Indians and 100,000 Chinese between 1963 and 1967, and, in consequence, lost a considerable entrepreneurial resource (ibid.: 219). A centralized socialist one-party state, based on the national ideology of the 'Burmese Way to Socialism', and the associated command economy were introduced in 1974 (Tin Maung Maung Than, 2004: 187,197, 209; 2005: 76–78). Overall 'the unitary structure of both the BSPP and government put an end to all discussion of rights of autonomy, secession or independent political representation' (Smith, 1991: 200).

The harshness of the regime and its uncompromising stand against ethnic self-determination and human rights meant that unrest continued apace. The government announced in 1981 that it was facing armed opposition from four major and eleven minor opposition groups, including the Karen (Kayin) National Liberation Army (KNLA), which was the armed force of the KNU, the Shan State Independence Army (SSIA), the Pao Nationalist Movement (PNM), the Karenni National Progressive Party (KNPP), the Lahu Nationalist United Party (LNUP), and the Wa National Army (WNA) (Owen, 2005: 500; Smith, 1991: 322–354). The Burma Communist Party (BCP) also served as a rallying point in the 1980s for disaffected members of the minorities including the Shan and Wa, and they were also allied to the Kachin Independence Army (KIA). However, these insurrections had depended substantially on Communist China's support, which was withdrawn in the mid-1980s as China reached a rapprochement with the Burmese government. During much of Ne Win's tenure the armed insurrections increased in scale, intensity and complexity, with fissions and factions occurring within ethnic groups as well (Smith, 1991: 96–9).

However, by the middle of the 1990s most of the ethnic insurgent groups had reached an agreement with the military-dominated State Law and Order Restoration Council (SLORC), which came to power in 1988, to cease hostilities in return for a measure of autonomy within their own areas, with authority given to the leaders of ethnic minorities within their defined territories, the promise of consultation, and the provision of government assistance in development (ibid.: 503; Tin Maung Maung Than, 2004: 207; 2005: 65–108). However, some groups like the KNU continued their struggle, and the fundamental grievances of the minorities have still not been satisfactorily addressed (Smith, 2001: 33). Ethnic-based resistance rumbles on, some cease-fires continue as among the Wa and Kokang, but some have collapsed, and defections within the minority areas and outbreaks of protest and discontent from armed organizations among such groups as the Karen, Shan, Karenni, Mon and Wa continue (Tin Maung Maung Than, 2004: 207; Smith, 2001: 33–39). There have also been recent reports of Burmese military operations, forced relocation and armed resistance from ethnic minorities in Karen and Karenni state and a continuing exodus of refugees. There are still some 140,000 Karen, Karenni and Mon refugees in Thailand and some 600,000 displaced persons in the upland areas (info@burmacampaign.org.uk, September 2006).

In summing up the situation in Burma or Myanmar, Brown states that 'ethnic-nationalist rebellion provided for both a response which offered a symbolic solution, – the assertion of group worth, status and rights – and also, potentially, a practical solution – authority positions for the elites and communal stability for the masses' (1994: 64). What the Burmese case demonstrates above all is that ethnic identity, as a principle of social organization, comprises 'the main structural basis for political alignments and for communal consciousness in independent Burma'. Indeed, it has become 'so institutionalized and ideologized [sic] that it constitutes, in the form of Burman ethnic nationalism, the core component of Burmese state identity' (ibid.:

36). It is also clear that Burmese state-building is so closely interwoven with inter-ethnic war and violence that it has imparted a certain character to the military government – inward-looking, coercive, preoccupied with counter-insurgency and unwilling to meet extra-state demands and interests. As Tin Maung Maung Than says, 'the military junta is determined to push forward the establishment of a highly centralized unitary state structure ... . They expect the ethnic groups to embrace "Union Spirit" – a constant refrain in the government-controlled media and the staple of the leaders' numerous speeches on national unity' (2005: 96).

Singapore

My final case study in this chapter presents interesting contrasts and comparisons with Malaysia and Burma, but like these two countries Singapore demonstrates how the state attempts to manage a national cultural identity (Clammer, 1985). Singapore comprises a primarily ethnic Chinese, urban or city state surrounded by territorially larger and more populous Muslim (Malay) neighbours (though Malaysia and Indonesia have significant resident ethnic Chinese communities as well). Ethnicity and national identity and resilience are therefore ever-present phenomena in the consciousness of Singaporeans and, in particular, in that of the political elite, which has to manage socio-political relations both domestically and regionally. Indeed, national leaders have 'developed a marked predisposition to depict and to organize Singaporean society along primarily ethnic lines' (Brown, 1994: 77; 1993). It has also been concerned to develop what Wee, with reference to the work of Appadurai (1996), calls a 'national culturalism', a state-generated national culture or identity based on the management of and reconfiguration of ethnicity (2002b: 130–133).

Singapore is a nation formed from immigration and commerce, and very much the creation of a Western power from the early nineteenth century, unlike Burma which had an established monarchy surrounded by diverse ethnic minorities, and Malay(si)a which had several established Muslim sultanates, although subject pro-gressively to Asian immigration. However, like the colonial experience in Burma and Malay(si)a, the colonial administration created and presided over an ethnic division of labour and justified it in terms of assumed, innate cultural and genetic characteristics. Singapore was also incorporated briefly into the Federation of Malaysia from 1963 to 1965 in which issues of ethnicity and its politicization, par-ticularly in the relations between Malays and Chinese, played a dominant role, and led ultimately to Singapore's expulsion from the then newly-created hotchpotch of former British territories.

Although Singapore's population of some 4 million, is approximately 78 per cent ethnic Chinese (internally differentiated into mainly Hokkien, Teochiu and Cantonese), it is, like its neighbours, a plural society, with the remainder of the population made up of Muslim Malays (some 14 per cent, comprising Malays proper and immigrants from the Indonesian islands, including Javanese), Indians (7 per cent, mainly Tamils, Malayalees, Bengalis, and Punjabis), and a diverse minority of 'others' comprising, in part, hybrid populations like the Eurasians. What the highly interventionist and centralist government of Singapore, dominated by Lee Kuan Yew's People's Action Party (PAP), has done – as it has in much of the state's social, cultural, economic and political life – is control, restructure and domesticate its pluralism to ensure that it does not become a source of tension, conflict and opposition (Brown, 1994: 66–67). Indeed, up until today '[t]he state remains a pervasive force in all aspects of economic, social, and political life in the city-state' (Rodan, 2006a: 160). This kind of political system has been styled 'corporatist' in that 'an avowedly autonomous state elite', comprised primarily of bureaucrats and technocrats, controls and organizes the various constituents of the state, limits popular participation and channels it through state-controlled institutions, develops an overriding loyalty and commitment to the state, constructs a national cultural identity, and builds through political mechanisms a unified, organic, harmonious society on the basis of a partnership between state and people (ibid.: 68–71; Tremewan, 1996). Whether or not Singapore is fully corporatist rather than straightforwardly authoritarian (Deyo, 1981; Rodan, 1989) has been the subject of intense debate, but the evidence suggests that the government and its supporting administration work through a variety of indirect and direct controls to ensure compliance and obedience. Brown argues that the state became increasingly corporatist from the early 1980s and prior to that was characterized more usually as 'bureaucratic', 'administrative' or 'bureaucratic-authoritarian' (1994: 78).

The state's energies in Singapore have therefore been directed to engineering ethnicity and to demand absolute political loyalty from the constituent ethnic communities; there is no encouragement or tolerance of potentially subversive 'competing sub-national loyalties, including ethnic loyalties' (ibid.: 76). In contrast to Burma where inter-ethnic conflicts have been largely uncontrolled and uncontrollable by the Burman-dominated government, and Malaysia where, after a period of tension and open conflict, they have been brought under some control by the Malay-dominated state, in Singapore the task adopted by the state has been 'to modify ethnic affiliations so that they can become compatible with, and component elements of, the organic national identity' (ibid.). The management of ethnicity in Singapore has been one of simultaneously 'seeking to erode ethnic political loyalties' whilst addressing the national political imperative to 'promote and develop the approved ethnic cultural values' (ibid.). Singapore could not structure its national identity on the basis of 'Chineseness' developing a Chinese state within a predominantly Muslim Malay–Indonesian region. Nor could it assimilate its minorities into Chinese culture, nor, given the sensitivities of a decolonizing region, could it promote Western values and culture as a means of unifying the nation. After the departure from Malaysia Singapore's leaders were also acutely conscious of the weakness and insecurity of their country in relation to their large ethnically different neighbours.

The state therefore initially adopted a national ideology based on ethnic diversity and 'multiracialism', in other words, on the notion of an 'ethnic mosaic', underpinned by mutual tolerance, accommodation and respect. The government decided to establish four official languages: Malay, Mandarin, Tamil and English, with Malay as the national language; political and administrative offices were allocated on the basis of a balanced 'ethnic arithmetic', the educational system was based on bilingualism (English plus an 'ethnic' or 'home' language) and on the existence of 'ethnic streams', and public housing policy was directed to promoting inter-ethnic residential arrangements (ibid.: 78–79, 281; Benjamin, 1975). However, from the 1970s multiracialism was integrated into an ideology of national development and progress which promoted the values of a meritocracy (the 'ethnically neutral state'), 'discipline and rugged self-reliance, pragmatism, egalitarian competition, and the pursuit of excellence'; there was an accompanying shift from calculations based on ethnic arithmetic to ones based on merit (Brown, 1994: 80; Wee, 2002b: 136–137). Ethnicity was increasingly neutralized and de-politicized; it became part of 'high culture' and its potential destabilizing, conflict-generating qualities were warned against and subsequently eliminated from the political scene. 'Singaporeans are still repeatedly reminded that ethnic political loyalties … constitute primordial and irrational bonds which are easy to ignite and which constantly threaten to explode' (Brown, 1994: 91).

Since the early 1980s there has been another shift in national policy in order to address the charge that Singapore was becoming too westernized and that ethnicity, in a meritocratic environment, had been assigned a too marginal position in the development of a national consciousness. Instead the racial groups have been incorporated into an overarching ideology focusing on common 'Asian values' as against 'Western values' (see Chapter 8). Asian values, principally derived from Confucianism, constitute the national consensus and identity in the process of 'Asianizing Singapore'. They comprise an ideological amalgam or composite of 'core values' of discipline, hard work, respect for authority, and community consciousness (including commitment to the family and the wider society) rather than 'hedonistic individualism'. They are also claimed to characterize a pan-Asian culture, and are conveniently encapsulated in Singapore's harmonious, balanced, hard-working, resilient and loyal Asian citizenry (Brown, 1994: 92–96; Wee, 2002b: 139). The principles of Asian-ness also drew on Japanese models of industrial and commercial organization with an emphasis on the state's role in the economy, consensus decision-making, and loyalty to the enterprise. As Wee has said 'Dramatic changes occurred in the … government's cultural management through ethnicity from the 1970s, when the state had an "ethnically neutral" policy undergirded by a rational commitment to cultural modernization, to the international appearance of the "Asian values" discourse and the 1980's re-ethnicization of Singaporeans into hyphenated identities' (2002b: 130; see also Wee, 2001: 248–253).

These shared Asian values provided a 'positive work ethic' which was seen to provide 'a bridge' between traditional Asian culture and a capitalist-oriented modernity, integrating different levels of identity and action, from the family at the lowest level through the four major racial groups to the wider nation (Wee,

2002b: 141; 1999; Chua, 1998: 34–36). They are also part of the more general process of 'othering' the West (Lee, 2001: 95–116). These values are in turn underpinned by the earlier notions of ethnic tolerance, consensus in decision-making and the importance of the family 'as the core unit of society' (Brown, 1994: 94).

The complexities of ethnic identity in Singapore were also progressively simplified, stereotyped and essentialized into a four-'race' model of society in which each major category – Chinese, Malay, Indian, and Other (CMIO) – was seen as culturally distinctive one from another and internally homogeneous, as well as separate from the political process; but ultimately they were mutually compatible (Wee, 2002b: 135). Singaporeans have been 'Asianized' through a long process set in motion during the British colonial period (Chua, 1998: 39–42,45; PuruShotam, 1998a: 51–94). There was firm state control of this process, through such things as 'licensed debates' on ethnic issues within parameters set and legitimized by the government, and individuals were pressed into identifying with one of these races and conforming to the characteristics, which government had designated and decreed, of that particular racial group. Siddique refers to this multiracial model as 'interactionist' rather than 'integrationist' or 'assimilationist' in that each race has been encouraged to retain its distinctiveness within an overarching national framework (1997: 109). In other words certain of the primary values which were seen by the government to characterize and underpin the constituent racial groups were also seen to depict and identify the national culture. Ethnic affiliation, therefore, has been engineered to form 'a cultural building block from which an Asian communitarian form of national identity can be created' (Brown, 1994: 106). However, the distinctions which the government draws between ethnicity as 'cultural anchor', as 'political loyalty' and as 'legitimate interest' are difficult ones to draw, and they have also caused confusion and tensions within Singaporean society (ibid.: 107). The government has been very successful in managing ethnicity in Singapore, but it runs the risk of depriving it of 'its intrinsic power and appeal, so that it becomes eventually a new source of anxiety and confusion rather than a source of security' (ibid.: 111). However, the government has been especially skilful in its development of 'national culturalism' and in the provision of the cultural 'ballast' and moral and spiritual support 'to further support discipline for a labour force that competes within global capitalism' (Wee, 2002b: 150). Wee argues that we cannot separate out the Singapore state's involvement in ethnic management from its need to secure capitalist modernity and 'to mobilize the country towards the economic goal of becoming a first-world society under the conditions of a burgeoning international economy' (ibid.: 132). Rodan too provides a broader contextualization of the political management of social change, when he points to the very limited nature of middle class activism in Singapore and the ways in which the government has not only controlled and co-opted ethnic interests, but also those of business, professional and women's groups (2001: 160).

What distinguishes Singapore has been its flexible approach to the construction of national symbolism which has been adjusted as domestic, regional and global circumstances require. Wee notes a further shift following the 1997 Asian economic crisis and the more general questioning of Asian values and the 'Asian way'. Although 'national culturalism' is still promoted the 'idea of pan-Asian capitalist culture started to weaken by the early 1990s' and a Singaporean 'multiculturalism', a 'common culture' was re-emphasized, but integrated into 'a universal neo-liberalism and the institutions of the global economy' (2002b: 148–149).

Conclusion

I have argued that ethnicity is an important social organizational principle in Southeast Asia, but it is subject to state action and to manipulation, construction and transformation to serve such needs as nation-building. We have seen how different nations within the region have addressed the issue of ethnic identity, some more successfully than others, and, even though it serves ideological purposes, it is a reference point for individuals and a means to mobilize and organize groups. It is difficult, for example, to explain the scale and intensity of conflict within Myanmar without addressing the importance of ethnicity and the willingness of people to struggle and lose their lives in fighting for ethnic self-determination, even though these identities must also be understood, at least in part, as products of external action and influence. With reference to the creation of 'colonial [ethnic] categories' and their subsequent use, Goh, for example, argues that these 'turn out to be a potential cultural framework for re-formed identities' (2002: 186). Wee also notes in relation to Singapore's 'national culturalism', that it is not merely 'pastiche', but is 'a significant site of cultural practice' (2002b: 151).

In comparison with class, 'ethnicity often appears to offer a more all-embracing and emotionally satisfying way of defining an individual's identity' (Brown, 1994: xviii). In addition, it is not merely an expression of class structures and struggle. It is 'in part generated by the political and socio-economic structure of society, but is also in part a "given" which plays a causal role; it is neither fully determined by the cultural structure of society, nor is it a totally elastic response to situational variations' (ibid.). It does, however, have a close relationship with the state, and I shall return to the theme of identity and state management in the concluding chapter. But now I turn to another organizational principle which cuts across class identities and that is patron–client relations.

7

Patronage and Corruption

Everywhere in the world, not only in the so-called underdeveloped countries, dependency relationships are being discovered, vertical lines crosscutting the social class divisions and providing a supplementary principle for an analysis of quite a number of societies ... Sociological theory has, thus far, neglected this more or less universal phenomenon, which is as fundamental as the principle of social stratification (Wertheim, 1993: 75, 78).

In post-war conditions we find various factors which clearly foster the phenomenon of corruption, such as the moral disruption caused by war and revolution, the extension of government intervention in economic life, the low remuneration of officials, and the lure of the way of life of certain groups. Moreover the great publicity given to corruption tends in itself to promote corruption (Wertheim, 1964a: 127).

Introduction

In the previous two chapters, I examined principles which create defined social groupings on the basis of class (status and power) and ethnicity. This chapter considers personal relations of a one-to-one kind (or dyads) (Scott,1972a [1977]). The literature on Southeast Asian societies, and particularly on political activity, has tended to concentrate not on group formation but on personal networks (Landé, 1965, 1968, 1973, 1977a; see also Eisenstadt and Roniger, 1981; Wolf, 1966). Indeed, Higgott and Robison were especially critical of political scientists like Riggs (1964, 1966), Wilson (1962), Jackson and Pye (1978) and Landé (1965) in their preoccupation with 'personal and inter-clique rivalry' and 'a personal client-patron relationship structured by the psychological or cultural attachments of individuals' at the expense of the study of class conflict and the state (1985c: 27–28). However, the study of political and economic structures on the one hand and personal networks of power and influence on the other are not mutually exclusive. We have to address structural relations within which individuals are embedded as well as their personal interests and strategies (Arghiros, 2001:

7; Kerkvliet, 1990; Khan and Jomo, 2000b; Wertheim, 1964a: 103–131; Wolters, 1983). The most common mechanism for pursuing personal rather than collective objectives is to form specific one-to-one relations with others, and exchange resources or favours on a complementary, self-interested basis (Landé, 1973, 1977a: xv; Wolf, 1966: 1–22).

These networks can be generated through kinship or family relationships, or through neighbourhood, friendship or ritual kinship. Indeed, it has been argued that one of the main reasons for corruption in the Philippines has been 'kinship politics' and its conflict with Western values (Roces, 2000: 181–221). However, one of the major forms of personal association is through patronage, and these ties usually cut across other kinds of allegiance such as social class and ethnicity. Riggs, in his study of the 'bureaucratic polity' in Thailand, coins the term 'pariah entrepreneurs' for those like Chinese businessmen who do not enjoy political legitimacy, but rather are outsiders who have to forge patron–client links with Thai bureaucrats across the ethnic divide in order 'to make mutually rewarding deals' (1964: 188–193; Searle, 1999: 7).

In this chapter I shall first consider the main characteristics of patronage, then discuss its relationships to political and bureaucratic corruption, and finally present case-study material from Indonesia, Malaysia, and Thailand (see Khan and Jomo, 2000b). In his discussion of the relations between the military, the state and development in Pacific Asia, Luckham places Indonesia, Malaysia and Thailand together in a category of relatively strong, though not necessarily highly militarized states, in which regimes enjoy some but not complete autonomy from social forces, are 'more prone to corruption', but nevertheless have enjoyed considerable success in securing economic development (1991: 23). On the other hand, the Philippines under Marcos is located, along with Myanmar, in a category of states which are weaker, repressive 'yet not powerful, interfering yet not autonomous' and where surpluses are appropriated not to generate development 'but to support corrupt regimes and parasitic ruling classes' (ibid.; (Hutchinson, 2006: 54).

Definitions and Concepts

Inequality

The main defining criterion of patron–clients relations is their asymmetrical character with regard to differentials in power, status and wealth (Landé, 1977a: xx–xxvii; 1973; Mulder, 1983: 9, 1989: 101–102). There is an inequality between patron and client in their respective access to, control over or possession of valued resources. As Hanks says of Thai society, 'Each Thai regards every other person in the social order as higher or lower than himself' (1975: 198; see also Doner and Ramsay, 2000: 146–147). The patron, who is typically a politician, senior bureaucrat, landowner or entrepreneur, has a greater ability to allocate or grant goods and services than the client, and he uses this discretion to acquire and develop a clientele. This capacity will, in turn, provide the patron with political and economic support, labour services and the means to consolidate and enhance his power. The client receives protection, social or crisis insurance and access to the patron's influence, connections and resources, including land and capital; the patron can, for example, act as an intermediary or 'broker' on behalf of the client, but a 'broker' need not be a patron, and need not control the exchange. The relationship comprises therefore an informal, personalized or particularistic, multifunctional, reciprocal exchange between those of unequal position; it is not usually based on legal norms or contractual written agreements (Hall, 1977: 510–512). The patron–client model is derived from Weber's concept of 'patrimonialism' (1947; Eisenstadt, 1973a, 1973b). In a patrimonial polity, the head of state, leader or patron maintains his position 'by dispensing rewards to members of the elite, which itself is divided into rival cliques that compete for the patronage of the ruler.' The system also comprises a 'pyramid-like network of patron–client relationships and the notion that politics is characterized not by conflict over issues of policy but by competition for material rewards' (Searle, 1999: 6).

Reciprocity and Exploitation

The two persons in the patron–client dyad evaluate each other's behaviour on the basis of their expectations and obligations within the relationship (Landé, 1977a: xiv–xix). The two people involved also maintain their separate identities as social actors, and enter into a personal (not a categorical) relationship with each other. But, in spite of notions of reciprocity and mutual obligation, the patron is the obvious overall beneficiary of this relationship, given the imbalance in power and wealth (ibid.: xx). The inequality in the relationship is, nevertheless, embedded in an ideology of mutual benefit and trust, which distorts the reality. Furthermore, in the process of modernization and in the commoditization of relationships, patron–client relations frequently tend to become more contractual and impersonal, and also more coercive and involuntary (Kerkvliet, 1977; Scott, 1972a, 1972b, 1972c; Arghiros, 2001: 7–9; Kerkvliet, 1990; Wolters, 1983). It is important then to analyse the nature and balance of the exchanges as well as the perceptions of the parties to this relationship because there is no clear dividing line between what might be seen as reciprocal and mutually supportive and that which is seen as exploitative. What is clear, however, is that beyond a certain limit the client will begin to perceive the relationship as exploitative and increasingly unacceptable.

Moral Economy

In his study of the 'moral economy' of the peasant, Scott examines in detail the nature and perceptions of the exchanges between land-holders and their dependents (1976; see also King and Wilder, 2003: 174–178). He argues that the crucial concern for certain sectors of the peasantry in 'precapitalist' society, particularly the 'poor peasant or tenant' (Scott, 1976: 25) is 'the desire for subsistence security' or alternatively 'the fear of dearth' (ibid.: vii, 6). One of the sets of mechanisms to ensure that subsistence needs are met is through social arrangements including reciprocity, forced generosity, sharing and paternalism; the crucial principle is 'the norm of reciprocity' (Gouldner, 1977: 28–43). These relationships, including that between the more wealthy rural patron and the dependent small cultivator, assist in evening out 'the inevitable troughs in a family's resources which might otherwise have thrown them below subsistence' (ibid.: 3). Patron–client bonds 'tempered the rough edges of inequality' and ensured that the patrons were 'disciplined by the prevailing moral consensus' (Boyce, 1993: 84).

However, it was the increasing intervention of the state and the market from the late colonial period onwards which shifted the balance in favour of the rural upper class and strengthened peasant perceptions and experiences of injustice and inequity. The development of new technologies and the displacement of labour also cemented these inequalities (ibid.: 137–155, 192–199). Landlordism, especially of the absentee variety, replaced patronage and paternalism, and was one of the most significant elements in the emergence of peasant protest movements in the region (Kerkvliet, 1977). 'A major cause for the unrest was the dramatic deterioration of traditional ties between local elites and peasants', and the decrease in, or the loss of the protection, sponsorship and financial assistance which those ties afforded (Scott and Kerkvliet, 1977: 439–458).

This changing landscape of vertical relations also alerts us to another issue: we should be wary of lumping together all kinds of unequal relations under the label of patronage. As Arghiros, following Kemp (1982, 1984), suggests, hierarchical relations can be arranged on 'a continuum of personalism', from close kinship exchanges at one end to 'relations of naked power at the other', with patron–client relations occupying the middle ground (2001: 7; Neher and Budsayamat, 1989). Arghiros demonstrates, in his study of local-level electoral politics in Thailand, that, although local politicians and their supporters might be characterized as patrons and they use the ideology of traditional patronage to justify this, the nature of recent political patronage and clientelism in rural central Thailand is very different. It is instead politically instrumental and pragmatic and local politicians 'make use of the idiom of the caring, generous patron with people in whom they wish to instil a sense of loyalty, and place in a relation of dependence' (Arghiros, 2001: 8). Therefore, political clientelism in the context of competition for votes in elections, for example, can usually be characterized as comprising relationships which are 'short-term, impersonal and mediated only by cash transactions'; this situation is rather different from the 'multi-faceted' and 'personalistic' patronage systems characteristic of 'traditional' Southeast Asian social systems (ibid.: 232). Arghiros's analysis echoes the subtle perceptions of Scott in his study of the shifting and complex nature of patronage and class and the ways in which these relations are thought about and expressed in a Malay village in Kedah (1985).

Interestingly in the course of the democratic transition and economic modernization in Cambodia and the position of a weak state having to negotiate with and try to control non-state actors, Hughes points to a similar translation of traditional ties of patronage to more instrumental ones (2003: 18–19, 60–67). She argues that the multiplex relations which bound 'the elite to the labourer in pre-modern times' have been transformed, in this situation of political and economic liberalization and uncertainty, into 'practices of corruption, rent-seeking and vote-buying, on the part of elites, and diffuse processes of negotiation, co-optation, passive resistance and periodic rebellion on the part of the peasantry' (ibid.: 19). This politico-bureaucratic patronage, based on access to the resources and privileges of the state, is, according to Hughes, 'purely extractive' though it uses the idiom of 'traditional' and personal support mechanisms (ibid.: 61–62). The same situation has developed in Laos, with its severe economic problems and poverty, and, which, in very strong terms, St John places at the door of 'a sclerotic political elite, centralised decision making, and corruption' (2006: 189).

Networks, Clusters and Pyramids

What is important about the dyadic tie between patron and client is that it is the basic building block of wider sets of relationship which, in theory at least, are unbounded. In other words, a patron will have linkages with more than one client to form a 'cluster' or 'entourage', and patron–client ties are usually arranged in 'pyramids' so that a client of one person will be the patron of another and the cluster is extended downwards in a tiered fashion (Hanks, 1977: 161–167). The overall pattern of relationships is the 'network' which embraces not only vertical ties but can also comprise horizontal ties between those of the same position and status (Landé, 1977a: xix–xx). Alliances between equivalent patrons with their clients in a competitive political system in which individuals and groups are struggling for power and other resources, therefore comprise 'factions' or 'cliques' which are impermanent groupings or 'quasi-groups', usually within a party structure, formed on the basis of sharing a common identity, purpose or interest (ibid.; Scott, 1972b: 96, 97; Stockwin, 1970; Mayer, 1977: 43–54; Nicholas, 1977: 55–73).

These networks can be relatively extensive and they are also flexible and adaptable. However, they can be fragile and conflict-ridden in that their instrumental, personal and unequal character can lead to rupture if one or both parties come to the view that their expectations are not being met because, for example, the clients feel increasingly exploited by ungenerous patrons, or the patrons perceive clients to be disloyal and insufficiently supportive. In other words, the balance of power may change; this may occur when the patron does not have a monopoly of a particular resource such as land if, for example, the resource is plentiful and labour scarce, and clients can seek out others for support. On the other hand, when resources are scarce, clients compete to secure the support of particular patrons and may be much more reluctant to leave their protection. In these fluid situations the relationship is subject to negotiation. Of course, there are ways of ensuring a greater degree of commitment between patron and client by reinforcing the relationship through social events and rituals and through the mechanism of 'fictive' or 'ritual kinship'. In the Philippines, for example, there is the institution of godparent or ritual co-parenthood (*compadrazgo* or *compadrinazgo*) between the patron and the child or children of clients. Therefore, relationships may exhibit considerable resilience, although they may also be relatively short-lived. Furthermore, when a patron dies it is very difficult for someone else to take over his clientele, given the personal ties involved.

Contexts of Patronage

Scott suggests that these kinds of relationships thrive in the absence of strong corporate groups or classes (1972a, 1972b). Where social classes are fluid and in the process of transformation and powerful individuals are in competition to build their bases of support then mobilizing clients through personal ties is a very effective strategy. Patron–client ties are also usually active in situations in which there are marked inequalities, and where there is a lack of government support or state provision of welfare or of other institutions to promote the security of the poor and the weak. Patronage thrives in authoritarian political contexts, where there are dominant bureaucratic structures and no or very little recourse to democratic processes or strong political parties, or access to the organs of the state on the part of citizens; people, therefore, have to fall back upon their own resources and those of others to survive in an unpredictable and threatening environment (Scott and Kerkvliet, 1977; Scott, 1969: 333–337). Patron–client ties also tend to form in contexts in which business, politics and the state are closely intertwined (McVey, 1992a, 1992b). Therefore, even when processes of decentralization and democratization are taking place in previously authoritarian polities and businessmen move into positions of political power and influence, patronage and clientelism, though different in form, may continue to have salience, and corruption and vote-buying become associated with electioneering (Arghiros, 2001; Hughes, 2003: 70–76, 80–81, 116–117).

Factions and Cliques

Patronage is closely linked to political factionalism and a faction is 'a self-consciously organized body, with a measure of cohesion and discipline' (Rose, 1964; Nathan, 1977). It is usually formed within a political party, but, in certain circumstances may form across party divides (Zariski, 1960: 33). Factions are conflict groups which operate in a politically competitive arena and engage in struggles for the control of political power and other resources. They are usually temporary, impermanent organizations, although sometimes they can transform themselves into a political party rather than remain as a smaller unit, or a sub-unit within a larger one (Boissevain, 1964: 275–287). They are also formed on the basis of personal relations between a political leader or 'boss' and his or her followers, and like patron–client links they can be either 'simple' (a patron with a collection of clients) or tiered and 'complex' (a patron with clients who are patrons of their clients and so on).

Factional politics therefore is characterized by personalized, particularistic relations and factions, usually as temporary coalitions, emerge for mainly instrumental reasons. They may have an ideological rationale, but they tend to focus on the control and distribution of resources, their membership is unstable, their duration uncertain, and individuals can move between factions and ally with former adversaries. In other words, their members have 'a greater concern with power and spoils than with ideology or policy' (Landé, 1977a: xxxii).

Political and Bureaucratic Corruption

Contexts of Corruption and Definition

Given the personal, self-interested character of patron–client relations and factional politics it is likely that they will give rise to 'corruption'. There is a substantial literature on political and bureaucratic corruption in Southeast Asia (Khan and Jomo, 2000a, 2000b; Kidd and Richter, 2003b; Palmier, 1985, 2003, 2006; Scott, 1972c; Wertheim, 1964a: 102–131). However, it is a peculiarly difficult phenomenon to define cross-culturally (Scott, 1969: 317–321). It is also not necessarily a symptom of personal failings, political dysfunction, imminent regime collapse, the persistence of 'traditional' cultural values, nor an obstacle to the process of modernization (Khan and Jomo, 2000a: 3–19; Doner and Ramsay, 2000: 145–147, 151–155; Hutchcroft, 2000: 210–241). As Scott suggests it is 'an informal political system' and one which is often 'an integral part' of the overall political system (1972c: 2–3; Wertheim, 1964a: 103). It is, therefore, very easy to adopt a Western-centred perspective of corruption, and evaluate it in negative terms, presupposing situations in which everyone's values and norms of behaviour are the same or similar. Nevertheless, the term 'corruption' has entered the everyday vocabulary of Southeast Asians, and accusations of corruption have been used rather frequently as justification to oust politicians and administrators and bring regimes to account. Robison, for example, draws attention to the cross-cultural problem we face when he says:

> Although it has been claimed by many liberal Western observers that corruption is culturally acceptable to Indonesians, this is both inaccurate and, to be quite blunt, rather racist. Corruption is not acceptable to Indonesians, apart from those engaged in it, for the very same reasons it is not acceptable to the average Westerner; it penalizes the poor, the politically weak and corrodes confidence and respect. Corruption is not a component of Indonesian culture but is an extra means of exploitation of the weak by the powerful, imposed by force. (1985: 323)

Robison's comments have particular relevance to what has been termed 'crony capitalism' or 'booty capitalism' in the Philippines, a phenomenon which emerged during Marcos's dictatorship, and demonstrated the interrelationships between a centralizing political system, patronage, factionalism and clique politics, and political and bureaucratic corruption on a massive scale (Yoshihara, 1988: 93; Clad,

1989: 29). Marcos built a domestic power base by establishing a patronage system among a select group of military officers, civilian technocrats and politicians, and intervened on behalf of family and friends, pursuing 'the logic of individual self-interest to its ultimate conclusion' (Boyce, 1993: 8; Hutchcroft, 2000). With reference to various historical analyses of Philippine politics and economy, Hutchinson examines the weakness of the state there and its recurring inability 'to steer the course of national economic development because it is constantly subject to the *particularistic* demands of a wealthy elite or oligarchy' and to 'the persistent encroachment of the personal and family-based interests of the oligarchy on government processes' (2001: 44). The Philippine case also refers to the scale of corruption, and it is perhaps appropriate to attempt a distinction, though not always easy to make, between modest gifts or benefits (bribes), and those which 'represent a substantial addition to legitimate income, and may therefore pose a risk to the faithful discharge of the duties of office' (Palmier, 1985: 2; 2003: 81–82).

There are several areas of social life which are usually included under the umbrella of corruption; they comprise transactions judged to involve 'a deviation from certain standards of behavior' (Scott, 1972c: 3). In other words, the behaviour is defined as illegal and goes against certain accepted norms of behaviour for which sanctions and punishment, at least in theory, can be applied. Corrupt behaviour is also usually undertaken covertly and, when discovered, denied or argued as justified in cultural terms. In examining corruption cross-culturally, Scott rejects definitions on the basis of public interest and opinion, and instead uses the earlier definition of Nye, based on legal norms, as referring to 'behavior which deviates from the formal duties of a public role (elective or appointive) because of private-regarding (personal, close family, private clique) wealth or status gains: or violates rules against the exercise of certain types of private-regarding influence' (1967: 416, cited in Scott 1972c: 4). This definition still presents problems in the comparative study of corruption with regard to the interpretation of formal duties and standards, the danger of assigning 'normative value to whatever standards of official conduct happen to prevail', the changing nature of norms and values, and the precise relations between the public and the private sector and the relative size of the two (Scott, 1972c). It should also be noted that while we tend to associate corruption with 'personal enrichment' in public office and 'the use of public office to obtain unauthorised emoluments', this also 'frequently occurs in private employment too, and in several countries the legal definition of the malpractice covers both areas' (Palmier, 1985: 1; 2003: 76; 2006: 147). However, Nye's and Scott's definition provides a reasonably effective means of understanding corruption as a mode of transaction in which influence or persuasion is exercised and, as a result, special consideration given and access to resources and services secured, in a particular politico-bureaucratic system.

Corrupt behaviour includes: first, 'extortion', when someone, who usually occupies a political or official position, uses that position to secure a payment or some other gift from someone who needs a service from them; second, 'bribery' when a payment is made or a gift given to induce someone in an official capacity to give special consideration to the interests of the donor; third, 'nepotism' when the act of gaining or being granted something is by virtue of a special link (shared ethnicity, kinship, friendship, for example) between the giver and the receiver; and, finally, 'embezzlement' or 'fraudulent corruption' when funds or goods to which one has access or responsibility for, but which are not one's own, are used covertly for one's own purposes (Palmier, 2003: 73–76, 81–82). The first three are of special interest to sociologists because they entail a transaction between at least two individuals; embezzlement may also involve a relationship but is frequently undertaken alone.

The emergence of corruption in Southeast Asia has invariably been linked with the establishment and growth of bureaucracies during the late colonial period, a form of administration which Weber styled 'rational authority' within the 'modern bureaucratic state' as against 'patrimonial bureaucracy' (Quah, 1982; Wertheim, 1964a: 106–111). This administrative system emerged in Western Europe primarily from the early nineteenth century, governed by formal rules and sanctions; a hierarchy of offices or positions with a fixed order of procedure recorded in formal minutes, documents and accounts; the importance of qualifications for office and recognized procedures to evaluate the suitability of an individual for promotion; and the specification of official tasks and responsibilities by a strict, exhaustive and comprehensive set of written regulations and codes (Wertheim, 1964a: 114–115). When this kind of system is imposed on one governed by non-bureaucratic, personalized values based on kinship, friendship, shared ethnicity, and patronage, then there is the strong likelihood in legal terms that behaviour that blurs the boundaries of the 'public' and 'private' sector will be designated as corrupt (Huntington, 1968; Palmier, 2003: 78–84; Sculli, 2003: 207–211; Wertheim, 1964a: 131). It is even more likely, as in many developing nations, when the state is the major player within the national economy and the most important supplier of goods, services and employment (Scott, 1969: 320; 1972c: 8–9; Sculli, 2003: 211–214). In other words, it is particularly prevalent when opportunities are presented by 'the direct involvement of public servants in the administration or control of lucrative activities', and Palmier argues that one crucial means to reduce corruption is by 'withdrawing officials from control over commercial activities so far as possible'; in other words, 'corruption is stimulated perhaps less by laxity of sanctions than by opportunities available' (Palmier, 1985: 271, 274; 2003: 76). Furthermore, in the context of modernization new groups or classes acquire wealth, and, if they are blocked from acquiring political power by vested interests, then one way to secure political office is to buy it.

An area which has attracted considerable interest in the Southeast Asian region more recently has been the extensive networks of 'money laundering', not only generated from corrupt practices, but also from criminal activities, drug and human trafficking and illegal arms sales in particular (Kidd and Richter, 2003a: 18; Lilley, 2003: 47–71). The problems are especially acute in the mainland Southeast Asian countries of Myanmar, Thailand, Laos and Cambodia, where corruption flourishes, as well as Indonesia and the Philippines, with Manila recently described as 'Asia's Money Laundering Capital' (Lilley, 2003: 64).

Corruption and the State

In Southeast Asia the state, whether 'soft' or 'hard, has played and continues to play a vital role in the economy. The control which politicians and senior bureaucrats have over access to resources, licences, permits, franchises, and contracts, as well as the regulation of the economy and business, invites behaviour, which in terms of the legal definition, can be considered as corrupt. This is compounded by the personal nature of politics and political alliances, and social arrangements which comprise the informal, 'surreptitious' dimension of the political system (Scott, 1972c: 2). Writing in the early 1970s Scott proposes that '[w]here, as in most new nations, loyalty to the nation-state is still tenuous, the individual feels little compunction to avoid acts that promote his personal or small-group interests at the expense of the state' (ibid.: 12). Nevertheless, his overall view is that the nature of political institutions and leadership are also important factors in determining whether corruption is amplified or reduced (ibid.: 16). It is by no means inevitable that the presence of the conditions of corruption will result in a corrupt regime because 'these conditions can be contained and effectively managed' (ibid.: 19). One important element in combating corruption is, according to many observers, the development of civil society and the increase in public accountability and scrutiny which accompanies it (Palmier, 2003: 88; Quinones, 2003: 44; Westcott, 2003: 255–257)

Country Case Studies

Indonesia

I have already examined the Indonesian case in some detail in Chapters 4 and 5 in relation to social class and the development of the Indonesian economy and polity under colonialism. However, we should not lose sight of the importance of personalized politics and patronage in Indonesia in the context of the increasing intervention of the government in economic affairs from the 1950s. The attempt to transform a 'colonial economy' into a 'national' one demanded the intervention of the state and the issuing of licences and contracts to well connected Indonesians who then indulged in rent-seeking (Palmier, 1985: 199). Then, later in the 1950s corruption increased because there were 'no social groups economically independent of government and with sufficient financial resources to support the political parties necessary for a parliamentary democracy' (ibid.: 201). As we have seen there were no indigenous business or landed classes strong enough to support effective political activity, and therefore, 'only by being in government could the parties lay their hands on the resources necessary for effective political activity' (ibid.; see also Crouch, 1988a: 54–55; Robison and Hadiz, 2006: 117).

Despite his criticisms of the inadequacy of analyses in terms of personal networks, Robison makes frequent reference to their importance in his class- and state-focused examination of social transformations in post-war Indonesia (e.g., see 1996b: 4). He turns a critical eye to the work of earlier observers, specifically Emmerson (1976) and Liddle (1973, 1989, 1991, 1992) who were concerned to understand the ways in which 'political order' and 'integration' were achieved in Suharto's New Order, and their conception of politics as 'structured in terms of personal relationships between clients and patrons' and 'harnessed to the needs of individual officials, political factions, patron–client groups and cultural streams'. Yet Robison also notes that '[t]he power and resources of the state are appropriated by state officials to further their personal and political advantage and that of their family, clique or political power base' (1985: 296). This observation is reinforced by Palmier's perceptive analysis of the roots of Indonesian corruption, in that the organizational principle which underpins the social structure, and more specifically the bureaucracy, is 'a network of patron–client relationships'. Appointment to office was based on ties of kinship, friendship and ethnicity, and '[i]t was hardly surprising ... if the loyalty of officials lay to those by whom they were appointed, promoted, and possibly dismissed, rather than to the state service as a whole ... These particularistic loyalties militated against the application of sanctions against the corrupt' (Palmier, 2003: 206, 207; 2003: 80–84).

Although Robison delineates and analyses class and power structures and the role of the Indonesian state in capitalist development, and class formation and conflict, he does not lose sight of personal networks, though he assigns them less importance than I have done in this chapter. What is clear is that at certain times class structures take on much greater salience and at others personalized patron–client relations assert or re-assert themselves. In his historical examination of Indonesian social structures Robison seems to have the view, though he recognizes that the process is rather more complex than a simple transition, of a primarily personalized system giving way, particularly from the 1960s, to an increasingly bureaucratic, class-structured one, 'politically dominated by the military but administered by technocrats' (Robison, 1985: 299; 1978, 1988).

Prior to the 1960s, Indonesian social classes were relatively 'weak' and there were no powerful, cohesive forces emerging from either urban or rural areas. Indeed, during much of Sukarno's Presidency the political system seems to have been characterized as patrimonial with party, bureaucrats and military officials using their positions to fund factions and increase their own 'personal wealth' (Robison, 1985: 302; Crouch, 1988a: 57). As early as 1951, 'corruption was well entrenched in the Government service' and this was in place even 'before the great expansion of the bureaucracy which proceeded apace over the next fifteen years, and which left the government in no position to pay adequate salaries' (Palmier, 1985: 198). Robison also explains the failure of social revolution during the early 1960s led by the Indonesian Communist Party, by reference to cross-cutting, inter-class relations or 'non-class divisions' in which the PKI was 'caught between alliance with the politico-bureaucrats and the bourgeoisie in the context of client-patron political structures and revolutionary action based upon a mass base of peasant and proletarian support' (Robison, 1985: 305; Wertheim, 1969). Moreover the nature of rural society at that time complicated class-based action because the peasantry comprised 'a complex and confused mass of small landlords, independent peasant owners, tenants and landless, tied together by various feudal and exchange networks' (Robison, 1985: 306). Robison clearly strains at a class analysis here.

Subsequently Robison discerns an emerging class structure during the 1970s and 1980s and focuses on this, but even here he reveals the significance of patron–client linkages between those who possessed capital and were involved in business, including the Chinese, and also indigenous capitalists, and 'politico-bureaucrats' (ibid.: 315–316; 1988: 59–63; Crouch, 1988a: 55). The latter comprised military commanders, senior politicians and leading state officials who had access to the state apparatus and its resources which they then deployed for 'private use' (Robison, 1985: 315–316). Recently Robison, along with Hadiz, reiterates his conclusions on developments in the 1970s up to the early 1980s that 'powerful corporate conglomerates and politico-business families began to emerge under the umbrella of nationalist policies of protection and subsidy, and within monopolistic structures controlled by patrons with their hands on the levers of state power' (Robison and Hadiz, 2006: 119).

As Crouch says of Indonesia in the 1980s, 'Corruption was widespread and many military officers holding civilian appointments routinely provided benefits to private companies with which they themselves, their relatives or their colleagues were associated' (1988a: 59). Of the patron–client alliances none were more important than those between 'generals and big Chinese business groups', exemplified by the Liem Sioe Liong/Suharto group, given that businesspeople of Chinese descent did not have access to political power other than through their links with indigenous politico-bureaucrats (Robison, 1985: 318; Crouch, 1988a: 63). In this regard so rife was patron-based corruption in New Order Indonesia that a substantial part of the proceeds of the 'oil bonanza' of the 1970s was lost, being 'associated with scandals in military-managed enterprises, including the ... state oil corporation, Pertamina' (Luckham, 1991: 25). Furthermore, an important dimension of the emergence of a landowning class in the countryside and small-scale entrepreneurs was their dependence on patronage from the military and its sponsored political party, Golkar (Robison, 1985: 320).

Clearly corruption was widespread in Suharto's Indonesia with the appropriation of the powers and resources of the state by those who occupied public offices for the purposes of capital accumulation, business development and the acquisition of personal wealth. This was expressed most directly in the 'blatant venality' of those who held political office, which undermined any 'attempt to cleanse the administration' and which weakened the 'moral authority' of government (Palmier, 1985: 280). For example, the provision of local level grants for development purposes under the programmes styled 'Presidential Instruction' and 'Presidential Assistance' were 'closely tied to patronage networks' and were 'subject to frequent allegations (both public and private) of corruption and manipulation' (Robison, 1985: 333–334, 320). Overall then it is difficult to explain satisfactorily the ways in which the Indonesian political economy during the first two decades under Suharto was structured and operated without recourse to the relations of patronage and the practices of corruption embedded in the system (Crouch, 1988a: 53). Emerging class structures can be identified but, significantly, military leaders, including above all Suharto, his family and immediate entourage, were distributing 'largesse or economic opportunities to political clients and family members' (Robison, 1985: 322; Robison and Hadiz, 2006: 119). Their powers were very substantial, having access to forestry and oil-drilling concessions, the allocation of distributorships of basic commodities, import and export licences and monopolies, sole agencies and bank credit, and contracts for supply and construction through the development budget. The widespread nature of corruption was also due to the relatively poor remuneration of public officials and the practice, established during Sukarno's time, of using an official position to supplement one's salary unofficially (Palmier, 1985: 271).

The general relationship between state and capital in developed industrialized societies through the operation of fiscal and monetary policies and a legal and administrative framework was replaced in Indonesia by alliances between particular power groups and business conglomerates whose fortunes were 'heavily dependent upon access to political patronage' (Robison, 1985: 323). Therefore, '[p]ayoffs, contributions, equity and directorships for military units, generals and other officials and their families have become simply another operating cost' (ibid.). The politico-bureaucrats therefore became major players in the process of capital accumulation and the development of state capitalism under a system of political authoritarianism.

Robison draws attention to a shift in the direction of the Indonesian economy following the collapse of oil prices in the 1980s. It was marked by increasing integration into international financial markets and economic liberalization, including the removal of various public-sector monopolies and reductions in import and export duties. However, market deregulation and the increasing privatization of the financial system did not result in a liberal market economy. Instead, public monopolies became private ones, and the power of the state was used to support 'powerful coalitions of private and public oligarchies' (2001: 106; Robison and Hadiz, 2006: 120–124). Robison refers to it as 'robber baron capitalism', based on 'predatory officials', 'political' or 'politico-business families' and '"rent-seeking" business interests' (2001: 106, 114–115). Tellingly Robison contrasts the process by which business conglomerates can emerge in a truly competitive open market and that in Indonesia where 'conglomeration' was the result of 'corruption, collusion, and nepotism' and where unsustainable levels of foreign and private domestic debt and inefficient business operations born out of private predatory interests eventually led to economic collapse in 1997 (ibid.: 114–117). The role of the alliance between the Suharto family and their business partners like Bob Hasan and Liem

Sioe Liong is assigned a significant role in Indonesian political economy in the 1980s and 1990s (Robison and Hadiz, 2006: 121; Robison, 1997: 39–41).

Even after the fall of Suharto and with increasing political democratization Robison presents evidence of structural continuity. Although politics came to be 'mediated through parties and parliament...[t]he system of predatory relations among officials, business, and political entrepreneurs continued to pervade Indonesian politics' (2001: 120). Efforts 'to bring to court and successfully prosecute most of the major corrupt figures of the old regime have been almost entirely unsuccessful ....monopolies, concessions, and off-budget funding persist' (Robison and Hadiz, 2006: 111). Palmier's recent observations of the persistence of corruption, the disappearance of international aid funds, and the general inability of the state to raise sufficient revenues to pay and reward its employees suggest that there will be no immediate end nor easy solution to these Indonesian practices (2006: 147–160). The networks of patronage and corruption in New Order Indonesia were so 'vast', and had penetrated to the middle and lower levels of the politico-bureaucratic and economic systems, that, following the undoubted decentralization of state power, 'local political operators and entrepreneurs, enforcers, and petty apparatchiks' managed to insert themselves into positions of power and influence at the local level (ibid.: 112; 133). I note here not so much a focus on class analysis but again on the struggles between political bosses, powerful families, gatekeepers, factions and cliques within a system of money politics and political violence (ibid.: 113; 129).

The issue of 'money politics' brings us to the case of Malaysia, which, though rather less extreme in its predatory characteristics, demonstrates some similarities in the ways in which the state intervenes in the economy, and politicians and bureaucrats develop stakes in business.

Malaysia

In his detailed study of 'the nexus between business, politics and the state' in Malaysia, Searle argues, contra the negative evaluation of Southeast Asian capitalism of such writers as Yoshihara (1988) and Clad (1989) as 'ersatz', corrupt, speculative, imitative, inferior, and fragile, that despite its unorthodox emergence out of political influence, cronyism, rent-seeking and patronage, it appears, at least in Malaysia, to be 'remarkably dynamic, vibrant and resilient' (Searle, 1999: 249; McVey, 1992b). Overall the Malay-dominated civilian government, supported by senior elements of the other major ethnic groups, has enjoyed considerable legitimacy and presided over a favourable economic environment for the development of capitalism during much of the period of independence (Crouch, 1988b). Searle's approach to the understanding of the dynamics of capital accumulation and socio-economic change suggests the kind of interrelationships between networks and class structures which, in my view, require exploration, though he does not provide a thoroughgoing analysis in these terms. What he does demonstrate is that the complexity of Malaysian society and capitalism cannot be captured by such simple categories as 'rentiers', 'crony capitalists', 'pariah entrepreneurs' and 'patrons' on the one hand and 'independent entrepreneurs' or 'real capitalists' on the other. Instead the interaction between politics and business or the state and capital 'has blurred the distinctions' (Searle, 1999: 22), and 'a core of productive investment and entrepreneurial activity is emerging from within the cocoon of state/UMNO-supported patronage networks and rent-seeking activity (ibid.: 17). Searle is acutely aware of the importance of personal networks and patronage for his analysis (see also Gomez, 1990, 1991, 1994; and Gomez and Jomo, 1999). White's work on the interaction between Chinese capital and indigenous Malay patronage, which, he argues began in the early years of independence when political alliances were formed between the Chinese bourgeoisie and Malay political leaders, demonstrates similar concerns (2004: 389–417).

The issue addressed by the Malaysian government from the 1970s was the perceived imbalance between ethnicity and economic function, and specifically between the economically more 'advanced' Chinese and the more 'backward' Malays (see Chapter 6). Its solution was seen to rest on the restructuring of society and economy through state intervention, and the imposition of a daunting range of requirements on business, both foreign and Chinese. State-directed positive discrimination generated the development of 'many powerful Malay business groups, but also the rise of new Chinese business groups', as well as changes in the composition of the Malay political class (Searle, 1999: 12; 58–102). The New Economic Policy strengthened the patrimonial character of the Malay-dominated state, and Malay businessmen relied on state patronage (Lim, 1985; Crouch, 1996; Gomez and Jomo, 1999). They were designated 'statist capitalists' or a 'bureaucratic bourgeoisie', and included politicians, bureaucrats and businessmen who accumulated capital through their access to the state apparatus (Jomo, 1986; Lim, 1985). The state 'gave aspiring Malay entrepreneurs financial assistance, credit facilities, contracts, preferential share allocations, subsidies, and training', and '[t]he result of this social engineering was a full range of Malay entrepreneurs and capitalists' (Khoo, 2001: 184).

The route to economic success and the corporate world was clear, it came through political connections and state patronage, but the extent of the connections between state and capital and its consequences have been a subject of intense debate and the precise nature of the merger between the state, UMNO and private business interests has been discussed at length (Searle, 1999: 15–16; Mehmet, 1988; Gomez, 1990, 1991, 1994). The complexity of these arrangements is also revealed by Jesudason, in his discussion of the Malaysian 'syncretic state' and political opposition up to the mid-1990s. He says:

> There is a rentier segment for accumulating resources for political patronage ..., a protected sector for politically important small and aspiring business men, a quasi-monopolistic segment for well-connected business men and large state companies, and a sizeable com-

petitive arena comprising multinationals, local Chinese companies, and a few Malay companies to ensure national competitiveness. (1996: 135)

He also notes that, although relations with the state are varied with tensions and conflicts between these different economic segments, 'each of these groups is dependent on the state to meet its particular interests' (ibid.).

In his examination of the development of the Malaysian political economy during the 1980s, Searle demonstrates the overwhelming importance of patronage under Prime Minister Mahathir, and the increasing power struggles within UMNO as a result of the increasing availability of state-generated business opportunities (1999: 46–47). Mahathir was also responsible for promoting an ever closer integration of politics and business and the appointment of politically loyal members of the Malay elite to powerful positions within those organizations which presided over the economy (including the Economic Planning Unit, the Central Bank [Bank Negara], and the Ministries of Finance and of Trade and Industry) (Jesudason, 1989: 78). These personal appointments were often drawn from the upper echelons of Malay business. It should not be forgotten that some Chinese enterprises with Malay equity and special relations with politicians and bureaucrats also did relatively well in this environment (Rasiah, 1997: 131). Chinese business groups ranged from those which depended on state support and had close relationships with the Malay political elite (some of these retained their 'pariah' status), and were particularly characteristic of the post-NEP period ('new' Chinese wealth), to those which either succeeded in retaining their independence from Malay patrons (some elements of 'old' Chinese wealth) or in increasing their economic autonomy following a period of dependence on Malay patrons (Searle, 1999: 177–240; Jesudason, 1989).

The shift in the Malaysian political system to one which took on 'an increasingly patrimonialist cast' was accompanied not only by a rapid expansion of business interests in the Malay political elite but also by changes in the Malay class structure with a substantial increase in the middle class, including increasing numbers of businesspeople, and the eclipse of traditional UMNO supporters such as village headmen and schoolteachers (Searle, 1999: 45–46; Jesudason, 1996: 129, 146–155). One of the main ways in which businesses could gain advantage in Malaysia was to employ or forge links with powerful state organs, specifically those regulatory agencies responsible for the management and development of the economy. Therefore, political criteria became much more important for decision-making in business and economic development than technical competence or entrepreneurial experience. This did not mean that corruption and nepotism took hold completely or that these practices necessarily spawned inefficiency and incompetence, but that patronage was an overriding concern for those who wanted access to government decision-makers in order to establish, develop and conduct business. Indeed 'many bureaucrats and state managers who were at the common frontier of the state and business in the government's efforts to expand Malay ownership have themselves become businessmen' (Searle, 1999: 81). Searle categorizes those Malays who form the nexus between government, administration, armed forces and business into five types: figurehead capitalists appointed to the boards of companies; executive-professional and executive-trustee directors; functional directors serving as advisers and brokers to the private sector; bureaucrats-turned-businessmen (some are rent-seekers whilst others have become entrepreneurs in their own right); and state managers-turned-owners through the process of privatization of state assets (ibid.: 81–102).

Following economic recession during the mid-1980s and the decline in Malaysian commodity prices, the Mahathir government pursued an agenda of economic reform and liberalization, including lowering interest rates, privatizing state assets, reducing public expenditure, reorganizing the bureaucracy and relaxing the NEP principle of redistribution between ethnic groups (Searle, 1999: 53; Rasiah, 1997: 131–136, 1995; Khoo, 1992). The change in economic policies had mixed consequences for the Malay business class; for the rentiers who were heavily dependent on state patronage, and who tended to be small and middle-level businesspeople, these were difficult times, but for those less dependent on the state and who comprised the more dynamic, bigger businesses the reforms provided opportunities for further growth and profit (Searle, 1999: 53–56; Khoo, 2001: 190–192). On a continuum of dependence on and independence from the state, Searle therefore classified Malay business as either 'rentier', 'transitional' or 'entrepreneur', and argues that, although political and bureaucratic patronage was the crucial factor in the early development of Malay capitalism, some Malay businesspeople have been able to secure greater independence from the state (Searle, 1999: 154–174). Moreover Malay business became increasingly entwined with Chinese and other business activities. In particular, the privatization policy gave rise to '[a] new category of politically connected Malay, non-Malay, or often interethnic conglomerates ... [which] evolved into privileged oligopolies' (Khoo, 2001: 193).

Searle's study demonstrates the important role of patronage in the development of capitalism in Malaysia, whilst avoiding the assumption that state–business and patron–client relations can only lead to a static, stunted kind of capitalism (ibid.: 241–249; McVey, 1992a, 1992b). Above all he warns against 'drawing sharp contrasts between dependency and self-reliance, between state and capital, and between rent-seekers and true productive capitalists' because the relationships between state and business and between Malays and Chinese are complex and dynamic (Searle, 1999: 249).

Thailand

I have already examined some post-war developments in Thailand and changing class structures in Chapter 5. In some respects, the situation in Thailand with regard to the position of the military is similar to that in Indonesia. From the revolution of 1932, when the power of the monarchy was removed, until the 1970s, and then irregularly through to the 1990s, 'the armed forces dominated the political arena without real challenges from the civil bureaucracy, political parties or other societal groups' (Suchit, 1991: 67). Patronage had been inherited from the traditional Thai social order where the king and nobility were at the pinnacle of a hierarchy of patron–client ties (the *sakdina* ['dignity marks'] system), and was continued in the post-1932 social order in which the military and senior bureaucrats wielded considerable power and based this, in part, on the size of their clienteles (Girling, 1985: 45–60). This system was in turn strengthened when the military expanded its role into the economic sphere in the 1960s and 1970s and '[l]eading members of the armed forces were appointed board members of state enterprises and private firms', and consequently controlled considerable resources to dispense patronage (Suchit, 1991: 67).

Studies of Thai society undertaken mainly by American social scientists in the 1950s and 1960s focused not on social class formation and struggle, but instead on individualistic, face-to-face, 'loose', fluid relationships, 'organised along patron–client lines, with class barriers being few and not impenetrable, and occupational stratification being limited'; social organizational arrangements were in turn often seen as a function of Thai culture and personality (Hewison, 1989a: 8, 1989b, 1997a: 3–6, 1997b, 2006: 76). I have referred to the work of Wilson (1962) and Riggs (1961, 1964, 1966) in this regard and their emphasis on political stability, consensus, and evolutionary change (see also Hewison, 1997b). Wilson argued that Thai society is dominated by a small elite competing for power and political spoils and organized into unstable and shifting cliques, factions and patron–client networks, and in which the popular support of a large constituency of ordinary citizens is unnecessary. These cliques 'are not motivated by policy or ideological differences, but are rather centered around a more or less amoral quest for power and spoils' (Scott, 1972c: 59). The spoils include personal access to state funds, political promotions and appointment to bureaucratic posts (Doner and Ramsay, 2000: 151–155).

This social pattern is given explicit attention in Hanks's work (1962, 1975, 1977; and Scott, 1972c: 57). For Hanks the whole of Thai society is ordered in terms of a hierarchy of deference and respect, based on voluntary, flexible, multifunctional, unbounded, personal relationships; these vary in the degree of affection, loyalty and trust between patron and client, and, according to circumstances, they may be terminated by one or both parties (1975: 198–199; Girling, 1985: 19). Positions of power also provided the means to accumulate merit, and the cultural expectations of the Thais, based on the traditional *sakdina* system, was one of presenting gifts to high officials in return for protection and favours (Hanks, 1962; Pasuk and Sungsidh, 1996: 3–4). Traditionally a person's status coincided with their power, wealth and merit, at least in principle, and labour resources were assigned to powerful people according to their social position (Girling, 1985: 20–29).

Hanks provides two concepts to analyse these patron–client relations: the 'entourage' comprising a patron and his immediate clientele, and the 'circle' which is, in effect, a pyramid, in which a dominant patron, builds a clientele, which, in turn, establish their own set of clients and so on (Hanks, 1975: 202). Therefore, instead of a system of social classes, for Hanks the 'Thai social order consists of a congeries of linked circles with minimal functional differentiation', and it is these not classes that are in conflict and competition (ibid.: 207). Indeed, he proposes that concepts of 'class, elite and specialized institution becloud our vision' (ibid.: 218). The Thai state then, which Hanks considers to be weak, with little capacity to support its general populace, is organized on the basis of autonomous circles which compete to secure monopolies of various state resources. In this situation 'petty warlordism, corruption and opportunism' thrive (ibid.: 216).

Furthermore, the Chinese business community, based primarily in Bangkok, is also linked into this system of patronage in which '[e]ach businessman received protection from an influential Thai official to carry out his business, and in return the Chinese businessman paid his protector or patron for the service' (Pasuk and Sungsidh, 1996: 3; Riggs, 1966: 251; Girling, 1985: 99–101). The ethnic Chinese did not hold or have access to formal positions of authority other than through informal links with Thai officials and politicians or by appointing the latter to the board of directors of Chinese-owned companies (Scott, 1972c: 22, 72–75). Senior Thai officials tended to treat their office as a personal space or domain which they could use to further their own interests as well as perform their public duties. Indeed, appointment to office in the traditional Thai monarchical-bureaucratic system did not provide remuneration from the state, but rather the right to retain a reasonable proportion of taxes levied and to charge fees for other official services (Maneewan and McLean, 2003: 323–327). It was only gradually in the modern period that the influence of Western values on the relationships between private interests and public duties began to lead the Thais to interpret certain kinds of exchanges as corrupt.

Pasuk and Sungsidh draw attention to the fact that particularly from the late 1980s corruption became a political issue. It became increasingly visible and was associated with the rise and fall of governments. In 1991 a military coup was justified on the grounds of the need to remove corrupt civilian politicians in order to restore democracy (1996: 1–2, 51). Subsequently the elected governments of Chuan Leekpai and Banharn Silpa-archa from 1992 to 1996 both 'fell amid accusations of corruption' (Hewison, 1997a: 2). Yet, it would seem that levels of corruption as a percentage of the annual government budget and GDP were higher under the military dictatorships of Sarit Thanarat (1957–63), Thanom Kittikachorn, Prapass Charusathiarana and Narong Kittikachorn (1964–73) than later elected governments (Pasuk and Sungsidh, 1996: 26–56). It was simply that it was more 'invisible' and difficult to detect in the period of dictatorship; only subsequently did it come to light, for example, that Sarit had diverted around US$ 140 million from state funds for his own personal use (ibid.: 14–15). 'The military domination of government ensured that the corruption money was not only controlled within a small group of appointed politicians and bureaucrats, but was also hidden from public knowledge' (ibid.). Subsequently, with the rise of businessmen and their involvement in the political process, the competition for revenue from corruption increased rapidly, as did the need for revenue to fund election campaigns and political parties. Some enterprising military leaders also left the armed forces, moved into politics full time and founded political parties.

Studies of Thai politics and political culture have revealed, therefore, that 'there is corruption in all levels of the bureaucracy and the political system, and that for many of those involved the practices are legitimate under the patronage system although illegal in the context of modern laws' (ibid.: 5). Other factors have also been used to explain the high incidence of corruption in Thailand: the low level of salaries for officials (though this applies much more to the lower levels of the administration), the legal limitations and the weakness of the police forces in combating corruption, the lack of strong countervailing forces or political opposition in drawing attention and seeking solutions to official corruption, and finally the lack of impersonal state-derived guarantees of security and rights (ibid.: 5–6). Clearly lack of accountability and weak enforcement are key elements in situations in which corruption thrives. Moreover, in certain circumstances, and particularly if the level of a bribe or personal favour is relatively modest, this may not occasion social opprobrium but rather be interpreted in terms of traditional culture (Siffin, 1966: 212–218).

Corruption has been closely associated with authoritarian and paternalistic governments – a very general feature of Southeast Asian society and politics. But even following the process of 'democratic decentralization' in Thailand, which commenced modestly from the 1970s and accelerated in the 1990s, the deep-seated values associated with patronage and reciprocity persist. Arghiros (2001) presents a detailed study of electoral processes, and the effects of the commercialization of agriculture and the shift from agriculture to capitalist relations of production on changing class formations at the provincial and sub-district levels in rural central Thailand in the 1980s and 1990s. He reveals that the movement towards democratic decentralization and the anticipated development of civil society and mass participation in political life have tended towards the 'extension of bureaucratic power into local communities' so that a certain kind of patronage relationship has been continued (ibid.: 5, 21–40). He says that at the local level, 'elections often yield representatives who are only a little more accountable than are non-elected civil servants: patronage and mutually beneficial relations between bureaucrats and a commercial elite can mean that power remains concentrated within this sphere' (ibid.).

As noted earlier, the ideology of patronage is still deployed in these new circumstances and its idiom invoked by a new breed of 'businessmen-politicians' to give rise to a 'new clientelist electoral politics' (ibid.: 72). The emergence of wealthy Thai and Sino-Thai entrepreneur-politicians has been particularly noteworthy as has the emergence into the political arena of businessmen more generally; two-thirds of all candidates returned in the 1988 elections, for example, were businessmen and they formed the most significant group in Parliament in the 1990s (ibid.: 18; Surin Maisrikod and McCargo, 1997: 141–142; Handley, 1997: 94–113). They began to make their appearance significantly in the 'democratic period' of 1973–76. The motivations of businessmen in seeking political office are complex ones and are not driven purely by materialist considerations; they frequently comprise considerations of prestige, status and respect. Nevertheless, the occupation of an official position does give access to public development funds and 'associated opportunities for graft' as well as access to influential bureaucrats (Arghiros, 2001: 126). Having invested funds in buying votes successful candidates wish to see some return on their investment, and electoral choice is restricted by the practice of 'purchasing power'. Yet there is a moral dimension to this; those who have sold their votes still hold 'views on what constitutes a good representative', and do expect some form of accountability (ibid.: 274).

In terms of the patron–client model, the increasing process of democratization has given rise to 'a new kind of politician', the 'godfather' (*jao pho*) (ibid.). The term is used to refer to provincial and district businessmen who either finance political party activity and control MPs or are politicians and political office-holders themselves; they have moved in to take over offices like the village and subdistrict head from such previous incumbents as rice farmers and landowners (ibid.: 60–68). These 'godfathers' have been able 'to develop mutually beneficial relationships with local officialdom and use those links to play a crucial intermediary role between the state and a wide array of local interests' (Pasuk and Sungsidh, 1996: 12; 57–107; Turton, 1989). This intervention of the wealthy in regional and local politics has, not unexpectedly, also led, as in the case of the emergence of a wealthy and well-connected Malay business group in Malaysia, to the increasing importance of money in elections. Arghiros examines the ways in which money has been used to buy votes, particularly in the countryside, to the extent that 'in the 1990s vote buying in local elections was ubiquitous', though he places a question mark over its long term effectiveness as an electoral strategy (2001: 71, 208–210; Callahan and McCargo, 1996; Surin and McCargo, 1997). Therefore, where no former relationships of a personal kind existed between a local constituency and a wealthy businessman, then, through the traditional idiom of patronage and the moral obligation underlying mutual reciprocity, a relationship was created through the distribution of money in vote-buying. Once money in the form of a bribe has been received and obligations established then, in most cases, the voters will feel a moral compulsion to vote for that candidate. In a case study of elections to a subdistrict headship, Arghiros notes that the candidates 'lacked reciprocal relations with the majority of landless households', with 'little basis for mutual exchange and sharing in the subdistrict' (2001: 125). In this regard, '[v]ertical networks held together by the distribution of money and development grants define the electoral politics of contemporary Thailand' (ibid.: 222). Buying electoral support can take the form of collective donations to the community or gifts of money to individuals (ibid.: 256–259).

These developments have led to questions about the utility of the 'bureaucratic polity' model and the dominance of bureaucrats in analysing the Thai political economy, given that 'the rise of provincial businessmen-politicians has been at the expense of the power and control of the bureaucracy' (ibid.: 20, 272). In addition, 'entrepreneurs collectively and individually convert their economic power into political power by buying votes, dispensing patronage and manipulating their workers'; networks of power, influence and wealth have been extended from the national arena of political competition to the provincial and local level in the search for voter support in elections (ibid.: 227, 231). Overall the Thai version of democracy has continued to uphold the principles of hierarchy, authoritarianism and patrimonial relations of deference and respect. It has done this in a rapidly changing and increasingly complex social order which comprises new and established socio-political forces which contend and ally one with another and which Pasuk and Baker categorize as the mandarins (civil and military officials), metropolitan businessmen and technocrats based in Bangkok, provincial businessmen, the salariat (popularly, the middle class), peasants, and urban workers (1997: 21–41; see also Chapter 5). The relatively recent rise and demise of Thaksin and his entrepreneurial allies, as representatives of crony capitalism, further demonstrate the power and the problems of patronage (Kasian, 2002: 323–356).

Conclusion

We have seen how personal relationships of a hierarchical kind interrelate with class formations, and that despite the importance of class in Southeast Asia, personal networks continue to have salience in the region's social systems. In addition, the prevalence of the related practices of corruption is also a very general feature of political and economic life. Read any recent overviews of Southeast Asia from the *Economist Intelligence Unit, Far Eastern Economic Review,* and *Asian Survey* and references to corruption and attempts to counter it are very common indeed, from the Communist Party systems of Laos and Vietnam, to the recent transition from one-party rule to a more democratic system in Cambodia, to the military dictatorship of Myanmar, to the politically pluralist systems of Thailand, Malaysia, Indonesia and the Philippines (Kidd and Richter, 2003b). Events in the Philippines, in particular, in 2005 with accusations of electoral fraud against President Gloria Macapagal-Arroyo, and attempts to impeach her, and continuing accusations of high-level political irregularities demonstrate above all else the salience of corruption in the region (Hedman, 2006: 187–189).

In order to ensure that we have a relatively comprehensive view of the changing political economies of Southeast Asia, I have advocated an approach which combines analysis of patron–client relations with social class. Arghiros argues along similar lines and proposes that 'we must meld perspectives on class with attention to the manipulation of personal relations' and, citing Brummelhuis and Kemp (1984), argues for an approach which emphasizes both 'structures' and 'strategies' (Arghiros, 2001: 7; Keyes, 1989: 136–137). Even in his thoroughgoing analysis of Thai political economy in terms of changing class structures, Hewison also examines the emergence and development of the Thai capitalist class, particularly in the finance and banking sector, during the nineteenth century from the perspective of families and personal networks (1989a: 99–116). It is worth dwelling on this perspective of patronage and personal linkage for a moment. Wealthy Chinese and Sino-Thai merchant families formed business alliances with and sought the patronage of the upper echelons of the Thai nobility and aristocracy, and subsequently the civilian and military bureaucracy (ibid.: 100). Hewison considers, for example, the case of the Sophonpanich family, of Chinese origin, their alliance with the Police-General Phao Sriyanon and their founding of the Bangkok Bank, and their subsequent links with the family business of General Prapass Charusathiarana (ibid.: 103). The Sophonpanich family was linked with another powerful family, the Tejapaibuls. In addition, the Ratanaraks who enjoyed business links with Police-General Prasert Rujirawongse, re-established the Bank of Ayudhya (ibid.: 105). Monarchical connections also continue to be of importance, and Hewison says of the situation in the 1970s that '[t]he role of the royal family [as patrons] in linking noble, military-bureaucratic and business families is of considerable importance in a society where the dominant ideology continues to emphasize the importance of the monarchy' (ibid.: 112). Most recently we have the examples of the Shinawatras and the Maleenonds, hugely wealthy capitalist families with strong political and bureaucratic connections, accumulating considerable capital from state concessions (Ockey, 2004: 151).

It has been said that attitudes of deference and respect to those of higher rank is a general and constant element within what has come to be referred to as 'Asian values'. I shall now turn to examine the relations between cultural and, more specifically, religious values and social and economic action in Southeast Asia.

8

Asian Values and Social Action

For every generalisation about Asia or America that is made, exceptions can be found. And yet, there is a body of common values and beliefs that can be called 'Asian', that most of us in Asia hold on to, in order to guide our way in the world, just as there is a body of common values and ways that can be called 'American' (Mahathir bin Mohamad, 1997: 5).

According to the conservative American political scientist Samuel Huntington, world politics is entering a new phase in which the fundamental source of conflict will be cultural rather than ideological or economic. ...[He] expects that there will be increasingly active conflict over the issue of Western cultural dominance and a heightening of inter-cultural friction around the globe (Rodan and Hewison, 1996: 31).

[I]n terms of religious content there is really little in common between Islam and Confucianism, or indeed between the Buddhism of the Theravada and Mahayanist persuasions (Spencer, 1971: 4).

Like the Arabian Phoenix of Mozart's opera, everyone knows abut Asian values, but nobody knows where they are. Worse still, fewer and fewer people seem to believe in them (Farish Noor, 1999: 171).

Introduction

This chapter addresses the 'Asian values' debate, but it relates to my earlier discussion of modernization and the relationships between cultural, particularly religious values and socio-economic change (Chapter 3; see also Alatas, 2002: 107–126;). Those who embraced the Western-derived modernization paradigm were concerned to uncover those cultural and psychological predispositions which encouraged economic growth and the adoption of modernity and the 'traditional' values which presented barriers to these processes. Based on Weber's work, though often in a rather crude fashion, one of the main foci of interest was the character of Asian religions and philosophies and the identification of elements within these, such as 'otherworldliness' and 'fatalism', the Hindu caste system, Muslim prescriptions against usury, Islamic religious law and attitudes towards women, and Theravada Buddhist merit-making, which were thought to stand in the way of modernization (von der Mehden, 1986: 5–9; McVey, 1992b: 9–10; Buss, 1984).

The focus was on religious beliefs and practices which diverted resources from so-called productive activities, seen in its most extreme form in Buddhism, which, it was argued, is 'anti-materialist', because it discourages consumption and production; as well as religious personnel who were perceived as 'parasitic' and wedded to tradition. Furthermore, the tendency in talking about culture as 'facilitator' or 'obstacle' was to associate it with something long-established ('traditional'), deeply embedded in people's psyche, generally resistant to change, and an essential part, if not the central part of the identity of a particular community or group. Therefore, the modernization perspective argued that traditional values did not provide incentive for material success and individual achievement (Hauser, 1959: 78–84). There was also a tendency to rejoice in the development of secularism and 'rational' organization and decision-making, and view with suspicion religious values and activities (von der Mehden, 1986: 10–13). What was also problematical was the position, actual or implied, that in some way basic religious doctrines were in a causal relationship with processes of modernization. This position must be firmly rejected (Wertheim, 1993: 45–56; 1964).

Asia Strikes Back

More recent debates about the relationships between values and action have been generated principally by scholars and politicians within Asia (Han, 1999a). They have turned the modernization position on its head and argued that, far from barriers to the achievement of modernity, Asian values, and more particularly Confucian culture, are appropriate for a thriving capitalist economy and the promotion of economic growth in the most recent developmental stages of the global economy. In other words, the Western-derived interpretations of Asia and the perspectives which came to be labelled as 'Orientalism' have undergone a process of inversion and those who have argued for the positive contribution of Asian values have developed a thesis which we now refer to as 'Occidentalism' (Lawson, 1996: 116). This is what Jayasuriya also refers to as the 'culturalist' argument in that values are conceived of as 'steering' other elements of the social system and as being 'traditional', unchanging and pervasive (1997: 21). The proponents of Asian values have, therefore, taken the debate to 'the West' and challenged the assumptions of the modernization paradigm, whilst retaining the central importance of culture; they have accommodated 'the requirements of global capitalism' as a natural part of indigenous culture (Wee, 2002a: 9; Chua, 1995: 150–153). They have also challenged the assumed pre-eminence of Western values and argued that rather than a solution to Asian social and economic problems, they are part of the problem. Indeed, it is precisely this complex of Asian values that has given rise to a 'distinctive modernity' and successful Asian economic development (Malhotra, 2002: 37; Yao, 2001a: 17). The promotion of Asian values, particularly in the early 1990s, was also interwoven with such 'triumphalist accounts' as 'The Pacific Century', 'The Asian Renaissance', and 'The Rise of East Asia', and processes of 'globalization' were seen to be working in favour of Asia (Wong, 2004: 56–57).

The Clash of Civilizations

One of the senior American figures in the formulation of the modernization paradigm in the 1960s, Samuel Huntington later issued a warning that 'civilizational' identity, which is 'the highest cultural grouping of people and the broadest level of cultural identity' will play an increasingly important role in global conflicts as various non-Western civilizations reaffirm their indigenous values and react against Western domination (1993: 22–25; 1996; Alatas, 2002: 117). Huntington, like those who argue for an opposition between Western and Asian values, presents a broadly homogeneous Western value complex. For him, it has a strong socio-political dimension and comprises 'individualism, liberalism, constitutionalism, human rights, equality, liberty, the rule of law, democracy, free markets, the separation of church and state' (Huntington, 1993: 40). In its global reach he summarizes it as 'human rights imperialism'. This complex he sets against other value systems such as 'the Islamic' and 'the Confucian' and even 'the rest', and argues that, though other civilizations have attempted to embrace modernity, they will endeavour 'to reconcile this modernity with their traditional culture and values'; in other words, they attempt to become 'modern' but not 'Western' (ibid.: 49). Huntington's thesis has been the subject of extended criticism (Lingle, 1996; Goldsworthy, 1994). It has also been pointed out by observers in Asia that his perspective is an expression of a European paranoia, increasingly embraced by the Americans, about Islam, 'perceived as a force of darkness hovering over a virtuous Christian civilization' and of an irrational, vacillating view of China, its increasing economic power, its attitudes towards human rights and its relations with Japan (Mahbubani, 1993: 12–13; Johnson, 1997: 3; Wong, 2004: 56). But Huntington's thesis did give comfort to those Asian leaders who were presenting a view of 'Asian-ness' as distinctive and as demarcating a clearly defined East-West divide (Searle, 1996: 72–73; Lawson, 1996: 112; Lingle, 1996). His culturalist approach was put to ideological use by certain political leaders in Southeast Asia to demonstrate the appropriateness of their political and economic strategies in relation to the values of their citizens (Ong, 1999: 48–72).

Spokespersons for Discipline

One of the most prominent advocates of 'Asian values', Mahathir Mohamad, the former Prime Minister of Malaysia, certainly supported the view that Western values are not universal, and that Western criticism of certain 'Asian' practices is therefore unwarranted, given that social and political life is culturally relative (1997: 3–10; see also Robison, 1996a: 309–327, 1996b: 5). Mahathir argued for mutual respect between the West and Asia, but held to the position that Asian values are broadly different and that they should and will persist. He also explicitly denied, contra Huntington, that Asian values justify dictatorship, authoritarianism, anti-democratic practices, and the suppression of human rights (1997: 7). Nevertheless, one of the main areas of contention in the debate is the Western ethos of individualism, liberalism and human rights as against the Asian emphasis on community, order, hierarchy, discipline and the oneness of state and society or 'organic statism' (Jayasuriya, 1997: 19; Robison, 1996b: 4; Lawson, 1996: 117; Lee, 2001: 108). Lee Kuan Yew, the former Prime Minister of Singapore, another ardent proponent of Asian values, and his successor Goh Chok Tong, similarly argued that only within an ordered and controlled environment, which recognizes individual responsibilities to the wider society and polity, can individual freedoms be enjoyed (Zakaria, 1994: 112; Jayasuriya, 1997: 19; Sebastian, 1999: 237–245). Lee and several other prominent Singaporean political leaders, sometimes styled the 'Singapore School', argued for discipline, which could not be guaranteed by the 'exuberance of democracy' (Sebastian, 1999: 238–239); this, in turn, guards against the break up of the family, falling educational standards and moral decline (Alatas, 2002: 119).

Modernization Revisited

The recent Asian values debate, which was the subject of intense scrutiny during the 1990s but which had already emerged as a significant focus of discussion in the 1970s and the 1980s, strikes one as surprisingly old-fashioned and ill-informed. On the surface it is difficult to comprehend why it has excited so much attention (Kessler, 1999; Alatas, 2002: 108). However, when the political and ideological context of modernization and the important role of the state in the later stages of the development of industrial capitalism are taken into account, the importance accorded to cultural values becomes clear (Robison, 1996b: 15–21; Chua, 1996: 93; Alatas, 2002: 120–121; Wee, 2002b: 130). Values, and more generally culture can be adapted, manipulated, transformed and symbolically attributed to serve political purposes. Although it is generally accepted that values have a bearing on what people do and on how they interpret and act in the world, they are also extraordinarily malleable. They can be symbolically created and re-created, re-ordered and re-classified in the course of social change and class conflict. Cultural traditions can be and are 'invented'; they are located in 'the field of language and discourse' (Farish Noor, 1999: 151; Jayasuriya, 1997: 21).

An interest in the relationships between values and socio-economic action has a long pedigree in sociological thought, and it was crystallized in the competing paradigms of Marx and Weber. Values were conceived of as either products of socio-economic processes or as providing certain preconditions for socio-economic action, though even this formulation does not do credit to the subtleties of Marx's and Weber's theories. However, the explanatory power accorded cultural values is somewhat diminished when, for example, on the one hand, Confucian culture was deployed by Weber to help explain Chinese backwardness, and on the other, more recent explanations for the economic development of such countries as South Korea,

Taiwan, Singapore and Hong Kong, and now China itself, refer precisely to those Chinese values which Weber saw as inimical to modernity (McVey, 1992b: 9–10).

But, more than anywhere else in Southeast Asia the problems occasioned by modernization (and explaining it) were exercising scholars and politicians in the 1970s in Singapore when the small island republic was going through a period of rapid economic growth and social change, and opening up to the global economy (Tham, 1972; Seah, 1977; Clammer, 1997: 502–505; Chua, 1995: 153–163). It is no coincidence that Singapore, as the first state in the region to adopt successfully an EOI strategy, should be preoccupied with the nature of globalization, processes of Westernization and the interplay of Western and local cultures. How could the political leaders of a 'global city' – interconnected to international flows of capital, labour, commodities, knowledge and information, and subject to cross-national power relations – retain and promote its own political, economic and cultural priorities?

These concerns were then reinforced by prominent politicians in neighbouring Malaysia, another Southeast Asian state which had embraced the global economy with some alacrity. In both Singapore and Malaysia there has also been considerable middle-class support for the dominant political party, and it is this middle class that is 'likely to be highly sympathetic to the logic and rationale of technocratic efficiency and managerialism' and to warnings about the danger to the state's security and stability from forces within and without (Jayasuriya, 1997: 25). Furthermore, the political leaders of Singapore and Malaysia were 'possibly the most articulate in English among leaders of East Asian states, giving them disproportional access and exposure in [the] international press', and they were buoyed by a new-found confidence in their economic achievements and the resurgence of Asia (Chua, 1996: 88; see also Bruun and Jacobsen, 2000a: 4; Mauzy, 1997). This was obviously not the case for the Philippines – most certainly an English-speaking Asian country, and one which, we might assume, shared Asian values. Yet it was predominantly Catholic, and had adopted a form of American republican democracy and an 'undisciplined' open-market capitalism after Marcos's downfall and the accession of Aquino (De Jesus, 2002: 62). Interestingly, the then Philippines President Fidel Ramos clashed with Lee Kuan Yew over the latter's conception of Asian values and the anti-democratic tendencies it entailed (Rodan, 1997: 164–167).

Finally, both Singapore and Malaysia comprised plural societies, which embraced several Asian cultures and, therefore, for the purposes of constructing a national identity, this cultural diversity encouraged their political leaders to present their local identities in terms of pan-Asian themes (ibid.). Nevertheless, we should not forget that the construction and development of the Indonesian state ideology – Pancasila – which reached its fullest expression under Suharto, goes back much earlier and is 'based on principles supposedly derived from local culture'; '[t]hese putatively Indonesian cultural principles will look familiar to students of the Asian values debate' (Halldorsson, 2000: 111–112). The overriding concern was economic development and political stability, based on consensus, community, social order and harmony, respect for authority, and a 'uniform understanding of both the nature of the Indonesian state and Pancasila as the state ideology' (Sukma, 1999: 124–126, 141).

Singapore's Contribution

Returning to Singapore in the 1970s, one of the prominent local academics in this debate, the sociologist Peter Chen posed the question of 'the feasibility of retaining Asian values in the process of modernization in the modernizing society of Singapore' (1976: 2). For him cultural values provide a crucial mechanism for maintaining the integrity, stability, identity and resilience of society. Therefore, how might these fast changing societies like Singapore retain order and harmony in an unpredictable future in which Western or modern values, and, one might add, 'cultural messages' from the globalized Western mass media, were threatening to sweep all before them, and for some local observers, 'pollute' and 'contaminate' Asian values (Yoshihara, 2004: 84)? And what precisely were these values which were in danger of being lost?

An obvious tendency in the debates about Asian values is to present these as positive and desirable; their loss would have serious consequences for the stability, harmony and identity of community and the nation-state (Diokno, 2000: 75–76). However, this new-found confidence in Asian ways and their suitability for attaining economic success require constant attention and vigilance. Mahathir has maintained on behalf of Asians that:

> Not only are we now convinced of the rightness of many of our Asian ways, but we are also convinced that these Asian ways are currently under attack ... We cannot avoid noticing the connection between our approach and our values with our success in many fields. Why then must we change ourselves to suit the West and their values? Why are so many in the West insisting that we become just like them? (1997: 4; see also Yao, 2001c: 53–56)

The former Malaysian Deputy Prime Minister, Anwar Ibrahim, before his incarceration, also conducted this dialogue with the West (Ang, 2001: 27–45). What is more when 'Eastern defects' are detected (and Mahathir, among others, admits to these), the argument presented in the 1970s by local politicians such as Rajaratnam, the then Foreign Minister of Singapore, was that these are also Western defects and the West should not criticize the East without first addressing its own problems (Clammer, 1997: 504–505).

All Values, Any Values

In the search for Asian values, Clammer makes reference to a speech delivered by the then Deputy Prime Minister of Singapore in 1976, Dr Goh Keng Swee, about the dangers of Western permissiveness, and the importance of upholding Eastern values of 'belief in hard work, thrift, honesty, self-discipline, regard for education, respect for enterprise and concern over family stability' (ibid.: 503). 'Respect and courtesy towards elders' was also mentioned in the local press (ibid.). As we shall see, senior political support for these values had been unwavering up to the 1990s. It was expressed most forcefully by Lee Kuan Yew when he said:

> Man [sic] needs a certain sense of right and wrong. There is such a thing called evil, and it is not the result of being the victim of society. You are just an evil man prone to do evil things, and you have to be stopped from doing them. Westerners have abandoned an ethical base for society, believing that all problems are solvable by good government, which we in the East never believed possible. (cited in Zakaria, 1994: 112)

Nevertheless, the discussion of Asian values in 1970s Singapore demonstrates just how diverse and difficult they are to pin down; other observers like Chen do not provide a value complex which maps directly onto that of Goh, though there is some overlap. Chen is concerned to explore how Asian values might be used to address the demands of modernization in Singapore, which include:

- Increasingly impersonal relations in the workplace.

- Labour mobility and the separation of work from family and community.

- Receptiveness to change, achievement orientation, materialism, and individualism.

- The attenuation of family and community relations, and the increasing importance of the nuclear family as against wider kinship and community relations.

- The widening of the 'generation gap'; and the importance of 'positivist', value-free enquiry (1976: 7–13).

The attributes of modernity are 'rationality, expediency, efficiency, flexibility and, to some extent, impersonality' which, according to Chen, are in tension with the more collectivist impulses in Asia (ibid.: 13).

Although Chen acknowledges that 'it is extremely difficult, if not impossible, to identify common Asian values' he decides to focus on those of East Asia, particularly China and Japan, which he sees as most relevant to Singapore's circumstances (ibid.: 7). These comprise:

- 'group spirit and paternalistic employer–employee relationships'.

- 'mutual assistance and community life'.

- parent–child relationships and family life, including filial piety, respect for elders and support within the family.

- 'friendship patterns' and the incorporation of friendship into the idiom of kinship.

- 'normative ideology and value concept', which addresses the moral dimension of Asian academic enquiry and how people ought to behave.

Chen argues that these five principles should have a role to play 'in rectifying the adverse effects of modernization' (ibid.: 14). In other words, he suggests that they must be retained in some form to improve relations in the work-place, the family and community, ensure that friendship thrives and provides mutual support, and encourages a moral dimension in decision-making.

Again, although there is overlap in their discussion of Asian values, Ho Wing Meng, of the Philosophy Department in the University of Singapore, arrives at a somewhat different set of values from Chen (Ho, 1976). His perception of modernity is also rather different in that, although it includes such principles as rationality, it also involves 'a set of policies and administrative measures' which include 'comprehensive state planning for economic development', policies to 'equalize economic and social opportunities', the reform of 'pernicious attitudes, beliefs and other forms of rigidities and inhibitions' so that programmes of national development can be promoted, and a commitment to nationalism and national consolidation (ibid.: 3–4). He formulates these principles from the perspective of modernizing and developing countries, but he is much more concerned about the need to overcome 'traditional' obstacles.

Ho recognizes the dangers of stereotyping Asians, but he arrives at three major problems which they have to overcome in their search for modernity:

- The population explosion and the positive cultural, as well as economic value of having children.

- The negative attitude to 'making a living by manual labour' and the positive value placed on academic, administrative, professional and religious careers (note the sharp distinction between this and the general principle enunciated in Singapore that Asians generally work hard and have respect for enterprise).

- The negative attitude towards saving for one's old age and towards various forms of investment in the capitalist economy (including 'bonds', 'insurance policies', 'certificates of stocks and shares', and 'other forms of income titles') (ibid.: 11–14).

Ho concludes in ambivalent fashion that Asians need to modernize, with all the 'unsettling and upsetting' consequences of this process, but, like Chen he hopes that local values will survive. For him these are 'cherished cultural, philosophical and religious values' which should not be sacrificed merely for material rewards (ibid.: 14). This is for the reason that 'if you care to examine the teachings of the great religions of both the East and the West, you will find that they invariably include a commandment to eschew the ephemeral values of modernization, materialism and scientific technology' (ibid.: 15).

It becomes even more complicated when a local politician like Mahathir seeks to identify what characterizes Asian culture (see also Hall, 1997). Interestingly, he relies on a comparative survey undertaken by David Hitchcock, the former Director of East Asian and Pacific Affairs at the United States Information Agency, which relates specifically to East Asian rather than Asian culture and to American rather than Western culture (Mahathir Mohamad, 1997: 5–6). Again there is some overlap with the findings of Chen and Ho, but for Mahathir Asian values conform very neatly to the desires and ideals of politicians: having an orderly society; societal harmony; the accountability of public officials; being open to new ideas; freedom of expression; and respect for authority (ibid.: 5). The personal values emphasized were hard work; respect for learning and education; honesty; self-reliance; and self-discipline (ibid.: 6). This fits well with the requirements of a modernizing, yet authoritarian polity like Malaysia, and it maps rather more satisfactorily onto Goh Keng Swee's model for Singapore: Asians are innovative, open to ideas, with a desire for education, but they value harmony and order; they are self-reliant, hard-working, disciplined and they respect those in authority.

Alatas has identified the discussions of the 1970s as crucial in shaping the later Asian values debate (2002). They commenced with the attempt to distinguish Westernization from modernization, based on the assertion that there is a form of modernization in Asia which can 'selectively' exclude certain Western influences and retain traditional values. They also identified particular Asian values as 'functional equivalents to the Protestant ethic', which could, in turn, be deployed in 'theoretical accounts of modernization in Asia' (ibid.: 109). However, the work of local Southeast Asian scholars also drew on an earlier body of Western research from the 1960s that claimed to have discovered positive relations between Asian, particularly Confucian ethics and economic growth and development in East Asia (ibid.: 113).

Culture or Politics?

The concept of Asian values gives rise to formidable difficulties, not just in the generalized way in which these underlying principles of action are presented (honesty, thrift, self-reliance, respect, and so on), but in delimiting what is and is not 'Asian' (Chen, 1997: 5–6). The concept of Asia as a cultural unit with defined characteristics is so vague and general, given that it is an artificially constructed entity, that it is of little analytical value. It is therefore somewhat surprising that, in a relatively recent overview of the relationship between Asian values, governance and development, Han, whilst fully recognizing the great variations among Asian countries in political and religious values, maintains that 'there are values which can be described as particularly Asian' (1999b: 8). He does, however, draw attention to the ways in which values can be sifted, adjusted, amplified, defined, created and implemented by a political leadership, and used to legitimize a particular political approach and set of policies (ibid.: 6). In this connection he refers especially to the success of the Singaporean government in 'deliberately emphasizing selective aspects of Asian (mostly Confucian) values while at the same time adapting them to the requirements of both initial industrialization and globalization' (ibid.).

The issue then becomes one of conveniently labelling a cultural characteristic as either 'Western' or 'Asian' to serve particular political and rhetorical purposes. In this regard, 'culture is being deployed as an instrument of political control' so that by categorizing a particular country as 'Asian' or 'Eastern' and therefore one that does not subscribe to certain universalist, Western-derived cultural values, political leaders can 'refashion and restructure the domestic economic and political process' (Jayasuriya, 1997: 21, 22). The proponents of Asian values also directly confront the thesis of Francis Fukuyama, his celebration of democracy as 'a universal form of social co-existence that expresses man's universal striving for happiness', and his relegation of cultural relativism and cultural diversity to 'the traditional and backward part of the world' (Ifversen, 2000: 49–50; Fukuyama, 1992; Bruun and Jacobsen, 2000a: 13). In Asian values discourse culture becomes a device in the construction of state and societal identity, and it justifies a corporatist, statist approach to the management of social, economic and political affairs. As Lawson proposes 'myths based on cultural interpretations are often invoked to legitimate a certain political order while at the same time portraying others as lacking legitimacy because they do not appear to resonate with certain cultural "givens"' (1996: 108).

Western and Eastern Interactions

What is clear is that the distinction between the 'West' and 'Asia' is ideologically generated. These are 'discursive constructs, relational and subject to constant negotiations and change' (Bugge, 2000: 65; Friedman, 2000: 22–25, 37). Mahathir, for example, notes that 'many of these "Asian values" were once also "Western values". Many of them are what would be termed "Victorian values". Many of today's Asian values were Western values which much of the West have successfully thrown off or "lost"' (1997: 7). Indeed, the 'suggestion that dedication to hard work and commitment to family are uniquely Asian ignores the Protestant ethics that are argued by many to have been an integral element in the modernization of western culture' (Lingle, 1996: 30, 48). Moreover it has also been argued that the basic tenets of Confucianism and Buddhism accord with notions of individualism and human rights, and, though 'the history of human rights thought is strongly linked with Western thinkers and nations, it is also compatible with at least two important Asian traditions that have profoundly influenced Asian thought and society' (Powers, 1997: 16; see also Chen, 1997: 5–6). Rather than such principles as individual rights and democracy being incompatible with Asian values, it has even been suggested that, in the case of the People's Republic of China, the difficulties of accommodating Western values stem not from the resistance of traditional Asian values but from the adoption of the competing Western ideological system of Marxism-Leninism (ibid.: 7–9). The same has been argued for Vietnam when Vo Van Ai proposes that, whilst invoking Vietnamese values, the country's communist leaders hold to the Western-derived ideology of Marxism-Leninism, and that 'individual rights and freedoms are a fundamental and ancient feature of Vietnamese culture, rooted in a cultural heritage [of Buddhism and Confucianism] over four thousand years old' (2000: 92–93, 102). In other words, there are competing and conflicting value systems in the West, just as there are in Asia, and a good deal of interconnection between Western and Asian value systems. Bruun and Jacobsen add that 'Northern European countries with massive state management are hard to fit into the East–West contention' (2000a: 6).

The problem of counterposing the categories 'Western' and 'Eastern' and defining them by a small number of contrasting characteristics is obvious. 'West' and 'East' are not homogeneous entities, cannot be separated neatly one from another, and have been interacting and influencing one another for a considerable period of time (Friedman, 2000: 37–41; Freeman, 2000: 50–56). The fallacious reasoning behind the construction of an Asian value system in opposition to a Western one, which can be traced in an unchanging fashion to a distant, pre-modern period, is easily criticized, as is the view of culture as 'essentialist', 'authentic' and coincident with an artificially constructed region (Bruun and Jacobsen, 2000a: 1, 8; Rodan and Hewison, 1996: 34; Chua, 1996: 94). However, once it is seen as a mechanism of political control in the context of a global debate about human rights and democracy, then much is explained (Robison, 1996; Jayasuriya, 1997: 21–23; Robison, 1996a, 1996b; Rodan and Hewison, 1996). The promotion of 'an immutable and discrete Asian set of values' has provided Asian political leaders with the means 'to deny legitimacy to domestic opponents, who can be dismissed as opposing the national interest or simply being un-Asian' (Robison, 1996b: 4; Lingle, 1996: 27, 34–35).

Furthermore, as Bruun and Jacobsen propose 'from a straightforward human rights point of view the real challenge embedded in Asian values is less their ideological content than the prominence they derive from being articulated in government rhetoric and official statements' (2000a: 1). It is also an attempt to impose boundaries between West and East, to eliminate ambiguity (occasioned by those who absorb or combine cultural elements of both East and West), and has been used as a means to control or at least socialize the citizens of certain Asian states to safeguard them against perceived undesirable influences emanating from the West. Clammer presents a very interesting analysis with reference to Singapore of the Asian values complex as a 'coherent and interlinked systematic network of beliefs and ideas ... which form the focus of the symbolic system, and the language of control of the leadership' (1997: 506). Government policies and pronouncements focus on notions of Western pollution, on demarcating and controlling this pollution, emphasizing discipline, vigilance and tidiness, and on constantly and pervasively socializing the citizens in this set of ideas which is presented as having an unshakeable moral foundation (ibid.). What we are dealing with here then, is, as Clammer indicates, 'an official culture', sanctioned and promoted by governments (ibid.: 510; Lingle, 1996). It is also one in which the 'theatrical and ritualistic nature' of symbolic action comes to the fore (Jayasuriya, 1997: 20). Ironically it is claimed that, despite the proclamations of the political leaders of Singapore on the importance of Confucianism to their Chinese citizens and its role in promoting the most positive aspects of Singaporean society, the 'Singaporean Chinese do not in fact have a particular traditional familiarity with Confucianism' (Lawson, 1996: 120). Furthermore, Chua has argued that Singapore's success lies in its ability to address and play to the logic of global capitalism; therefore, for him:

> ... the singularly most significant cultural contribution of the govern-
> ment is in its concerted effort at actively transforming a population
> into a disciplined industrial work-force. This has been achieved
> through legislative measures and securing the co-operation of labour;
> the role of Confucian values, in whatever guise, was never pressed
> into service' (1995: 167).

An Asian Trajectory of Modernity and Reactionary Modernism

The use of cultural strategies in debates about modernity and morals has also been explained in terms of the concept of 'reactionary modernism' (or 'radical conserva-tism'), which combines certain strands of political thinking and practice in both the East and the West (Jayasuriya, 1997: 22–26; Lingle, 1996: 39, 61–85). This is a par-ticular 'trajectory of modernity' and indeed 'an ideology born of modernity' (Wee, 1996). It is one which embraces 'conservative political values' and seeks to promote the market economy, but in conjunction with the conceptualization of the future as an embodiment of unchanging traditional values, and the government as the guardian of those values essential to the maintenance of the integrity of the state, the stability and health of society, and the success of the economy (Lawson, 1996: 23, 26). In this regard, 'culture strengthens the economy' so that, Lew Kuan Yew claims that 'Confucian ideas of family loyalty have fostered a sense of discipline and individual responsibility that has created strong incentives for hard work and thrift in East Asian societies' (ibid.: 24). Mahathir too, in his continuing dialogue with Islam and Malay values and their relationship with economic change, has claimed that the Muslim faith embodies 'the virtues of individual responsibility, discipline and thrift' (ibid.).

The theme of ideological interconnection between political strands of thinking in both the West and the East is pursued by Rodan and Hewison (1996). Jayasuriya too has drawn parallels between the Asian values complex and 'fascist and other organic ideologies that dominated Western Europe in the inter war period' (1997: 26). Rodan and Hewison argue that it is precisely the culturalist debates of Huntington and his 'clash of civilizations' thesis and Asian political leaders and their assertion of Asian as against Western cultural values which 'masks conver-gences of political ideologies across nations' (1996: 48; see also Lawson, 1996: 112; Lingle, 1996: 37). These ideologies are conservative ones. They demonstrate a commitment to traditional values and a desire to conserve them, especially those based on the traditional 'patriarchal' family; the need to control the 'anarchic' and 'natural' impulses of human beings through discipline and a sense of community responsibility, rather than allowing the free rein of individualism, and the belief that there is a natural tendency to commit evil deeds; the importance of continuity and avoidance of conflict and instability; and the crucial role played by such social institutions as the 'community', 'society', 'nation' and 'family' as against the individual who has 'duties' to these larger corporate bodies rather than rights and freedoms (Rodan and Hewison, 1996: 36–48). In their focus on the vital role of the family as an embodiment and carrier of 'traditional' values, these ideologies are profoundly gendered, and they assign women a particular role and function within the family (Brooks, 2003: 86–106; see Chapter 9).

The Singaporean government has focused directly on building community self-help organizations and disciplining and organizing the family as a basic building block of society (Chua, 1996: 94–98; see Chapter 10). According to the advocates of Asian values, good government, based on a firm, long-established cultural matrix, does not necessarily require a democratic framework, and the notion of democracy is itself extraordinarily flexible (Lawson, 1996: 113–115). Indeed, the encouragement of individual rights within Western democracies was identified by Asian political leaders as the root cause of social and moral breakdown. Lee Kuan Yew again drew attention to aspects of American culture – 'guns, drugs, violent crime, vagrancy, unbecoming behaviour in public' – which are symptomatic of the triumph of the individual – 'to behave or misbehave as he pleases' – over the community (cited in Zakaria, 1994: 111). Lee's view of Western democracies is unequivocal: 'Too much democracy leads to homosexuality, moral decay, racial intolerance, economic decline and single-parent families' (cited in Lawson, 1996: 121; Lingle, 1996).

The 'culturalization' of political and economic life is illustrated by a further development. The free market, non-socialist, authoritarian political system of a state like Singapore, which has always remained within the orbit of Western capitalism now serves as 'an attractive model of development for the socialist states in Asia, which are trying to maintain their authoritarian political structures with capitalist economies, such as China and Vietnam' (Chua, 1996: 99; 1995). The emphasis on the community, nation, and state therefore shades comfortably into ideologies of socialism and communism.

Yet the constructions of politicians still seem to be more than that. What is it that leads large numbers of people to accept them, other than political coercion and the threat of sanctions? Lawson ponders the problem of the constructed nature of 'East' and 'West', and the dynamic, ever-changing, malleable character of culture. She says, 'Yet the grand, monolithic and apparently eternal constructions ... and the polarities and stereotypes they generate, are [so] readily accepted into play in everyday politics, that they cannot be dismissed summarily as having no consequence' (1996: 123). But it is not, I think, only about the cunning and sophistication of politicians in creating these myths, as Lawson seems to suggest, or that there are easily identifiable cultural universals (ibid.). There is something else about culture that gives it such influence: it is its ability to give meaning and 'realness' to people's lives and provide a means to interpret the world and our place within it. Perhaps this is what Han has in mind when he refers to the utility, salience and relevance of

Asian values in relation to economic and political behaviour (1999a: 4). What also needs further investigation is the complexity of the interrelationships between particular values and socio-economic action and to take account of the fact that value complexes are different between different Asian countries and cultures; and that even within one country there are different values competing one with another.

With the economic crisis in Asia in 1997, 'the Asian miracle economies began to crack up, sending shock waves out in all directions irrespective of the East–West divide' (Bruun and Jacobsen, 2000a: 16). This had a significant effect on the confidence of some of those political leaders who had championed Asian values as a rationale for economic success and the robustness of the model of the Asian developmental state (Abdul Rahman Embong, 2005: 27–28, 31–36). Various economies, which, it had been argued, had enjoyed economic success on the back of a particular value complex, were in trouble. Bruun and Jacobsen suggest that '[a]t the opening of the new millennium, Asian states as a united front of Asian values proponents is an unlikely scenario'. Instead they think that 'the Asian values discourse will gradually be replaced by more localized debates on culture, self and modernity' (Bruun and Jacobsen, 2000a: 17). Following the Asian financial crisis of the late 1990s, Mahathir, for example, has shifted the grounds of the debate on globalization, arguing that rather than Asia being a beneficiary of this process, it is 'a specifically western project' designed to revive 'European imperialism' (Wong, 2004: 57). In addition, there are academic observers who suggest that the economic crisis signals that the Southeast Asian developmental state, based on corruption, nepotism and political repression 'is on its way out'. 'The economic meltdown, while it brought untold hardships to many, was nonetheless a salutary development since it helped to dismantle authoritarian regimes ... and thereby advance the trajectory of democratisation' (Saravanamuttu and Loh, 2004: 363; see also Loh, 2000, 2002).

I shall take up recent work on globalization in Southeast Asia in the concluding chapter. Nevertheless, let me now return to the theme of values and socio-economic action, and consider in the final section of the chapter some observations which arose from the modernization paradigms of the 1950s and 1960s.

Religion and Modernization

Von der Mehden has explored the complexities of the relationships between religion and modernization (1986; Alatas, 2002: 109–119). In my view, his subtle analysis of the relationships between beliefs, values and socio-economic behaviour in Southeast Asia has not been surpassed. I must also emphasize that religion, far from becoming less important in an increasingly secularizing and modernizing world, has assumed a much more significant role in Southeast Asia and a fundamental one in the political life of the newly-independent nations. Not only did it provide a crucial rationale for anti-Western nationalist movements, enabling the development of a distinctive anti-Western identity, but the representatives of Asian religions have subsequently responded to the pressures placed on local communities by globalization and the continuing dominance of the West in scientific and technological fields, by re-invigorating local commitments to Islam and Buddhism (von der Mehden, 1968: 8). As George and Willford propose, religion is 'an enduring and increasingly significant precinct of Southeast Asian politics and public life' (2005: 9). Although the impact of modernization on religion has been mixed, 'the area where [it] has probably strengthened religious commitment the most is in the realm of ideology' (ibid.: 195). We are well aware that religion played a vital role in unifying emerging nationalist forces in such places as Burma, Indonesia and the Philippines (von der Mehden, 1968; Spencer, 1971: 3). Von der Mehden also argues that religion filled a gap in the process of moving from tradition to modernity (1968: 9). Indeed, for the populations in these countries the 'manifestations of their religion and of the hold which it continues to have on their consciousness are everywhere readily apparent' (ibid.: 3). Religion therefore has been used as a weapon in political struggles. It also gives communities a perspective on their past and a means of interpreting, understanding and coming to terms with it.

We have moved from the perspective of religion as either 'promoting' or 'hindering' change or as promoting 'societal stability' (Spencer, 1971: 3) to a much more sophisticated position, as exemplified by von der Mehden, in that 'the very complexity of the process of change defies most efforts to formulate over-arching theories that integrate religion and modernization' (1986: vii). The indeterminacy of the influence of religion and other cultural values on economic action, for example, is amply illustrated by the early inconclusive debate between Parkinson and Wilder on the relationship between Islam and economic development among the rural Malays of Malaysia (Parkinson, 1967, 1968; Wilder, 1968). From Parkinson's macro-level modernization and economic growth perspective and his definition of capitalism in terms of individual risk-taking and entrepreneurship, the religio-cultural, social and psychological predispositions of the rural Malays, in contrast to the Chinese, do not encourage positive attitudes to modernization and capitalist relations of production; rural Malays suffer, therefore, from 'economic retardation'. They are passive, fatalistic, crave for security and stability, and are therefore, resistant to change. They do not supply the creative individuals that capitalism demands (1967: 40–41). On the other hand, from Wilder's local-level, culturally sensitive, anthropological perspective, there is considerable evidence of Malay involvement in the market economy and the relationship between religious motivations and economic behaviour. Religious goals such as the imperative to undertake the pilgrimage to Mecca provide incentives to generate income (1968: 163–164). In one sense the two protagonists are arguing at cross-purposes; Parkinson ends the debate by stating that he believes the rural Malays to be resistant to change, whilst Wilder does not (1968: 267–272). But this misses the point. Their debate needs to be contextualized within the historical circumstances of the respective roles of the Malays and the Chinese within the emerging colonial economy, as well as to address issues to do with the distinctions and interrelationships between doctrine and practice, and the considerable variations in economic behaviour within and between different Malay-Indonesian and, more widely, Muslim communities in Southeast Asia (Clammer, 1978b).

It is especially problematical to explain the central role of the Chinese in Southeast Asian economies, and until recently the relative absence of native entrepreneurs in business in terms of cultural values. As McVey has noted the emphasis on Chinese cultural values which promote success in business and entrepreneurship fail to acknowledge properly that 'the overseas Chinese economic role is relatively recent and was determined by historical-political factors which had little to do with Chinese culture. There was nothing particularly entrepreneurial about the China from which the immigrants to Southeast Asia came' (1992b: 18). Much of the Chinese experience and the differences between immigrant and indigenous communities were down to colonial policy and the nature of migrant as against established societies.

As von der Mehden indicates, religion (and culture), as a crucially important element of Asian value systems, needs to be deconstructed into several separate but interrelated components. It is therefore essential to determine which dimension of religion one is addressing when attempting to relate it to socio-economic change. He discerns five main elements which comprise:

- 'basic tenets' ('more or less consistently held across time and sect as the essential dogma of the religion', though even here there are conflicting interpretations and uncertainties about what constitutes a religious core, and some of the tenets, such as 'do good and not evil', are so broad as not to be easily related to socio-economic change).

- 'religious institutions' (religious hierarchies and structures and the relationships between religious personnel and laypeople).

- 'popular beliefs' (including the reinterpretation, or even rejection of basic tenets).

- 'popular practices' ('popular reinterpretations of basic dogma', including rites of passage, rituals to propitiate spirits, specific interventions related to sickness, fertility and agriculture; and calendrical rites).

- 'symbolic manipulation' (which, as we have seen in the Asian values debate, relates to the use which political leaders make of religion as a means of legitimization, to promote national consciousness and unity, encourage or discourage specific political programmes, especially in the sphere of economic development, or lend weight to or undermine particular political organizations). (Ibid.: 47)

Clearly religion, in its close relationship with the state, can be used to encourage or discourage certain developmental objectives. The best examples of deploying religion for socio-economic development purposes can be found in Burma, Malaysia and Thailand, where Buddhism and Islam have been used to provide justification and a rationale for the projects of the nation-state, promoted by the political leadership with the support of the religious leadership. Despite the doctrinal prescriptions, some Thai Buddhist monks, for example, have been used, and have been active in community development projects, whereas Muslim religious teachers and mosque leaders in Malaysia have tended to be more conservative (von der Mehden, 1986: 81–90). Nevertheless, examples of Muslim teachers 'with strong interests in modernization exist' (ibid.: 90).

Von der Mehden proposes that the basic tenets of religion have probably 'had the least impact on the modernization process in Southeast Asia', and the main influences come from popular beliefs and practices, religious institutionalization and symbolic manipulation (ibid.: 53). Tambiah too draws attention to the exaggerated focus on the religious canon, and, in the case of Theravada Buddhism in Thailand, the failure to locate it in the political and economic environment of the country (1973: 3–5; see also Alatas on Confucianism, 2002: 115–116). The practice of Buddhism and its encounter with this world will not be fully understood if one follows the canonical guidance on the 'illusory nature of the world and the individual's self' and the importance of 'detachment' (Tambiah, 1973).

A complicating factor in this is the difficulty of determining to what extent and in what ways the fundamental values of a religion (and the motivations which arise from them) have been internalized by a given population. All one can say with confidence is that this process of internalization is variable: there are those who embrace and absorb more than others, and the normative religion competes with other beliefs and practices. Spiro demonstrates this aptly in his distinction between those who hold to the doctrine of nirvana (nibbanic Buddhism) and seek to achieve it, and those who are in the majority and oriented to the accumulation of merit (karma), the avoidance of demerit, and the securing of a better rebirth (kammatic Buddhism) (1970). Moreover, there is strong evidence for materialism in Buddhist societies in Southeast Asia, even though in theory Theravada Buddhism rejects an orientation to the material world; specifically an emphasis on achieving a better rebirth suggests a positive incentive to secure economic success. The important area for examination is the relationship between doctrine and practice, and whether or not certain practical outcomes arise from the original doctrines (von der Mehden, 1986: 57). In Islam, for example, the levying of tithes (*zakat* and *fitrah*) which should go to the needy and to the administration of its collection; the fast (Ramadan); and the pilgrimage (*haj*) have obvious implications for social and economic affairs. But even here the outcomes of these rituals in relation to modernization vary considerably. In addition, in analysing religious expenditures it is by no means clear that these invariably have a negative impact on modernization and, indeed, they may also 'encourage entrepreneurial attitudes and behaviour as well as provide services needed by the community' (ibid.: 143).

Conclusion

What emerges from the debate on values and economic modernization is the intimate relationship between political action and motivation and the ways in which cultural, including religious values are deployed to support particular political positions and policies. Nevertheless, provided one makes a distinction between doctrine and practice and recognizes that religious values are malleable, it is clear that values have motivational force, but their influence and effects are complex, they may work directly or indirectly, and at times they may have no consequence at all.

With regard specifically to religious values and their direct relevance to the Asian values debate, von der Mehden proposes that 'Southeast Asians, like people elsewhere, may conceptualize, publicly promote, and otherwise verbalize values that they may practice intermittently, if at all' (ibid.: 71). Furthermore, depending on one's perspective and on the element of religious belief and practice one focuses on in relation to socio-economic change 'cogent arguments can be presented to characterize religion as both a positive and negative force in the modernization process' (ibid.: 199). McVey, in similar vein, proposes that 'values *are* important, but they must be observed in social and historical context ... Any cultural tradition has many strands of meaning, which may be emphasized, forgotten, and reinterpreted over time, providing legitimacy for quite contrary modes of behavior' (1992b: 18; see also Tham, 1980: 8). There is the mistaken tendency then to 'essentialize' values, draw on certain canononical or textual traditions, homogenize cultures and religions, and emphasize their directly instrumental effects and functions (Alatas, 2002: 114–117).

In his analysis of studies of the relationships between religion and the development of capitalism in Asia, particularly the work of Norman Jacobs (1958) on China and Japan and Robert Bellah on Tokugawa religion (1957), Wertheim seizes on a somewhat different issue and warns that we should not view the relationships through a Eurocentric lens and in terms of the development of 'private capitalism' (1993: 47; 1964a: 146–163; Alatas, 2002: 114). Instead capitalism has been very much a state project in Asia, and, for Bellah, it was the relationship between religion and bureaucracy which was crucial in Japan's industrialization and economic growth, and not that between a Weberian religious ethic and a capitalist spirit (Wertheim, 1993: 47–49). This, for Wertheim, referring warmly to Bellah's observations on the shortcomings in the orthodox view of European history concerning the problematical role of the state in economic development, is the Achilles heel in Weber's weighty studies of religion and economic activity. Wertheim proposes that Weber's study of Western capitalism neglects the bureaucracy and the role of state intervention in the economy, and focuses on the attitudes of private capitalists (Wertheim, 1993: 50–51). For Wertheim, Weber and others have therefore been relating religious values and practices to the wrong social groups. Instead, spiritual forces may play a role in the attitudes and behaviour of 'efficient administrators' in that:

> Without their Spartan sobriety and their strict devotion to their cause, the builders of modern industrial states in the East would never have been able to build a counterpart of the imposing edifice

of British eighteenth-century industrial society, which, according to
Max Weber, was based on the Protestant ethic. (ibid.: 54, 56).

This may be so, but we must also acknowledge that politicians and administrators have used elements of religious ideology for particular policy objectives rather than necessarily being guided, directed and influenced by them.

9

Transformations in the World of Work: Gender Issues

Southeast Asia has long been identified as an area where women enjoy high status. From Burma to the islands of Indonesia and the Philippines this alleged high status is accentuated by the contrasting male dominance characteristic of traditional Indian and Chinese societies (P. van Esterik, 1996: 1).

Western analytical concepts such as women's invisible work and the opposition between productive and reproductive work, and public and private domains of women's work are inappropriate for the analysis of gender in Southeast Asia (P. van Esterik, 1995: 253).

[I]t makes sense to think about gender not in terms of discrete exclusive categories, but rather in terms of one or more dimensions along which differing degrees of 'maleness' or 'femaleness' may be plotted (Helliwell, 1993: 264).

Introduction

During the past three decades we have witnessed a burgeoning of the literature on women's changing roles in Southeast Asia, and, in particular the consequences for them of agricultural commercialization, the expansion in factory- and urban-based employment, and the increase in affluence in a modernizing and globalizing region (Chipp and Green, 1980b; Heyzer, 1986; Karim, 1993, 1995; Manderson, 1983a, 1983b; Nagata and Salaff, 1996; Stivens, 1998a; Wolf, 1990, 1992, 1996). The background to these developments is that traditionally women were seen to be primarily involved 'in a private, domestic sphere', focused on 'housework' and child-bearing and -rearing, which was separate from 'the public world of capitalist production', politics and the wider society (Stivens, 1991a: 13; 1998a: 3–4; Branson and Miller, 1988: 1; Helliwell, 1993: 266–274). In other words, gender difference was used to explain the division of labour in that certain kinds of work, activities and responsibilities were deemed appropriate for women, and other kinds were located within the domain of men.

Private-Public, Nature-Culture

The characterization of women in terms of the division between the 'domestic' or 'private' and the 'public' sphere, which has tended to render women as low status, oppressed subjects, has been unduly influenced by Western perceptions of gender. It was expressed early on in gender studies by such writers as Rosaldo (1974: 17–42). The private/public distinction was also closely interrelated with and reinforced by the dichotomy between 'nature' and 'culture'. It was Ortner's chapter, published in the same volume as Rosaldo's influential piece, which drew attention to the association of women with the 'natural' rather than the 'cultural'; it was used to help explain the universal subordination of women (Ortner, 1974: 56–87; Chipp and Green, 1980a: 2–6). Generally domestic functions associated with physical reproduction, nurturing, eating and sustenance, and the satisfying of bodily, sexual and emotional needs, were seen to be rooted in biology, and therefore universally part of nature, whilst the world of men, beyond the family, directed to politics, religious life and economic production, were part of the world of culture, of which men were the bearers and reproducers; they had transcended nature and therefore were superior to women.

These broad categorizations have been subject to criticism, particularly in relation to the claims for their universality, the assumption that they are homogeneous and unchanging and that, as categories influenced by Western conceptions of gender, their meaning is amenable to cross-cultural translation. Indeed, both Rosaldo and Ortner revised their views subsequently (Helliwell, 1993). In other words, it is extremely difficult to generalize about women's experiences and the categories 'woman', 'the feminine' or 'female', given the differences that exist between women in terms of ethnicity, religion, age, stage of the life-cycle, class, social status (lifestyle, education, occupation), marital and family status, residential location and the different opportunities and constraints they face (Sears, 1996a, 1996b). As Helliwell remarks '[d]ifferent cultures place quite different constructions on what it is to be a woman', and the category 'woman' is subject to economic and political change (1993: 265). 'No person is *simply* a woman...' (ibid.). Wazir Jahan Karim warns that the constructs or categories 'male' and 'female', and the relations between men and women are not universally the same (1995a: 13–14, 1992; Errington, 1990: 8–9,24–26; Stivens, 1998a: 21). This diversity is captured very well in the work by Lebra and Paulson on Chinese women in Southeast Asia (1980). Helliwell too notes that many cultures do not make distinctions between 'private' and 'public' and 'nature' and 'culture' – or, if they do, they assign them different meanings: they do not differentiate them in an absolute, oppositional way, nor do they necessarily associate them ideologically with female-male distinctions; they are subject to contestation, negotiation and reformulation (1993: 276–278; Karim, 1995a: 13–15; Peletz, 1995b: 102–105; Stivens, 1998a: 3–4).

The notion that women are removed from the public and cultural sphere, even in a symbolic sense, seems absurd given their crucial role in the market-place, in socialization processes and as purveyors of cultural knowledge to pass on to their children. Indeed, as Stivens remarks in relation to recent transformations in Southeast Asia, 'such dualities are collapsing completely', and concepts of the domestic are being reformulated in debates about middle classness, lifestyle and consumption, notions of female beauty, the desirability of certain kinds of family life, and concepts of romantic love and sexuality (1998a: 4,7–8). The recent rapid expansion in scholarly interest in sexuality (or 'sites of desire'), and in sexual orientations and practices among young people in Asia is obviously germane to the understanding of gender relations (Manderson and Jolly, 1997b; Manderson and Pranee, 2002). From a sociological perspective sexuality is also 'embedded in a social world structured ... by relations of power, not just of gender and sexual orientation but also of race and class' (Manderson and Jolly, 1997a: 26; see also Sears, 1996a); it 'only exists through its social forms and social organization' (Manderson and Pranee, 2002: 5).

An interesting dimension in recent debates about gender and sexuality is that middle-class women, in particular, are very much involved in them, and play active roles in 'reforming groups' (ibid.: 22, 24). Even in Vietnam, which has emerged only recently from a state socialist system, the images and practices of women are being re-worked, with the rise of a middle class and consumerism in the context of a globalizing capitalist modernity. As Fahey demonstrates, the representations of Vietnamese women have shifted from those which focus on them as heroines of the revolution, peasant and urban workers, and dutiful and responsible wives, mothers and sisters, to those which concentrate on women, especially young, urban, working women, as objects of beauty, harnessing female sexuality to promote fashion, cosmetics, hairdressing, health clubs, exercise equipment, and beauty contests (1998: 229–237; see also Earl, 2004: 351–379; Jamieson, 1993: 1–41; Nghiem, 2004: 297–324). Fahey remarks, 'Vietnamese women seem to be increasingly conscious of fashion and body shape' and oriented to notions of romantic love and passion so that 'the beauty contest is replacing the revolutionary war as the battleground for defining femininities in Vietnam' (ibid.: 228, 234, 245). More dramatically, Nghiem suggests that in Vietnam 'unmarried women, still living in their parents' home, are often compared to bombs that can explode at any minute' (2004: 297).

Women as Victims

Continuing the early theme in gender and feminist studies of female subordination, there were those who continued to see women as marginalized and exploited, and, *in extremis*, as anonymous even in their involvement in the modernization process (Blackburn, 1991). Heyzer proposes, in her wide-ranging study of working women, that with regard to 'power relationships, women remain subordinates', and she lists several areas in which women continue to suffer subordination as well as new areas of difficulty:

- Loss of decision-making in the household, in agriculture and urban occupations.

- Increase in the burden of work.

- Limited participation in newly formed organizations.

- Lack of alternative roles and regular employment.

- Reinforcement of gender inequalities.

- Contradictions and conflicts in patterns of behaviour and roles.

- Limited social advancement.

- Low wages (1986: 16, 113–118).

Furthermore, Bell's evaluation of the incorporation of women in Thailand into export-oriented growth in the 1970s and 1980s is that, in comparison with men, they have been 'disadvantaged in almost every way' and, more generally, 'marginalized, exploited, and oppressed' (1991: 61–82). They are victims of the 'feminization of poverty' (Blackburn, 1991: 61–62). Coyle and Kwong too, in examining Thai women's contribution to work outside the home and their continuation of domestic and 'traditional' female roles, propose that the subordination to men continues through women's 'commitment to the hegemonic ideology of Thai society' (2000: 504–505). According to this view women continue to lack economic power and political and bureaucratic representation (Blackburn, 1991: 63–64). Manderson's volume on women's work and roles in Indonesia, Malaysia and Singapore, although with qualifications, presents a similarly depressing picture: 'women have increasingly been marginalized and circumscribed in economic life; consistently they are seen in terms of idealized roles; the realities of their lives, especially if they are poor, are continually overlooked or ignored' (1983b: 13; see also Keng, 1998: 484–497 on Singapore). In Malaysia specifically, the circumstances of women caught up in rapid socio-economic change in both agriculture and industry, are said to be located 'in the less prestigious, less well paid positions throughout the labour force of Peninsular Malaysia [and this] is at once a reflection of the lower status of women in society and related to the maintenance of female subordination' (O'Brien, 1983: 213).

It is a bleak picture of oppression, marginalization and invisibility, and, according to this view, the process advocated by the international development institutions, including the World Bank and the United Nations from the 1970s with the 'women in development' paradigm and the efforts to promote gender equality and integrate women into the modern sector on the assumption of the invisibility and the low value placed on women's work, has made the situation worse (P. van Esterik, 1995: 252–253). As many observers have noted this 'integrationist' view has failed to recognize that women have always been involved in economic activities (formal and informal, market-related and domestic), and economic growth in developing countries has depended significantly on the contribution of women in the non-market sector, and in small-scale manufacture, market-trading and wage work. Therefore, the issue is not the degree or lack of integration of women into the national and international economy, but the nature of this integration (Heyzer, 1986: vii–x, 3–8). The 'women in development' approach has also failed to address the emancipatory consequences of modernization in terms of such developments as female role freedom, new occupations in the professions and access to education, changes which Barbara Ward pointed to as long ago as the early 1960s (1963; see also Stivens, 1998a, 1998b).

Women Strike Back: Reconceptualizing the Domestic

These particular views of women have, of course, been subject to extensive commentary and criticism subsequently, and, in particular, the tendencies in the earlier literature to 'essentialize' what has been termed 'the domestic' as an arena of female subordination and dependence (Stivens, 1991a: 15, 17–21). More recently, observers have pointed to many cases where women in Southeast Asia have enjoyed 'relative autonomy', and 'a degree of economic and social power in the household and village economy' (Stivens 1988: 80; Stoler, 1977; Peletz, 1987). In the absence of men, women will also invariably assume the responsibilities and decision-making powers of household heads (Barnard, 1983: 132–133). Moreover, with increasing affluence, middle class women, working outside the home, are re-working the domestic sphere; some also hire other women to release them from housework, either to take up paid work or remain at home with children (Stivens, 1998a: 7). But a major issue for working women more generally is the relationship between work within and beyond the home (Stivens, 1998b: 89).

In this connection it is important to note whether analytical perspectives view women as 'victims', 'survivors', and passive recipients of change, or as active agents, turning potential disadvantage into opportunity, resisting oppression and subordination, and able to take control of their circumstances. What is stressed increasingly is 'the versatility of the strategies adopted by the women in coming to terms with problems in their relationships with the world of men' (Nagata and Salaff, 1996: 3). Obviously gender ideologies inform and constrain women's decision-making, but various studies reveal that women's decisions may be just as likely to challenge as to reinforce these perspectives (Crane and Nadeau, 2004: 171–174). One's findings and conclusions will therefore depend partly on whether or not one adopts an emic perspective, listens to the voices of women and attempts to understand how they evaluate and represent their own circumstances; this, in turn, involves a more complex rendering of such concepts as 'work' and 'the domestic'. Ong and Peletz make the point that gender identities, in the fast-changing postcolonial world of Southeast Asia, are subject to contestation and negotiation and are constantly changing, and these processes operate at different levels or scales, from the national to the local (1995a: 1–5; Stivens, 1998a); in Sears's words they are 'fragile' (1996a). Even in the alienating situations of international labour migration of female domestic workers, there is evidence of active response and resistance (Lindio-McGovern, 2004: 217–238). Furthermore, gender ideologies usually involve much more than gender, and invariably embrace issues to do with broader kinship and family relations, personalities and human nature, religious and political ideologies and practices, class and status (Peletz, 1995a, 1995b).

Southeast Asian conceptions of 'domestic work' suggest that it is not easily differentiated from other productive activities; it is part of a continuum of or rather integrated into a range of income-generating activities, and is usually positively evaluated (Karim 1995a: 28; Barnard, 1983: 133–134). For example, women may be engaged in 'unpaid' work within the home, as well as being involved both in home-based activities, like handicraft production, and in paid work outside the home, like market-trading, factory employment or agricultural labouring (Helliwell, 1993: 270; Alexander, 1987; Dewey, 1962; Willner, 1980: 185). They also often have a period of time working outside the home, with a degree of independence, then return to a domestic situation, whilst retaining paid work; this usually involves a re-negotiation and broadening of domestic gender roles (Esra, 2004: 199–216).

The involvement of women in the 'public' sector, in wage-work and in generating income from such activities as small-scale trading is a very widespread feature of Southeast Asian economies. As Sen has said of Indonesia, 'in the 1990s, in sharp contrast to the 1970s, the working woman is replacing the "housewife" as the paradigmatic female subject in political, cultural and economic discourses', although Sen recognizes that 'the domestic sphere continues to frame many constructions of femininity' (1998: 35). Yet, there are increasing numbers of Indonesian women in a range of white-collar occupations, and a not insignificant number in the emerging middle class, 'whose earning capacity is not only greater than that of the vast majority of working women, but also the vast majority of working men' (ibid.: 39–40).

Moreover, although domestic tasks might superficially look the same everywhere, detailed comparative research on domestic economies has revealed significant differences in what is classified as 'domestic' and 'housework' across various cultures, the meanings and values attached to these activities, and who is responsible for performing them (Helliwell, 1993: 267–269; Karim, 1995a: 28–29). In certain cultures, no distinction is drawn between the 'domestic' and the 'public' in local language and thought, and the concept of 'work' is broadly and flexibly conceived as applying to activities within and beyond the home (Helliwell, 1993: 268, 278; P. van Esterik, 1995: 253–255; Illo, 1995: 209–210, 222). In addition, rather than a fixed division of labour, in certain circumstances both men and women perform various tasks around the home, and men cook, mind children and shop (Helliwell, 1993: 271). Van Esterik argues that in Southeast Asia women's work is 'neither invisible nor undervalued'; indeed, in village Malaysia '[m]en acknowledge that women are superior to them in their ability to use money judiciously' (Strange, 1980: 129). Furthermore, in Thailand, the concept of work, whether in or outside the home, refers to accomplishing something in social settings; it is to be enjoyed and can apply to a secular job or task as well as to ceremonies and festivals (P. van Esterik, 1995: 253–255). Women's housework and other activities are also essential in peripheral capitalist economies not just to reproduce and maintain the labour force, but also to compensate for the low wages that are often paid to labourers, which are usually insufficient for survival.

Social transformations have also influenced the nature and the extent of involvement of women in domestic activities. For socially mobile and well-to-do households, women may be released from many home-based tasks by the hiring of domestic help or bringing in an older member of the family (usually a woman) to provide assistance; this is especially so in the case of women engaged in full-time work outside the home. Unmarried women too have been drawn increasingly into full-time, paid employment and they are often exempted from domestic work because they are making sufficient contribution in their wages to the support of the household.

Status and Male–Female Equality

Are Southeast Asian Women Equal?

There is a long-standing debate about the relative equality and high status of women in Southeast Asia in comparison with women in East and South Asia. More specifically, male–female roles are claimed to be complementary, 'with a lack of exaggerated opposition between male and female ideologies' (P. van Esterik, 1995: 248; Errington, 1990: 1–3; Atkinson and Errington, 1990). The issues are complex, and as Penny van Esterik suggests, there is no agreed definition of status or the means to measure it, and no agreement on the criteria for evaluating differential positions between men and women, socially, culturally, economically, and politically (1996: 9; Stoler, 1977). Separate spheres of life can be subject to different evaluations, not comparable one with another nor arranged on a unified scale of superior–inferior. In other words, we might have to address issues of difference and complementarity rather than relative status. Although male–female relations may appear formally as hierarchical, 'in day-to-day activity, through the family and social life, men and women go about doing things which are important to them without asserting who are or which sets of activities are more valuable or indispensable' (Karim, 1995a: 26; 1992).

However, in determining levels of status, what is usually considered is the relative worth or value placed on women and what they do (including the place that they are assigned in religious and political ideologies and practices), the kinds and extent of control they are able to exercise over their lives and those of others (in other words, whether or not they are independent or relatively independent, and what kinds and degrees of power they might exercise and authority they possess), and the rights which they have in law and over such things as property.

Gender and Power

The possession and exercise of power is especially problematic; there are different arenas within which power operates (Stivens, 1998b: 90). For Southeast Asia the situation is even more complex because there is considerable flexibility in the interpretation of prestige and power and their different dimensions, women often exercise power informally, and such devices as 'silence', 'withdrawal' and 'non-cooperation' are also 'strategies of power' (Karim, 1995a: 12, 18–19). These informal processes may also be related to spiritual power and potency. In other words, the exercise of power, forcefully, explicitly and actively, in the sense that we would identify 'powerfulness' in the West, 'reveals a lack of spiritual power and effective potency, and consequently diminished prestige' (Errington, 1990: 5; Roces, 1998: 294). Karim emphasizes that '[d]eferment, patience, spirituality, invisibility, transference and other social intangibles are intrinsic features of a Southeast Asian social system, and become sources of resistance and strength' (1995a: 19–20). When women wish to express their disagreement with or resist the 'authoritarian man' they often deploy strategies of 'hostile harmony' or 'friendly animosity' (ibid.: 18).

It has also been argued that women's influence on public affairs in Indonesia, for example, has been considerable, though this has been 'indirect' or 'concealed' rather than through the exercise of power in formally elective or appointive offices (Willner, 1980: 187). In Malaysia too, although there have been studies of women's formal involvement in political life, specifically in their participation in official political organizations, their influence 'continues to be exercised primarily at the household level, with women seeking to affect the direction and substance of local and party politics by influencing their husbands' (Manderson, 1991: 48; 1980). Women's general public profile in Malaysia has increased during the past two decades, especially in the female auxiliary organizations of political parties such as Wanita UMNO, but 'it remains generally true that politics is still men's business' (ibid.: 58). There are also many examples of politically ambitious women running for public office, but again 'their relegation to structural subordinate sections within party organisations restricts their access to and exercise of power' (ibid.).

A similar situation prevails in the Philippines. Although there are prominent examples of women occupying public offices, even at the presidential level, Roces suggests that they usually operate 'behind the scenes predominantly within the confines of the kinship group' (1998: 292). Men who seek political office depend on the mobilization and support of networks of kin dominated and mediated by women (ibid.: 296). Men occupy most of the formal political and bureaucratic offices, but Roces demonstrates the influence of women on their husbands, and the close relationship between women and civic and charity work (ibid.: 302). Interestingly most of the small number of women who achieved high political office had a background in social welfare and community work, and were embedded in a moral universe which countered the corruption and violence of male-dominated politics (ibid.: 302–304).

Women and the Economy

The proposition about women's relatively high status in Southeast Asia in comparison with women elsewhere in Asia is based primarily on their role in economic production (specifically in small-scale marketing, agriculture, and household management), the predominance of bilateral kinship, matrilocal post-marital residence practices, and the discretion given to women in the inheritance of property, particularly land (Karim, 1995a: 39–40; P. van Esterik, 1995: 249; Errington, 1990: 3–4). 'All of these practices combine to give women psychological importance and decision-making authority over real wealth – including cash, land, and other valuable property' (Chipp and Green, 1980a: 105). Nevertheless, the dimensions of politics, wider decision-making, and the religio-ideological definitions of men and women appear to provide a rather different picture (P. van Esterik, 1995: 248; 1996: 2). We are presented with an ambivalent, shifting frame of reference when attempting to determine issues of gender equality and inequality, but despite the considerable discretion and influence which women exercise and the availability of fields of action which provide them with a significant level of autonomy, there are areas of life in which they are subordinated, exploited and marginalized. Ong and Peletz capture this complexity when they state, with reference to the edited book by Atkinson and Errington (1990), that the volume 'does in fact emphasize that many insular Southeast Asian cultures stress gender equality and complementarity, but it also illustrates, albeit perhaps less emphatically, that the prerogatives, spiritual power or "potency", and overall prestige enjoyed by men ... typically exceed those of women' (1995a: 7–8).

Women and Religion

With regard to Muslim and Buddhist ideology, the position of women is seen to be, with certain qualifications, inferior. Hantrakul claims that in Buddhist Thailand women 'are viewed as second-class citizens' and suffer from 'religious inferiority' because, at least doctrinally, women are assigned 'a lower moral status' and are 'denied admission to the Buddhist Order' (1988: 115; see also Keyes, 1977: 161, 1984; P. van Esterik, 1996: 3; Kirsch, 1985, 1996). Their role as wives and mothers is emphasized. Hantrakul argues further that, in cultural terms, 'Thai society still very much flatters men for their promiscuity and polygamy' (1988: 117). Yet all of this is highly equivocal, ideological, and generalized; as van Esterik says, 'Buddhist doctrine appears to be sufficiently paradoxical to allow for alternative representation' (1996: 3). We must address the complex relationships between doctrine and practice and between what texts and certain Buddhist scholars say and what happens in practice. The complexity of male–female relations in Buddhism is revealed in John van Esterik's paper on female meditation teachers in Bangkok in that women do not see themselves straightforwardly as women but as practitioners who are gradually transcending gender distinctions (J. van Esterik, 1996: 33–41). Furthermore, women play crucial roles in important rituals and merit-making (Karim, 1995a: 21).

We can see similar complexities in Muslim societies. In the contradictory processes of transforming young Muslim Malay women into 'factory daughters', they are increasingly subject to the constraints of Muslim morality and the control of men, given that as 'free' wage labourers they are depicted as sexually promiscuous and liable to bring dishonour on men (Ong, 1995: 165–167, 171–172; Ackerman, 1984). The resurgence or revival of a patriarchal, disciplined and pure form of Islam in Southeast Asia, based on the direct engagement with holy texts, a deepening of the understanding of the faith, and a stricter observation of its tenets, which in Malaysia (and Indonesia) is primarily an urban-based, middle-class phenomenon, has reinforced images of women as wives and mothers and not as daughters and sisters. In particular, it has worked to restrict female sexuality, emphasizing women's roles in procreation and child-rearing (Ong, 1995; Blackwood, 1995: 126; Stivens, 1998b: 103–111; Woodcroft-Lee, 1983: 174–175, 177). The close relationship between the emerging middle class and its roots in the rural areas is significant in understanding the increasing emphasis on strengthening Malay identity through recourse to an Islamic morality critical of the decadence, inequality and secularism spawned by a rampant capitalism (Ong, 1995: 174–175).

From the 1970s, the Islamic Youth Movement of Malaysia, its membership comprising young Malays who had benefited from the government's promotion of Malay education and employment in the modern sector of the economy, gave expression to these re-discovered Muslim values (ibid.). Educated young women, in particular, responded to these changes and the contradictions and alternatives generated by modernity by covering their heads and bodies, some in Middle Eastern or Arabic style, and a 'hyperethnicized feminine identity (the veiled, modest, maternal Malay-Muslim woman)' began to take precedence over other kinds of female identity (Maznah, 2001: 115). Ong argues that this cultural reaction 'registered the multiple effects of cultural disorientation, protest, and intimidation, enfolding them in a moral community'; it served to demarcate the Malays from other ethnic groups and became a symbol of class mobility and 'depeasantization' (1995: 180,181).

Women and State-Led Development

Much has been written about the local responses to the Malaysian government's policies of modernization, particularly in restructuring Malay society and culture to bring Malays into the mainstream of capitalist development. Young Malay men and women were increasingly drawn into urban society and, through its welfare and family planning policies, the state increasingly intervened in family and village life. In this context Islamic resurgence and the criticisms levelled at Western-derived modernity have been interpreted, by some authors as an anti-government protest on the part of the 'politically marginalized' (Nagata, 1984; Chandra Muzaffar, 1986). Ong claims that this has served, among other things, 'to neglect the gender dimension of these responses in the negotiation and reformulation of Malay identity, and the ideological struggles over the concepts of family, gender and race' (1995: 161). She proposes instead that state intervention, especially with the influx of large numbers of young unmarried women into the industrial sector, challenged men's rights over female sexuality and their authority over their daughters. She says 'For the first time in Malay history, a large number of nubile women had the money and social freedom to experiment with a newly awakened sense of self' (ibid.: 172). These contestations were further complicated by the emergence of a middle class and the debates about female sexuality and women's role in the Malay family (Stivens, 1998b: 116–117).

However, the promotion of Asian values from the 1980s brought certain Islamic values together with the 'communal spirit' which was presumed to infuse Japanese-owned (and other East Asian-owned) enterprises operating in Malaysia. Japanese companies were seen as organized on the basis of a family system, but this was a patriarchal one, which served to reinforce the emphasis on male authority in the household (Ong, 1995: 172–173). The Malaysian government also appropriated various Islamic revivalist themes, including the importance of the home-oriented woman and her contribution to the strengthening of the Malay community and the nation.

As in Malaysia, women in Indonesia, and their 'private lives', have been brought decisively into the national arena. Similarly, this has served, in a strongly nationalist and development-oriented Indonesian state ideology, to present a particular view of women's contribution to processes of modernization, which locates them in a 'traditional' context of marginality and subordination (Sullivan, 1983: 169). These ideologies are forged in the context of capitalist development in developing societies in that women are represented in particular ways and encouraged to meet the perceived needs of national development, unity and security (Blackwood, 1995: 125–126; Stivens, 1998a: 7,17). They have also been heavily influenced by Western-derived, 'economistic' development theories, which assigned those activities in the home to the 'private' and non-economic sphere. This perspective is seen very clearly in the images of womanhood constructed by Suharto's New Order. Indonesia's post-1965 ideology was in marked contrast to that of Sukarno's regime, which, at least in its rhetoric, expressed support for female equality and the full participation of women in national life; reference was also made to their contribution to the anti-Dutch nationalist struggle (Douglas, 1980: 154–155, 159–164,165–166).

Suharto's government, or rather a senior male political elite, regulated personal and family relations in Muslim communities; it issued the Marriage Act of 1974 which affirmed men as household heads, producers and protectors, and women as nurturers and national reproducers; and it encouraged the more general separation of the roles of men and women so that women could direct their energies to supporting families and producing and socializing future generations, 'as wives, housekeepers, mothers, child-rearers, and ultimately as "citizens"'(Robinson, 2001: 27–29; see also Hull, 1976: 21–22; Rochayah Machali, 2001: 1–16; Sullivan, 1991: 62–68; Branson and Miller, 1988: 12–13). The domestic role of women was built firmly into the country's second Five-Year Development Plan from 1974 (Sullivan, 1983: 149).

In the programme for the promotion of family welfare, which the Indonesian government launched from 1973, married women were seen as crucial to the success of this initiative, and to achieve the aims of the programme they were organized into non-political women's movements such as Dharma Wanita (Suryakusuma, 1996). However, in national development they were seen 'not as fully fledged, responsible citizens, but as the dependent assistants of males' (Sullivan, 1991: 70; Sunindyo, 1996). Women as the key agents of the family were assigned the role of supporters to their husbands, household caretakers, producers of future generations, and socialization agents (Sullivan, 1983: 148–149). They had a central role in Indonesia's family planning programme, responsible for the 'spiritual, moral, mental, and physical welfare of their families and for producing good future citizens' (ibid.). National development, bolstered by Islamic discourse, was seen as a male arena of political and economic activity. The women's social movement, organized to deliver the family welfare programme, tended also to reinforce state ideology in that it was dominated by wealthier, educated women, whose husbands were usually state employees; many were themselves employed by the state, whilst others stayed at home, but could afford to engage domestic help to relieve them of the burdens of housework (ibid.: 163).

Despite these national representations of gender, many observers have revealed different images and practices, particularly at the local level, and as counters to New Order ideology. Blackwood, in exploring customary practices among the matrilineal Minangkabau, demonstrates that 'women continue to wield significant power within the village', although some of them, especially well-to-do women might pay lip-service to the state ideology of female domesticity (1995: 150–151). Senior women exercise considerable control over their households and property, although there are various ways in which they might present gender relations, given the multiple, contradictory discourses on gender available. In spite of Muslim law in Indonesia generally favouring men over women in inheritance, in many parts of the country, including Minangkabau, it is local customary inheritance laws which have precedence or act to modify religious law. In this regard, women are given equal rights, or in some cases are favoured over men in inheritance (Willner, 1980: 184–185).

Indonesian women are also increasingly evident in a range of 'public' activities. Not only are they involved in the market sector as factory workers and street sellers, but there are increasing numbers employed in middle class, white collar occupations. The state ideology also began to shift from the late 1980s, in part to accommodate these changes, and the role of women as wives and mothers decreased whilst their role as 'workers' outside the home became more prominent. Men are also brought into the domestic frame, having a shared responsibility with women for child-care and socialization (Sen, 1998: 41–46). Representations of women in the media also reflected this increasing emphasis on 'new wealthy working women' as 'advertisers, architects, femocrats and high income consumers of goods and services' (ibid.: 57).

Overall women are seen as (and are increasingly) active agents and negotiators in these processes of change. But, in their responses to state ideologies of modernity and national unity, they are also deployed as symbols of change (Ong, 1995: 187). They are negotiating their own positions in relation to ethnic, class and national interests, and in the case of middle class women, they are playing a crucial role in the reproduction of that class and in shaping its future (PuruShotam, 1998b: 158–162).

Factory Women

The forces of change and capitalist development are uneven and contradictory and impact on women in different ways at different times in different places. We therefore see a complex picture of women drawn into the capitalist economy and experiencing both opportunities and constraints: some women secure benefits and succeed; others suffer and lose out; and there are those who both gain in some areas and lose in others.

With the development of the new international division of labour and the promotion of Export Oriented Industrialization strategies in the low wage economies of Southeast Asia, women became a much sought-after labour resource (Bell, 1988: 68–69; Fatimah, 1983; Heyzer, 1986; Rigg, 1997: 211–236; Yun, 1984). Prior to this, manufacturing industry was primarily import substitution-oriented, capital intensive, employing mainly male workers (Lie and Lund, 1994: 38). The export processing or free trade zones established in such countries as Malaysia and the Philippines to attract multinational manufacturers, in the early stages mainly from the USA and Japan, became the major sites for the incorporation of young, unmarried, unskilled or semi-skilled, and non-unionized women into the modern sector (Lim, 1978; Ong, 1987, 1988, 1990; Pineda-Ofreneo, 1988). Assembly plants using labour-intensive methods, in such fields as electronics, computers, textiles, toy manufacture and food-processing were established to take advantage of the ample supplies of low-cost labour, much of it female. Indeed, '[m]anagers argue that electronics assembly work is suitable for women, who like routine manual work, and have been socialised to work obediently for others' (P. van Esterik, 1995: 251; see also O'Brien, 1983: 203). Young Malay girls working in the factories of multinational companies are seen as biologically conditioned for this work; they are 'patient', have 'nimble fingers', 'fine eyesight', and 'the passivity to withstand low-skill, unstimulating work' (Ong, 1990: 396; O'Brien, 1983: 203).

The involvement of young women in export production is substantial. In the Philippines, for example, in the 1980s, about 60 per cent of workers were women and in garments a not unsurprising 90 per cent (Pineda-Ofreneo, 1988: 20, 24). There is evidence in the electronics sector of women in the Philippines and elsewhere working long hours for low pay, with a demanding quota system, in a controlled and monitored environment, in conditions which did not meet reasonable health and safety requirements (ibid.: 20, 24; Wolf, 1993: 135). In the garments industry women are 'generally the ones relegated to monotonous, tiresome work requiring finger dexterity' (Pineda-Ofreneo, 1988: 24). Overall female labour costs less than that of men; this is a crucial factor in the decisions of certain kinds of manufacturing enterprise. What follows from this is that employers will usually secure the services of higher qualified and educated women at lower costs. They acquire the female skills of endurance, patience, obedience, respect for authority and punctuality.

Wolf notes in her study of female factory workers in Central Java that production workers tend to be young, single women, often from poor, landless families at later stages in the life-cycle when there are fewer dependents (1993: 137; 1990, 1992). Interestingly, she points out that usually the very poorest households could not afford to release labour to factories, and the displacement of female labour in agriculture and cottage industries was not made good directly by factory employment because those employed were usually 'unmarried daughters', whilst those who were unemployed or underemployed were usually 'older sisters and mothers' (Wolf, 1992: 180–188). The very low female wage rates and the differentials between men and women were justified on the basis of 'conceptions of gender relations in Java, particularly a daughter's dependence upon her father' (Wolf, 1993: 145). Female wages, sometimes at least 50 per cent below male rates, were rationalized as pocket money and a useful surplus for households because young women were considered as primarily provided for by their families, and particularly male household heads. Wolf argues that factory-based gender relations under the New Order were part of a complex of relations in which the state, in partnership with industrial capitalism, served to exploit, control and discipline young, female rural workers (1996: 142, 148–159). Similar patterns of gendered factory labour can also be seen in Vietnam's recent experience of industrialization (Nghiem, 2004).

These manufacturing operations were usually organized on the basis of joint ventures, subcontracting with local capitalists, or establishing branches and subsidiaries. Depending on the production process, modes of organization differed. For example, subcontracting of garment manufacture could take the form of large-scale, factory-based production, producing for high-volume customers in the West. In some of the higher-quality textile production for export there is also evidence of a preference for larger factories where monitoring is more feasible. Nevertheless, larger production units also encouraged the greater representation and coordination of labour and the need for employers to deal with organized labour (Hutchinson, 1992: 479–482). However, production is usually organized on a multi-level basis with a system of outworking or domestic production at the local level so that only a small core of staff is required in the main plant and overheads are kept to a minimum. Thus, we find in the Philippines 'Manila-based supplier firms subcontracting to provincial manufacturers or agents, who further farm out the jobs all the way down to the rural households' (Pineda-Ofreneo, 1988: 23). In this regard, women (and children) perform such tasks as finishing and assembling garments, footwear, and even electrical goods in their own homes on an individual basis (Heyzer, 1986: 44–45).

Nevertheless, the patterns of employment generated by the new international division of labour and the transnational relocation of production were not the only processes absorbing female labour. The internationalization of capital has taken different forms. Lie's and Lund's study in the late-1980s reveals there were also smaller companies established, some serving a local market, and not necessarily in search of cheap labour but seeking 'access to local raw materials and local markets, as well as utilization of discarded technology' (1994: 5, 149). In their study, six Norwegian-owned companies, which were not major international players, were investigated with labour forces ranging from 25 to 776, manufacturing fishing tackle, rubber boots, cane furniture, paint, and wheelbarrows and trolleys; some were oriented to export, others to the local market using local materials; some employed mainly male labour, whilst others employed a mix of male and female labour. However, there was a relatively clearly defined gender division of labour in the mixed plants; men usually worked with large, heavy machinery and women were involved in assembly work ('the least mechanized parts of production'), mainly based on manual, repetitive, unskilled or low skill operations, with a tendency to work individually, and with wages 'dependent on individual performance by production incentives and merit systems' (ibid.: 47, 150). We should, however, query what we define as unskilled or semi-skilled and recognize 'the special qualifications women possess' (ibid.: 150).

In their detailed case study of the Norwegian company making fishing tackle in Johor, Lie and Lund found that the majority of the 190 workers were young, unmarried Malay women, performing low-skill tasks. The company produced for export, using cheap female labour. The women were overseen by female managers rather than male, and their parents, who were concerned about the moral environment and the safety of factory work, were satisfied because their daughters still lived at home, close to their place of employment, travelled daily to work, were supervised by women, permitted to wear traditional Malay dress, and worked in a largely young, female Malay environment in which most employees were friends and relatives. The young employees saw themselves as 'daughters' at work, and their employment as temporary with few prospects; most of them intended to marry and leave their employment anyway (ibid.: 65–69). The company viewed them as 'girls', and the main criteria of recruitment were gender and age rather than qualifications and experience.

The wages were low and insufficient to support an independent existence. The remuneration was viewed as a useful supplement to the household economy; their parents saw their daughters as gainfully employed, providing something for the household budget instead of staying at home undertaking domestic chores and looking after younger siblings. Thus, overall these young women continued to be integrated into the domestic and village economy, and were part of a strategy to pool both internal and external resources to meet the household needs of the generally less wealthy; the industrial workers were drawn from the surrounding farms and Federal Land Development Authority settlement schemes (ibid.: 70). In line with the integration of the local household economy with the nearby factory, the female employees spent very little on themselves, instead surrendering the major part of their earnings to their parents (ibid.: 115, 119). The study revealed that in the late 1980s many in the rural economy were struggling to make ends meet and the contributions of working children both within and outside the local economy were needed and diversification of income sources imperative (ibid.: 93–95). Lie and

Lund indicate that this diversification in rural Johor was the product of 'economic recession, underemployment in agriculture and a surplus population' (ibid.: 99).

Ironically the very company that Lie and Lund chose to demonstrate the virtues of a small, non-transnational operation breaking the pattern of multinational activity turns out to be something different a few years later. Indeed, it conforms to the patterns of multinational companies reported elsewhere. Subsequently it was established in Singapore to secure a foothold in the Southeast Asian market; it farmed out its labour-intensive operations to Malaysia, based on low-cost female labour; then it moved these operations to the Philippines when labour became much more expensive in Malaysia (ibid.: 150). Revealingly Lie and Lund observe that these changes and interconnections demonstrate 'the footloose character of the industrialization process now taking place in Southeast Asia' (ibid.: 151). What it demonstrates is the difficulty of drawing general conclusions from a limited case study. We would need to explore the involvement of women in the multinational sector to be able to say something about the future trajectories of Malay women in modernizing Malaysia. But what Lie and Lund suggest is that the process of industrialization is constraining, at least in the small factory that they investigate, but also just possibly liberating.

Returning to the complexities of the multinational sector, however, systems were established in which the differentiation of workers at different levels of the production process could be used by employers to play one set of workers off against another. Outworkers, for example, are by definition, atomized or individualized production units, working without the benefit of cooperation and sharing information with others, and without knowledge of the more general economic environment within which they work. They are, therefore, in a relatively weak position, usually on low wages and piece-rates, without security of employment and access to any social or other employment benefits. This is in the context of the shedding of labour in agriculture with the advent of technological innovation and other changes in the rural sector (Heyzer, 1986: 37–50).

Ong's study of the processes of change involved in the movement of young Malay women from the village to factory work ably illustrates the contradictory processes affecting their lives; young women find some elements of their lives liberating and others constraining and controlling (1987, 1988, 1990, 1995; see also Heyzer, 1986: 100–103; Karim, 1992; O'Brien, 1988). Overall Ong is concerned with the effects on women of capitalist forms of discipline in industrial work situations, the loosening of relations in the village in which women are subordinate, and the imposition of new relations of superiority and inferiority between men and women in the factory. The question which she addresses is 'Why are Malay women workers periodically seized by spirit possession on the shopfloor of modern factories?' (1987: xiii). In attempting to address it, Ong examines the links between material relations, power and cultural attitudes and practices. She is especially concerned with the cultural construction of gender and the contradictory images of sexuality generated in the transition from village life to factory organization (1995: 171–172).

Her study, conducted in the late 1970s, focused on communities in Kuala Langat, a district of coastal Selangor. Since 1972, three Japanese multinational micro-component assembly factories had been established there. They employed about 2,000 workers, mostly young women from the surrounding villages. Ong remarks that the scenes of young factory women 'uniformly clad ... looking rather like schoolgirls' are now very common in the free trade zones of Malaysia (1987: 179). The movement from the supervision of the village to certain social and economic freedoms on the one hand and new controls in the factory on the other produced conflicting images of gender, and tensions arising from the changing roles of women.

Ong traces the changes in Malay peasant society resulting from the increasing integration of farmers into the market economy. Gradually rural dwellers moved from a mainly subsistence economy to one concentrated on the production of commodities. The village economy had declined in importance for many people, with population increase, land fragmentation, concentration of land in fewer hands, and land shortage and landlessness. Ong found that, among poorer households in particular, there was a growing dependence on wage-work outside the village, especially undertaken by young unmarried women who commuted daily to work. This reliance on paid work led to differentiation in domestic relations. When the village economy was focused on agriculture, young women were home-centred, assisting senior women in domestic activities, child-rearing and farming. Women also usually married at a young age. Closely interrelated with the social and residential fixity of women was a host of cultural ideas and practices which constrained and controlled women. Men were seen as morally superior and responsible for protecting the virtue of their womenfolk; indeed, 'all village men were responsible for the moral status of all village women' (Ong, 1995: 165, 166). Young women were encouraged to be modest and shy and not to roam too far from the safety of the home. They behaved and dressed with decorum. The maintenance of female virtue was inextricably linked with male honour. Ong states that '[y]oung women are believed to be particularly weak in spiritual essence (*lemah semangat*), a condition which makes women susceptible to irrational and disruptive behaviour' (1987: 88). These cultural constructions of gender and concepts of female vulnerability and unpredictability served to justify the close supervision of young girls by fathers, brothers and other male relatives (1990: 387, 388–392). Married women were also under the protection and moral authority of their husbands, who, in turn were expected to provide for their wives in all respects. Women were therefore socialized into roles which were characterized as subordinate, submissive, passive, obedient and home-centred.

Ong argues that changing economic relations have begun to affect these cultural constructions of gender. In village and domestic life, female employment in factories has meant that male power and influence over women have been to some extent undermined. Female labour has become increasingly important in providing supplementary income for rural households. According to Ong, young women are therefore able to challenge male power at home. Their income-earning capacities give them some leverage over fathers and brothers; they now have some independence to form relations with members of the opposite sex. Similar observations have been made by Wolf with regard to the increase in personal freedoms and material benefits of young Javanese industrial labourers and some 'factory daughters' decided to take up paid employment in the face of parental opposition (1992: 180–188). Yet they find one kind of freedom only to subject themselves to another kind of control. They are increasingly tied to the disciplines engendered in the work situation; capitalism demands a fixed working day, shift-work, monotonous productive activities, a fragmented work process, and supervision by men (Heyzer, 1986: 104–105, 108–110). Ong says:

> Placed under continued male supervision, the meaning of work is reduced to repetitive time-motion manipulations, and factory operators have little sense of the entire production process and how the microcomponents they assemble are fitted into the larger scheme of manufactured things and social relationships. (1987: 112)

What are the cultural expressions of these changing relationships? Ong shows that young women have begun to restructure marital strategies, viewing marriage in terms of the logic of the market-place. It becomes a transaction governed by the images of commodities and market exchange. Women have room for manoeuvre in deciding their preferred partners, marriage ceremony and post-marital residence. Nevertheless, women's working roles are expressed and legitimized in a range of cultural images designed to control them further. Employed women are seen as pleasure-seekers, increasingly oriented to money and Western ways. Therefore they must be supervised carefully by men. Peletz puts it more strongly when he refers to the 'denigration of such women', who are 'among the most exploited members of the Malaysian workforce'; it is, therefore, the 'victims' who are blamed for threatening the Malay moral and social order (1995b: 111). These constraints have evoked responses from women in their attempts to construct and reconstruct images of themselves against those promoted by men. For example, many women have positively embraced Islamic values and emphasized the importance of Malay Muslim culture as against Western consumer culture, and the values of hard work, virtue and purity expressed in Islam. This has helped many of them adjust to the pressures of their contradictory status between home and factory. In responding to accusations of moral looseness and social freedom, many women have sought to resist these cultural constructions by emphasizing their self-discipline and purity within Islam.

Ong argues that these cultural images do not constitute an emerging class consciousness. Rather they are part of contradictions or tensions between men and women, and are concerned with cultural constructions of gender inequality. They are attempts by women to assert themselves in relation to the controls placed upon them. In other words, women are not engaged in a struggle against class inequalities, but rather in reconstituting an image of themselves as moral, worthy and dignified human beings in dehumanizing work situations. Their changing status and position are expressed in terms of moral values which serve to resist the cultural images constructed by men, images designed to control and undermine what is perceived to be emerging female autonomy.

Other consequences of female control and the changes in their circumstances are 'spirit possession' and 'mass hysteria' on the factory floor. In meeting the contradictions produced by the movement between village and factory, young women at work succumb to the displeasure of 'angry spirits', which express ideas of pollution, violation and possession. Spirit possession is also a cultural construction representing a mode of female resistance against factory discipline and male authority. These spirit beliefs express notions of 'social dislocation, draining of their essence, and violation of their humanity' (1987: 220). Aside from this cultural resistance young female workers also adopt other responses to overbearing male management: various forms of dissimulation, foot-dragging, ignoring orders, excusing themselves and spending time in the locker room or prayer room, and surreptitiously damaging machinery and products (ibid.: 203–211); they 'daily engage in covert boundary-setting rituals to limit management control' (1990: 417). This is part of the process of redefining identities and interests and demonstrates that women are actively engaged in this process and not merely passive victims.

Prostitution and Sex Tourism

Another area of female employment and contribution to national development is prostitution. It was estimated conservatively that some half to three-quarters of a million women were working as prostitutes in Thailand in the 1980s (Hantrakul, 1988: 121). A much more pessimistic estimate puts the number at possibly up to three million (Bell, 1991: 66). Their contribution to the service industry and to Thailand's economic growth is presented in a stark and uncompromising fashion by Bell in that women have 'generated the capital needed for industrial development through their employment as prostitutes and, in related service employment, as dancers, waitresses, masseuses, hotel maids, cleaners, and tour guides' (ibid.: 65–66). A major point to establish is that prostitution in such places as the Philippines and Thailand has been exacerbated but not generated by interaction with foreign tourists. There is a substantial and long-established domestic prostitution industry for local customers (ibid.; Hamilton, 1997: 146; Law, 1997).

Above all women are attracted to prostitution by the economic gains; it provides means of employment, especially for rural women who have few skills to deploy in the modern economy and usually a low level of education (Hantrakul, 1988: 120; Cook, 1998: 259). Indeed, a considerable number of studies of prostitution concentrate on the economics of the activity (Heyzer, 1986: 54). A vital role is that prostitution provides resources which can be sent to dependents (parents, siblings and children) in the home community, to repay debts, contribute to Buddhist merit-making, and pay taxes and school fees. Women may eventually return to their home village, set up in small businesses and reintegrate into village life. In some cases, parents have also wittingly or unwittingly sold their daughters into prostitution (P. van Esterik, 1995: 252; Cook, 1998: 251). It is claimed that an overriding motivation in young women entering prostitution appears to be not so much an escape from an oppressive rural society, but rather 'an entrepreneurial move to improve their economic situation', though there are clearly a range of factors at work including the 'limitation of alternative courses of action, lack of opportunity for marriage, unemployment, lack of education, persuasion or coercion by a pimp or other prostitutes, and severe economic pressure' (Heyzer, 1986: 57, 63–66). Furthermore, the positive view of prostitution as an avenue for economic improvement should not lead to the conclusion that all prostitutes view themselves and their work in a positive light, although some do (Cook, 1998: 267–268). Overall, one finds an ambivalent view: they tend to emphasize the economic benefits of prostitution and the independence which it provides, whilst accepting the morally negative aspect of their lives. '[I]n many cases prostitutes conceal how they earn their money' (ibid.: 268). In Thailand, they meet their obligations as dutiful daughters, yet they put at risk their reputation and moral worth (Rigg, 2001: 46–47).

Although there are numerous examples of abuse, coercion and exploitation in the sex trade, some observers have issued warnings about generalizing its impacts and viewing it from a purely Western perspective. Van Esterik, for example, has indicated the 'wide range of conditions for women who work as prostitutes', and that the 'Thai perspective on prostitution as work which is "family-supporting" should be compared to the external media view of sexual oppression and exploitation' (1995: 252). In her study of Philippine prostitution, Law suggests that, while women 'engage in sex for money, many perceive their employment as encompassing a variety of functions, including tour guide, interpreter, girlfriend, and prospective wife' (1997: 241).

In his study in Bangkok in the 1980s, Cohen has demonstrated the differences in opportunities, risks, income and self-perceptions between those prostitutes who worked in brothels and massage parlours and served a mainly local clientele, and the smaller number of 'tourist-oriented' prostitutes, 'the elite of the trade', who worked independently from bars and coffee shops (1993: 157–159). The latter practices Cohen refers to as 'open-ended prostitution' which does not conform to the standard perception of prostitution as the provision of an 'emotionally neutral' sexual service 'with a transient partner for monetary gains' (ibid.: 160; Heyzer, 1986: 57). Although it may start 'as a specific neutral service', an open-ended relationship 'may be extended into a more protracted, diffused and personalised liaison, involving both emotional attachment and economic interest' (Cohen, 1993: 57). Prostitutes range from those who are more or less independent full-time or part-time operators to those who are more dependent and work through intermediaries, club-owners, tour-guides, taxi-drivers and pimps (Heyzer, 1986: 58–59). As Hamilton has observed 'there is a very wide range of activities and conditions which are lumped together as "prostitution" in Thailand, obscuring the significant differences both for sex workers and clients' (1997: 146).

Yet, we must still recognize the extreme health risk which prostitution constitutes in Thailand with the rapid spread of AIDS/HIV, the physical dangers, the incorporation of very young girls and children into the trade, as well as such issues as 'the low esteem in which prostitutes are held in urban Thai society [which] is exacerbated by their mostly rural origins' (Cook, 1998: 253, 255). Thai men 'associate their wives with respectable domestic life and reproductive sex ... and prostitutes with recreational sex' (ibid.: 261). This cultural devaluation of women has also been linked to the lower status of women within Buddhism (ibid.). Cook argues that an important reason for the involvement of educated middle class women in debates about prostitution in Thailand, stressing its roots in rural poverty, the victimization and exploitation of women and parental and patriarchal oppression, is the international popular image of all Thai women as in some way associated with sexually permissive behaviour (ibid.: 256, 270–271, 277–279; Hamilton, 1997: 145–146; Manderson, 1997: 143).

Women, Agriculture, Non-Farm Work and Migration

Despite the relative decline in the contribution of agriculture to the economies of Southeast Asia, it still plays a significant role in the region, and particularly in the less developed countries of Myanmar, Vietnam, Cambodia and Laos, and even in Indonesia, the Philippines and Thailand. Women continue to perform important roles in rural household economies and agriculture, especially when men are away working in towns. They undertake essential tasks in rice-farming, animal husbandry, gardening, gathering materials for the domestic economy, and in child care and other domestic chores. Heyzer says that '[t]he most characteristic feature of rural women is their long and arduous working day' (1986: 12). This is particularly so in poorer households, and 'farming cannot be dealt with in isolation since it is interrelated tightly to all other aspects of life like child care, nutrition, home-budgeting, handicrafts, water and fuel collection' (ibid.: 15).

Nevertheless, the changing relations between men and women are conditioned to some extent by a long-established gender division of labour – in agriculture, other rural-related activities, and small-scale trading and commerce – even though this division is not rigid or absolute (Branson and Miller, 1988: 4–6; O'Brien, 1982, 1983, 1988). There is a temptation to evaluate the changing circumstances of women in negative terms in that in societies in which 'women are already unequal to men, capitalist penetration seems, in most instances, to further undermine their position' (O'Brien, 1988: 41; 1983: 193–201). However, as Penny van Esterik demonstrates the effects tend to be complex and variable. In agriculture, for example, the introduction of high-yielding rice varieties has in some cases provided more employment opportunities for women in weeding, harvesting and post-harvest processing, but, in others where such processes as mechanical threshing and harvesting, operated usually by men, have been introduced, labour demands have been reduced (1995: 250–251; Rigg, 2001: 113; Stoler, 1975; Sullivan, 1983: 156). Indeed, Hart has analysed these changing practices in the Muda Irrigation Scheme in Kedah, northern

Peninsular Malaysia in terms of a gendered struggle between poor female work-ers resisting the introduction of mechanization by rich male landowners whose own wives increasingly confine themselves to domestic affairs (1992; Rigg, 2001: 112–115). Changes in land rights and the registration of communally-owned land have also tended to work in favour of men, who receive land titles rather than women, and can access credit, extension services and other forms of assistance (Heyzer, 1986: 17–33).

One major survival strategy for women has been to diversify their sources of income, such as in small-scale food production and marketing, and for younger women to take up wage work. Women of a certain age range, principally below the age of 25, have become very mobile, so that 'young women now form a major proportion of the rural–urban drift', attracted by the greater demand for cheap labour in the manufacturing and service sectors, and the need to increase the household income where there is a reduction in opportunities in agriculture and on the land (ibid.: 36, 37–38). Another important category comprises older unmar-ried, divorced and widowed women who may also be less tied to the home, as well as single women with children and married women with unemployed or lowly paid husbands who are forced to migrate for work because of their straitened circum-stances (ibid.: 49).

In rural development, the bureaucracies promoting and organizing these en-deavours tend to be dominated by men, and women are assigned roles in develop-ment programmes, based on their association with the domestic sphere, and usually receive training in domestic tasks (ibid.: 25, 27; P. van Esterik, 1995: 249, 252; Boserup, 1970). This approach to training and education began to be institutionalized in the colonial period (O'Brien, 1983: 196). Furthermore, in countries like Malaysia, with a 'conservative Muslim rural populace', the direction of agricultural development programmes fits more appropriately into a situation 'in which senior men represent the household in its external social and economic relations' (Barnard, 1983: 130). Development programmes and training courses for women in the Muda Scheme were heavily directed to domestic matters including cooking, sewing, handicrafts, and social activities, and not instruction in improving knowledge of rice farming, nor basic literacy and numeracy classes (ibid.: 141). The introduction of mechanization also tends to be directed towards men 'who learn to use mechanical equipment while women continue to use traditional means of agricultural production' (Strange, 1980: 147). However, since the 1980s in countries like Malaysia, there has been a gradual shift in emphasis, following the establishment of women's organizations at the lo-cal level (co-operative and credit associations, and local political party branches for women), to the provision of technical training for women using female instructors, though these organizations have tended to be dominated by more well-to-do women from the village elite (Heyzer, 1986: 27–29).

Robinson's study of the introduction of a foreign-owned nickel mining com-pany in Soroako, a rural area of Sulawesi in Indonesia, dependent on agriculture and with limited involvement in the market, illustrates a rather different set of circumstances for women (1983). However, there are particular features of mining as an industry and of the region and local economy of Soroako, which generated difficulties for women (1986, 1998). Previously men and women were partners in agriculture and 'equally important', men generally undertaking the more heavy physical work and women being primarily responsible for such tasks as weeding and harvesting (1983: 113, 118). Women tended to be confined to the village and its environs whilst men were responsible for hunting, gathering and trade. In agriculture women 'had an equal though different participation with men' (ibid.). They also identified their primary task as mothers providing care for their children, although this did not indicate a lowly status because children were 'highly valued' (ibid.: 117–118).

The introduction of mining involved taking over prime wet-rice lands with a dramatic effect on the local agricultural economy. Households could no longer meet all their food needs and had to diversify into other activities, including casual wage work, small-scale trading, the sale of agricultural and other produce, and renting rooms to immigrants working for the company. About a third of the households had their menfolk, mainly young men from 16 to 35 years of age, employed in the company (ibid.: 119). Several other young men were at school. In these circumstances women had to take on work previously done by men in a much changed, marginalized and decreasing agricultural sector, and they had only very limited employment opportunities in the mining company, as secretaries, nurses and teachers; a few also worked as domestic servants in the company town (ibid.: 122). The general attitude of the company management was that the work was inappropriate for women, and Indonesian labour law did not allow women to work in mines. The presence of the company and the expansion of a money economy also led to increasing social differentiation between households; in the case of those households with limited availability of wage work, women were increasingly confined to the domestic sector and a reduced agricultural economy, with the segregation of male and female work (ibid.: 124). Robinson concluded that 'the erosion of the possibilities for women to be independent producers through the decline in the agricultural sector will have the consequence of making them more dependent on men' (ibid.: 125). However, with the opening of Soroako to the outside world, there appeared to be a greater degree of personal freedom for some, particularly younger women to move outside the household, meet strangers, arrange their own marriages, and enjoy more leisure time. As we have seen already in relation to middle class and working women, changing definitions of femininity are increasingly in evidence (1998: 77–83).

Another area of work for mainly rural unemployed or underemployed women is in the domestic service sector 'where women are already skilled as a result of task allocation by the sexual division of labour within the household' (Heyzer, 1986: 46). Paid domestic labour is usually a relatively insecure form of employment, often not tied to specific contracts and subject to the whims of the employer. Usually migrant female labour, either within or across countries, is employed on a full-time, live-in basis, whilst women who live locally are employed part-time (ibid.: 47). Wages are also highly variable, with domestic employees who work for urban-based expatriates usually commanding the highest wages, and new migrants working in local homes receiving the lowest remuneration. Several countries in the region have attempted to regulate the sector and introduce minimum wages, but, by the very nature of the work, regulation is extremely difficult. Nevertheless, countries like the Philippines and Indonesia and to a lesser extent Thailand are heavily dependent economically on revenues from their female labour force working as overseas domestic helpers. Much has been written about the crucial role they play in supporting the economy of the Philippines through remittances; and numbers of overseas workers vary between 7.4 to 9 million, a very significant proportion of them women (Choy, 2003; Hedman, 2006: 192). It has also been calculated that in the first 10 months of 2005 remittances were worth about US$8.8 billion to the Philippine economy (Hedman, 2006: 192).

A considerable amount of research has been undertaken on the working conditions of domestic workers and their responses to these circumstances. As Young says, in his study of Indonesian and Philippine domestic servants in Hong Kong and Taiwan, they are subject to certain national contractual and legal arrangements, even though these are difficult to regulate and enforce; but they are also incorporated into the most intimate arena of social life (2004: 287–303). If they work full-time and live in with the family, they become part of a kin-based, child-rearing unit, as well as an economic and administrative one. In East Asia, despite the changes occasioned by modernization, patriarchal elements still survive in household affairs (ibid.: 301).

A concern for governments and those who employ domestic servants is that the changing nature of local women's work and the demands of working outside the home require the hiring of domestic help. On the other hand, foreign domestic workers bring with them different cultural values and are often involved in the care and rearing of children. Although they are of generally low status and subject to abuse and exploitation, domestic workers have their own perspectives on kinship, gender and work: they can exercise influence within the household; some fight for their rights and benefits; they have their own organizational arrangements for sustaining their identities and their own codes of discipline (Guy, 2004: 501–518). There are also considerable variations in the experiences of domestic workers. In the case of Thai women in Hong Kong, Hewison suggests that, for the sector, they are relatively well paid in comparison with their wages back home; and they are generally respected by their employers (2004: 318–335). On the other hand, they face considerable hardship both in their living and working conditions and being away from home, and overall they have very low status in Hong Kong society (ibid.).

Another area of interest is the way in which cross-national encounters are transforming national identities, or as Healey terms it, 'imaginaries', as well as serving to draw boundaries between, in her case, 'Malaysian' and 'non-Malaysian' (2000: 222). For example, the high levels of labour immigration into Malaysia, comprising mainly single, unskilled and semi-skilled men and (increasingly) women, have given rise to national debates about the nature of Malaysian relations with people who are (in one sense) perceived as 'undesirable aliens', 'unwelcome guests', and increasingly 'feminized aliens' (ibid.: 223–225, 246; Azizah Kassim, 1987: 265–278). Economic migrants usually from the poorer countries of the region – the Philippines, Indonesia, Myanmar – and large numbers of women, in particular, move into the Malaysian domestic service sector and the entertainment industry. The Malaysian national media has expressed ambivalent views about 'alien' migrants, as essential to economic development, but also as sources of social and cultural problems (Healey, 2002: 237–242). The anxieties focus, among other things, on the inculcation in Malaysian children of 'foreign' values, given the importance of the family's role in the socialization of new generations of responsible and loyal citizens, and the closeness of maids to the intimate and private affairs of the family and its children. Foreign maids are also 'portrayed as impoverished, greedy humans because of their foreignness, and sexualized temptresses of Malaysian men. They are held to be responsible for the break up of Malaysian marriages and even the abandonment of Malaysian wives and children' (ibid.: 242).

Usually, the receiving societies construct stereotypes of migrant workers and, in Taiwan, labour brokers tend to categorize economic migrants from different countries in different ways, allocating them to particular areas of employment. For example, Indonesian women are usually placed in domestic service and in the most exploited areas of the market (Loveband, 2004: 337–338). This is not to say that women are passive or lack agency in this situation; there are ample cases of Indonesian domestic workers absconding and taking up illegal work in the black economy (ibid.: 343–345). Female workers do seize opportunities in overseas markets; they play crucial roles in their home economies by providing much needed foreign exchange, and they are a source of small-scale entrepreneurship on their return and important stakeholders in their home economy (Weekley, 2004: 349–363).

Women, Small-Scale Production and Trade

Women have a significant role in home-based manufacture. Some of these activities are long established, as in cloth manufacture and handicrafts, originally for local use, whilst others are newly acquired in the context of industrialization and the putting-out system. There has also been the adoption of new technology in traditional village industries, in such areas as the improvement in handlooms and batik printing (Price, 1983: 97). However, these are complex processes and, in certain cases, the growth of new manufacturing industries has replaced village-based enterprises, given that large-scale production, with economies of scale can undercut small businesses.

In her study of changing batik manufacture in a north coast Central Javanese village, Price indicates that Chinese and Arab cotton merchants began to take over Javanese-owned batik stamp production units on a putting-out basis during the inter-war years. At that time some enterprising local Javanese men also began to sell supplies of cloth, dyes and wax to small-scale entrepreneurs in a cooperative shop arrangement (ibid.: 100–101). In the post-independence period there has been a move, supported by government, to develop large-scale factory production, using high technology weaving processes financed by foreign capital. Smaller, home-based production units have had to specialize in such areas as hand-drawn art and screen-printing to survive.

These changes have resulted overall in women performing the lowest paid and most menial production tasks whilst men have moved into the arrangement of contracts and sales outside the village. Sometimes women will also be engaged in some petty trading of textiles in their home area (ibid.). In stamped batik production, based on more complex and differentiated technology, men have tended to take over the higher skilled, better paid jobs. Similarly in mechanized weaving and factory production, men have increasingly replaced women. However, in home-based industries there has been social differentiation between women, with some taking on the roles of small-scale managers and employers of other female labour (ibid.: 102–103). They have begun to form an elite group within village society, more wealthy, and with political influence through their husbands. Therefore, the consequences for women of technological and social transformations have been mixed. Generally these changes have resulted in women losing 'their pre-eminence in cloth production' (ibid.: 108). The majority have been relegated to village-focused and factory-based labouring tasks. However, a group of women have been relatively successful, attaining higher status as managers and traders 'with very different skills to those of the employees' (ibid.: 109).

Rutten's study of commercialization and socio-economic differentiation in Philippine rural craft industries in Nabas, northern Panay and Malilipot in the Bicol region of southern Luzon demonstrates the importance of women, particularly married women, in these activities, and their crucial role in the village and household economy (1990: 1–4). Handicraft production was taking place in the context of increasing population pressure and inequalities in land ownership, and the commercialization and technological development of cultivation which reduced demand for labour in certain operations (ibid.: 241). Nabas women, primarily involved in rice- and coconut-growing, worked part-time from home in making plaited hats and sleeping mats for the domestic market, using local raw materials. They could not support themselves on the basis of craft production alone. The wholesale trade was controlled by village traders, buyers and larger entrepreneurs, some of whom were well-to-do women (ibid.: 246–247). Bicol women, either from home or in small workshops, made Western-style placemats, shopping bags and other giftware for export, based on a sub-contracting or putting out-system. The producers depended on wages from large-scale, urban-based exporters and smaller-scale suppliers who recruited labour, provided raw materials, paid wages, and assembled the finished products (ibid.). Although some producers were involved in agriculture, they tended to spend more time on craft manufacture, production was organized by entrepreneurs who had invested in looms, sewing machines, and workshops, and there was a higher level of specialization. The wages were higher than in Nabas, but as a result of dependence on export, demand tended to be more unpredictable and insecure. In addition, there was more scope for social mobility, and examples of capital accumulation among some previously poor and landless shop- and home-workers (ibid.: 217). Some households could also earn sufficient from craft production. In Bicol, loom-weavers were men, based at home or in workshops, who produced a coarse fabric, which was then machine-sewn mainly by women into placemats and bags.

Rutten reveals the unequal relations between small-scale producers and workers on the one hand and the group of entrepreneurs and traders on the other. Remuneration was generally very low but these craft industries provided an important source of income and daily subsistence. Women were also found at all levels of these industries, and, although most of them were producers and workers, there were those who had succeeded as entrepreneurs and traders. There was also evidence of some women moving upwards in class terms, accumulating capital and employing others. Generalizations about craft production are therefore difficult to make, given the socio-economic differentiation among women.

Contradictory transformations are also seen in the small-scale trading sector. A characteristic feature of women in Southeast Asia is their significant involvement in market trading (O'Brien, 1983: 202; King and Kim, 2005). As Branson and Miller say of the Balinese market of Pekengede, women are 'very much the dominant presence ... at all levels of trading, the decision-makers as far as capital outlay and the expenditure of profits are concerned, few seeing reference to their husbands as relevant' (1988: 10). However, with the incorporation of smaller markets into more extensive commercial networks focused on urban markets, and in the context of Indonesian government policy which stressed at that time the family-based roles of women and the public roles of men, it was discovered that men were making inroads into certain sectors of this female domain. However, other opportunities have opened up for women, and recent changes in agriculture and a reduction in female employment in rice cultivation, for example, have resulted in a shift of women into urban-based petty trading, the sale of cooked food, fruit and vegetables, and handicrafts. They undertake precisely those activities 'which involve skills developed within the household' (Heyzer, 1986: 43–44). The Indonesian crisis of 1997–98, with fluctuating household incomes, soaring inflation, deterioration in the terms of trade, and increased pressures on agriculture also generated a positive response by women. In the Minahasan area of north Sulawesi, for example, women, especially married women, took on the role of 'socio-economic buffers', adopting 'economizing' roles in household financial management, utilizing reciprocal credit associations and moving more decisively into the petty trading and retailing sector (King and Kim, 2004, 2005).

Conclusion

Three important general issues have emerged from the consideration of the changing circumstances of women in Southeast Asia. First, the impacts on women's lives are extremely variable across the region. In both the rural and urban sectors we find cases of women, depending on such factors as their age, education, and class position, benefiting from modernization; in other cases, exploitation, subordination and marginalization have increased. The effects on women, as in the case of young Muslim factory girls, can be contradictory, both liberating in certain areas of their lives and constraining in others; more generally, for young women in Southeast Asia there are tensions and conflicts between 'modern women' and 'dutiful daughters' (Mills, 1997; Rigg, 2001: 45–46). Women's changing circumstances cannot be straightforwardly captured by either the concept of subordination or that of emancipation (Crane and Nadam, 2004: 171–174; Esra, 2004: 199–216; Lindio-McGovern, 2004: 217–238).

Second, changing gender relations cannot be understood in isolation and are part of transformations in such areas of life as class, status and power relationships. A significant development affecting women's roles and status in Southeast Asia is the emergence of educated, middle-class, well-to-do women employed in the professions and white collar jobs, as well as women working more generally in the urban sector and engaging with the globalized world of consumption, image-making and lifestyles. Third, gender has become a site of debate, contestation and negotiation, and categories such as 'woman', 'family' and 'sexuality' have come to symbolize changing gender relations and notions of femininity and masculinity. In this process, the weight of opinion suggests we should not conceptualize women as 'victims', but as active agents in making their own lives and futures. Even Heyzer, who focuses on the struggles of Southeast Asian women against poverty and adversity, proposes that, although 'forms of work are directed by structural and ideological systems, women are seldom passive agents of these forces' (1986: 50).

In the penultimate chapter, I shall consider urbanization and the transformations and transitions between 'the rural' and 'the urban' which brings together themes and discussions in earlier chapters, distilling some of the major changes Southeast Asians have experienced during the post-independence period.

10

Transformations in Urban Worlds

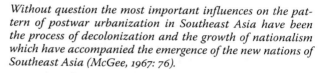

Without question the most important influences on the pattern of postwar urbanization in Southeast Asia have been the process of decolonization and the growth of nationalism which have accompanied the emergence of the new nations of Southeast Asia (McGee, 1967: 76).

[W]hile urban life is embedded in indigenous meanings, urban studies have been embedded in Western meanings, specifically the belief in a single, fixed and knowable underlying reality ... In many modern studies it is the market that makes the city what it is (O'Connor, 1983: 2, 3).

The readiness with which people depart rural areas and migrate to towns and cities exposes fundamental processes of social, economic, and spatial restructuring. It emphatically dispels Arcadian myths about bucolic village life (Forbes, 1996: 24).

Introduction

The major part of this book has been concerned with large-scale transformations in Southeast Asia, and the changing principles of social organization which are an integral part of these wider changes. I have also examined changes generated by government policies to promote national consciousness, resilience and security, and direct and support development and economic growth.

This chapter focuses on an aspect of transformation which has been touched on in other chapters: issues to do with the state, class, ethnicity, gender, patronage, corruption and cultural values tend to be at their most magnified and intense in urban Southeast Asia. Urban space is structured and expressed very explicitly in terms of such organizational principles as class, gender and ethnicity. It has been remarked with reference to the urbanized society of Singapore, that given its physical and socio-political 'compactness', the changes introduced by the government in the context of global processes, have given rise to 'highly interac-

225

tive effects and end results' (Ong et al., 1997a: xvi). Indeed, most, if not all of the major changes in the region have their sources in the capitals and other main cities and towns, and these urban concentrations serve as intermediaries and filters for new ideas, values, institutions, technology, and commodities disseminated through global transport and communication networks. Urban areas are also veritable 'theatres of accumulation' (Armstrong and McGee, 1985).

Cities and towns in Southeast Asia have therefore been conceptualized as 'centres of change' and as catalysts 'intellectually, socially and politically' (Dywer, 1972a: viii). Urban areas and their influence will continue as their boundaries are extended through suburbanization and the creation of satellite towns, as mechanization in agriculture and demographic and economic pressures push labour into urban-based occupations, and as rural people take conscious decisions to migrate in search of work, education and new opportunities. In a global and electronic world, cities and towns above all are centres of information, image and symbol construction and dissemination; major activities located there are in publishing, television and film production, the arts, entertainment, advertising, education, training and government.

From a modest 15 per cent of the total Southeast Asian population living in urban areas in 1950, the proportion has increased to well over 40 per cent today; 50 per cent is anticipated by 2010, with countries like Malaysia and the Philippines having already reached over 60 per cent by 2005 and Indonesia nearly 50 per cent, though we should recognize that there is considerable variation in the definition of urban areas from country to country (McGee, 2002: 21; Owen et al., 2005: 400, 419; United Nations, 2006; Evers, 1978c: 324). The urban conglomerations of Jakarta, Metro Manila, Bangkok and Ho Chi Minh City each had populations of over five million in 2005, with Greater Jakarta estimated at 17 million and the Bangkok Metropolitan area between 6.5 to 9 million (United Nations, 2006). Even Rangoon (Yangon) was above four million, whilst Singapore stands at over four million; the urban sprawl of Kuala Lumpur and the Klang Valley is now approaching three million, Hanoi over two million, and the Cambodian capital of Phnom Penh, in a still predominantly agrarian country, is today over one million (ibid.). We are now in the era of megacities, supercities and urban corridors characterized as zones of movement, especially for young migrant labour (Vickers, 2004: 314–315).

The Historical Context

Pre-Colonial Urban Areas

Recognizably urban areas have been long-established in Southeast Asia and there is a large literature on pre-colonial urban forms, politico-ritual centres and commercial emporia in the 'classical' period (McGee, 1967: 29–41; Geertz, 1980; Kathirithamby-Wells and Villiers, 1990; O'Connor, 1983, 1995; Reid, 1980, 1988, 1993). As we saw in Chapter 1, the rulers of these states adopted Indian politico-religious models of statehood. But what is of crucial importance is that the early urban areas had already emerged from local socio-economic and political transformations; they were then 'indigenous growths, not Indic imports' (O'Connor, 1983: 37).

A basic division made in the study of early urbanization is that between the concentrations of population which arose from the conditions of irrigated rice agriculture in the rice-bowl areas of mainland Southeast Asia and Java, and those which coalesced around trade in the harbour and coastal principalities. The agricultural-, land-based state of the Indianized Khmers of Angkor, focused on a ruling elite and administrative and religious specialists (the 'sacred city'), and the trade-based, coastal state of the Malays of Srivijaya and its successor Malacca, represented by the merchant and trader (the 'market city'), have become the type cases of the pre-colonial state and its associated urban forms (O'Connor, 1983: 61–70; Osborne, 2004: 25–34; McGee, 1967: 30).

Colonial Cities

Nevertheless, it was the arrival of the Europeans, with their commercial interests, and the later impetus of the industrial revolution and the need for raw materials and markets which led to major changes in urbanization. '[A]t the heart of the new towns lay not the monarchy but money [and] the citadel was forced to give way to the market' (Owen, 2005: 256). Early urban centres, like Portuguese/Dutch/British Malacca and Dutch Batavia were European 'transplants' (Grijns and Nas, 2000). The colonial powers also increasingly established centralized colonial bureaucracies and encouraged the migration of coolie labour from China and India. The colonial capitals, as economic and administrative centres, like Rangoon, Singapore, Saigon-Cholon, Manila and Batavia (Jakarta), and even Bangkok under European influence, became firmly oriented to the coast. They looked out to the sea and beyond, and, with the influx of labour from outside the region along with the gradual movement of people from the rural areas, developed relatively segregated, ethnic-based residential enclaves (McGee, 1967: 24–25, 42–75).

This pluralism, in turn, had a rather loose relationship with the social class system, differentiated into a Western upper or ruling class, and a mixed middle and lower class of Asians (migrants and locals). The plural character of the colonial cities and towns and their residential and occupational segregation have commanded considerable attention, and as a very significant urban structural feature have persisted to some extent since independence (Bruner, 1973; Clammer, 1985; Evers and Korff, 2000; Geertz, 1965; Goh, 1998, 2002; Jenkins and King, 2003; Nagata, 1979). Urban centres took on an alien appearance with European colonial landscapes, Chinatowns, and, in the British dependencies, Indian commercial and residential areas (Owen, 2005: 257).

This multi-ethnic environment was interrelated with the distinction between, in very broad terms, a modern, Western-dominated economic sector focused on the central business district and the Asian-dominated trading and craft centres, characterized by smaller-scale businesses (Guinness, 1993: 311–312). The centralization of urban activities in the capital, and the low level of industrialization in colonial dependencies, still heavily dependent on agriculture and resource extraction, meant that there was little basis for widespread urbanization and the establishment of thriving provincial centres. Instead, the capital cities grew much more rapidly than other centres and took on 'primate' characteristics (ibid.: 312; Wertheim, 1964a: 178). They were also more closely tied, as suppliers of raw materials and channels for imported goods, to the West than they were to their rural hinterlands, and were not themselves centres of industrial innovation and growth (McGee, 1967: 18).

Having said this there are exceptions to the colonial roots of cities and to the feature of primacy. Bangkok, though a primate city, was a locally founded, indigenous capital as well as subsequently the centre of the emerging modern state of Siam/Thailand. It therefore performed multiple functions in the modern period: first, as a national and sacred focus for Theravada Buddhism and the monarchy, seen in the royal temple and palace complexes; second, as the national capital and the centre of government and administration from the late eighteenth century, it expressed through its architecture and urban landscapes, which subsequently combined Western and indigenous elements, the identity of a modern Buddhist nation-state; and, finally, it was a major nineteenth-century economic, commercial and financial centre, with its central business district, port and service areas, which became ever closely integrated into the global market-place (Evers and Korff, 2000: 92–95). Bangkok therefore demonstrates continuity with the past, although the city was modernized rapidly from the late nineteenth century.

Furthermore, in Vietnam primacy is not such an obvious feature of its urbanization, given its colonial and immediate post-war history of division between north and south (up to 1975). Hanoi in the north is the centre of government in the cultural heartland of the Vietnamese people, whilst Ho Chi Minh City (Saigon) is the city of commerce in the more aggressively pioneering and free-wheeling south, which was more subject to French influence (Forbes, 1996).

Another major transformation occasioned by colonial capitalism was not simply the restructuring of spatial relationships but also their commoditization, and their 'creolization' or 'hybridization' combining globalized, modernized and indigenous cultural elements (Yeoh, 2001: 103; see also Hannerz, 1992). Western concepts of private property meant that urban land was mapped, registered and controlled, and divided into privately owned segments (Yeoh, 2001: 104–109). It could be leased, rented, mortgaged, sold or transferred. By rendering land as private, either owned by individuals, organizations or the state, those who did not have legal access to urban land and accommodation, and occupied land which was not theirs were therefore deemed 'squatters'. The colonial urban project also extended its influence and power to the furthest corners of the realm, demarcating, and controlling, much more effectively than hitherto, the margins of the state (O'Connor, 1983: 73; Scott, 1976).

Yet despite the inclination to see Southeast Asian cities as 'alien growths' and 'the bastard offspring of colonialism and capitalism', even the centres of colonial control contained and expressed indigenous elements or symbolic complexes of community (networks of family, friends, neighbours and common ethnicity) and hierarchy (O'Connor, 1983: 1, 5, 28–38, 43–50). Thus, such characteristics of colonial urbanism as immigration, pluralism and primacy, 'were not new to indigenous urbanism' because urban areas under colonialism 'merely magnified and ossified these long-standing patterns', and they remained centres of 'wealth, power and prestige' (ibid.: 71; Goh and Yeoh, 2003a: 3–4).

The Post-Independence Legacy

The newly-independent governments of Southeast Asia inherited the urban-based and related infrastructure bequeathed them by the departing colonial powers, and when ISI strategies were introduced, activities were drawn to existing urban centres where housing, transport and communication systems, energy supplies, labour, and supporting financial and other services were available. Primacy and urban concentration also continued to be a significant feature of urbanization (Evers, 1978c: 325–326; Ho, 2002: 1–7). As industrialization proceeded, the major centres developed into 'the employment centres for an industrial workforce increasingly attracted from the rural hinterland' (Guinness, 1993: 312). Pre-independence Chinese and Indian immigration was replaced by internal rural–urban migration and natural population increase. The capital cities were also 'the locale of other lucrative employment, [for] public servants, or providers of services to the public and capitalist sectors' (ibid.).

Young people came to the urban areas looking for new opportunities and adventure, and also to escape parental and other constraints. Nevertheless, in the early years of independence the rapid increase in population was matched neither by employment and industrial growth nor by the provision of adequate services and facilities. Affluence and poverty were sharply juxtaposed; rural migrants found what work they could in the service sector (as hawkers, street vendors, trishaw drivers, shop-workers, prostitutes), and suffered from the lack of essential urban infrastructure. The term 'pseudo-urbanization' was coined (McGee, 1967: 18–20; Evers, 1978c: 326–327; Sukamdi, 1996: 73; Mantra and Keban, 1988); the relationship between 'primacy' and the 'parasitic' character of cities was explored (London, 1980). Furthermore, the labour absorption capacity of the informal sector was a focus of interest, given the problems of employment generation in the formal sector (Forbes, 1996: 43; Armstrong and McGee, 1985: 220–234; Sukamdi, 1996: 72).

Rural–Urban Migration

Much has been written about rural–urban migration in Southeast Asia, and I do not propose to dwell on the issue here. However, a few remarks need to be made in relation to urbanization processes. Early work tended to employ simple push-pull models, identifying those factors which attracted rural migrants to urban areas, and those which forced them from the village (McGee, 1972; Wertheim, 1964a: 169–173). The weight of opinion was that it was economic and demographic pressures in the countryside (lack of employment, low remuneration in agriculture, landlessness and poverty) which forced 'peasant' households to release labour to the towns and cities (McGee, 1972: 109). Rigg refers to processes of de-agrarianization, de-peasantization, counter-urbanization and agro-industrialization so that overall the term 'peasant' (and indeed 'rural') seems a misnomer in a modern context; 'events have consigned the peasantry as a social formation, to history' (2001: 6–7, 10, 16–18, 41).

However, gradually the complexities of the decision-making processes of migrants were recognized, as well as the range of individual circumstances of a mobile population, the combination of reasons and changing motivations which made migration a likely option, and the structural conditions which generated physical relocation (McGee, 1972: 121–122). Changing relationships of production and exchange, uneven development, rural differentiation and changes in the class structure (with the emergence of different land-owning classes and rural wage labourers, as well as tenants and sharecroppers) resulted in changes in the character and the motivations of the labour force and affected the relationships between town and countryside (Scott, 1976, 1985; Kerkvliet, 1977, 1990). Rural households have diversified their modes of livelihood, often combining farm and non-farm, and rural and non-rural activities. Rigg says that research across the Southeast Asian region has shown 'consistently – an increase in the contribution of non-farm incomes to total incomes' (2001: 83). These processes were set in train during the colonial period, with changes in land ownership, agricultural technology and crops, and in levels of commercialization and commoditization.

The influence of education, the media and, more broadly, globalization has resulted in a shift in the aspirations of young people, the desire to find 'clean' employment in the non-agricultural sector, acquire modern consumer goods and lifestyles and achieve social mobility (Rigg, 2001: 42–45, 50–56). It has also been discovered that migration is not a one-off event; migrants often return periodically or, some of them permanently to their home villages after periods of residence in towns; some people commute daily from rural areas, with improvements in transport and infrastructure (ibid.: 139, 141). There was and is constant interaction between the rural and the urban and increasing spatial interpenetration through such processes as suburbanization, the relocation of urban activities, including tourist resorts, retail outlets, and factories to the countryside and extended metropolitan regionalization in such urban agglomerations as Jakarta, Metro Manila and Bangkok. Urban-based industries employ rural workers in a putting-out system; rural craft industries grow in scale and export to urban markets.

Thus, 'the rural may no longer be very distinctive from the urban in terms of economy and society' and it is mistaken to conceive of two very different, homogeneous worlds in some sort of conflict, competition, or opposition (ibid.: 3, 27, 57–61; Wertheim, 1964a: 174–178). This is even more so in situations in which rural migrants become absorbed into 'urban villages' and sustain or re-create something approximating rural life in the towns and cities (Evers, 1978c: 326–327; Provencher,

1971). Vickers has referred to the collapse of urban–rural boundaries in Java, and Nas and Boender (2002) and McGee (2002) have drawn attention to the combined Indonesian concept of 'desakota' (village-town) to reflect the merging and inter-penetration of the urban and the rural. Nas goes further and suggests that 'town and countryside as such do not exist. They are concepts, like village, peasant and state' (1989: 29; see also Kemp, 1989a, 1989b).

Nevertheless, we can make useful rough-and-ready discriminations; there are broadly distinguishable social and cultural patterns and 'moral worlds' between the face-to-face, small-scale nature of the village and the large-scale, more impersonal life of urban populations, although notions of the village as self-sustaining, subsist-ence-oriented, and inward-looking have long been discarded (Rigg, 2001: 29,31; Vickers, 2004: 304–317). Indeed, there have been vigorous debates about the ways in which the colonial powers 'invented', for administrative, economic, historical and symbolic reasons, the concept of the unchanging 'traditional village' (Breman, 1982; Hoadley and Gunnarsson, 1996; Kemp, 1989a, 1989b, 1991; Shamsul, 1989). In contrast, more recent research on the pre-colonial village has revealed a complex, stratified, diverse and dynamic community interacting with surrounding com-munities and the state, and involved in commercial relations (Rigg, 2001: 36–37). There is also considerable structural variation between villages and in their levels of integration with the state and the market.

Concepts and Perspectives

Large–Small, Formal–Informal

There are two broad sociological approaches in the study of urbanization in Southeast Asia: one has tended to adopt a macro-level perspective and the other has deployed a local or micro-level one, although Goh suggests a more differenti-ated and complex analytical field of research, comprising demographic, coloni-alist-historical, culturalist-anthropological, political-economic and structuralist approaches (2001a: 159–162).

The Large-Scale

Macro-sociological approaches have concentrated on the large-scale processes of change within and beyond urban communities. These examine the location, character and interconnections of urban areas in broader political and economic processes and transformations in class, status and power relations (Evers, 1978a, 1978c). Early modernization theorists tended to view the role and function of urban centres in a positive transformative light. Therefore, although urban sites had their problems, they were seen as generators and disseminators of modernity (Dwyer, 1972a, 1974). On the other hand, dependency theorists and radical political economists saw them as 'parasitic' head-links in the global economy extracting surplus value from marginal and dependent populations and generating uneven development (Frank, 1969a, 1969b; Yeoh, 2001: 102–103). McGee says 'they were the centres from which excessive depletion of natural resources and the exploitation of peasants and primary producers were carried on' and the 'imported manufactured goods which were channelled through the great city to the countryside shattered the domestic industry of the rural areas' (1967: 61; see also Armstrong and McGee, 1985).

In his classic study of the Southeast Asian city, McGee raises the issue of urban areas as centres of change, 'with their growing middle class, their aggressive modernism and signs of Westernization', but questions whether these changes are replicated in the wider society and draws attention to the problematical linkages between urban elites and rural dwellers (1967: 27). Korff also focuses on the articulation of global, national and local discourses, and the construction of a 'global society', although globalization affects only parts of a city, and the perspectives on the city of different socio-economic groupings are conflicting and contradictory (1996: 288–289, 294). He relates these urban constituencies to different levels or sectors: professionals, businesspeople and technocrats at the global level and in the trans-national corporate culture; a political elite and middle class elements in the national sphere; and those in the low-class slums and squatter areas situated in the local sector (ibid.: 294–295). Korff interestingly maps social classes, class fractions and strategic groups and the communities and discourses to which they give rise on to particular segments of urban life, locating them on a scale of activity from the local to the international.

The Small-Scale

The other approach at the micro-sociological or anthropological level has examined the characteristics of different communities and economic sectors in urban areas, and their different adaptations to urban ways of life (including studies of the 'formal' and 'informal' sectors; ethnic communities; factory and office workers; small-scale traders and street vendors; shanty town dwellers and squatters; high-rise apartment residents; and upper and middle class suburbia). Major interests here are continuities and changes in identities and socio-cultural patterns (Nagata, 1979; Provencher, 1971). Of course, there are researchers who have combined both micro- and macro-level perspectives (Evers and Korff, 2000; Yeoh, 2001). Askew, for example, has examined the internal structure of Bangkok – its slums, middle class estates, condominiums, sex workers' communities, backpacker areas, and the rural–urban fringe – in a wider socio-economic and political context (2002).

In focusing on the internal structure of urban areas, Clifford Geertz's study of small-scale Muslim merchants in an east Javanese provincial town of the 1950s has been most influential (1963b: 28–29; 1965). He divides the urban economy there into two sectors and distinguishes the risk-spreading, flexible, fluid, face-to-face, highly competitive, ad hoc, labour-intensive 'bazaar' sector from the profit-seeking, impersonal, corporate, specialized, regulated, rational 'firm-centred' sector. This modified version of Boeke's dual-economy concept was translated subsequently by the International Labour Organization into the distinction between the 'informal' and 'formal' (or 'small-scale' and 'large-scale') sectors (Jellinek, 1991: xx; Sethuraman, 1974; Moir and Wirosardjono, 1977). However, Geertz also pointed to other sectors or classes in small town Java; the administrator-bureaucrats (an urban, white-collar middle class) and the low-class, wage-labouring communities (1965: 4). At this time in Indonesia's struggles to achieve economic development, Geertz searched for potential growth points or facilitators in the modernization process, and identified pious Muslim shopkeepers and traders as one such promising agent of change. Although he wanted to understand the ways in which the small-scale sector can increase its scale of operations, his division between two sectors does not capture the fluidity and variations across urban areas, the dynamic transformations in the scale and character of different enterprises, the complex interconnections between the 'informal' and 'formal', and the multiple activities in which a given urban household can be engaged (Roberts, 1978).

As we saw in Chapter 9, the putting-out system in such operations as textile manufacture within the new international division of labour embraces both small- and large-scale production and is not captured by notions of 'informal' and 'formal'. In other words, the small-scale sector, some parts more than others, is sustained by and integrated into capitalist production and the market, although certain activities are also subject to displacement and marginalization as consumer tastes change, urban areas are redeveloped and large-scale production of previously small-scale manufactured commodities becomes feasible and profitable (ibid.: 112–117; Jellinek, 1991). Petty commodity producers also become involved in the consumption of goods generated in the large-scale sector, and those who work outside the informal sector consume goods and services provided by family enterprises, self-employed workers, artisans and casual workers. Moreover, in identifying the seeds of a capitalist spirit in the Muslim ethics of small traders, Geertz failed to take sufficient account of the ways in which the scale and the nature of petty commodity production and trade are constrained and changed by the external political and economic environment (Wertheim, 1964b: 307–311; Kahn, 1980).

These processes of change in Indonesia's informal sector in the context of wider political and economic changes (in global supply and demand, competition, and laws, taxes, regulations, and government support) have been captured in several studies, including Forbes's work on peddlers and trishaw drivers in Ujung Pandang, south Sulawesi (1979, 1981), van Dijk's study of small enterprises in the Central Javanese town of Salatiga (1986), and Jellinek's engagement with an 'urban village' in Jakarta (1991). Jellinek demonstrates that from the 1960s this urban community experienced rising incomes and an increase in general well-being, but by the late 1970s some economic activities were suffering from competition from the large-scale manufacturing and service sector. Some residents, because of a lack of education and skills, were experiencing difficulties in securing employment; changes in urban consumer tastes led to a decline in demand for some informal sector products and services; and government controls and regulations had put pressure on some activities (ibid.: 95–122). Nevertheless, some households adapted better than others, and even prospered. Overall, changes in the scale of operations, produced a continuum of enterprises from the smallest to the largest, with many enterprises combining features of both 'informality' and 'formality', and individual households pursuing a range of income-generating activities.

The investigation of internal urban structures has also focused not on economic and employment sectors and ethnic quarters but on social class formation. Evers has analysed the ways in which earlier forms of urban ethnic segregation have given way to social class differentiation (1978c: 328–331). Ethnicity still shapes some patterns of social interaction where there is ethnic clustering in particular urban areas, but increasingly urban growth and redevelopment, and particularly new residential developments and high-rise living have tended to break down spatial–ethnic divides. Residential areas therefore express and structure class and status relationships so that there is an increasing differentiation into upper-class areas, civil-service and professional quarters, lower-middle-class housing estates and squatter settlements (ibid.: 331).

Finally, the concentration on the local level has embraced 'local histories and particularities' and 'heterogeneous racial, religious and linguistic conditions' (Goh and Yeoh, 2003a: 3–4). Goh and Yeoh draw attention to the contribution of Evers and Korff (2000) in locating the broader processes of change within 'local traditions, ritual structures and the struggles among social groups' (ibid.: 5). Their concerns overlap with earlier studies concerned with the multiple constituencies of urban areas, be they ethnic quarters, squatter settlements or inner-city slums.

Cultures of Hope and Despair

In earlier sociological studies of urban areas, the phenomenon of rural–urban migration and the social problems of the in-migrant, urban unemployment and underemployment, pressures on urban services and housing, the illegal occupation of land in squatter and 'spontaneous' settlements, the characteristics of the informal sector and life in low-class neighbourhoods attracted considerable attention (Korff, 1996; Yeoh, 2001). The long-established, overcrowded Asian residential areas, the slums and shanty towns, especially the Chinatown tenements, were also a focus of study (Kaye, 1960). Rather than notions of a 'culture of poverty' and slums and squatter settlements as centres of despair, deprivation, disease and delinquency, which was a very general view of governments from the 1960s, sociological work saw these areas, inhabited usually by low-paid workers, small traders and street vendors, as pragmatic, creative, flexible and positive adaptations to the vagaries and pressures of urban life and the shortage of decent, affordable public housing (Dwyer, 1972b; Jocano, 1975: 7; Korff, 1996: 306–309). Jocano says of the Manila slum of Looban in the 1970s that it 'has its own social organization, standards of values, expectations, normative behaviour, moral order and system of reward and punishment' (Jocano, 1975: 6; Decaesstecker, 1978: 337). These studies also attempted to counter government policies which were generally hostile to 'the spreading mass of dense, low-cost, unregulated and unserviced housing' (Guinness, 1993: 317; Laquian, 1969).

Instead, these urban 'ways of life' were seen as a means not only to survive, and sometimes progress, but also to support and integrate newly arrived rural migrants through networks of kinship, friendship and shared ethnicity (Wertheim, 1964a: 168–169). Jellinek says of her Jakarta urban kampong that the residents saw their community as 'a place of hope, a stepping stone to a better standard of living' (1991: xix). It also facilitated entry into a more general urban world, partaking of both modernity and indigenous culture, and providing a personal, socially supportive learning ground for adjustments to urban life (Hollnsteiner, 1972: 29–40).

They were, in other words, functioning communities, providing crucial welfare services which governments and urban employers did not provide. Urban residents maintained links with their home villages, often retaining a stake in property, returning home for special occasions, and sending remittances to their families. These networks of reciprocity and support have been the subject of study in many parts of the region, in Jakarta (Bruner, 1973; Jellinek, 1991; Nas, 1986, 1987), Manila (Laquian, 1979; Hollnsteiner, 1972), Kuala Lumpur (Brookfield, Abdul Samad Hadi and Zaharah Mahmud, 1991) and Bangkok (Pasuk, 1982).

As another example, the problem of squatting escalated dramatically in Malaysia following the introduction of the NEP in 1970. This policy resulted in the influx of large numbers of Malays into Kuala Lumpur and the Klang Valley (Yeoh, 2001: 109–120). But with the lack of affordable housing and for financial reasons, 'a significant majority' resorted to 'self-help housing', settling around established Malay 'urban villages' or 'clearing new areas for habitation' (ibid.: 109). They then developed personal networks to support their adaptation to urban ways of life.

Nevertheless, we should not equate these residential areas straightforwardly with the informal sector, because they are socially and economically diverse; there are those who work both in small-scale enterprises, often part-time and casually, as well as full-time in the manufacturing and service sector. There are those who own and operate small businesses, those who advance socially, and those who struggle against adversity (Sukamdi, 1996: 73; Korff, 1996: 299–300). There are communities with a high level of integration and shared cultural values, and those in which there are tensions and conflicts. Some are physically and socially stable, whilst others are fluid with a mobile and transient population (King, 1999: 246–247). Korff draws a distinction between long-established communities with relatively strong social networks, and more recently established ones where social linkages are more transitory (1996: 296–298). Even in cases in which social ties are strong and supportive, it is misleading to see these communities as 'corporate units' because relationships are invariably selective, and usually formed with a sub-set of residents; they also tend to be activated and maintained through women rather than men (ibid.: 299; Sullivan, 1992).

After an earlier period in the 1960s when governments usually pursued policies of eviction and demolition, there was a shift in emphasis and recognition of the positive dimensions of low class urban areas. In some cases, governments provided land titles and services, and made efforts to develop low-cost public housing schemes (Yeoh, 2001: 110; Sternstein, 1972). The granting of a measure of security and the provision of facilities also usually resulted in squatter households refurbishing and extending their houses and improving their neighbourhoods. Where there are large numbers of low-paid residents and deficiencies in urban services, there is little incentive for private developers to clear slum and squatter areas and build affordable accommodation. Instead, the private sector has focused on housing for the better-off middle and upper classes.

Governments have therefore, in some cases, moved residents into low-cost, public housing schemes and demolished and redeveloped their former home areas. Nowhere has this been done on such a large scale and with such speed than in Singapore. At various times Manila, Jakarta and Bangkok have also seen aggressive evictions and demolitions, particularly in the 1960s and 1970s, and local organizations have struggled to resist these policies (Korff, 1996: 308–309). But even in a changed atmosphere of support for squatters, governments, on occasion, have continued to employ forced relocation measures when these communities occupy valuable real estate needed for development and their residences are considered to be an eyesore and have a negative effect on tourism and other foreign exchange-generating activities.

The Malaysian government, for example, introduced a mix of measures from the late 1970s in Kuala Lumpur, comprising the improvement of facilities in squatter areas, reduction in numbers by a phased programme of relocation, and the monitoring and containment of existing areas to prevent uncontrolled expansion (Yeoh, 2001: 110–111).

> To ensure that squatter houses and even small colonies did not materialize overnight in the capital city, [from 1984] an enforcement unit was formed to patrol and keep a close surveillance on the growth of *rumah kilat* ("lightning houses") and to remove any unauthorized repairs and extensions to dwellings'. (ibid.: 111)

Despite this more enlightened approach, Yeoh has drawn attention to the recent intensification of evictions to enhance Kuala Lumpur's image as a 'garden city' and 'a squatter-free city'; squatter areas have been replaced with 'monumentalist architectural structures, mega-shopping complexes, condominiums, the light-rail transit' (ibid.: 115). The modernization of cityscapes, the symbolic function of cities and urban redevelopment are themes to which I shall now turn.

Urban Areas as Centres of Symbols, Control and Contestation

During the colonial period, urban areas, particularly capital cities – with their impressive administrative and religious buildings: the governor's residence, the city or town hall, the cathedral and church, the European club, the statues of former

European pioneers, founders of colonies and of monarchs and administrators – were the symbols of European power and authority. Similarly, in the pre-colonial period, urban centres expressed the position and status of rulers, often in religious monuments, temples and palaces, closely associated with the assumed divinity or semi-divinity of the monarch. Those in power shaped and constructed the urban environment to symbolize and sustain particular political and other hierarchies. As Goh says, 'the cityscape is the place where identity finds concrete expression' (1998: 169). Moreover urban redevelopment and the promotion of modernization through transformations in the built environment are never purely economic processes but involve the 'politics of representation', and a 'rhetoric of culture and identity' (2001a: 159). Goh, for example, proposes that urban areas are a product of larger-scale political and economic processes as well as human agency at the local level involved in struggle and conflicts over the use of space and the symbolisms and identities attached to it and to urban built forms (ibid.: 161–162; Goh and Yeoh, 2003a: 1–11).

Jakarta

In the period of independence the political elites of the newly- independent countries of Southeast Asia felt an even greater need to decorate or embellish their capitals and other urban areas with symbols of nationhood. It involved the achievement of scale in prominent, central locations, and the presentation of a 'clear message', usually embedded in history and myth as well as in national awakening and anti-colonial struggle (McGee, 1967: 76–105; Laquian, 1972: 44–48; Nas, 1992, 1993). Often street names were changed, and new buildings and monuments erected to express and display the new national identity. Perhaps the most significant of the monument-builders was Indonesia's first President, Sukarno. As Leclerc notes, the pre-colonial urban centres of the Indonesian islands were arranged according to cosmological principles and the 'royal or holy city' planned on the basis of 'concentric circles representing the cosmos'. At the powerful and sacred centre were the royal buildings and main temples, later mosques, 'surrounded by the dwellings of the nobility and religious leaders'. Beyond were the artisans' dwellings, and beyond them the foreign traders (1997: 206). However, Sukarno's capital, with its origins in Dutch Batavia, did not have these roots in the traditional polity and religion, and 'Sukarno appears to have been aware of the need to fill a symbolic void' (ibid.). Jakarta was to become the capital city of an independent nation, to commemorate that independence, and 'serve as a lasting symbol of urban, progressive civilization' (ibid.; see also Nas, 1992, 1993).

The obsession with the planning, arrangement and control of space in Sukarno's Jakarta resulted in the construction of broad avenues and monumental architecture, and the use of avenues, esplanades, circuses and pillars, and Italian marble, harking back to the triumphal urban landscapes of ancient Rome and the baroque city. Pillars were surmounted by statues and sculptures commemorating important national events such as the West Irian monument with the prisoner breaking his chains (Leclerc, 1997: 207). The National Monument in Independence Square reflected the 'basic Hindu figure of the world binarity: male *linggam* and female *yoni* ... an abstraction of centrality and origin' (ibid.). Sukarno therefore created a city 'saturated with signs and symbols' to express nationhood and secure Indonesia international recognition as a modern and 'grand' state (Nas, 1992: 175). This preoccupation with the need to symbolize and legitimize the nation-state in its capital city, and focus on themes of freedom, nation-building and moderniza-tion was continued by Suharto's New Order government (ibid.: 175–207).

Kuala Lumpur and Penang

In the case of Kuala Lumpur, and especially from the early 1990s when the Malaysian Prime Minister set his country on the path to fully industrialized status by 2020, the cityscape was transformed. Malaysian modernity was not merely about eco-nomic development; it also involved a range of social, cultural and political objec-tives (Goh, 2001a: 163; 2001b). A national preoccupation or 'fetish' with building 'the tallest, the biggest, the longest and the widest' began to take hold (Goh, 1998: 171–172; 2001a: 164). The Kuala Lumpur Tower, the Petronas Towers and other 'modern icons' began to appear to express and symbolize this anticipated status of modernity. They provided the focal points for a range of other modern devel-opments, multi-level shopping malls, office blocks, luxury apartments and hotels (Goh, 2001a: 163). Goh also detects a correlation between this spate of construction and the celebration of modernity with the flow of foreign capital into the Malaysian property market, following economic liberalization (ibid.: 173–174).

Malaysian national identity has been elaborated further by the extension of Kuala Lumpur from the modernist icons of the 'twin towers' to the new Kuala Lumpur International Airport, conjoined by the Multimedia Super Corridor, and the construction of two new 'high-tech' cities – Cyberjaya and Putrajaya – though Putrajaya also combines a traditional Muslim impulse with a modern, planned administrative space. As Bunnell suggests, Malaysia is developing a dimension of national identity based on 'intelligent citizenship' and 'informationalism', and ulti-mately presenting Malaysia as a globalized nation (2003: 109–133). The problem with these efforts to transform national identity is obvious.

A modern Malaysia has also to be rooted in an identity which cannot only be expressed in towering celebrations of technology, globalization and capital. There is a parallel concern to preserve, and often enhance buildings and urban areas des-ignated as 'heritage'. Heritage can be used to make statements about national iden-tity and status, but it can also be used for tourism and other commercial purposes. It can provide the focus for opposition to the government by minorities whose heritage is under threat, and it gives opportunities for groups within civil society to raise issues, principles and ideas which the state has ignored, neglected or abused (Hitchcock and King, 2003; Nagata, 2001). In the encounter with development, the concept of 'heritage' is then used by diverse interest groups to promote particular agendas because 'new icons of modernity can encroach on neighbourhoods and uproot communities, creating cultural contestations in the urban terrain' (Goh, 2001a: 166).

Penang provides an excellent case of this tension and conflict between the modern and the traditional. Its long history of settlement by immigrants from diverse parts of Asia has resulted in a number of distinct communities with their own architectural styles, religious buildings and ways of life (Nagata, 2001: 188). Furthermore, although until very recently Penang's old colonial centre of George Town had not changed much during the property boom because of the protection afforded by the 1948 Rent Control Act (which was only repealed in January 2000) and the need to retain heritage buildings for tourism, the fringe of the urban core witnessed the rapid expansion of high-rise office, hotel, retail and residential developments from the 1980s. Penang has also experienced rapid economic growth, the expansion of the middle class, and pressures to cater for modern consumer lifestyles (Goh, 1998: 179–180; 2001b; Jenkins and King, 2003). In the mid-1980s, two massive construction projects were completed, the Penang Bridge, and the 65-storey KOMTAR project, the latter located in a long-established, low-rise shophouse area that was demolished to make way for the development (Goh, 1998: 180). Goh demonstrates the ways in which these developments are generated by political decisions to represent and express modernity, the financial interests of the developers and the desire of the increasingly affluent middle class for up-market facilities. But they produce conflicts with the established communities which wish to retain the identity and character of their areas and preserve their cultural heritage (ibid.: 182–193). Goh suggests, therefore, that modernity in Malaysia is 'bounded by contradictory claims, making impossible one homogeneous or coherent meaning of modernity' (2002: 185).

One such set of conflicts focused on the Pulau Tikus area of the city where luxury residences for the wealthy had been built, but poorer, long-established communities in 'urban-village' dwellings still lived there, and developers were anxious to secure further land for development (Goh, 2001a: 168–172). A settlement of Portuguese-Eurasians who were ground tenants of the local landowner, the Roman Catholic Church, were to be evicted as a result of a property development agreement between the Church and an Indonesian–domestic joint-venture company. The local community was represented by the Penang Eurasian Association (PEA). The PEA made claims for compensatory low-cost housing for those to be evicted on the basis of the unique history of the settlement, including the proposal that the first Eurasian school which had been founded there should be preserved as a heritage museum. The Association also played on the Portuguese-Eurasians' close connections with indigenous Malay culture in Malacca, the cradle of Malay civilization (ibid.). Goh suggests that this is an example of the re-working of ethnicity, presenting Eurasians as part of a broader national Malay population in the context of struggles over local urban space and identities (2002: 185–189).

Nevertheless, despite the pressures encroaching on 'old Penang', and the serious threats to the colonial core of the city with the repeal of the Rent Control Act, much of the urban heritage remains. It is also currently the focus of struggles and debates about heritage, identity, urban land use, tourism, and development among a host of political and non-political organizations – local, national and international. Nagata says: 'Whether "heritage" is to be consumed by tourists, lived in by locals, preserved for an elite few, or used to score political points, is still open' (2001: 198).

The situation has been rather different in Singapore where, with few exceptions, the urban heritage has been discarded in a massive programme of social, political and economic engineering.

Singapore

Singapore, as a city-state, provides a fascinating example of both the creation of an urban and national identity, and the transformation of urban society under the strongly centralized government of the People's Action Party (PAP). A major problem that Singapore faced was how to create an identity from a plural society dominated by ethnic Chinese and surrounded by predominantly Muslim Malay-Indonesian neighbours. Singapore's political leaders were constrained in the kind of national identity and symbols they could deploy, following their separation from a Malay-dominated Malaysia (Chan and Evers, 1978). In a country comprising immigrants from other parts of Asia, they could not easily refer back to a primordial, traditional identity. Nor could they project a forward-looking revolutionary socialist-communist ideology (as a 'third China'). They therefore developed an 'ideology of pragmatism', 'development' and 'economic success', or a 'non-ideological national identity', based on universalistic, modern values. Symbolic of these were the modern, high-rise Housing and Development Board (HDB) flats, the planned industrial estates, the 'clean' image which Singapore projected, and its multi-racialism (ibid.: 119–123; Chua, 1995: 1–8;1997a, 1997b). To ensure the 'survival of the nation', the PAP government through its pragmatic, common-sense approach to development and national security was able to justify an increase in state intervention and constraints on personal freedoms, which the electorate was willing to accept in return for increases in material and social well-being and full employment (Chua, 1995: 17–20, 37–38, 44–48, 57–78, 95–99). Tay and Goh draw attention to the departure from Malaysia in 1965 as both a political and a cultural break, and the abandoning of a colonial-Malayan identity, which at least is still expressed in a place like Penang (2003: 14–15). Under the influence of Western-trained 'modernist' architects and planners and political leaders who embraced global capitalism and the imperatives of international tourism Singapore expunged its past and embarked on constructing a tightly planned and integrated cityscape of high-rise glass, steel, aluminium and concrete (ibid.: 16–17).

The government's housing policy has been a central element in its nation-building agenda, in securing legitimacy, restructuring social, family and community life, and in its economic growth strategy since 1960 when the HDB was established (Hill and Lian, 1995; Chua, 1995,1997a, 1997b; Wang, 1987). As Chua says:

... the overwhelming presence of more than half a million completed dwelling units is a constant reminder to the population of the PAP government's achievement ... [they are] symbolically, hence ideologically, a powerful sign of the existing regime's ability to fulfil its promise to improve the living conditions of the entire nation. (1995: 139; 1997b: 1–4, 12–26)

The apartment blocks were modelled on Western 'Garden City Modernist' approaches, and by 1970 about a third of the population had been re-housed in 120,000 new units (Chua, 1991; Tai, 1988). In its early days the government's housing policy was, in part at least, a response to population growth and the need to re-house its citizens as rapidly as possible in low-cost units, comprising one- to three-room flats, from the overcrowded, long-settled, squalid Chinese and Indian slum areas of central Singapore, and the squatter settlements and villages on the semi-urban fringe (Phillips and Yeh, 1987; Wong and Yeh, 1985). Substantial numbers of people in squatter areas were employed in the urban sector, in, for example, the British military bases, trade and services (Tremewan, 1996: 46; Chua, 1995: 81–87). However, a significant proportion of the Malay population lived in the rural areas, engaged in fishing and agriculture. Housing policy was also an important tool in promoting economic growth and expanding employment, given the enormous resources generated in the local construction industry (Tremewan, 1996: 49). The estates furnished the labour supply essential to the government's economic strategy, which from 1965 required a disciplined, relatively cheap workforce to support Export Oriented Industrialization strategies. Industrial estates and residential areas were closely integrated.

However, the political and ideological elements of housing policy should also be emphasized, and the HDB's role as an agent of social control (Tremewan, 1996: 45). During the early years of the consolidation of PAP power, it faced considerable opposition from left-wing Socialist Front and local community and labour organizations which drew much of their support from the old working-class slums and peri-urban squatter settlements. A policy of resettlement or 'forced suburbanisation' and compulsory land acquisition, not without resistance and violence, resulted in the demolition of existing settlements, the re-housing of the population in high-rise estates and new towns, and the break-up of established communities, ethnic groups and social networks (Yeung, 1973: 14–15, 78). The population was relocated in compact, dispersed, publicly-owned and state-controlled apartment blocks; pre-existing extended family structures were also reorganized into nuclear family units (Tremewan, 1996: 46–47, 50–52; Lim, 1989: 183). Community centres, management committees and constituency committees under PAP control were established in the estates to rebuild and restructure community relations in close tandem with the government's objective of instilling a sense of loyalty and commitment to the nation and government. These artificially created community organizations were continued and adjusted through the later 1970s and the

1980s with emphasis on such bodies as residents' committees and town councils, as government strategies for the restructuring of Singapore society were developed and modified in response to changing class structures, electoral and modest civil society pressures, and the requirements of the economy (Tremewan, 1996: 48–49, 66–68; Hill and Lian, 1995: 125). Therefore, housing development was a means to create 'new Singaporeans' and a 'new society', sweeping away traditional communities and values, mobilizing the population in support of the government and working for a modern, multiracial, economically robust and nationally secure Singapore.

From the 1970s the PAP's housing policy continued to be deployed to achieve national objectives. One of these was to transform society on the basis of harmonious multiracialism and break down the ethnic segregation that had characterized residential areas prior to the 1960s. The residential mixing of households from different ethnic groups was planned, and subsequently 'racial quotas' were introduced into housing estates (Chua, 1991: 343, 347, 1995: 140–141; Ooi et al., 1993; Tremewan, 1996: 65–66). Clammer has noted that

> ... the government through its own housing policy is attempting to
> create a sense of community and ethnic integration within its estates
> by grouping dwellings around common facilities such as a market,
> hawkers' centres selling cooked food, a community centre, children's
> playground and other recreational facilities. (1985: 143)

The social research undertaken during the 1960s and 1970s on HDB communities, some of it commissioned by the Board itself, produced mixed results. Overall the population, in a relatively short time, had experienced a massive change in ways of living, from mainly low-rise, privately-owned, vernacular housing to high-rise, publicly-owned, modern dwellings (Tai, 1988). A major focus was on the transition from one lifestyle to another and the processes, problems and adaptations involved. Some early research pointed to the financial and social difficulties which some sections of the population, especially poorer households, experienced when they were forced to move and their land and businesses compulsorily purchased (Buchanan, 1972; Gamer, 1972; Spiro, 1977; Hassan, 1976, 1977). There were reports of people feeling lonely and isolated, particularly the elderly and the disabled, as well as experiences of powerlessness and insecurity. Hassan argued that there had been a loss of community spirit, a decline in neighbourliness, an increase in psychological problems and stress- and anxiety-related illnesses, and an increase in suicide and delinquency (1976: 254; 1977: 199–206; 1983: 161–162; Chen and Tai, 1978). Despite government efforts at building communities and encouraging ethnic integration, there was also evidence that members of different ethnic groups for religious and other reasons were not interacting more frequently (Chua, 1988, 1991: 350; Li, 1989; Ooi et al., 1993: 75–76; Tai, 1988: 268–276).

These were hardly unexpected consequences of relocation, and accord with the more general literature on the social problems of urban and rural resettlement

(King, 1999: 78–112). Clearly there were some general improvements in physical facilities, but these were countered by the loss of community and a sense of belonging (Austin, 1989: 918–919). In addition, from 1968 residents had also been encouraged to purchase their flats from the Board using their savings through the government-administered Central Provident Fund as down-payments and mortgage redemptions, so that they would have a stake in the community and the nation (Chua, 1995: 132–136). This, in turn, gave the government an enormous leverage on owners in that the HDB continued to regulate and administer its accommodation (Tremewan, 1996: 53–58). Ultimately, housing was still under state control in that the owner-occupiers are in effect lease-holders of government property. There are regulations covering the size and family status of households in relation to the accommodation they can buy or rent, and the process of sale, renovation and altering a flat. Moreover, the HDB has the power to evict residents considered to be undesirable, though this option is in practice difficult to implement because of the absence of alternative accommodation (Tai, 1988: 5). The HDB also instituted a policy of restricting flats for rent and directing people into purchase (Purushotam, 1997: 545–546).

Having transformed 'traditional family structures' and focused on the nuclear family unit (with a preferred maximum of two children) in the 1960s and 1970s, the government then introduced measures to encourage married children to live near or with their aged parents and increase their family size. The 'normal' family became the traditional extended family, and the ideal number of children was raised to three or more. Government perceptions of family size and structure shifted with changes in the wider economy and society, but the family remained as one of the basic building blocks of the nation (Chua, 1995: 141–143). The HDB and the government also promoted the family values of love and concern for others, mutual respect, and filial responsibility based on Asian values (King, 1999: 253; Chapter 8). These changes in policy in relation to HDB residence also had consequences for women, particularly in the tensions between their domestic role and their role in the labour market in that the cost of living in a highly urbanized environment puts pressure on them to earn money (PuruShotam, 1997: 545–549).

By 1985, over 80 per cent of Singapore's population, comprising the working class and a good proportion of the middle class, lived in HDB housing. By 1995 the HDB had over 700,000 flats and 55,000 other properties, housing some 86 per cent of the population, and it continued its massive programmes of renovation and urban redevelopment (King, 1999: 252). The general rise in prosperity and aspirations in Singapore, and the increase in the middle class also put pressure on the HDB to improve not only the quality and size of accommodation, but also enhance the quality and facilities of the surrounding environment.

Most certainly in the early history of relocation there was considerable hardship and dislocation, although some research proposed that adaptation to high-rise living had been much more successful and smoothly instituted than Hassan and others had argued (Quah, 1983, 1985). Other research in the 1980s also suggested that the experiences of different categories of those relocated (according to age, gender, occupation, income, ethnicity, length of residence, family structure) have varied considerably (Tai, 1988). Yet clearly there has been a gradual acceptance of high-rise living, given that there is little alternative, and the HDB has continued with a programme of renovation and improvement, and using more variety in design and spatial arrangement (Chua, 1988: 5). There has also been research which suggests that over time, and with the careful planning of services, facilities, thoroughfares and meeting places, a sense of community can develop and has developed in the estates, though it will be more selective and restricted in scope than in former vernacular communities (Chua, 1997b: 441–442). There is also variation in the extent, intensity and character of neighbourly relations depending on whether an individual is more bound to an estate (such as housewives, the elderly and primary-school children) or whether one works or accesses services beyond the estate (as with some working adults, youths and older school-children) (Tai, 1988; Chua, 1995: 124–146). Goh's analysis of the ground floor 'void deck' of apartment complexes also suggests that, whilst they might provide spaces for informal encounters and were intended to promote inter-communal relations, they do not encourage 'more permanent expressions and interventions ... onto the built environment', and instead constitute areas of 'dissonance, awkwardness and contradiction' (Goh, 2003: 56–63).

Undoubtedly the Singapore government has skilfully managed the provision of services and facilities for its citizens. Even Tremewan, who has been very critical of the social control processes instituted by the PAP through its housing policy, recognizes that it 'has supplied a comparatively high material standard of housing' (1996: 72). Public housing serves as a powerful symbolic vehicle in the modernization, economic development and identity of Singapore, and an effective mechanism of social engineering. In its scope and intensity the HDB programme provides a focused social laboratory to explore some of the processes which I have examined in this book: economic change, nation-building, and changes in class, ethnicity, cultural values and identity.

Conclusion

I have ranged over several dimensions of urbanization and touched on certain issues of rural transformation. The interconnections between the urban and the rural and the rapid pace of change in which urban forms expand and embrace previously rural areas suggest that the broad distinction, though still heuristically useful, is becoming more problematical. An indisputable fact is that urbanization will accelerate and increasing numbers of Southeast Asians will reside and work in urban locations, though this does not mean that all urban areas in Southeast Asia will become increasingly alike (McGee, 2002: 8–22). Demographic projections suggest that in 25 years time more than three-quarters of the population of Malaysia and the Philippines, and nearly 70 per cent of Indonesians, will reside in urban areas. Myanmar will have about 50 per cent of its population in urban areas, with Thailand and Vietnam not far behind (United Nations, 2006). Agriculture will continue to decline in importance in national economic terms, and more people will be absorbed in the industrial, commercial and service sectors. Debates about cities as centres of change suggest that the dimension of opportunity and adventure holds sway and continues to provide attractions for rural people. Pressures on housing and urban infrastructure, and for certain urban residents the difficulties in securing employment and even eking out a livelihood still do not dissuade large numbers of people from 'becoming urban'.

One of the important dimensions of urbanization in Southeast Asia has been its role in symbolizing the nation and projecting images and identities of nationhood in a modernizing and globalizing world. In the final chapter, I shall examine, among other things, some recent work in the politics of culture, identity and globalization.

11

Conclusions: Modernity, Globalization and the Future

Recently I have proposed that there is no dominant research style, tradition or perspective in the anthropology of Southeast Asia. Like the region itself, scholarly approaches in studying it are equally diverse (King and Wilder, 2003: 308–319; King, 2001, 2006a, 2006b). The same applies to the related discipline of sociology. There are some anthropologists who have made a strong claim that 'interpretive approaches to culture' and 'comparative studies of culture in context' provide a distinctive regional contribution (Bowen, 1995: 1047; 2000: 11–13). In my view, the comparative study of culture does not indicate a dominant theoretical perspective or regional style either in the anthropology or the sociology of Southeast Asia.

A Sociological Style?

Having said this, there are some prominent readily identifiable sociological approaches. The early post-war scholarly concerns in Southeast Asia were directed by, in McVey's terms, 'the regnant paradigm' of modernization theory (1995: 1–2; King and Wilder, 2003: 313–314). This might lay claim to the status of a dominant sociological style but it was not long enduring, it was heavily criticized by radical traditions of scholarship, and even in the 1950s it competed with other perspectives particularly evident in Europe. Nevertheless, early on modernization theory raised major research issues which needed to be addressed. These included:

- the nature of the responses of local communities and new nation-states to modernization;
- prospects for the development of democratic political systems;
- the role of cultural values in modernization;

- the interaction between modern and traditional values and institutions and the nature of acculturation processes; and

- the mechanisms providing social and political stability in a changing context.

These concerns are seen in both the anthropological and sociological literature. American social science occupied an especially strong position in research on the Philippines, Vietnam, Thailand, and Indonesia. Even in the former British possessions of Malaysia, Singapore and Burma, there was a formidable American scholarly presence. Given that local scholars in these countries were trained primarily in American institutions or by American social scientists in situ, then they too gave expression to the early interest in modernization and nation-building. Commenting on the development of local scholarship, Taufik Abdullah also notes that:

> National integrity and stability were the common overriding concerns. If the 1950s and 1960s were characterized by the search for a proper academic perspective, then in the 1970s one can say it was the ideologically inspired notion of national identity and culture translated into academic enterprises that dominated the agenda of cultural policy.

These concerns continue to occupy an important place in local research agendas (n.d.: 3–4).

There was an unmistakable interest in modernization theory among Singaporean sociologists in the 1960s and 1970s, although this began to change under the influence of Hans-Dieter Evers as Professor of Sociology there in the 1970s, with his background in European sociology and his scepticism of modernization theory. The work of other expatriates like John Clammer and his interest in political economy was also influential, as was the historical-sociological perspective of Syed Hussein Alatas. However, the political and economic environment in newly independent Singapore dictated local research agendas. A major orientation was 'the conception of Singapore society as being in a dynamic equilibrium, needing a constant balancing of the social vectors and requiring strong governing and controlling forces to maintain the social stability' (Ong et al., 1997b: xii).

As we have seen, the focus on processes of modernization and nation-building is located firmly in the work of Clifford Geertz, who spoke to both an anthropology audience interested primarily in local-level communities and their increasing incorporation into a national and global society and economy, and to those who were focusing on broader issues of social change. For this reason I have given Geertz's work ample attention because of the importance of his concept of involution and, however imperfect, his historical analysis of the effects of Dutch colonialism on Indonesian societies, his work on urbanization and social class, and his attempt to identify socio-economic groups capable of promoting the modernization process.

The early, mainly American concerns with processes of modernization, the facilitators and obstacles to economic growth, and the problems of nation-building, were subsequently overtaken by, among others, those who were critical of the American involvement in Indochina and the inadequacy of the modernization approach in explaining transformations in the developing world. Criticisms came from both within American academe and from outside. As in anthropology, an important though very different academic tradition emerged early on in European social science. In anthropology, it was structuralism, and a Marxist variant of this; in sociology, it was a Marxist-influenced underdevelopment-dependency and political-economy approach. French structuralism and structural Marxism also played an important role in the development of European sociology and anthropology from the 1970s. These radical concerns generated an intellectual ferment among some local Southeast Asian scholars (Reynolds and Hong, 1983). A flurry of local contributions began to appear in such radical journals as the *Journal of Contemporary Asia* and the *Bulletin of Concerned Asian Scholars* (e.g. see Cham, 1975; Lim, 1980, 1985).

However, one European tradition which has not been given the attention it deserves and which embraced a more radical sociological perspective was the Dutch sociological-historical school of Wertheim. I also suggest that Evers's venture in Bielefeld elaborates interestingly on several of the themes which Wertheim addressed in the 1950s, 1960s and 1970s. Wertheim's sociology presents a trans-Atlantic contrast: early post-war American scholarship looked to the future through a generally optimistic lens, whilst Dutch scholarship, increasingly critical of the effects of European intervention, looked, in part at least, to the past to analyse the colonial experience and the problems which it posed for those newly-independent countries in achieving modernity. We have also seen critical approaches to the understanding of the effects of colonialism in Indonesia and Burma from two colonial writers, Boeke and Furnivall, one Dutch the other British, in their respective concepts of dualism and pluralism and their view of the divisive, disruptive consequences of the European encounter. Of course, having said this, my distinction between American and European scholarship is far too simple; there were American scholars who adopted a more historical perspective and Europeans who embraced modernization approaches.

Modernity, Post-Modernity and Globalization

An important trend in the recent sociology of Southeast Asia (and in anthropology) has been the concern with 'culture', 'identities', 'discourse' and 'multiple narratives', deploying various strands of post-modernism, post-structuralism, post-colonial studies and cultural, literary and globalization theory (Harvey, 1989; Pels and Salemink, 1999). A noticeable characteristic of these approaches is their adoption of multi- and interdisciplinary perspectives to deconstruct and 'read' cultural narratives. Joel Kahn's work has been particularly important in this regard in his focus on the interrelationships between culture, politics, the state and identity, and the ways in which identities are 'disembedded', 're-embedded' and 're-localized' in regional and international contexts (1995, 1998a, 1998b, 2006; Kahn and Loh,

1992). Kahn refers to 'the culturalization of the political landscape' in Southeast Asia, and explores the formation and transformation of 'cultural identities' rather than focusing on the political economy of change (1998a: 2, 15; Yao, 2001a: 15). He has revealed recently how complex the 'racial' concept of 'Malayness' is, and what it suppresses and promotes (2006: 1–28). The influence of Anderson's concept of 'imagined communities' (1991) and of identities as 'products of discourse' is very apparent in this subsequent work (Kahn, 1998a: 16; Thongchai, 1994). These interests mesh with my concerns in several of the chapters of this book, on social class identities (Chapter 5), ethnicity and national identities (Chapter 6), gender identities (Chapter 9), urban identities and symbolism (Chapter 10), and more generally Asian values and Asian-ness (Chapter 8).

The concepts of 'cultural identities' and 'cultural politics', though I find them problematical, have served as convenient cover terms to embrace the diverse character of identity construction and transformation in Southeast Asia, and the interactions, tensions and conflicts between ethnic groups, men and women, social classes, the state and ethnic constituencies, urban and rural communities, and between national identities and global cultural flows (Kahn, 1998a: 8–9). Aside from Kahn there have been numerous other contributions in this field, notably Maznah and Wong (2001a), Shamsul (2001), Tanabe and Keyes (2002), Wee (2001a, 2001b, 2001c), and Yao (2001a, 2001b), exploring, in different ways, the 'politics of representation', cultural invention and the interrelationships between identities, politics, state action, modernity and globalization. They are also concerned to address the debate about Asian values, the state and authoritarianism; the ways in which, following Hefner (1998), capitalism, as a cultural form, is embedded in particular societies and given cultural meaning; the relationships between the state, either in its 'weak' or 'strong form' and its constituent cultures (or ethnic groups), and the creation of a national culture and identity. As with Kahn's work on Malaysia (2006) there has been some excellent research on national identity in Thailand in this field, and specifically the shifting discourses and different frames of reference (traditional, monarchical, statist, democratic, globalized) relating to Thai identity (Connors, 2003a; Kasian, 2002; Reynolds, 1998, 2002; Thongchai, 1994). Another body of work focusing on the fluidity, invention and transformation of identities comprises the study of cultural and ethnic tourism (Hitchcock, King and Parnwell, 2008a, 2008b).

Rather than the concepts of 'cultural identities' and 'cultural politics' I have continued to prefer the concept of ethnicity in discussing these matters (Chapter 6) and examined other kinds of identity (including class and gender) separately. I have also explored issues to do with the relationships between the state, national identity and minorities elsewhere (King and Wilder, 2003: 193–230). There are, in my view, even greater problems engendered in using the broader concept of 'cultural identities', not least because of its elasticity, ambiguity and range (Maznah and Wong, 2001a: 24–26). Wee, for example, wants to promote our understanding of 'not only how states (from "on top", as it were) may attempt to re-tool local cultures to fit capital's cultural specificities, but also, how (from "the bottom", as it were) local cultures either may resist *or* enable the development process' (2002a: 3). For him the definition of 'culture' is equally broad and vague; it comprises 'value systems and local traditions' (ibid.). I prefer more precise specifications, and I think we can arrive at these if we examine the several dimensions of identity separately and then in interrelationship.

Let me now turn briefly to the issue of globalization. As Reynolds says, globalization is 'not only a historical process bound up with capitalism and telecommunications technology but also a way of looking at the world which sees opportunities as well as perils in the changes taking place' (1998: 141; George, 2004). It entails 'the search for new, authentic selves at the personal, community, and national levels' and, in the case of Thailand, for example, involves, among other things, a discourse about 'Thai-ness' (ibid.: 134, 141; Kasian, 2002). Moreover modernity and the conceptualization of 'being modern' are deeply implicated in global processes and the development of civil society (Chayan, 2003; Mulder, 2004). Mee reminds us that 'to be modern is to be global' (1998: 227), and there is an ongoing interaction between global cultural processes generated primarily in the West and local responses to these (Lee, 2001: 95–116; Kasian, 2001: 153–165). Kasian argues, for example, that, through the interaction with the international media and consumerism, Thai identity has been released from its formerly state-controlled national and ethnic roots; it has become 'a changeable, malleable, reimaginable object of cultural politics in the hands of an increasingly wider range of rival, independent socio-economic and ethno-cultural groups in civil society, especially the Sino-Thai middle class' (2002: 219). As well as in the realm of perceptions, identities, images, and representations – in short, culture – globalization operates in political and economic arenas. We have already seen that more recent contributions to political-economy analyses of Southeast Asia have been addressing the effects of globalization on Southeast Asian communities (Rodan et al., 2006a). Yet it seems to me that there should be greater interaction between those concerned with the cultural dimensions of transformation and development and those more interested in political and economic processes.

Work on globalization in Southeast Asia has become increasingly prominent from the 1990s. Some of the debates, both in academic and popular discourse, on the character, consequences and direction of globalization have become almost obsessive. As we have seen in Chapters 4 and 5 the processes or phenomena have assumed earlier guises in such notions as 'world systems', 'metropolis and satellite', 'centre and periphery' and 'the new international division of labour'; in its original form it was also a concept focused primarily on economic relationships. Globalization in its current form is usually associated with a host of related concepts: localization, decentralization, democratization (and popular participation), privatization, deregulation and the new middle class(es), as well as the now familiar triad – civil society, state and market (Chua, 2005; Khondker, 2001; Chayan, 2003). These ideas are well illustrated in Loh's and Öjendal's comparative book on

Southeast Asian responses to globalization which emerged from a multi-country research programme on democratic discourses and practices in Southeast Asia (2005b).

It is worth dwelling on this edited volume because it captures a considerable amount of work on globalization in Southeast Asia, broadly in political economy rather than in culture, undertaken during the past decade or so. It confirms some of the most recent thinking, concentrating on the particular, the specific, the local in a comparative and historical context, and arguing that there is no simple pattern of capitalist convergence and liberal democratization (see Robison, 2003: 162–171). It echoes earlier analyses of processes of democratization, the fitful emergence of civil society and its uneven character (given the ways in which authoritarian governments can accommodate political pressures, co-opt opposition, open up democratic spaces selectively, in the context of the varying interests and actions of different segments of civil society) (Lee, 2005; Rodan, 1997: 156–178; see Ockey on Thailand, 2004). The overall conclusion offered by Öjendal on the process of democratization in the region is that it is patchy and varied; in a globalizing, post-modern world we now emphasize uncertainty, complexity, 'diversity', 'plurality', 'fragmentation', 'paradoxes', and 'ambiguities'; we examine changes which are not uniform and unidirectional and are increasingly 'culturally flavoured' (2005a: 346; see also Maznah and Wong, 2001a).

We have become familiar with the observation that globalization and capitalist development are not necessarily accompanied by increasing democratization or cultural homogenization, but that rather globalization may strengthen the state and local identities, and generate new or modified responses. Loh's and Öjendal's book confirms this (2005a: 7–9). The main case given here which de-links globalization and democratization is that of Singapore where the PAP government has maintained a strict separation between state, society and economy and a firm grip on political expression, though Chua notes that a degree of cultural liberalization has been permitted (2005: 61–72; Rodan, 2006b: 180–186). In his earlier detailed studies of ideology and democracy in Singapore (1995, 1997a, 1997b), Chua also demonstrates how difficult it is even to employ the terms 'authoritarian' and 'democratic', though we continue to do so for convenience, because whilst we can readily identify anti-democratic policies and practices in Singapore, since 1959 the government has achieved a broad consensus around the ideology of 'economic pragmatism' (1995: viii; Chapters 6, 8 and 10). The population has also become 'more pluralistic in interests based on class, ethnicity and religion', and, although the government, through legislation and ideological construction, has kept ethnic and religious issues in check, the development of a capitalist meritocracy has led to an increase in class divisions and pressures on government to respond to different demands and interests (Chua, 1995: ix). Chua says that the government, despite continuing its close monitoring of its citizens, has 'developed policies and programmes to alleviate grievances which surfaced during each general election' (ibid.: viii, 205–207).

To a significant extent, the Malaysian government has also managed to retain an authoritarian stance, accompanied here by cronyism and political patronage, in the context of economic development, privatization and deregulation, and the growth of a civil society (Khoo, 2005: 83–137; Saliha and Lopez, 2005: 110–137; Derichs, 2006: 168–174). In other recent surveys of Southeast Asia, it is also an obvious fact that Vietnam and Laos continue as one-party Communist-governed states with little sign of opposition and a civil society (Luong, 2006: 148–154; Forbes and Butler, 2006: 175–179; Rodan, 1997: 173). Nevertheless, there has been modest decentralization of decision-making and some room for manoeuvre at the grass-roots level in Vietnam (Jørgensen, 2005: 316–342), and perhaps even more so in the former Communist state of Cambodia (Öjendal, 2005b: 287–315; Weggel, 2005). Myanmar's military leaders too continue the process of asserting firm control of politics, society and the economy, with the purging of former Prime Minister Khin Nyunt's supporters, the stranglehold on political opposition, and the recent actions against ethnic minorities (James, 2006: 162–167).

On the other hand, the grip of the state has been significantly loosened in Thailand (Connors, 2003b, 2005: 259–286; Chayan, 2003). Even with the recent military intervention, the state has opened itself to criticism and there has been a greater pluralization of politics and more scope for participation. In the Philippines, too, there is evidence of a more robust civil society: witness the moves not only to impeach the President in 2005, but also the expression of popular protest or 'people power' in public demonstrations against political leaders (Hedman, 2005, 2006). And, despite the enormous problems of conflict and violence in Indonesia since the crisis of 1997–98 and the fall of Suharto, there has been a significant degree of liberalization (Anwar, 2005: 201–229; Antlöv, 2005: 233–258; Ganesan, 2004: Liddle and Saiful Mujani, 2006). Yet on the other hand after 9/11 and the West's confrontation with international terrorism, its increasing obsession with security, religious fundamentalism and political extremism, and its willingness to use political and military rather than economic means to achieve international objectives, it has been suggested that pro-Western authoritarian regimes in Southeast Asia may well be given a greater degree of support and freedom of manoeuvre (Rodan and Hewison, 2004: 385, 399; Rodan, 2004: 479–499). The trajectories of democracy and authoritarianism are becoming even more difficult to predict.

We do know that, in certain cases and at certain times, the state is (or has been) in retreat, succumbing to supranational organizations and forces and yielding some discretion to sub-national localisms and identities and to various elements of civil society. Yet, the road is a difficult and bumpy one, and not every state has taken it, or at least not travelled far along it, although across the region there is evidence of a more general freeing up. Maznah and Wong capture this tension and contradiction very well in their assessment of Malaysia when they say '[t]here is a clash between the inexorable and inevitable universalization of worldviews instilled within civil society and the manufactured and reconstituted national identity and culture that leaders are determined to promote in order to avoid their own displacement'

(2001a: 39). Overall, Asian modernity is 'always an ambiguous mixture of local needs and global ambitions, national/communal aspirations and a desire for their transcendence' (Yao, 2001b: 15).

Whither Southeast Asian Sociology?

I have already indicated some of the concerns which will exercise those of us interested in sociological issues in Southeast Asia during the next decade or so. Some merely continue what McVey anticipated in the mid-1990s, including interest in the media and modern culture, gender, literature, the arts and performance, and urban and industrial life (1995: 8). Proposals for the future agenda in Singaporean sociology comprise a similar range of topics: class and gender inequality, the arts and political economy, globalization and local responses, and more detailed historical studies (Ong et al., 1997b: xx–xxi, 6, 66, 412). As Kahn has indicated, we shall continue to explore multi- and interdisciplinary approaches in such fields as cultural, media and gender studies. The politics of culture and identity in a globalizing world will loom large in the near future, especially in the fields of class, gender and local–state relationships. Political economy perspectives will also continue to flourish and the significant influence of personal relations in the political and bureaucratic fields in Southeast Asia will mean that issues of corruption and factionalism will not disappear from our agenda. Moreover, despite the measure of relative stability that has been secured within ASEAN, at least when we compare the current regional situation with the four decades up to the 1980s, there are still numerous and widespread cases of conflict, struggle and violence, particularly between ethnic groups and those of different religions and world-views. The subject of ethnic and religious violence will remain at the forefront of sociological and other research agendas in the foreseeable future (Cady and Simon, 2007a; Hefner, 2007; Kusuma and Scott Thompson, 2005a)

I do not see our interest in the middle classes waning either, and their identities, consumption practices, lifestyles and role in civil society promise to be a major focus of concern in the next decade (Hsiao, 2006). This will, in turn, generate a much greater interest than hitherto in youth and the young middle class, an area of work which has been relatively neglected, including sexual behaviour and values, occupations and careers, family life, consumerism, and political and civic values and practices (Manderson and Pranee 2002; Nguyen, 2002, 2003, 2006). An emerging body of work, focusing on urban youth in particular, also interrelates nicely with more general studies of urban culture and consumption (Drummond and Thomas, 2003). The recent post-renovation period in Vietnam has provided an ideal laboratory for exploring the interactions between capitalism, globalization and youth, and the changing identities, values and behaviour of young people (ibid.; Nguyen, 2003). Indeed, the Institute of Sociology in Hanoi and the Population Council in New York have been undertaking major collaborative studies of youth and the family in Vietnam, examining issues to do with reproductive health, premarital sex, abortion and family planning, as well as the problems of adolescence in a time of rapid social change (Long et al., 2000). The (Southern) Institute of Social Sciences in Ho Chi Minh City has also been involved during the past decade or so in 'life history' research with a focus on rural transition, migration, gender, entrepreneurship and poverty (1991).

We shall obviously be exercised by the ways in which Southeast Asians, not just young people, will respond to and interact with processes of globalization and the role of the state in mediating these powerful influences. In this regard I hope that sociological studies will be boldly comparative, seeking to draw out the similarities and differences between people's experiences across Southeast Asia. Unfortunately, we still have a rather unbalanced view of the region, given that large areas have not been accessible to researchers until relatively recently. In most books, including this one, which present themselves as addressing regional issues, there is a concentration on only certain countries. We have been overwhelmingly influenced by studies of only four or five countries in Southeast Asia, and the influence of Singaporean sociology. Other major social science programmes at the National University of Singapore and the Institute of Southeast Asian Studies have been very significant in shaping regional research agendas as well. In a more modest way, the work of the Institute of Malaysian and International Studies and sociologists at Universiti Kebangsaan Malaysia, and the social sciences at Universiti Malaya have also provided some direction in regional sociological studies. On the other hand, more national-based sociological studies have been undertaken by local sociologists at such universities as Chulalongkorn (Social Research Institute and the Institute of Asian Affairs), Thammasat and Chiang Mai in Thailand; the Department of Sociology and the Population Studies Centre, Gadjah Mada University, the Faculty of Social Sciences at the University of Indonesia, and the national research centres at the Indonesian Institute for Sciences (LIPI-LEKNAS/LRKN); and in such institutions as the Institute of Asian Studies and the Department of Sociology at the University of the Philippines (Taufik, nd; Chayan, 2003; Bautista, 1994). With the expansion of the membership of ASEAN during the 1990s, Singapore, in particular, has strengthened its position as a focus for local researchers from across the region and in supporting and disseminating their research. But it is encouraging that we are now beginning to see more sociologically-oriented research emerging or re-emerging on Myanmar, Cambodia, Laos and Vietnam, though Brunei is still very quiet. Nevertheless, we still seem only to be scratching the surface.

A Final Thought

My call for a region-wide vision echoes, though perhaps for different reasons, the efforts of Ong, Tong and Tan, to map out the future of Singaporean sociology. They were clearly concerned about the parochial tendencies in studying a 'unique case', and argued for the need to compare Singapore as an 'anchoring case' with neighbouring countries. They proposed cross-national research on newly-industrializing countries to understand better 'the interconnections between culture, economic development, democracy and class formation' (1997b: xx). I endorse their proposal. But this is where we must return to the problematical character of Southeast Asia as a region. We do indeed need region-wide research. On occasion this will be confined within Southeast Asia, as this present book is, and I hope that the benefits of adopting this broader sociological perspective will be obvious to the reader. In this respect I am only echoing earlier calls for region-wide comparative social, cultural and historical studies (e.g. see Cohen, 1991; Mulder, 1983). We shall not get very far if we focus on one country, case or community.

Comparative work will also need to consider, at the very least, recent social, cultural, economic and political developments in East Asia and the increasing interconnections between China, Japan, Taiwan, Korea and the Southeast Asian countries. I am, of course, close to calling for a general sociology of East and Southeast Asia, though it is not a book that I am capable of writing. What I can promise is a sequel to this book, another comparative sociological volume on Southeast Asia. Reflecting on the arduous process of writing a general text of this kind, and deciding what to address, I acknowledge that I have still left out too much. In recognition of this I have begun to plan my encounter within the next two to three years with the sociological literature on culture and identity (including the examination of religion, the arts, literature, media, consumerism, lifestyle, youth, gender and education). A culturally focused companion volume to this already lengthy introductory book (with its historical and political economy emphases) is urgently required.

Images of Southeast Asia

(All photographs courtesy of Dr Michael Parnwell, Leeds University)

Novice cameraman near Yangon, Myanmar.

Wat Thaalaat, Yasothon Province, northeast Thailand.

Transplanting rice, Yasothon Province, northeast Thailand.

Reflections: Buddhist monks
in Siem Reap, Cambodia;
cyclists in Kunming, China.

Mosque and boat, Padang, Sumatra, Indonesia.

Carrying offerings, Bali, Indonesia.

Offering devotions, Bali, Indonesia.

Akha girls, Chiang Rai, northern Thailand.

Boat women, Hoi-An, Vietnam.

Klong slum, Bangkok.

Democracy monument, Bangkok.

Singapore skyline.

Boat people, Hue.

Tanjung Pagar shophouses, Singapore.

HDB housing, Singapore.

Chinatown, Bangkok.

Chinatown, Singapore.

Slum housing in Smokey Mountain, Manila.

Round the bend: street vendor in Hanoi.

Air pollution, Hanoi.

Stevedore, Padang, Sumatra, Indonesia.

Hanoi street vendors.

Water collectors, Makassar, Sulawesi, Indonesia.

Child ice cream vendor, Bac Ha
market, northern Vietnam

Globalization, Indonesia.

Cool dude, Phnom Penh.

Taxi rank, Bangkok.

References

Abdul Rahman Embong (ed.) (2001a) *Southeast Asian Middle Classes. Prospects for Social Change and Democratisation*. Bangi: Penerbit Universiti Kebangsaan Malaysia, Malaysian and International Studies Series.

—— (2001b) 'Middle Class Politics, Democracy and Civil Society in Malaysia'. In Hsiao (2001), pp. 343–377.

—— (2002) *State-led Modernization and the New Middle Class in Malaysia*. Houndmills and New York: Palgrave.

—— (ed.) (2004) *Globalisation, Culture and Inequalities: In Honour of the Late Ishak Shari*. Bangi: Penerbit Universiti Kebangsaan Malaysia, Malaysian and International Studies Series.

—— (2005) *Development and Well-being: Mankind's Agenda for the Twenty First Century*. Bangi: Penerbit Universiti Kebangsaan Malaysia, Malaysian and International Studies Series.

—— (2006a) 'Malaysian Middle Classes Studies: A New Research Agenda'. In Hsiao (2006), pp. 155–165.

—— (2006b) 'Between Optimism, Contestation and Caution: The Second Generation Middle Classes in Malaysia'. In Hsiao (2006), pp. 133–154.

Abrams, P.H. (1982) *Historical Sociology*. Ithaca: Cornell University Press.

Ackerman, Susan (1984) 'The Impact of Industrialization on the Social Role of Rural Malay Women'. In Hing Ai Yun, Nik Safiah Karim and Rokiah Talib (eds), *Women in Malaysia*. Petaling Jaya: Pelanduk Publications, pp. 40–70.

Adas, Michael (1974) *The Burma Delta: Economic Development and Social Change on an Asian Rice Frontier, 1852–1941*. Madison, WI: University of Wisconsin Press.

Alatas, Syed Farid (2000) 'An Introduction to the Idea of Alternative Discourses'. *Southeast Asian Journal of Social Science*, Special Focus 'Alternative Discourses in the Social Sciences', vol. 28, pp. 1–12.

—— (2002) 'Religion, Values, and Capitalism in Asia'. In Wee (2002c), pp . 107–126.

Alatas, Syed Hussein (1972) *Modernization and Social Change. Studies in Modernization, Religion, Social Change and Development in South-East Asia*. Sydney: Angus and Robertson.

—— (1977) *The Myth of the Lazy Native: A Study of the Image of the Malays, Filipinos, and Javanese from the Sixteenth to the Twentieth Century and Its Functions in the Ideology of Colonial Capitalism*. London: Frank Cass.

—— (2000) 'Intellectual Imperialism: Definition, Traits, and Problems'. *Southeast Asian Journal of Social Science*, Special Focus 'Alternative Discourses in the Social Sciences', vol. 28, pp. 23–45.

Albritton, Robert B. (2006) 'Thailand in 2005. The Struggle for Democratic Consolidation'. *Asian Survey*, vol. 46, pp. 140–147.

Alexander, J. (1987) *Trade, Traders and Trading in Rural Java*. Singapore: Oxford University Press.

Alexander, J. and P. Alexander (1978) 'Sugar, Rice and Irrigation in Colonial Java'. *Ethnohistory*, vol. 25, pp. 207–223.

—— (1979) 'Labour Demands and the "Involution" of Javanese Agriculture'. *Social Analysis*, vol. 3, pp. 22–44.

—— (1982) 'Shared Poverty as Ideology: Agrarian Relationships in Colonial Java'. *Man*, vol. 17, pp. 597–619.

Allen, Douglas (1976) 'Universities and the Vietnam War: A Case Study of a Successful Struggle'. *Bulletin of Concerned Asian Scholars*, vol. 8, pp. 2–16.

—— (1989) 'Antiwar Asian Scholars and the Vietnam/Indochina War'. *Bulletin of Concerned Asian Scholars*, vol. 21, pp. 112–134.

Amara Prasithrathsint (1993) 'The Linguistic Mosaic'. In Evans (1993), pp. 63–88.

Amin, Samir (1974) *Accumulation on a World Scale*. New York: Monthly Review Press, originally published in French in 1970.

—— (1976) *Unequal Development: An Essay on the Social Formation of Peripheral Capitalism*. Sussex: Harvester Press, and New York: Monthly Review Press, originally published in French in 1973.

—— (1990) *Delinking: Toward a Polycentric World*. London and New York: Zed Books.

Anderson, Benedict R. (1977) 'Withdrawal Symptoms: Social and Cultural Aspects of the October 6 Coup'. *Bulletin of Concerned Asian Scholars*, vol. 9, pp. 13–30.

—— (1982) 'Perspective and Method in American Research on Indonesia'. In Anderson and Kahin (1982), pp. 69–83.

—— (1984) 'Politics and Their Study in Southeast Asia'. In Ronald A. Morse (ed.), *Southeast Asian Studies: Options for the Future*. Lanham, New York and London: University Press of America, The Wilson Center, pp. 41–51.

—— (1988) 'Cacique Democracy in the Philippines: Origins and Dreams'. *New Left Review*, vol. 169, pp. 3–31.

—— (1991) *Imagined Communities: Reflections on the Origin and Spread of Nationalism*. London and New York: Verso, revised and expanded edition, originally published in 1983.

—— (1998) *The Spectre of Comparisons. Nationalism, Southeast Asia and the World*. London, New York: Verso.

—— (ed.) (2001) *Violence and the State in Suharto's Indonesia*. Ithaca, New York: Cornell University Press.

Anderson, Benedict R. and Audrey Kahin (eds) (1982) *Interpreting Indonesian Politics: Thirteen Contributions to the Debate*. Ithaca: Cornell University, Southeast Asia Program.

Andrus, J.R. (1948) *Burmese Economic Life*. Palo Alto: Stanford University Press.

Ang, Ien (2001) 'Desperately Guarding Borders: Media Globalization, "Cultural Imperialism", and the Rise of Asia'. In Yao (2001b), pp. 27–45.

Antlöv, Hans (2005) 'Filling the Democratic Deficit: Deliberative Forums and Political Organizing in Indonesia'. In Loh and Öjendal (2005b), pp. 233–258.

Anwar, Dewi Fortuna (2005) 'The Fall of Suharto: Understanding the Politics of the Global'. In Loh and Öjendal (2005b), pp. 201–229.

Appadurai, Arjun (1996) *Modernity at Large: Cultural Dimensions of Globalisation*. Minneapolis and London: University of Minnesota Press.

Apter, David (1965) *The Politics of Modernization*. Chicago: University of Chicago Press.

—— (1987) *Rethinking Development: Modernization, Dependency and Postmodern Politics*. London: Sage Publications.

Arghiros, Daniel (2001) *Democracy, Development and Decentralization in Provincial Thailand*. Richmond: Curzon Press.

Armstrong, W. and T.G. McGee (1985) *Theatres of Accumulation: Studies in Asian and Latin American Urbanisation*. London: Methuen.

Aseniero, George (1996) 'Asia in the World-System'. In Chew and Denemark (1996b), pp. 171–199.

Askew, Marc (2002) *Bangkok: Place, Practice and Representation*. London and New York: Routledge.

Atkinson, Jane Monnig and Shelly Errington (eds) (1990) *Power and Difference in Island Southeast Asia*. Stanford: Stanford University Press.

Aung-Thwin, Michael (1990) *Irrigation in the Heartland of Burma: Foundations of the Pre-colonial Burmese State*. Northern Illinois University: Center for Southeast Asian Studies, Monograph Series on Southeast Asia, Occasional Paper No. 15.

Austin, W. Timothy (1989) 'Crime and Control'. In Kernial Singh Sandhu and Paul Wheatley (eds), *Management of Success: The Moulding of Modern Singapore*. Singapore: Institute of Southeast Asian Studies, pp. 913–927.

Ayal, E.B. (1963) 'Value Systems and Economic Development in Japan and Thailand'. *Journal of Social Issues*, vol. 19, pp. 35–51.

Azizah Kassim (1987) 'The Unwelcome Guests: Indonesian Immigrants and Malaysian Public Responses'. *Southeast Asian Studies*, vol. 25, pp. 265–278.

Baran, Paul (1957) *The Political Economy of Growth*. New York: Monthly Review Press.

Barnard, Rosemary (1983) 'Housewives and Farmers: Malay Women in the Muda Irrigation Scheme'. In Manderson (1983a), pp. 129–145.

Barth, Fredrik (1969) 'Introduction'. In Fredrik Barth (ed.), *Ethnic Groups and Boundaries: The Social Organization of Culture Difference*. Bergen and Oslo: Universitets Forlaget and London: George Allen and Unwin, pp. 9–38.

Batan, Clarence M. (2006) 'Thinking and Doing Sociology in the Philippines: A Personal Reflection'. Dalhousie University: Department of Sociology and Social Anthropology, class presentation.

Bautista, Cynthia (1994) 'Reflections on Philippine Sociology in the 1990s'. *Journal of Philippine Development*, vol. 21, pp. 3–20 (with Comments by Sylvia H. Guerrero, pp. 21–24)

—— (2001a) 'Methodological Notes of the Philippine Middle Class Survey'. In Hsiao (2001), pp. 41–89.

—— (2001b) 'Composition and Origins of the Philippine Middle Classes'. In Hsiao (2001), pp. 91–149.

—— (2006a) 'Beyond the EDSA Revolts: The Middle Classes in Contemporary Philippines Development and Politics'. In Hsiao (2006), pp. 167–186.

—— (2006b) 'Preliminary Thoughts on a Research Agenda for the Philippines Middle Classes'. In Hsiao (2006), pp. 187–196.

Globalization, Indonesia.

Cool dude, Phnom Penh.

Taxi rank, Bangkok.

References

Abdul Rahman Embong (ed.) (2001a) *Southeast Asian Middle Classes. Prospects for Social Change and Democratisation*. Bangi: Penerbit Universiti Kebangsaan Malaysia, Malaysian and International Studies Series.

—— (2001b) 'Middle Class Politics, Democracy and Civil Society in Malaysia'. In Hsiao (2001), pp. 343–377.

—— (2002) *State-led Modernization and the New Middle Class in Malaysia*. Houndmills and New York: Palgrave.

—— (ed.) (2004) *Globalisation, Culture and Inequalities: In Honour of the Late Ishak Shari*. Bangi: Penerbit Universiti Kebangsaan Malaysia, Malaysian and International Studies Series.

—— (2005) *Development and Well-being: Mankind's Agenda for the Twenty First Century*. Bangi: Penerbit Universiti Kebangsaan Malaysia, Malaysian and International Studies Series.

—— (2006a) 'Malaysian Middle Classes Studies: A New Research Agenda'. In Hsiao (2006), pp. 155–165.

—— (2006b) 'Between Optimism, Contestation and Caution: The Second Generation Middle Classes in Malaysia'. In Hsiao (2006), pp. 133–154.

Abrams, P.H. (1982) *Historical Sociology*. Ithaca: Cornell University Press.

Ackerman, Susan (1984) 'The Impact of Industrialization on the Social Role of Rural Malay Women'. In Hing Ai Yun, Nik Safiah Karim and Rokiah Talib (eds), *Women in Malaysia*. Petaling Jaya: Pelanduk Publications, pp. 40–70.

Adas, Michael (1974) *The Burma Delta: Economic Development and Social Change on an Asian Rice Frontier, 1852–1941*. Madison, WI: University of Wisconsin Press.

Alatas, Syed Farid (2000) 'An Introduction to the Idea of Alternative Discourses'. *Southeast Asian Journal of Social Science*, Special Focus 'Alternative Discourses in the Social Sciences', vol. 28, pp. 1–12.

—— (2002) 'Religion, Values, and Capitalism in Asia'. In Wee (2002c), pp . 107–126.

Alatas, Syed Hussein (1972) *Modernization and Social Change. Studies in Modernization, Religion, Social Change and Development in South-East Asia*. Sydney: Angus and Robertson.

—— (1977) *The Myth of the Lazy Native: A Study of the Image of the Malays, Filipinos, and Javanese from the Sixteenth to the Twentieth Century and Its Functions in the Ideology of Colonial Capitalism*. London: Frank Cass.

—— (2000) 'Intellectual Imperialism: Definition, Traits, and Problems'. *Southeast Asian Journal of Social Science*, Special Focus 'Alternative Discourses in the Social Sciences', vol. 28, pp. 23–45.

References

Albritton, Robert B. (2006) 'Thailand in 2005. The Struggle for Democratic Consolidation'. *Asian Survey*, vol. 46, pp. 140–147.

Alexander, J. (1987) *Trade, Traders and Trading in Rural Java*. Singapore: Oxford University Press.

Alexander, J. and P. Alexander (1978) 'Sugar, Rice and Irrigation in Colonial Java'. *Ethnohistory*, vol. 25, pp. 207–223.

—— (1979) 'Labour Demands and the "Involution" of Javanese Agriculture'. *Social Analysis*, vol. 3, pp. 22–44.

—— (1982) 'Shared Poverty as Ideology: Agrarian Relationships in Colonial Java'. *Man*, vol. 17, pp. 597–619.

Allen, Douglas (1976) 'Universities and the Vietnam War: A Case Study of a Successful Struggle'. *Bulletin of Concerned Asian Scholars*, vol. 8, pp. 2–16.

—— (1989) 'Antiwar Asian Scholars and the Vietnam/Indochina War'. *Bulletin of Concerned Asian Scholars*, vol. 21, pp. 112–134.

Amara Prasithrathsint (1993) 'The Linguistic Mosaic'. In Evans (1993), pp. 63–88.

Amin, Samir (1974) *Accumulation on a World Scale*. New York: Monthly Review Press, originally published in French in 1970.

—— (1976) *Unequal Development: An Essay on the Social Formation of Peripheral Capitalism*. Sussex: Harvester Press, and New York: Monthly Review Press, originally published in French in 1973.

—— (1990) *Delinking: Toward a Polycentric World*. London and New York: Zed Books.

Anderson, Benedict R. (1977) 'Withdrawal Symptoms: Social and Cultural Aspects of the October 6 Coup'. *Bulletin of Concerned Asian Scholars*, vol. 9, pp. 13–30.

—— (1982) 'Perspective and Method in American Research on Indonesia'. In Anderson and Kahin (1982), pp. 69–83.

—— (1984) 'Politics and Their Study in Southeast Asia'. In Ronald A. Morse (ed.), *Southeast Asian Studies: Options for the Future*. Lanham, New York and London: University Press of America, The Wilson Center, pp. 41–51.

—— (1988) 'Cacique Democracy in the Philippines: Origins and Dreams'. *New Left Review*, vol. 169, pp. 3–31.

—— (1991) *Imagined Communities: Reflections on the Origin and Spread of Nationalism*. London and New York: Verso, revised and expanded edition, originally published in 1983.

—— (1998) *The Spectre of Comparisons. Nationalism, Southeast Asia and the World*. London, New York: Verso.

—— (ed.) (2001) *Violence and the State in Suharto's Indonesia*. Ithaca, New York: Cornell University Press.

Anderson, Benedict R. and Audrey Kahin (eds) (1982) *Interpreting Indonesian Politics: Thirteen Contributions to the Debate*. Ithaca: Cornell University, Southeast Asia Program.

Andrus, J.R. (1948) *Burmese Economic Life*. Palo Alto: Stanford University Press.

Ang, Ien (2001) 'Desperately Guarding Borders: Media Globalization, "Cultural Imperialism", and the Rise of Asia'. In Yao (2001b), pp. 27–45.

Antlöv, Hans (2005) 'Filling the Democratic Deficit: Deliberative Forums and Political Organizing in Indonesia'. In Loh and Öjendal (2005b), pp. 233–258.

Anwar, Dewi Fortuna (2005) 'The Fall of Suharto: Understanding the Politics of the Global'. In Loh and Öjendal (2005b), pp. 201–229.

Appadurai, Arjun (1996) *Modernity at Large: Cultural Dimensions of Globalisation.* Minneapolis and London: University of Minnesota Press.

Apter, David (1965) *The Politics of Modernization.* Chicago: University of Chicago Press.

—— (1987) *Rethinking Development: Modernization, Dependency and Postmodern Politics.* London: Sage Publications.

Arghiros, Daniel (2001) *Democracy, Development and Decentralization in Provincial Thailand.* Richmond: Curzon Press.

Armstrong, W. and T.G. McGee (1985) *Theatres of Accumulation: Studies in Asian and Latin American Urbanisation.* London: Methuen.

Aseniero, George (1996) 'Asia in the World-System'. In Chew and Denemark (1996b), pp. 171–199.

Askew, Marc (2002) *Bangkok: Place, Practice and Representation.* London and New York: Routledge.

Atkinson, Jane Monnig and Shelly Errington (eds) (1990) *Power and Difference in Island Southeast Asia.* Stanford: Stanford University Press.

Aung-Thwin, Michael (1990) *Irrigation in the Heartland of Burma: Foundations of the Pre-colonial Burmese State.* Northern Illinois University: Center for Southeast Asian Studies, Monograph Series on Southeast Asia, Occasional Paper No. 15.

Austin, W. Timothy (1989) 'Crime and Control'. In Kernial Singh Sandhu and Paul Wheatley (eds), *Management of Success: The Moulding of Modern Singapore.* Singapore: Institute of Southeast Asian Studies, pp. 913–927.

Ayal, E.B. (1963) 'Value Systems and Economic Development in Japan and Thailand'. *Journal of Social Issues,* vol. 19, pp. 35–51.

Azizah Kassim (1987) 'The Unwelcome Guests: Indonesian Immigrants and Malaysian Public Responses'. *Southeast Asian Studies,* vol. 25, pp. 265–278.

Baran, Paul (1957) *The Political Economy of Growth.* New York: Monthly Review Press.

Barnard, Rosemary (1983) 'Housewives and Farmers: Malay Women in the Muda Irrigation Scheme'. In Manderson (1983a), pp. 129–145.

Barth, Fredrik (1969) 'Introduction'. In Fredrik Barth (ed.), *Ethnic Groups and Boundaries: The Social Organization of Culture Difference.* Bergen and Oslo: Universitets Forlaget and London: George Allen and Unwin, pp. 9–38.

Batan, Clarence M. (2006) 'Thinking and Doing Sociology in the Philippines: A Personal Reflection'. Dalhousie University: Department of Sociology and Social Anthropology, class presentation.

Bautista, Cynthia (1994) 'Reflections on Philippine Sociology in the 1990s'. *Journal of Philippine Development,* vol. 21, pp. 3–20 (with Comments by Sylvia H. Guerrero, pp. 21–24)

—— (2001a) 'Methodological Notes of the Philippine Middle Class Survey'. In Hsiao (2001), pp. 41–89.

—— (2001b) 'Composition and Origins of the Philippine Middle Classes'. In Hsiao (2001), pp. 91–149.

—— (2006a) 'Beyond the EDSA Revolts: The Middle Classes in Contemporary Philippines Development and Politics'. In Hsiao (2006), pp. 167–186.

—— (2006b) 'Preliminary Thoughts on a Research Agenda for the Philippines Middle Classes'. In Hsiao (2006), pp. 187–196.

Bauzon-Bautista, Ma. Cynthia Rose (1987) 'The Teaching of Sociology in the Philippines: Some Notes on a Survey of Sociology Teachers'. *Philippine Sociological Review*, vol. 35, pp. 7–10.

Bell, Peter F. (1978) '"Cycles" of Class Struggle in Thailand'. *Journal of Contemporary Asia*, vol. 8, pp. 51–79.

—— (1982) 'Western Conceptions of Thai Society: The Politics of American Scholarship. *Journal of Contemporary Asia*, vol. 12, pp. 61–74.

—— (1991) 'Gender and Economic Development in Thailand'. In Penny and John van Esterik (eds), *Gender and Development in Southeast Asia*. McGill University: Canadian Asian Studies Association, Proceedings of the Twentieth Meetings of the Canadian Council for Southeast Asian Studies, York University, 18–20 October, 1991, pp. 61–82.

Bellah, Robert N. (1957) *Tokugawa Religion: The Values of Pre-industrial Japan*. Glencoe: The Free Press.

—— (1965) 'Epilogue'. In Robert N. Bellah (ed.), *Religion and Progress in Modern Asia*. New York: The Free Press, pp. 168–229.

Bellwood, Peter (1985) *Prehistory of the Indo-Malaysian Archipelago*. Sydney: Academic Press.

—— (1995) 'Austronesian Prehistory in Southeast Asia: Homeland, Expansion and Transformation'. In Peter Bellwood, James J. Fox and Darrell Tryon (eds), *The Austronesians: Historical and Comparative Perspectives*. Canberra: Department of Anthropology, Australian National University, pp. 96–111.

Benda, Harry J. (1962) 'The Structure of Southeast Asian History: Some Preliminary Observations'. *Journal of Southeast Asian History*, vol. 3, pp. 106–138.

—— (1972) *Continuity and Change in Southeast Asia: Collected Journal Articles of Harry J. Benda*. New Haven: Yale University Press, Southeast Asia Studies.

Bendix, Reinhard (1964) *Nation Building and Citizenship*. New York: John Wiley and Sons.

Benjamin, Geoffrey (1975) *The Cultural Logic of Singapore's 'Multiracialism'*. University of Singapore: Department of Sociology, Working Papers No. 44.

Beresford, Melanie (2006) 'Vietnam: The Transition from Central Planning'. In Rodan, Hewison and Robison (2006a), pp. 197–220.

Berger, Mark T. (2001) '(De)constructing the New Order: Capitalism and the Cultural Contours of the Patrimonial State in Indonesia'. In Yao (2001b), pp. 191–212.

—— (2002) 'Battering Down the Chinese Walls: The Antinomies of Anglo-American Liberalism and the History of East Asian Capitalism in the Shadow of the Cold War'. In Wee (2002c), pp. 77–106.

Bernstein, Henry (1979) 'Sociology of Underdevelopment vs Sociology of Development'. In D. Lehmann (ed.), *Development Theory*. London: Frank Cass, pp. 77–106.

Béteille, André (1969a) 'Introduction'. In Béteille (1969b), pp. 9–14.

—— (ed.) (1969b) *Social Inequality. Selected Readings*. Harmondsworth: Penguin Books.

Bit, Seanglim (1991) *A Psychological Perspective of Cambodian Trauma*. El Cerrito: Seanglim Bit.

Blackburn, Susan (1991) 'How Gender Is Neglected in Southeast Asian Politics'. In Stivens (1991b), pp. 25–42.

Blackwood, Evelyn (1995) 'Senior Women, Model Mothers, and Dutiful Wives: Managing Gender Contradictions in a Minangkabau Village'. In Ong and Peletz (1995b), pp. 124–158.

Boeke, J.H. (1910) 'Tropisch-Koloniale Staathuishoudkunde: Het Probleem'. Leiden University: PhD Dissertation.

—— (1953) *Economics and Economic Policy of Dual Societies as Exemplified by Indonesia.* New York: Institute of Pacific Relations.

—— (1980) 'Dualism in Colonial Societies'. In Evers (1980b), pp. 26–37.

Boissevain, Jeremy (1964) 'Factions, Parties and Politics in a Maltese Village'. *American Anthropologist*, vol. 66, pp. 1275–1287.

Booth, Anne (2003) 'The Burma Development Disaster in Comparative Historical Perspective'. *South East Asia Research*, vol. 11, pp. 131–171.

Booth, David (1985) 'Marxism and Development Sociology: Interpreting the Impasse'. *World Development*, vol. 13, pp. 761–787.

—— (1993) 'Development Research: from Impasse to New Agenda'. In Schuurman (1993a), pp. 49–76.

Boserup, Esther (1970) *Women's Role in Agricultural Development.* London: Allen and Unwin.

Bottomore, T.B. (1965) *Classes in Modern Society.* London: George Allen and Unwin Ltd.

Bouvier, Hélène, Huub de Jonge and Glenn Smith (eds) (2006) 'Violence in Southeast Asia'. Special issue, *Asian Journal of Social Science*, 34.

Bowen, John R. (1995) 'The Form Culture Takes: A State-of-the-Field Essay on the Anthropology of Southeast Asia'. *The Journal of Asian Studies*, vol. 54. pp. 1047–1078.

—— (2000) 'The Inseparability of Area and Discipline in Southeast Asian Studies: A View from the United States'. *Moussons. Recherche en sciences humaines sur l'Asie du Sud-Est*, vol. 1, pp. 3–19.

Boyce, James K. (1993) *The Philippines. The Political Economy of Growth and Impoverishment in the Marcos Era.* Honolulu: University of Hawai'i Press.

Braighlinn, G. (1992) *Ideological Innovation under Monarchy. Aspects of Legitimation Activity in Contemporary Brunei.* Amsterdam: VU University Press, Comparative Asian Studies 9.

Branson, Jan and Don Miller (1988) 'The Changing Fortunes of Balinese Market Women'. In Chandler, Sullivan and Branson (1988), pp. 1–15.

Breman, Jan (1982) 'The Village on Java and the Early Colonial State'. *Journal of Peasant Studies*, vol. 9, pp. 189–240.

Brennan, Martin (1985) 'Class, Politics and Race in Modern Malaysia'. In Higgott and Robison (1985a), pp. 93–127.

Brewer, Anthony (1980) *Marxist Theories of Imperialism. A Critical Survey.* London: Routledge and Kegan Paul.

Brookfield, Harold, Abdul Samad Hadi, and Zaharah Mahmud (1991) *The City in the Village – the In-situ Urbanization of Villages: Villagers and their Land around Kuala Lumpur.* Malaysia and Singapore: Oxford University Press.

Brooks, Ann (2003) 'The Politics of Location in Southeast Asia: Intersecting Tensions around Gender, Ethnicity, Class and Religion'. *Asian Journal of Social Science*, vol. 31, pp. 86–106.

Brown, D.E. (1970) *Brunei, The Structure and History of a Bornean Malay Sultanate.* Brunei: The Brunei Museum, Monograph of the Brunei Museum Journal, 2-II.

Brown, David (1988) 'From Peripheral Communities to Ethnic Nations: Separatism in Southeast Asia'. *Pacific Affairs*, vol. 61, pp. 51–77.

—— (1994) *The State and Ethnic Politics in Southeast Asia*. London and New York: Routledge.

Brummelhuis, Han ten and Jeremy H. Kemp (1984) 'Introduction'. In Han ten Brummelhuis and Jeremy H. Kemp (eds), *Strategies and Structures in Thai Society*. Amsterdam: Anthropological-Sociological Centre, pp. 11–18.

Bruner, E.M. (1973) 'The Expression of Ethnicity in Indonesia'. In A. Cohen (ed.), *Urban Ethnicity*. London: Tavistock, pp. 251–280.

Bruun, Ole and Michael Jacobsen (2000a) 'Introduction'. In Jacobsen and Bruun (2000b), pp. 1–20.

—— (eds) (2000b) *Human Rights and Asian Values. Contesting National Identities and Cultural Representations in Asia*. Richmond: Curzon Press, Nordic Institute of Asian Studies, Democracy in Asia series, No. 6.

Buchanan, Iain (1972) *Singapore in Southeast Asia*. London: G. Bell and Sons.

Bugge, Peter (2000) 'The Idea of Europe – Europe and its Others'. In Irene Norlund and Pham Duc Thanh (eds), *Asian Values and Vietnam's Development in Comparative Perspectives*. Hanoi: National Center for Social Sciences and Humanities, pp. 64–83.

Bukharin, Nikolai (1972) *Imperialism and World Economy*. London: Merlin Press, originally published in Russian in 1917.

Bunnell, Tim (2003) 'Malaysia's High-tech Cities and the Construction of Intelligent Citizenship'. In Goh and Yeoh (2003b), pp. 109–133.

Burling, Robbins (1965) *Hill Farms and Padi Fields. Life in Mainland Southeast Asia*. Englewood Cliffs, New Jersey: Prentice-Hall, reprint 1992, Arizona State University, Program for Southeast Asian Studies.

Burma Campaign UK (2006) *Ethnic Minorities*. Info@burmacampaign.org.uk.

Buss, Andreas (1984) 'Max Weber's Heritage and Modern Southeast Asian Thinking on Development'. *Southeast Asian Journal of Social Science*, vol. 12, pp. 1–15.

Cady, Linell E. and Sheldon W. Simon (eds) (2007a) *Religion and Conflict in South and Southeast Asia. Disrupting Violence*. London and New York: Routledge, Center for the Study of Religious Conflict, and National Bureau of Asian Research.

—— (2007b) 'Introduction: Reflections on the Nexus of Religion and Violence'. In Cady and Simon (2007a), pp. 3–20.

Callahan, Mary P. (2003) *Making Enemies: War and State Building in Burma*. Ithaca, New York: Cornell University Press.

Callahan, William A. and Duncan McCargo (1996) 'Vote-buying in Thailand's Northeast'. *Asian Survey*, vol. 36, pp. 376–392.

Carino, Ledevina V. (1980) 'Research under Martial Law: The Tasks and Risks of the Filipino Social Scientist. *Philippine Sociological Review*, vol. 28, pp. 3–18.

Catley, Bob (1976) 'The Development of Underdevelopment in South-East Asia'. *Journal of Contemporary Asia*, vol. 6, pp. 54–74; and in Evers (1980b), pp. 262–276.

Carroll, John J. (1968) *Changing Patterns of Social Structure in the Philippines 1896–1963*. Quezon City: Ateneo de Manila University Press.

Cham, B.N. (1975) 'Class and Communal Conflict in Malaysia'. *Journal of Contemporary Asia*, vol. 5, pp. 446–461.

Chan Heng-Chee and Hans-Dieter Evers (1978) 'National Identity and Nation Building in Singapore'. In Chen and Evers (1978b), pp. 117–129.

Chan Kwok Bun and Ho Kong Chong (eds) (1991) *Explorations in Asian Sociology*. Singapore: Chopmen Publishers, Special Issue, Sociology Working Papers Series No. 100, Department of Sociology, National University of Singapore.

Chandler, Glen, Norma Sullivan and Jan Branson (eds) (1988) *Development and Displacement: Women in Southeast Asia*. Monash University: Centre of Southeast Asian Studies, Monash Papers on Southeast Asia, No. 18.

Chandra Muzaffar (1986) 'Malaysia: Islamic Resurgence and the Question of Development'. *Sojourn. Journal of Social Issues in Southeast Asia*, vol. 1, pp. 57–75.

Chattip Nartsupha, Suthy Prasartset and Montri Chenvidhakarn (eds) (1978/1981) *The Political Economy of Siam, 1851–1910*, and *The Political Economy of Siam, 1910–1932*. Bangkok: Social Science Association of Siam, 2 vols.

Chayan Vaddhanaputi (2003) 'The Role of the Social Sciences in Emerging Civil Society in Thailand'. *Asian Journal of Social Science*, vol. 31, pp. 155–161.

Chen Maiping (1997) 'What are "Asian Values"?' *NIASnytt, Nordic Newsletter of Asian Studies*, No. 2, pp. 5–6.

Chen, Peter S.J. (1976) *Asian Values in a Modernizing Society: A Sociological Perspective*. Department of Sociology, University of Singapore: Chopmen Enterprises, Sociology Working Paper No. 51.

—— (1978a) 'The Power Elite in Singapore'. In Chen and Evers (1978b), pp. 73–82.

—— (1978b) 'Professional and Intellectual Elites in Singapore'. In Chen and Evers (1978b), pp. 27–37.

—— (1980) 'The Cultural Implications of Industrialization and Modernization in South-East Asia. In Evers (1980b), pp. 236–246.

—— (ed.) (1983) *Singapore. Development Policies and Trends*. Singapore: Oxford University Press.

Chen, Peter S.J. and Hans-Dieter Evers (1978a) 'Introduction'. In Chen and Evers (1978b), pp. xiii–xx.

—— (eds) (1978b) *Studies in ASEAN Sociology. Urban Society and Social Change*. Singapore: Chopmen Enterprises.

Chen, Peter S.J. and Tai Ching Ling (1978) 'Urban and Rural Living in a Highly Urbanised Society'. In Chen and Evers (1978b), pp. 406–421.

Cheng Siok-Hwa (1968) *The Rice Industry of Burma, 1852–1940*. Kuala Lumpur: University of Malaya Press.

Chew, Sing C. and Robert A. Denemark (1996a) 'On Development and Under-development'. In Chew and Denemark (1996b), pp. 1–16.

—— (eds) (1996b) *The Underdevelopment of Development. Essays in Honor of Andre Gunder Frank*. Thousand Oaks, Calif.: Sage Publications.

Chipp, Sylvia A. and Justin J. Green (1980a) 'Introduction. Women's Changing Roles and Status', and 'Southeast Asia'. In Chipp and Green (1980b), pp. 1–11, 105–107.

—— (eds) (1980b) *Asian Women in Transition*. University Park and London: The Pennsylvania State University Press.

Chong, Terence (2005) *Modernization Trends in Southeast Asia*. Singapore: Institute of Southeast Asian Studies.

Chou, Cynthia and Vincent Houben (2006a), 'Introduction'. In Chou and Houben (2006b), pp. 1–22.

References

——(eds) (2006b) *Southeast Asian Studies. Debates and New Directions.* Leiden: International Institute for Asian Studies, and Singapore: Institute of Southeast Asian Studies.

Choy, Catherine Ceniza (2003) *Empire of Care: Nursing and Migration in Filipino-American History.* Durham: Duke University Press.

Chua Beng Huat (1988) 'Adjusting Religious Practices to Different House Forms in Singapore'. *Architecture and Behaviour*, vol. 4, pp. 3–25.

—— (1991) 'Race Relations and Public Housing Policy in Singapore'. *The Journal of Architectural and Planning Research*, vol. 8, pp. 343–354.

—— (1995) *Communitarian Ideology and Democracy in Singapore.* London: Routledge, paperback edition, 1997.

—— (1996) 'Culturalisation of Economy and Politics in Singapore'. In Robison (1996c), pp. 87–107.

—— (1997a) 'Still Awaiting New Initiatives: Democratisation in Singapore'. *Asian Studies Review*, vol. 21, pp. 120–133.

—— (1997b) *Political Legitimacy and Housing: Stakeholding in Singapore.* London: Routledge.

—— (1998) 'Racial-Singaporeans. Absence after the Hyphen'. In Kahn (1998b), pp. 28–50.

—— (2005) 'Liberalization without Democratization: Singapore in the Next Decade'. In Loh and Öjendal (2005b), pp. 57–82.

Clad, James (1989) *Behind the Myth: Business, Money and Power in Southeast Asia.* London: Unwin Hyman Press.

Clammer, John (1978a) 'Sociological Analysis of the Overseas Chinese in Southeast Asia'. In Chen and Evers (1978b), pp. 170–183.

—— (1978b) *Islam and Capitalism in Southeast Asia.* Singapore: Chopmen Enterprises.

—— (1980) *Straits Chinese Society.* Singapore: Singapore University Press.

—— (1985) *Singapore: Ideology, Society, Culture.* Singapore: Chopmen Publishers.

—— (1986) 'Ethnic Processes in Urban Melaka'. In Lee (1986c), pp. 47–72.

—— (1996) *Values and Development in Southeast Asia.* Petaling Jaya: Pelanduk Publications.

—— (1997) 'Culture, Values and Modernization in Singapore: An Overview'. In Ong et al. (1997b), pp. 502–512, extracted from *Singapore: Ideology, Society and Culture*, 1985, pp. 22–30.

—— (2000) 'Cultural Studies/Asian Studies: Alternatives, Intersections, and Contradictions in Asian Social Science'. *Southeast Asian Journal of Social Science*, Special Focus 'Alternative Discourses in the Social Sciences', vol. 28, pp. 47–65.

Clifford, James and George Marcus (eds) (1986) *Writing Culture: The Poetics and Politics of Ethnography.* Berkeley: University of California Press.

Cohen, Erik (1991) *Thai Society in Comparative Perspective. Collected Essays.* Bangkok and Cheney: White Lotus, Studies in Contemporary Thailand.

—— (1993) 'Open-ended Prostitution as a Skilful Game of Luck. Opportunity, Risk and Security among Tourist-oriented Prostitutes in a Bangkok Soi'. In Michael Hitchcock, Victor T. King and Michael J.G. Parnwell (eds), *Tourism in South-East Asia.* London: Routledge, pp. 155–178.

Collier, W.L. (1981) 'Agricultural Evolution in Java'. In G. Hansen (ed.), *Agricultural and Rural Development in Indonesia.* Boulder, Colorado: Westview Press, pp. 147–173.

Collier, W.L., Soentoro, Gunawan Wiradi, Effendi Pasandaran, Kabul Santoso and Joseph F. Stepanek (1982) 'Acceleration of Rural Development in Java'. *Bulletin of Indonesian Economic Studies*, vol. 18, pp. 85–101.

Connors, Michael Kelly (2003a) *Democracy and National Identity in Thailand*. London: RoutledgeCurzon, revised paperback edition by NIAS Press, 2007.

—— (2003b) 'Goodbye to the Security State: Thailand and Ideological Change'. *Journal of Contemporary Asia*, vol. 33, pp. 431–448.

—— (2005) 'Democracy and the Mainstreaming of Localism in Thailand'. In Loh and Öjendal (2005b), pp. 259–286.

Cook, Nerida (1998) '"Dutiful Daughters", Estranged Sisters: Women in Thailand'. In Sen and Stivens (1998), pp. 250–290.

Cordero, Felicidad V. and Isabel S. Panopio (1967) *General Sociology: Focus on the Philippines*. Manila: College Professors' Publication Corporation; third edition, 1994, Quezon City: Ken Incorporated.

Coyle, Saowalee and Julia Kwong (2000) 'Women's Work and Social Reproduction in Thailand'. *Journal of Contemporary Asia*, vol. 30, pp. 492–506.

Crane, Hillary and Kathleen Nadeau (2004) 'Crafting Gender: Women Making Decisions in Asia'. *Critical Asian Studies*, vol. 36, pp. 171–174.

Crawfurd, John (1967) *History of the Indian Archipelago Containing an Account of the Manners, Arts, Languages, Religions, Institutions and Commerce of its Inhabitants*. London: Frank Cass, 3 vols., reprint, first published 1820.

Crouch, Harold (1991a) 'Military-Civilian Relations in Indonesia'. In Selochan (1991), pp. 51–66.

—— (1991b) 'The Military in Malaysia'. In Selochan (1991), pp. 121–137.

—— (1992) 'Authoritarian Trends, the UMNO Split and the Limits to State Power'. In Kahn and Loh (1992), pp. 21–43.

—— (1993) 'Malaysia: Neither Authoritarian nor Democratic'. In Hewison, Robison and Rodan (1993), pp. 133–158.

—— (1996) *Government and Society in Malaysia*. Ithaca, New York, and London: Cornell University Press.

Cullinane, Michael (1971) 'Implementing the "New Order": The Structure and Supervision of Local Government During the Taft Era'. In Owen (1971c), pp. 13–75.

Cushner, Nicholas P. (1971) *Spain in the Philippines. From Conquest to Revolution*. Quezon City: Institute of Philippine Culture, Ateneo de Manila University, PIC Monographs No. 1.

Dahrendorf, R. (1969) 'On the Origins of Inequality among Men'. In Béteille (1969b), pp. 16–44.

Davidson, Jamie S. (2000) 'The Politics of Violence on an Indonesian Periphery'. *South East Asia Research*, vol. 11, pp. 59–89.

Decaesstecker, Donald Denise (1978) *Impoverished Urban Filipino Families*. Manila: U.S.T. Press.

De Jesus, Edilberto C. (2002) 'Muddling Through: Development under a "Weak" State'. In Wee (2002c), pp. 51–73.

Derichs, Claudia (2006) 'Malaysia in 2005. Moving Forward Quietly'. *Asian Survey*, vol. 46, pp. 168–174.

Dewey, Alice G. (1962) *Peasant Marketing in Java*. New York: Free Press of Glencoe.

Deyo, Frederic C. (1981) *Dependent Development and Industrial Order: An Asian Case Study*. New York: Praeger.

Dhakidae, Daniel (2001) 'Lifestyles and Political Behavior of the Indonesian Middle Classes'. In Hsiao (2001), pp. 475–513.

Diamond, Larry (ed.) (1994) *Political Culture and Democracy in Developing Countries*. London: Lynne Rienner.

Dick, Howard (1985) 'The Rise of a Middle Class and the Changing Concept of Equity in Indonesia: An Interpretation. *Indonesia*, No. 39, pp. 71–92.

Diokno, Maria Serena I. (2000) 'Once Again, the Asian Values Debate: The Case of the Philippines'. In Jacobsen and Bruun (2000b), pp. 75–91.

Doner, Richard F. (1991) 'Approaches to the Politics of Economic Growth in Southeast Asia'. *The Journal of Asian Studies*, vol. 50, pp. 818–849.

Doner, Richard F. and Ansil Ramsay (2000) 'Rent-seeking and Economic Development in Thailand'. In Khan and Jomo (2000b), pp. 145–181.

Dore, Ronald P. (1973) 'The Late Development Effect'. In Evers (1973b), pp. 65–80.

Douglas, Stephen A. (1980) 'Women in Indonesian Politics: The Myth of Functional Interest'. In Chipp and Green (1980b), pp. 152–181.

Drummond, Lisa B.W. and Mandy Thomas (eds) (2003), *Consuming Urban Culture in Contemporary Vietnam*. London and New York: RoutledgeCurzon.

Durkheim, Emile (1984) *The Division of Labour in Society*. London: Macmillan, and New York: The Free Press, trans. W.D. Halls, originally published in French in 1893.

Dwyer, D.J. (1972a) 'Introduction. The City as a Centre of Change in Asia'. In Dwyer (1972c), pp . vii–xvi.

—— (1972b) 'Attitudes towards Spontaneous Settlement in Third World Cities'. In Dwyer (1972c), pp. 166–178.

—— (ed.) 1972c) *The City as a Centre of Change in Asia*. Hong Kong: Hong Kong University Press.

—— (1974) *The City in the Third World*. London: Macmillan.

Earl, Catherine (2004) 'Leisure and Social Mobility in Ho Chi Minh City'. In Taylor (2004a), pp. 351–379.

Eisenstadt, S.N. (1964) 'Breakdowns of Modernization'. *Economic Development and Cultural Change*, vol. 12, pp. 345–367.

—— (1966) *Modernization: Protest and Change*. Englewood Cliffs, N.J.: Prentice-Hall.

—— (ed.) (1970) *Readings in Social Evolution and Development*. Oxford: Pergamon.

—— (1973a) 'The Influence of Traditional Colonial Political Systems on the Development of Post-traditional Social and Political Orders'. In Evers (1973b), pp. 3–18.

—— (1973b) *Traditional Patrimonialism and Modern Neo-Patrimonialism*. Beverly Hills, Calif.: Sage Research Papers in the Social Sciences, Vol. 1, Series No. 90-003.

—— (1973c) *Tradition, Change and Modernity*. New York: John Wiley and Sons.

—— (ed.), 2002, *Multiple Modernities*. New Brunswick and London: Transaction Publishers.

Eisenstadt, S.N. and L. Roniger (1981) 'The Study of Patron-client Relations and Recent Developments in Sociological Theory'. In S.N. Eisenstadt and R. Lemarchand (eds), *Political Clientelism, Patronage and Development*. London: Sage Publications, pp. 271–295.

Elson, R. (1978) *The Cultivation System and 'Agricultural Involution'*. Clayton, Vic.: Monash University, Centre of Southeast Asian Studies Working Paper 14.

—— (1984) *Javanese Peasants and the Colonial Sugar Industry: Impact and Change in an East Java Residency, 1830–1940*. Singapore: Oxford University Press.

Emmanuel, Arghiri (1972) *Unequal Exchange. A Study of the Imperialism of Trade*. London: New Left Books, and New York: Monthly Review Press, originally published in French in 1969.

Emmerson, Donald K. (1976) *Indonesia's Elite: Political Culture and Cultural Politics*. Ithaca, New York: Cornell University Press.

—— (1978) 'The Bureaucracy in Political Context: Weakness in Strength'. In Jackson and Pye (1978), pp. 82–136.

Errington, Shelly (1990) 'Recasting Sex, Gender and Power: A Theoretical and Regional Overview'. In Atkinson and Errington (1990), pp. 1–58.

Esra, Pilapa (2004) '"Women Will Keep the Household". The Mediation of Work and Family by Female Labor Migrants in Bangkok'. *Critical Asian Studies*, vol. 36, pp. 199–216.

Evans, Grant (1986) *From Moral Economy to Remembered Village. The Sociology of James C. Scott*. Clayton, Victoria: Monash University, Centre of Southeast Asian Studies, Working Paper No. 40.

—— (ed.) (1993) *Asia's Cultural Mosaic. An Anthropological Introduction*. New York: Prentice Hall

—— (1998) *The Politics of Ritual and Remembrance. Laos since 1975*. Chiang Mai: Silkworm Books.

—— (ed.) (1999) *Laos. Culture and Society*. Chiang Mai: Silkworm Books.

Evers, Hans-Dieter (1973a) 'Introduction: Modernization and Development'. In Evers (1973b), pp. xii–xix.

—— (ed.) (1973b) *Modernization in South-East Asia*. Singapore, Institute of Southeast Asian Studies: Oxford University Press.

—— (1973c) 'Group Conflict and Class Formation in South-East Asia'. In Evers (1973b), pp. 108–131.

—— (1978a) 'The Role of Professionals in Social and Political Change'. In Chen and Evers (1978b), pp. 3–13.

—— (1978b) 'The Formation of a Social Class Structure: Urbanization, Bureaucratization and Social Mobility in Thailand'. In Chen and Evers (1978b), pp. 83–95.

—— (1978c) 'Urbanization and Urban Conflict in Southeast Asia'. In Chen and Evers (1978b), pp. 323–332.

—— (1980a) 'Editor's Introduction'. In Evers (1980b), pp. ix–x.

—— (ed.) (1980b) *Sociology of South-East Asia. Readings on Social Change and Development*. Kuala Lumpur: Oxford University Press.

—— (1980c) 'The Challenge of Diversity: Basic Concepts and Theories in the Study of South-East Asian Societies'. In Evers (1980b), pp. 2–7.

—— (1980d) 'Group Conflict and Class Formation in South-East Asia'. In Evers (1980b), pp. 247–261.

—— (2000) 'Globalization, Local Knowledge, and the Growth of Ignorance: The Epistemic Construction of Reality'. *Southeast Asian Journal of Social Science*. Special Focus 'Alternative Discourses in the Social Sciences', vol. 28, pp. 13–22.

Evers, Hans-Dieter and Rüdiger Korff (2000) *Southeast Asian Urbanism. The Meaning and Power of Social Space.* New York: St. Martin's Press, and Munster: Lit Verlag.

Evers, Hans-Dieter and Daniel Regan (1978) 'Specialization and Involvement: The Modernizing Role of Doctors in Malaysia and Indonesia'. In Chen and Evers (1978b), pp. 14–26.

Fahey, Stephanie (1998) 'Vietnam's Women in the Renovation Era'. In Sen and Stivens (1998), pp. 222–249.

Farid, Hilmar (2005) 'The Class Question in Indonesian Social Sciences'. In Hadiz and Dhakidae (2005b), pp. 167–195.

Farish A. Noor (1999) 'Values in the Dynamics of Malaysia's Internal and External Political Relations'. In Han (1999b), pp. 146–176.

Fasseur, Cornelis (1992) *The Politics of Colonial Exploitation. Java, the Dutch, and the Cultivation System.* Ithaca, New York: Cornell University, Southeast Asia Program, Studies on Southeast Asia, trans. by R.E. Elson and Ary Kraal, edited by R.E. Elson.

Fast, Jonathan and Jim Richardson (1979) *Roots of Dependency. Political and Economic Revolution in 19th Century Philippines.* Quezon City: Foundation for Nationalist Studies.

Fatimah Halim (1983) 'Workers Resistance and Managerial Control: A Case Study of Male and Female Workers in West Malaysia'. *Journal of Contemporary Asia*, vol. 13, pp. 131–150.

Fenichel, Allen and Gregg Huff (1975) 'Colonialism and the Economic System of an Independent Burma'. *Modern Asian Studies*, vol. 9, pp. 321–335.

Ferrer, Miriam Coronel (2005) 'The Moro and the Cordillera Conflicts in the Philippines and the Struggle for Autonomy'. In Kusuma and Thompson (2005a), pp. 109–150.

Fieldhouse, D.K. (1967) *The Theory of Capitalist Imperialism.* London: Longman.

Fischer, Joseph (ed.) (1973) *Foreign Values and Southeast Asian Scholarship.* Berkeley: University of California, Center for South and Southeast Asian Studies.

Fisher, Charles (1962) 'South East Asia: The Balkans of the Orient?' *Geography*, vol. 47, pp. 347–367.

—— (1964) *South-East Asia: A Social, Economic and Political Geography.* London: Methuen.

Forbes, D.K. (1979) *The Pedlars of Ujung Pandang.* Melbourne, Monash University: Centre of Southeast Asian Studies, Working Paper No. 17.

—— (1981) 'Petty Commodity Production and Underdevelopment: The Case of Pedlars and Trishaw Riders in Ujung Pandang, Indonesia. *Progress in Planning*, vol. 16, pp. 105–178.

Forbes, Dean (1996) 'Urbanization, Migration, and Vietnam's Spatial Structure. *Sojourn. Journal of Southeast Asian Social Issues*, vol. 11, pp. 24–51.

Forbes, Dean and Cecile Butler (2006) 'Laos in 2005. 30 Years of the People's Democratic Republic'. *Asian Survey*, vol. 46, pp. 175–179.

Fox, Richard (2006) 'Strong and Weak Media? On the Representation of "Terorisme" in Contemporary Indonesia'. *Modern Asian Studies*, 40: 993–1052.

Frank, Andre Gunder (1969a) *Capitalism and Underdevelopment in Latin America, Historical Studies of Chile and Brazil.* New York: Monthly Review Press, revised edition.

—— (1969b) *Latin America: Underdevelopment or Revolution: Essays on the Develop-ment of Underdevelopment and the Immediate Enemy.* New York: Monthly Review Press.

—— (1971) *Sociology of Development and Underdevelopment of Sociology*. London: Pluto Press.

—— (1972) *Lumpenbourgeoisie-Lumpendevelopment: Development, Class, and Politics in Latin America*. New York: Monthly Review Press.

—— (1975) *On Capitalist Underdevelopment*. Bombay: Oxford University Press.

—— (1978a) *Dependent Accumulation and Underdevelopment*. London and Basingstoke: Macmillan.

—— (1978b) *World Accumulation, 1492–1789*. New York: Monthly Review Press, and London: Macmillan.

—— (1981) *Crisis: In the Third World*. London: Heinemann, and New York: Monthly Review Press.

—— (1996) 'The Underdevelopment of Development'. In Chew and Denemark (1996b), pp. 17–55.

—— (1998) *ReOrient: Global Economy in the Asian Age*. London and Los Angeles: University of California Press.

Frank, Andre Gunder and B.K. Gills (eds) (1993) *The World System: Five Hundred Years or Five Thousand?* London and New York: Routledge.

Freeman, Michael (2000) 'Universal Rights and Particular Cultures'. In Jacobsen and Bruun (2000b), pp. 43–58.

Friedman, Edward (2000) 'Since There is No East and There is No West, How Could Either Be the Best?' In Jacobsen and Bruun (2000b), pp. 21–42.

Frobel, F., J. Heinrichs and O. Kreye (1980) *The New International Division of Labour*. Cambridge: Cambridge University Press.

Fukuyama, Francis (1992) *The End of History and the Last Man*. London: Hamish Hamilton.

Furnivall, J.S. (1939) *Netherlands India. A Study of Plural Economy*. Cambridge: Cambridge University Press.

—— (1942) 'The Political Economy of the Tropical Far East'. *Journal of the Royal Central Asian Society*, vol. 29, pp. 195–210.

—— (1956) *Colonial Policy and Practice: A Comparative Study of Burma and Netherlands India*. New York: New York University Press, first published 1948, Cambridge University Press.

—— (1957) *An Introduction to the Political Economy of Burma*. Rangoon: People's Literature House.

—— (1980) 'Plural Societies'. In Evers (1980b), pp. 86–96.

Gamer, Robert E. (1972) *The Politics of Urban Development in Singapore*. Ithaca, New York: Cornell University Press.

Ganesan, N. (2004) 'The Collapse of Authoritarian Regimes in Indonesia and Thailand: Structural and Contextual Factors'. *Asian Journal of Social Science*, vol. 32, pp. 1–18.

Geertz, Clifford (1956) *The Development of the Javanese Economy: A Socio-cultural Approach*. Cambridge, Mass.: MIT Center for International Studies.

—— (1963a) *Agricultural Involution. The Process of Ecological Change in Indonesia*. Berkeley and Los Angeles: University of California Press.

—— (1963b) *Peddlers and Princes: Social Development and Economic Change in Two Indonesian Towns*. Chicago and London: University of Chicago Press.

—— (ed.) (1963c) *Old Societies and New States: The Quest for Modernity in Asia and Africa.* New York: Free Press of Glencoe.

—— (1964) 'A Study of National Character'. *Economic Development and Cultural Change*, vol. 12, pp. 205–209.

—— (1965) *The Social History of an Indonesian Town.* Cambridge, Mass: MIT Press.

—— (1980) *Negara: The Theatre State in Nineteenth-Century Bali.* Princeton, NJ: Princeton University Press.

—— (1984) 'Culture and Social Change: The Indonesian Case'. *Man*, vol. 19, pp. 511–532.

George, Cherian (2004) 'Understanding the Internet's Political Impact in Asia'. *Asian Journal of Social Science*, vol. 32, pp. 519–529.

George, Kenneth M. and Andrew C. Willford (2005) 'Introduction: Religion, the Nation, and the Predicaments of Public Life in Southeast Asia'. In Andrew C. Willford and Kenneth M. George (eds), *Spirited Politics. Religion and Public Life in Contemporary Southeast Asia.* Ithaca, New York: Cornell University, Southeast Asia Program, Studies on Southeast Asia, No. 38.

Gerke, Solvay and Hans-Dieter Evers (2006) 'Globalizing Local Knowledge: Social Science Research on Southeast Asia, 1970–2000'. *Sojourn. Journal of Social Issues in Southeast Asia*, vol. 21, pp. 1–21.

Girling, John L.S. (1981) *The Bureaucratic Polity in Modernizing Societies.* Singapore: Institute of Southeast Asian Studies, Occasional Paper No. 64.

—— (1985) *Thailand. Society and Politics.* Ithaca and London: Cornell University Press, paperback edition.

—— (1988) 'Development and Democracy in South East Asia'. *The Pacific Review*, vol. 1, pp. 332–340.

Gladney, Dru C. (1998a) 'Making and Marking Majorities'. In Gladney (1998b), pp. 1–9.

—— (ed.) (1998b) *Making Majorities. Constituting the Nation in Japan, Korea, China, Malaysia, Fiji, Turkey, and the United States*, Stanford, California: Stanford University Press.

Glassman, Jim (2004) 'Economic "Nationalism" in a Post-Nationalist Era: The Political Economy of Economic Policy in Postcrisis Thailand'. *Critical Asian Studies*, vol. 36, pp. 37–64.

Goh Beng Lan (1998) 'Modern Dreams: An Enquiry into Power, Cityscape Transformation and Cultural Difference in Contemporary Malaysia'. In Kahn (1998b), pp. 168–202.

—— (2001a) 'Rethinking Urbanism in Malaysia: Power, Space and Identity'. In Maznah and Wong (2001b), pp. 159–178.

—— (2001b) *Modern Dreams: An Enquiry into Power, Cultural Production and the Cityscape in Contemporary Urban Penang.* Malaysia, Ithaca, New York: Cornell University Press, Southeast Asia Publications.

—— (2002) 'Rethinking Modernity: State, Ethnicity, and Class in the Forging of a Modern Urban Malaysia'. In Wee (2002c), pp. 184–216.

Goh, Robbie B.H. (2003) 'Things to a Void: Utopian Discourse, Communality and Constructed Interstices in Singapore Public Housing'. In Goh and Yeoh (2003b), pp. 51–75.

Goh, Robbie B.H. and Brenda S.A.Yeoh (2003a) 'Urbanism and Post-colonial Nationalities: Theorizing the Southeast Asian City'. In Goh and Yeoh (2003b), pp. 1–11.

—— (eds) (2003b) *Theorizing the Southeast Asian City as Text: Urban Landscapes, Cultural Documents and Interpretative Experiences.* Singapore: World Scientific Publishing Co. Pte. Ltd.

Goldsworthy, David (1994) 'Huntington's "Clash of Civilizations"? An Overview'. *Asian Studies Review*, vol. 18, pp. 3–9.

Gomez, E.T. (1990) *Politics in Business: UMNO's Corporate Investments*. Kuala Lumpur: Forum.

—— (1991) *Money Politics in the Barisan Nasional*. Kuala Lumpur: Forum.

—— (1994) *Political Business: Corporate Involvement of Malaysian Political Parties*. Townsville: Centre for Southeast Asian Studies, James Cook University of North Queensland.

Gomez, E.T. and Jomo K.S. (1999) *Malaysia's Political Economy: Politics, Patronage and Profits*. Cambridge: Cambridge University Press, second edition.

Gordon, Alec (1992) 'The Poverty of Involution: A Critique of Geertz' Pseudo-history'. *Journal of Contemporary Asia*, vol. 22, pp. 490–513.

Gouldner, Alvin W. (1977) 'The Norm of Reciprocity: A Preliminary Statement'. In Schmidt, et al. (1977), pp. 28–43.

Grijns, Kees and Peter J.M. Nas (eds) (2000) *Jakarta-Batavia: Socio-cultural Essays*. Leiden: KITLV Press.

Guinness, Patrick (1993) 'People in Cities: Anthropology in Urban Asia'. In Evans (1993), pp. 307–323.

Gunn, Geoffrey C. (1993) 'Rentier Capitalism in Negara Brunei Darussalam'. In Hewison, Robison and Rodan (1993), pp. 111–132.

Guy, Michelle Lee (2004) 'Gossiping Endurance: Discipline and Social Control of Filipina Helpers in Malaysia'. *Asian Journal of Social Science*, vol. 32, pp. 501–518.

Hadiz, Vedi R. (2004) 'Indonesian Party Politics. A Site of Resistance to Neoliberal Reform'. *Critical Asian Studies*, vol. 36, pp. 615–636.

Hadiz, Vedi R. and Daniel Dhakidae (2005a) 'Introduction'. In Hadiz and Dhakidae (2005b), pp. 1–29.

—— (eds) (2005b) *Social Science and Power in Indonesia*. Singapore: Institute of Southeast Asian Studies and Jakarta: Equinox Publishing.

Hajime, Shimizu (2005) 'Southeast Asia as a Regional Concept in Modern Japan'. In Kratoska et al. (2005b), pp. 82–112.

Hall, Anthony (1977) 'Patron–Client Relations: Concepts and Terms'. In Schmidt, et al. (1977), pp. 510–512.

Hall, Ivan P. (1997) 'Japan's New Cultural Push toward Asia: Partner, Hegemon, or Perpetual Outsider?' *Pacific Rim Report*, No.3, pp. 1–8.

Halldorsson, Jon O. (2000) 'Particularism, Identities and a Clash of Universalisms: Pancasila, Islam and Human Rights in Indonesia'. In Jacobsen and Bruun (2000b), pp. 111–133.

Hamilton, Annette (1997) 'Primal Dream: Masculinism, Sin, and Salvation in Thailand's Sex Trade'. In Manderson and Jolly (1997b), pp. 145–165.

Han Sung-Joo (1999a) 'Asian Values: An Asset or a Liability?' In Han (1999b), pp. 3–9.

—— (ed.) (1999b) *Changing Values in Asia. Their Impact on Governance and Development*. Singapore: Institute of Southeast Asian Studies, and Tokyo and New York: Japan Center for International Exchange.

Handley, Paul (1997) 'More of the Same? Politics and Business, 1987–96'. In Hewison (1997b), pp, pp. 94–113.

Hanks, Lucien, M. (1962) Merit and Power in the Thai Social Order'. *American Anthropologist*, vol. 64, pp. 1247–1261.

—— (1975) 'The Thai Social Order as Entourage and Circle.' In Skinner and Kirsch (1975), pp. 197–218.

—— (1977) 'The Corporation and the Entourage: A Comparison of Thai and American Social Organization.' In Schmidt, et al. (1977), pp. 161–167.

Hannerz, Ulf (1992) *Cultural Complexity. Studies in the Organisation of Meaning.* New York: Columbia University Press.

Hantrakul, Sukanya (1988) 'Prostitution in Thailand.' In Chandler, Sullivan and Branson (1988), pp. 115–136.

Hart, Gillian (1992) 'Household Production Reconsidered: Gender, Labor Conflict, and Technological Change in Malaysia's Muda Region.' *World Development*, vol. 20, pp. 809–823.

Harvey, David (1989) *The Condition of Postmodernity: An Enquiry into the Origins of Cultural Change.* Oxford: Basil Blackwell.

Hashim Hussin Yaacob (1977) 'Development and Restructuring of Society: Some Social and Cultural Dilemmas in a Transitional State.' *Persatuan Ekonomi Malaysia*, May, pp. 394–416.

Hassan, Riaz (ed.) (1976) *Singapore: Society in Transition.* Kuala Lumpur: Oxford University Press.

—— (1977) *Families in Flats: A Study of Low Income Families in Public Housing.* Singapore: Singapore University Press.

—— (1983) *A Way of Dying: Suicide in Singapore.* Kuala Lumpur: Oxford University Press.

Hauser, Philip (1959) 'Some Cultural and Personal Characteristics of the Less Developed Areas.' *Human Organization*, vol. 18, pp. 78–84.

Hawes, Gary (1992) 'Marcos, His Cronies, and the Philippines' Failure to Develop.' In McVey (1992a), pp. 144–160.

Healey, Lucy (2000) 'Gender, "Aliens", and the National Imaginary in Contemporary Malaysia.' *Sojourn. Journal of Social Issues in Southeast Asia*, vol. 15, pp. 222–254.

Hedman, Eva-Lotta E. (2001) 'Contesting State and Civil Society: Southeast Asian Trajectories.' *Modern Asian Studies*, vol. 35, pp. 921–951.

—— (2005) 'Global Civil Society in One Country? Class Formation and Business Activism in the Philippines.' In Loh and Öjendal (2005b), pp. 138–172.

—— (2006) 'The Philippines in 2005. Old Dynamics, New Conjuncture.' *Asian Survey*, vol. 46, pp. 187–193.

Hefner, Robert W. (ed.) (1998) *Market Cultures: Society and Morality in the New Asian Capitalisms.* Boulder, Colorado: Westview Press.

—— (2007) 'The Sword against the Crescent. Religion and Violence in Muslim Southeast Asia.' In Cady and Simon (2007a), pp. 33–50.

Helliwell, Christine (1993) 'Women in Asia. Anthropology and the Study of Women', in Evans (1993), pp. 260–286.

Heng Pek Koon (1992) 'The Chinese Business Elite of Malaysia.' In McVey (1992a), pp. 127–144.

Heryanto, Ariel (2005) 'Ideological Baggage and Orientations of the Social Sciences in Indonesia.' In Hadiz and Dhakidae (2005b), pp. 57–89.

Hettne, B. (1990) *Development Theory and the Three Worlds.* Harlow: Longman.

Hewison, Kevin J. (1985) 'The State and Capitalist Development in Thailand'. In Higgott and Robison (1985a), pp. 266–294.

—— (1987) 'National Interests and Economic Downturn: Thailand'. In Robison, Hewison and Higgott (1987a), pp. 52–79.

—— (1989a) *Power and Politics in Thailand: Essays in Political Economy*. Manila and Wollongong: Journal of Contemporary Asia Publishers.

—— (1989b) *Bankers and Bureaucrats: Capital and the Role of the State in Thailand*. New Haven: Yale University Southeast Asia Monograph No. 34.

—— (1993) 'Of Regimes, States and Pluralities: Thai Politics Enters the 1990s'. In Hewison, Robison and Rodan (1993), pp. 159–189.

—— (1996) 'Emerging Social Forces in Thailand. New Political and Economic Roles'. In Robison and Goodman (1996b), pp. 135–160.

—— (1997a) 'Introduction. Power, Oppositions and Democratisation'. In Hewison (1997b), pp. 1–20.

—— (ed.) (1997b) *Political Change in Thailand. Democracy and Participation*. London and New York: Routledge.

—— (2001) 'Thailand's Capitalism: Development Through Boom and Bust'. In Rodan, Hewison and Robison (2001a), pp. 71–103.

—— (2004) 'Thai Migrant Workers in Hong Kong'. *Journal of Contemporary Asia*, vol. 34, pp. 318–335.

—— (2006) 'Thailand: Boom, Bust and Recovery'. In Rodan, Hewison and Robison (2006a), pp. 74–108.

Hewison, Kevin, J., Richard Robison and Garry Rodan (eds) (1993) *Southeast Asia in the 1990s: Authoritarianism, Democracy and Capitalism*. St Leonards: Allen and Unwin.

Heyzer, Noeleen (1986) *Working Women in South-East Asia. Development, Subordination and Emancipation*. Milton Keynes and Philadelphia: Open University Press.

Higgins, Benjamin (1963) 'Foreword'. In Clifford Geertz, *Agricultural Involution. The Processes of Ecological Change in Indonesia*. Berkeley and Los Angeles: University of California Press, pp. vii–xv.

—— (1980) 'The Dualistic Theory of Underdeveloped Areas'. In Evers (1980b), pp. 46–56.

Higgott, R. and R. Robison (1985a) 'Introduction'. In Higgott and Robison (1985a), pp. 3–15.

—— (eds) 1985b) *Southeast Asia. Essays in the Political Economy of Structural Change*. London: Routledge and Kegan Paul.

—— (with Kevin J. Hewison and Gary Rodan) (1985c) 'Theories of Development and Underdevelopment: Implications for the Study of Southeast Asia'. In Higgott and Robison (1985a), pp. 16–61.

Hilferding, Rudolf (1981) *Finance Capital: A Study of the Latest Phase of Capitalist Development*. London: Routledge and Kegan Paul, originally published in German in 1910.

Hill, Michael and Lian Kwen Fee (1995) *The Politics of Nation Building and Citizenship in Singapore*. London: Routledge.

Hirschman, Charles (1986) 'The Making of Race in Colonial Malaya: Political Economy and Racial Ideology'. *Sociological Forum*, Spring, pp. 330–361.

—— (1987) 'The Meaning and Measurement of Ethnicity in Malaysia'. *The Journal of Asian Studies*, vol. 46, pp. 555–582.

—— (2001) 'Internationalising Social Science: Problems and Prospects'. In Jomo (2001), pp. 114–133.

Hitchcock, Michael and Victor T. King (2003) 'Discourses with the Past: Tourism and Heritage in South-East Asia'. *Indonesia and the Malay World*, special issue 'Tourism and Heritage in South-East Asia', Michael Hitchcock and Victor T. King (eds), vol. 31, pp. 3–15.

Hitchcock, Michael, Victor T. King and Michael J. G Parnwell (eds) (2008a) *Tourism in Southeast Asia*. Copenhagen: NIAS Press, and Honolulu: University of Hawai'i Press, forthcoming.

—— (2008b) *Tourism and Heritage in Southeast Asia*. Copenhagen: NIAS Press, forthcoming.

Ho, K.C. (2002) 'Globalization and Southeast Asian Urban Futures'. *Asian Journal of Social Science*, vol. 30, pp. 1–7.

Ho Wing Meng (1976) *Asian Values and Modernisation – A Critical Interpretation*. Department of Philosophy, University of Singapore: Chopmen Enterprises, Occasional Paper No .1.

Hoadley, Mason C. and Christer Gunnarsson (eds) (1996) *The Village Concept in the Transformation of Rural Southeast Asia, Studies from Indonesia, Malaysia and Thailand*. Richmond: Curzon Press.

Hobsbawm, Eric J. (1987) *The Age of Empire, 1875–1914*. London: Weidenfeld and Nicolson.

Hollnsteiner, Mary R. (1963) *The Dynamics of Power in a Philippine Municipality*. Quezon City: Community Development Research Council.

—— (1972) 'Becoming an Urbanite: The Neighbourhood as a Learning Environment'. In Dwyer (1972c), pp. 29–40.

Hong Lysa (1984) *Thailand in the Nineteenth Century. Evolution of the Economy*. Singapore: Institute of Southeast Asian Studies.

—— (2004) '"Stranger within the Gates": Knowing Semi-colonial Siam as Extraterritorials'. *Modern Asian Studies*, vol. 38, pp. 327–354.

Hoogvelt, Ankie M.M. (1978) *The Sociology of Developing Societies*. London: Macmillan, second edition.

—— (1982) *The Third World in Global Development*. London: Macmillan.

—— (2001) *Globalization and the Postcolonial World: The New Political Economy of Development*. Basingstoke: Palgrave Macmillan, second edition.

Hoselitz, Bert F. (1952) 'Non-Economic Barriers to Economic Development'. *Economic Development and Cultural Change*, vol. 1, pp. 8–21.

—— (1960) *Sociological Aspects of Economic Growth*. Glencoe: The Free Press.

Hsiao, Hsin-Huang Michael (ed.) (1999) *East Asian Middle Classes in Comparative Perspective*. Taipei: Institute of Ethnology, Academia Sinica.

—— (ed.) (2001) *Exploration of the Middle Classes in Southeast Asia*. Taipei: Program for Southeast Asian Area Studies, Academia Sinica.

—— (ed.) (2006) *The Changing Faces of the Middle Classes in Asia-Pacific*. Taipei: Center for Asia-Pacific Studies, Academia Sinica.

Hsiao, Hsin-Huang Michael and Wang Hong-Zen (2001) 'The Formation of the Middle Classes in Southeast Asia: An Overview'. In Hsiao (2001), pp. 3–38.

Hughes, Caroline (2003) *The Political Economy of Cambodia's Transition, 1991–2001*. London and New York: RoutledgeCurzon.

Hull, V.J. (1976) *Women in Java's Rural Middle Class: Progress or Regress?* Yogyakarta: Gadjah Mada University Working Paper Series No. 3.

Hulme, David and Mark Turner (1990) *Sociology and Development. Theories, Policies and Practices.* Hemel Hempstead: Harvester Wheatsheaf.

Hunt, Chester L. (and Agaton P. Pal, Richard W. Coller, Socorro C. Espiritu, John E. de Young and Severino F. Corpus) (1954) *Sociology in the Philippine Setting*. Manila: Alemar's.

—— (1963) *Sociology in the Philippine Setting*. Quezon City: Phoenix Publishing House, revised second edition.

—— (1976) *Sociology in the New Philippine Setting*. Quezon City: Phoenix Press.

—— (1987) *Sociology in the Philippine Setting: A Modular Approach*. Quezon City: Phoenix Publishing House, fourth edition.

Hunt, Chester L. and Dylan Dizon (1978) 'The Development of Philippine Sociology'. In Donn V. Hart (ed.), *Philippine Studies: History, Sociology, Mass Media and Bibliography*. Northern Illinois: Northern Illinois University, Centre for Southeast Asian Studies, Occasional Paper 6, pp. 98–232, and addendum, 232A–232D (see also 'Response to Weightman's Comments', as Appendix C, pp. 180–183).

Huntington, Samuel P. (1968) *Political Order in Changing Societies*. New Haven: Yale University Press.

—— (1993) 'The Clash of Civilizations?' *Foreign Affairs*, vol. 72, pp. 22–49.

—— (1996) *The Clash of Civilizations and the Remaking of World Order*. New York: Simon and Schuster.

Husin Ali, S. (1981) *The Malays. Their Problems and Future*. Kuala Lumpur, Singapore, Hong Kong: Heinemann Educational Books (Asia).

Hüsken, F. (1979) 'Landlords, Sharecroppers and Agricultural Labourers: Changing Labour Relations in Rural Java'. *Journal of Contemporary Asia*, vol. 9, pp. 140–51.

Hutchcroft, Paul D. (2000) 'Obstructive Corruption: The Politics of Privilege in the Philippines'. In Khan and Jomo (2000b), pp. 207–247.

Hutchinson, Jane (1992) 'Women in the Philippine Garments Export Industry'. *Journal of Contemporary Asia*, vol. 22, pp. 471–489.

—— (1993) 'Class and State Power in the Philippines'. In Hewison, Robison and Rodan (1993), pp. 191–212.

—— (2001) 'Crisis and Change in the Philippines'. In Rodan, Hewison and Robison (2001a), pp. 42–70.

—— (2006) 'Poverty of Politics in the Philippines'. In Rodan, Hewison and Robison (2006a), pp. 39–73.

Huxley, Tim (1996) 'International Relations'. In Mohammed and Huxley (1996b), pp. 224–246.

Hwang, In-Won (2003) 'Authoritarianism and UMNO's Factional Conflicts', *Journal of Contemporary Asia*, vol. 33, pp. 206–230.

Ifversen, Jan (2000) 'European Values and Universal Values'. In Irene Norlund and Pham Duc Thanh (eds), *Asian Values and Vietnam's Development in Comparative Perspectives*. Hanoi: National Center for Social Sciences and Humanities, pp. 48–63.

Illo, Jean Frances (1995) 'Redefining the *Maybahay* or Housewife: Reflections on the Nature of Women's Work in the Philippines'. In Karim (1995b), pp. 209–225.

Institute of Social Sciences (1991) *Vietnam Life History Survey 1991*. Ho Chi Minh City: Institute of Social Sciences.

Jackson, Karl D. and Lucian W. Pye (eds) (1978) *Political Power and Communications in Indonesia*. Berkeley and Los Angeles: University of California Press.

Jacobs, Norman (1958) *The Origin of Modern Capitalism and Eastern Asia*. Hong Kong: Hong Kong University Press.

—— (1971) *Modernization without Development: Thailand as an Asian Case Study*. New York: Praeger.

James, Helen (2006) 'Myanmar in 2005. In a Holding Pattern'. *Asian Survey*, vol. 46, pp. 162–167.

Jamieson, N. (1993) *Understanding Vietnam*. Berkeley and Los Angeles: University of California Press.

Jayasuriya, S.K. (1987) 'The Politics of Economic Policy in the Philippines during the Marcos Era'. In Robison, Hewison and Higgott (1987a), pp. 80–112.

—— (1997) 'Asian Values as Reactionary Modernization'. *NIASnytt, Nordic Newsletter of Asian Studies*, No. 4, pp. 19–27.

Jellinek, Lea (1991) *The Wheel of Fortune: The History of a Poor Community in Jakarta*. Sydney: Allen and Unwin, Asian Studies Association of Australia, Southeast Asia Publications Series No. 18.

Jenista, Frank, Jr. (1971) 'Conflict in the Philippine Legislature: The Commission and the Assembly from 1907 to 1913'. In Norman G. Owen (ed.), *Compadre Colonialism. Studies on the Philippines under American Rule*. Ann Arbor, Michigan: The University of Michigan, Centre for South and Southeast Asian Studies, Michigan Papers on South and Southeast Asia, No. 3, pp. 77–101.

Jenkins, Gwynn and Victor T. King (2003) 'Heritage and Development in a Malaysian City: George Town under Threat?' *Indonesia and the Malay World*, special issue, 'Tourism and Heritage in South-East Asia', Michael Hitchcock and Victor T. King (eds), vol. 31, pp. 44–57.

Jesudason, James V. (1989) *Ethnicity and the Economy: The State, Chinese Business, and Multinationals in Malaysia*. Singapore: Oxford University Press.

—— (1996) 'The Syncretic State and the Structuring of Oppositional Politics in Malaysia'. In Garry Rodan (ed.), *Political Oppositions in Industrialising Asia*. London and New York: Routledge, pp. 128–160.

Jocano, F. Landa (1975) *Slums as a Way of Life: A Study of Coping Behaviour in an Urban Environment*. Quezon City: University of the Philippines Press.

Johnson, Chalmers A. (1997) 'The Empowerment of Asia'. *Pacific Rim Report*, No. 1, pp. 1–12.

Jomo, Kwame Sundaram (K.S.) (1986) *A Question of Class: Capital, the State and Uneven Development in Malaya*. Singapore: Oxford University Press.

—— (1987) 'Economic Crisis and Policy Response in Malaysia'. In Robison, Hewison and Higgott (1987a), pp. 113–148.

—— (ed.) (2001) *Reinventing Malaysia: Reflections on Its Past and Future*. Bangi: Penerbit Universiti Kebangsaan Malaysia.

Jones, D. and D. Brown (1994) 'Singapore and the Myth of the Liberalizing Middle Class'. *The Pacific Review*, vol. 7, pp. 79–87.

—— (1997) 'Democratization, Civil Society and Illiberal Middle Class Culture in Pacific Asia'. *Comparative Politics*, vol. 30, pp. 147–169.

Jørgensen, Bent D. (2005) 'Democracy among the Grassroots: Local Responses to Democratic Reforms in Vietnam'. In Loh and Öjendal (2005b), pp. 316–342.

Juree Namsirichai and Vicharat Vichit-Vadakan (1973) 'American Values and Research on Thailand'. In Fischer (1973), pp. 82–89.

Kahn, Joel S. (1980) *Minangkabau Social Formations: Indonesian Peasants and the World-Economy*. Cambridge: Cambridge University Press, Cambridge Studies in Social Anthropology, 30.

—— (1992) 'Class, Ethnicity and Diversity: Some Remarks on Malay Culture in Malaysia'. In Kahn and Loh (1992), pp. 158–178.

—— (1995) *Culture, Multiculture, Postculture*. London: Sage Books.

—— (1996) 'Growth, Economic Transformation, Culture and the Middle Classes in Malaysia'. In Robison and Goodman (1996b), pp. 47–75.

—— (1998a) 'Southeast Asian Identities: Introduction'. In Kahn (1998b), pp. 1–27.

—— (ed.) (1998b) *Southeast Asian Identities. Culture and the Politics of Representa-tion in Indonesia, Malaysia, Singapore, and Thailand*. Singapore and London: Institute of Southeast Asian Studies.

—— (2006) *Other Malays. Nationalism and Cosmopolitanism in the Modern Malay World*. Singapore: Singapore University Press, and Copenhagen: NIAS Press, Asian Studies Association of Australia, Southeast Asia Publications Series.

Kahn, Joel S. and Francis Loh Kok Wah (eds) (1992) *Fragmented Vision. Culture and Politics in Contemporary Malaysia*. Sydney: Allen and Unwin, Asian Studies Association of Australia, Southeast Asia Publications Series, 22.

Karim, Wazir Jahan (1992) *Women and Culture: Between Malay Adat and Islam*. Boulder: Westview Press.

—— (1993) 'Gender Studies in Southeast Asia'. *Southeast Asian Journal of Social Science*, vol. 21, pp. 98–113.

—— (1995a) 'Introduction: Genderising Anthropology in Southeast Asia'. In Karim (1995b), pp. 11–34.

—— (ed.) (1995b) *'Male' and 'Female' in Developing Southeast Asia*. Oxford and Washington: Berg Publishers.

Kasian Tejapira (2001) 'The Post-modernization of Thainess'. In Yao (2001b), pp. 150–170.

—— (2002a) 'Post-crisis Economic Impasse and Political Recovery in Thailand. The Resurgence of Economic Nationalism'. *Critical Asian Studies*, vol. 34, pp. 323–356.

—— (2002b) 'The Postmodernisation of Thainess'. In Tanabe and Keyes (2002), pp. 202–227.

Kathirithamby-Wells, J. and J. Villiers (eds) (1990) *The Southeast Asian Port and Polity: Rise and Demise*. Singapore: Singapore University Press.

Kaye, Barrington (1960) *Upper Nankin Street Singapore: A Sociological Study of Chinese Households in a Densely Populated Area*. Singapore: University of Malaya Press.

Kemp, Jeremy H. (1982) 'A Tail Wagging the Dog: The Patron–Client Model in Thai Studies'. In Christopher Clapham (ed.), *Private Patronage and Public Power: Political Clientelism in the Modern State*. London: Frances Pinter, pp. 60–74.

—— (1984) 'The Manipulation of Personal Relations: from Kinship to Patron-clientage'. In Han Ten Brummelhuis and Jeremy Kemp (eds), *Strategies and Structures in Thai Society*. Amsterdam: Anthropological-Sociological Centre, pp. 55–69.

—— (1989a) *Seductive Mirage: The Search for the Village Community in Southeast Asia*. Dordrecht: Foris Publications Holland, Comparative Asian Studies 3.

—— (1989b) 'Peasants and Cities: The Cultural and Social Image of the Thai Peasant Community. *Sojourn. Journal of Social Issues in Southeast Asia*, vol. 4, pp. 6–19.

—— (1991) 'The Dialectics of Village and State in Modern Thailand'. *Journal of Southeast Asian Studies*, vol. 22, pp. 312–326.

Keng, William Mun Lee (1998) 'Gender Inequality and Discrimination in Singapore'. *Journal of Contemporary Asia*, vol. 28, pp. 484–497.

Kerkvliet, Benedict J. Tria (1977) *The Huk Rebellion. A Study of Peasant Revolt in the Philippines*. Berkeley, California: University of California Press.

—— (1990) *Everyday Politics in the Philippines: Class and Status Relations in a Central Luzon Village*. Berkeley: University of California Press.

Kessler, Clive S. (1999) 'The Abdication of the Intellectuals: Sociology, Anthropology, and the Asian Values Debate'. *Sojourn. Journal of Social Issues in Southeast Asia*, vol. 14, pp. 295–312.

Keyes, Charles F. (1977) *The Golden Peninsula: Culture and Adaptation in Mainland South-East Asia*. New York: Macmillan; revised edition, 1995, Honolulu: University of Hawai'i Press.

—— (1984) 'Mother or Mistress but Never a Monk: Buddhist Notions of Female Gender in Rural Thailand'. *American Ethnologist*, vol. 11, pp. 223–241.

—— (1989) *Thailand: Buddhist Kingdom as Modern Nation-State*. Bangkok: Editions Duang Kamol.

Khan, Mushtaq H. and Jomo K.S. (2000a) 'Introduction'. In Khan and Jomo (2000b), pp. 1–20.

—— (eds) (2000b) *Rents, Rent-seeking and Economic Development. Theory and Evidence in Asia*. Cambridge: Cambridge University Press.

Khondker, Habibul Haque (2000) 'Sociology in Singapore: Global Discourse in Local Context'. *Southeast Asian Journal of Social Science*, Special Focus 'Alternative Discourses in the Social Sciences', vol. 28, pp. 105–122.

—— (2001) 'Environmental Movements, Civil Society and Globalization: An Introduction'. *Asian Journal of Social Science*, vol. 29, pp. 1–8.

Khoo Boo Teik (2001) 'The State and the Market in Malaysian Political Economy'. In Rodan, Hewison and Robison (2001a), pp. 178–205.

—— (2005) 'Capital Controls and *Reformasi*: Crises and Contestations over Governance'. In Loh and Öjendal (2005b), pp. 83–109.

—— (2006) 'Malaysia: Balancing Development and Power'. In Rodan, Hewison and Robison (2006a), pp. 170–196.

Khoo Kay Jin (1992) 'The Grand Vision: Mahathir and Modernization'. In Kahn and Loh (1992), pp. 44–76.

Khwin Win, U (1991) *A Century of Rice Improvement in Burma*. Manila: International Rice Research Institute.

Kidd, John B. and Frank-Jürgen Richter (2003a) 'Introduction: Corruption and its Measures'. In Kidd and Richter (2003b), pp. 1–25.

—— (eds) (2003b) *Fighting Corruption in Asia. Causes, Effects and Remedies*. Singapore: World Scientific Publishing Co. Pte. Ltd.

Kiely, Ray (1995) *Sociology and Development. The Impasse and Beyond*. London: UCL Press.

King, Victor T. (1981) 'Sociology in South-East Asia: A Personal View'. *Cultures et développement*, vol. 13, pp. 391–414.

—— (1986) 'Review Article. Southeast Asia: Essays in the Political Economy of Structural Change'. *Journal of Contemporary Asia*, vol. 16, pp. 520–533.

—— (1996) 'Sociology'. In Mohammed and Huxley (1996b), pp. 148–188.

—— (1999) *Anthropology and Development in South-East Asia: Theory and Practice*. Kuala Lumpur: Oxford University Press.

—— (2001) 'Southeast Asia: An Anthropological Field of Study?' *Moussons. Recherche en sciences humaines sur l'Asie du Sud-Est*, vol. 3, pp. 3–31.

—— (2005) *Defining Southeast Asia and the Crisis in Area Studies: Personal Reflections on a Region*. Lund University: Centre for East and South-East Asian Studies, Working Papers in Contemporary Asian Studies 13.

—— (2006) 'Southeast Asia. Personal Reflections on a Region'. In Cynthia Chou and Vincent Houben (eds), *Southeast Asian Studies. Debates and New Directions*. Leiden: International Institute for Asian Studies, and Singapore: Institute for Southeast Asian Studies, pp. 23–44.

King, Victor T. and Ye-kyoum Kim (2004) 'Regional Development Programmes and the Life-dynamics of Tomohonese Women'. *Sojourn. Journal of Social Issues in Southeast Asia*, vol. 19, pp. 254–287.

—— (2005) '"Reflexive" Reactions of Eastern Indonesian Women to the Economic Crisis: An Ethnographic Study of Tomohon, Minahasa, North Sulawesi'. *Indonesia and the Malay World*, vol. 33, pp. 307–325.

King, Victor T., Phuong An Nguyen and Nguyen Huu Minh (2007) 'Professional Middle Class Youth in Post-reform Vietnam: Identity, Continuity and Change'. *Modern Asian Studies*, vol. 41, pp. 1–31 (website).

King, Victor T. and William D. Wilder (2003) *The Modern Anthropology of South-East Asia: An Introduction*. London: RoutledgeCurzon.

Kirsch, A. Thomas (1975) 'Economy, Polity and Religion in Thailand'. In Skinner and Kirsch (1975), pp. 172–196.

—— (1985) 'Text and Context: Buddhist Sex Roles/Culture of Gender Revisited'. *American Ethnologist*, vol. 12, pp. 302–320.

—— (1996) 'Buddhism, Sex Roles and the Thai Economy'. In Penny van Esterik (ed.), *Women of Southeast Asia*. Northern Illinois University: Center for Southeast Asian Studies, Monograph Series on Southeast Asia, Occasional Paper No. 17, pp. 13–32.

Koentjaraningrat (1963) 'Review, The Religion of Java, Clifford Geertz'. *Madjalah Ilmu-Ilmu Sastra Indonesia*, vol. 1, pp. 188–191.

—— (1975) *Anthropology in Indonesia: A Bibliographical Review*. The Hague: Nijhoff, KITLV, Bibliographical Series 8.

—— (1980) 'The Theory of Indonesia's Tropico-Colonial Economy'. In Evers (1980b), pp. 38–45.

Koo, Hagen (2006) 'Globalization and the Asian Middle Classes'. In Hsiao (2006), pp. 9–24.

Korff, Rüdiger (1996) 'Global and Local Spheres: The Diversity of Southeast Asian Urbanism'. *Sojourn. Journal of Social Issues in Southeast Asia*, vol. 11, pp. 288–313.

Kratoska, Paul H., Remco Raben and Henk Schulte Nordholt (2005a) 'Locating Southeast Asia'. In Kratoska et al. (2005b), pp. 1–19.

—— (eds) (2005b) *Locating Southeast Asia: Geographies of Knowledge and Politics of Space*. National University of Singapore: Singapore University Press and Athens: Ohio University Press, Research in International Studies, Southeast Asia Series, No. 111.

Kusuma Sintwongse and W. Scott Thompson (eds) (2005a) *Ethnic Conflicts in Southeast Asia*. Chulalongkorn University: Institute of Security and International Studies and Singapore: Institute of Southeast Asian Studies.

—— (2005b) 'Introduction'. In Kusuma and Thompson (2005a), pp. vii–xii.

Kyaw Yin Hlaing (2003) 'Reconsidering the Failure of the Burma Socialist Programme Party Government to Eradicate Internal Economic Impediments'. *South East Asia Research*, vol. 11, pp. 5–58.

Laclau, Ernesto (1971) 'Feudalism and Capitalism in Latin America'. *New Left Review*, vol. 67, pp. 19–38.

Landé, Carl H. (1965) *Leaders, Factions and Parties: The Structure of Philippine Politics*. New Haven: Yale University Press.

—— (1968) 'Parties and Politics in the Philippines'. *Asian Survey*, vol. 8, pp. 242–247.

—— (1973) 'Networks and Groups in Southeast Asia: Some Observations on the Group Theory of Politics'. *American Political Science Review*, vol. 62, pp. 103–127; republished (1977b) in Schmidt, et al. (1977), pp. 75–99

—— (1977a) 'Introduction. The Dyadic Base of Clientelism'. In Schmidt, et al. (1977), pp. xiii–xxxvii.

—— (2001) 'The Philippines and the United States'. *Philippine Studies*, vol. 49, pp. 518–539.

Laquian, Aprodicio A. (1969) *Slums Are for People: The Barrio Magsaysay Pilot Project in Urban Community Development*. Manila: College of Public Administration, University of the Philippines.

—— (1972) 'The Asian City and the Political Process'. In Dwyer (1972c), pp. 41–55.

Larkin, John A. (1972) *The Pampangans. Colonial Society in a Philippine Province*. Berkeley, Los Angeles: University of California Press.

Law, Lisa (1997) 'A Matter of "Choice": Discourses on Prostitution in the Philippines'. In Manderson and Jolly (1997b), pp. 233–261.

Lawson, Stephanie (1996) 'Cultural Relativism and Democracy: Political Myths about "Asia" and the "West"'. In Robison (1996c), pp. 108–128.

Leach, E.R. (1954) *Political Systems of Highland Burma. A Study of Kachin Social Structure*. London: G. Bell and Son,

Leaver, Richard (1985) 'Reformist Capitalist Development and the New International Division of Labour'. In Higgott and Robison (1985a), pp. 149–171.

Lebra, Joyce and Joy Paulson (eds) (1980) *Chinese Women in Southeast Asia*. Singapore: Times Books International.

Leclerc, Jacques (1997) 'Jakarta in Sukarno's Image'. In Michael Hitchcock and Victor T. King (eds), *Images of Malay-Indonesian Identity*. Kuala Lumpur: Oxford University Press, pp. 203–208.

Lee Hock Guan (ed.) (2005) *Civil Society in Southeast Asia*. Copenhagen: NIAS Press.

Lee, Raymond L.M. (1986a) 'Introduction'. In Lee (1986c), pp. iv–viii.

—— (1986b) 'Symbols of Separatism: Ethnicity, and Status Politics in Contemporary Malaysia'. In Lee (1986c), pp. 28–46.

—— (ed.) (1986c) *Ethnicity and Ethnic Relations in Malaysia*. Northern Illinois University: Center for Southeast Asian Studies, Monograph Series, Occasional Paper No. 12.

Lee Sheng Yi (1978) 'Business Elites in Singapore'. In Chen and Evers (1978b), pp. 38–60.

Lee Weng Choy (2001) 'McNationalism in Singapore'. In Yao (2001b), pp. 95–116.

Lehman, F.K. (1963) *The Structure of Chin Society: A Tribal People of Burma adapted to a Non-Western Civilization*. Urbana, Illinois: The University of Illinois Press.

—— (1967) 'Ethnic Categories in Burma and the Theory of Social Systems'. In Peter Kunstadter (ed.), *Southeast Asian Tribes, Minorities and Nations*. Vol. 1, Princeton, NJ: Princeton University Press, pp. 93–124.

—— (1979) 'Who are the Karen, and if so, why'? Karen Ethnohistory and a Formal Theory of Ethnicity'. In Charles F. Keyes (ed.), *Ethnic Adaptation and Identity: The Karen on the Thai Frontier with Burma*. Philadelphia: Institute for the Study of Human Issues, pp. 215–253.

Lenin, Vladimir I. (1950) *Imperialism. The Highest Stage of Capitalism*, in *Selected Works, Volume 1*. Moscow: Foreign Languages Publishing House, first published in Russian in 1917.

Lerner, Daniel (1958) *The Passing of Traditional Society: Modernizing the Middle East*. New York: Free Press.

Li, Tania Murray (1989) *Malays in Singapore: Culture, Economy and Ideology*. Singapore: Oxford University Press.

Lian Kwen Fee (1997) 'Introduction: Ethnic Identity in Malaysia and Singapore'. *Southeast Asian Journal of Social Science*, vol. 25, pp. 1–6.

Liddle, R. William (ed.) (1973) *Political Participation in Modern Indonesia*. New Haven: Yale University Southeast Asian Studies, Monograph Series, No. 19.

—— (1989) 'Development or Democracy?' *Far Eastern Economic Review*, vol. 9, November, pp. 22–23.

—— (1991) 'The Relative Autonomy of the Third World Politician: Soeharto and Indonesian Economic Development in Comparative Perspective'. *International Studies Quarterly*, vol. 35. pp. 403–427.

—— (1992) 'The Politics of Development Policy'. *World Development*, vol. 20, pp. 793–807.

Liddle, R. William and Saiful Mujani (2006) 'Indonesia in 2005. A New Multiparty Presidential Democracy'. *Asian Survey*, vol. 46, pp. 132–139.

Lie, Merete and Ragnhild Lund (1994) *Renegotiating Local Values. Working Women and Foreign Industry in Malaysia*. Richmond: Curzon Press, Nordic Institute of Asian Studies, Studies in Asian Topics, 15.

Lieberman, Victor B. (1978) 'Ethnic Politics in Eighteenth-Century Burma'. *Modern Asian Studies*, vol. 12, pp. 455–482.

Likhit Dhiravegin (1985) 'Social Change and Contemporary Thai Politics: An Analysis of the Inter-relationship between the Society and the Polity'. In Likhit Dhiravegin (ed.), *Thai Politics: Selected Aspects of Development and Change*. Bangkok: Tri-Sciences Publishing House, pp. 294–331.

Lilley, Peter (2003) 'The Asian Money Laundering Explosion'. In Kidd and Richter (2003b), pp. 47–71.

Lim, Linda (1978) *Women Workers in Multinational Corporations: The Case of the Electronics Industry in Malaysia and Singapore*. Ann Arbor: University of Michigan, Michigan Occasional Papers in Women's Studies, No. 9.

Lim Mah Hui (1980) 'Ethnic and Class Relations in Malaysia'. *Journal of Contemporary Asia*, vol. 10, pp. 130–154.

—— (1985) 'Contradictions in the Development of Malay Capital: State, Accumulation and Legitimation'. *Journal of Contemporary Asia*, vol. 15, pp. 37–63.

Lim Yuen-Ching (1989) 'Social Welfare' In Kernial Singh Sandhu and Paul Wheatley (eds), *Management of Success: The Moulding of Modern Singapore*. Singapore: Institute of Southeast Asian Studies, pp. 171–197.

Lindio-McGovern, Ligaya (2004) 'Alienation and Labor Export in the Context of Globalization. Filipino Migrant Domestic Workers in Taiwan and Hong Kong'. *Critical Asian Studies*, vol. 36, pp. 217–238.

Lingle, Christopher (1996) *Singapore's Authoritarian Capitalism. Asian Values, Free Market Illusions, and Political Dependency*. Barcelona: Edicions Sirocco, S.L., and Fairfax, VA: The Locke Institute.

Liow, Joseph Chinyong (2007) 'Violence and the Long Road to Reconciliation in Southern Thailand'. In Cady and Simon (2007a), pp. 154–173.

Loh Kok Wah, Francis (2000) 'State-Societal Relations in a Rapidly Growing Economy: The Case of Malaysia 1970–97'. In R.B. Klienberg and J. Clark (eds), *Economic Liberalisation, Democratisation and Civil Society in the Developing World*. New York: St. Martin's Press, pp. 65–87.

—— (2002) 'Developmentalism and the Limits of Democratic Discourse'. In Francis Loh Kok Wah and Khoo Boo Teik (eds), *Democracy in Malaysia: Discourses and Practices*. Richmond: Curzon Press, pp. 19–50.

Loh Kok Wah, Francis and Joel S. Kahn (1992) 'Introduction: Fragmented Vision'. In Kahn and Loh (1992), pp. 1–15.

Loh Kok Wah, Francis and Joakim Öjendal (2005a) 'Introduction'. In Loh and Öjendal (2005b), pp. 1–54.

—— (eds) (2005b) *Southeast Asian Responses to Globalization. Restructuring Governance and Deepening Democracy*. Copenhagen: NIAS Press.

London, Bruce (1980) *Metropolis and Nation in Thailand: The Political Economy of Uneven Development*. Boulder, Colorado: Westview Press.

Long, Lynellyn D., Lyn Nguyen Henderson, Le Thi Phuong Mai and Carl Haub (2000) *The Doi Moi Generation: Coming of Age in Vietnam Today*. Hanoi: Population Council.

Loveband, Anne (2004) 'Positioning the Product: Indonesian Migrant Women Workers in Taiwan'. *Journal of Contemporary Asia*, vol. 34, pp. 336–348.

Luckham, Robin (1991) 'Introduction: The Military, the Developmental State and Social Forces in Asia and the Pacific: Issues for Comparative Analysis'. In Selochan (1991), pp. 1–49.

Luong, Hy V. (2006) 'Vietnam in 2005. Economic Momentum and Stronger State-Society Dialogue'. *Asian Survey*, vol. 46, pp. 148–154.

Luxemburg, Rosa (1951) *The Accumulation of Capital*. London: Routledge and Kegan Paul, originally published in German in 1913.

Luxemburg, Rosa and Nikola Bukharin (1972) *Imperialism and the Accumulation of Capital*. London: Allen Lane.

Lynch, Frank and Mary Hollnsteiner (1961) 'Sixty Years of Philippine Ethnology: A First Glance at the Years 1901–1961'. *Science Review*, vol. 2, pp. 1–5.

Macaraig, Serafin E. (1938) *Introduction to Sociology*. Manila: Educational Supply Company.

McCargo, Duncan (2002) 'Security, Development and Political Participation in Thailand: Alternative Currencies of Legitimacy'. *Contemporary Southeast Asia*, vol. 24, pp. 50–67.

—— (2006a) 'Introduction: Rethinking Thailand's Southern Violence'. In McCargo (2006b), pp. 3–9.

—— (ed.) (2006b) 'Patani Merdeka – Thailand's Southern Fire'. *Critical Asian Studies*, special issue, vol. 38.

McCarthy, Stephen (2006) 'Prospects for Justice and Stability in Burma'. *Asian Survey*, vol. 46, pp. 417–436.

McGee, T. (1967) *The Southeast Asian City: A Social Geography of the Primate Cities of Southeast Asia*. London: G. Bell and Sons.

—— (1972) 'Rural-urban Migration in a Plural Society. A Case Study of Malays in West Malaysia'. In Dwyer (1972c), pp. 108–124.

—— (2002) 'Reconstructing *The Southeast Asian City* in an Era of Volatile Globalization'. *Asian Journal of Social Science*, vol. 30, pp. 8–27.

McVey, Ruth T. (ed.) (1992a) *Southeast Asian Capitalists*. Ithaca, New York: Cornell University Southeast Asia Program, Studies on Southeast Asia.

—— (1992b) 'The Materialization of the Southeast Asian Entrepreneur'. In McVey (1992a), pp. 7–33.

—— (1995) 'Change and Continuity in Southeast Asian Studies'. *Journal of Southeast Asian Studies*, vol. 26, pp. 1–9.

—— (2005) 'Afterword: in Praise of the Coelacanth's Cousin'. In Kratoska et al. (2005b), pp. 308–319.

Magdoff, Harry (1978) *Imperialism: From the Colonial Age to the Present*. New York and London: Monthly Review Press.

Mahathir bin Mohamad (1997) *The Asian Values Debate*. Kuala Lumpur: Institute of Strategic and International Studies, The Perdana Papers.

Mahbubani, Kishore (1993) 'The Dangers of Decadence. What the Rest can Teach the West'. *Foreign Affairs*, vol. 72, pp. 10–14.

Malhotra, Kamal (2002) 'Development Enabler or Diasbler? The Role of the State in Southeast Asia'. In Wee (2002c), pp. 31–50.

Mandel, Ernest (1971) *The Formation of the Economic Thought of Karl Marx, 1843 to Capital*. London: Monthly Review Press.

Manderson, Lenore (1980) *Women, Politics and Change: The Kaum Ibu UMNO Malaysia 1945–1972*. Singapore: Oxford University Press.

—— (ed.) (1983a) *Women's Work and Women's Roles. Economics and Everyday Life in Indonesia, Malaysia and Singapore*. Canberra and New York: The Australian National University, Development Studies Centre Monograph No. 32.

—— (1983b) 'Introduction'. In Manderson (1983a), pp. 1–14.

—— (1991) 'Gender and Politics in Malaysia: Reflections on Order, Knowledge and Enquiry'. In Stivens (1991b), pp, pp. 43–60.

—— (1997) 'Parables of Imperialism and Fantasies of the Exotic: Western Representations of Thailand – Place and Sex'. In Manderson and Jolly (1997b), pp. 123–144.

Manderson, Lenore and Margaret Jolly (1997a) 'Sites of Desire/Economies of Pleasure in Asia and the Pacific'. In Manderson and Jolly (1997b), pp. 1–26.

—— (eds) (1997b) *Sites of Desire, Economies of Pleasure. Sexualities in Asia and the Pacific*, Chicago and London: University of Chicago Press.

Manderson, Lenore and Pranee Liamputtong (2002) 'Youth and Sexuality in Contemporary Asian Societies'. In Leonore Manderson and Pranee Liamputtong (eds), *Coming of Age in South and Southeast Asia*. Richmond: Curzon Press, pp. 1–15.

Maneewan Chat-uthai and Gary N. McLean (2003) 'Combating Corruption in Thailand: A Call to an End of the "White Buffet"'. In Kidd and Richter (2003b), pp. 317–348.

Manlove, Robert Fletcher (2002) 'Social Inequality in Urban Philippines'. *Philippine Studies*, vol. 50, pp. 451–495.

Mantra, Ida Bagoes and Yeremias T. Keban (1988) *Urbanization in Indonesia*. Yogyakarta: Gadjah Mada University, Population Studies Center.

Marr, David G. (1973) 'Institutionalized Value Imbalances in Vietnam Studies'. In Fischer (1973), pp. 95–102.

Marsden, William (1975) *The History of Sumatra, Containing an Account of the Government, Laws, Customs and Manners of the Native Inhabitants, with a Description of the Natural Productions and a Relation of the Ancient State of That Island*. Kuala Lumpur: Oxford University Press, reprint, first published 1783.

Martinussen, John (1997) *Society, State and Market. A Guide to Competing Theories of Development*. London and New Jersey: Zed Books.

Marx, Karl (1964) *Pre-Capitalist Economic Formations*. London: Lawrence and Wishart, trans. and ed. Eric Hobsbawm.

—— (1972) *On Colonialism: Articles from the New York Tribune and Other Writings*. New York: International Publishers.

Marx, Karl and Frederik Engels (1971) *On Ireland*. London: Lawrence and Wishart.

—— (1978) *Ireland and the Irish Question*. London: Lawrence and Wishart.

Mauzy, Diane K. (1997) 'The Human Rights and "Asian Values" Debate in Southeast Asia: Trying to Clarify the Key Issues'. *The Pacific Review*, vol. 10, pp. 210–236.

Mayer, Adrian C. (1977) 'The Significance of Quasi-groups in the Study of Complex Societies'. In Schmidt, et al. (1977), pp. 43–54.

Maznah Mohamad (2001) 'Women in the UMNO and PAS Labyrinth'. In Maznah and Wong (2001b), pp. 112–138.

Maznah Mohamad and Wong Soak Koon (2001a) 'Malaysian Culture, Politics and Identity: A Reappraisal'. In Maznah and Wong (2001b), pp. 23–41.

—— (eds) (2001b) *Risking Malaysia. Culture, Politics and Identity*. Bangi: Penerbit Universiti Kebangsaan Malaysia.

Mee, Wendy (1998) 'National Difference and Global Citizenship'. In Kahn (1998b), pp. 227–258.

Mehmet, Ozay (1988) *Development in Malaysia: Poverty, Wealth and Trusteeship*. Kuala Lumpur: Insan.

Mills, C. Wright (1967) *The Power Elite*. New York: Oxford University Press.

Mills, Mary Beth (1997) 'Contesting the Margins of Modernity: Women, Migration, and Consumption in Thailand'. *American Ethnologist*, vol. 24, pp. 37–61.

Milner, Anthony (1998) 'Ideological Work in Constructing the Malay Majority'. In Gladney (1998b), pp. 151–169.

Mohammed Halib and Tim Huxley (1996a) 'Introduction'. In Mohammed and Huxley (1996b), pp. 1–9.

—— (eds) (1996b) *An Introduction to Southeast Asian Studies*. London: I.B. Tauris Publishers.

Moir, H. and Wirosardjono, S. (1977) *The Jakarta Informal Sector*. Jakarta: ILO-LEKNAS.

Moore, Wilbert E. (1963) *Social Change*. Englewood Cliffs, New Jersey: Prentice Hall.

Morell, David, and Chai-anan Samudavanija (1981) *Political Conflict in Thailand. Reform, Reaction, Revolution*. Cambridge: Oelgeschler, Gunn and Hain.

Morin, Alexander J. (1952) 'Editorial'. *Economic Development and Cultural Change*, vol. 1, pp. 3–7.

Mortimer, Rex (ed.) (1973) *Showcase State: The Illusion of Indonesia's 'Accelerated Modernisation'*. Sydney: Angus and Robertson.

Muhammad Ikmal Said (1992) 'Ethnic Perspectives of the Left in Malaysia'. In Kahn and Loh (1992), pp. 254–281.

Mulder, Niels (1979) *Everyday Life in Thailand: An Interpretation*. Bangkok: Editions Duang Kamol.

—— (1983) *Java-Thailand: A Comparative Perspective*. Yogyakarta: Gadjah Mada University Press.

—— (1989) *Individual and Society in Java: A Cultural Analysis*. Yogyakarta: Gadjah Mada University Press.

—— (1990) *Appreciating Lowland Christian Filipino Culture*. Bielefeld: University of Bielefeld, Faculty of Sociology, Sociology of Development Research Centre, Working Paper No. 141.

—— (1998) ' The Legitimacy of the Public Sphere and Culture of the New Urban Middle Class in the Philippines'. In Schmidt, Hersh and Fold (1998a), pp. 98–113.

—— (2004) *Southeast Asian Images:Towards Civil Society?* Chiang Mai: Silkworm Books.

Mya Maung, U (1962) 'Cultural Values and Economic Change in Burma'. *Asian Survey*, vol. 4, pp. 757–764.

Myint, Hla (1972) *Southeast Asia's Economy: Development Policies in the 1970s*. Harmondsworth: Penguin Books.

Myint, Maung (1966) *Agriculture in Burmese Economic Development*. University of California, Berkeley, PhD thesis.

Nagata, Judith A. (1974) 'What is a Malay? Situational Selection of Ethnic Identity in a Plural Society'. *American Ethnologist*, vol. 1, pp. 331–350.

—— (1975a) 'Introduction'. In Judith A. Nagata (ed.), *Pluralism in Malaysia: Myth and Reality*. Leiden: E.J. Brill, pp. 1–16.

—— (1975b) 'Perceptions of Social Inequality in Malaysia'. In Judith A. Nagata (ed.), *Pluralism in Malaysia: Myth and Reality*. Leiden: E.J. Brill, pp. 113–136.

—— (1979) *Malaysian Mosaic: Perspectives from a Poly-ethnic Society*. Vancouver: University of British Columbia Press.

—— (1984) *The Reflowering of Malaysian Islam*. Vancouver; University of British Columbia Press.

—— (2001) 'Heritage as a Site of Resistance: from Architecture to Political Activism in Urban Penang'. In Maznah and Wong (2001b), pp. 179–201.

Nagata, Judith A. and Janet W. Salaff (1996) 'Strategies of Adjustment: Lives of Southeast Asian Women'. *Southeast Asian Journal of Social Science*, vol. 24, pp. 1–17.

Naroll, Raoul (1964) 'On Ethnic Unit Classification'. *Current Anthropology*, vol. 5, pp. 283–291, 306–312.

—— (1968) 'Who the Lue are'. In June Helm (ed.), *Essays on the Problem of Tribe*. Washington, DC: University of Washington Press, pp. 72–79.

Nas, Peter J.M. (ed.) (1986) *The Indonesian City. Studies in Urban Development and Planning*.

Dordrecht and Cinnaminson: Foris, Verhandeligen van het Koninklijk Instituut voor Taal-, Land- en Volkenkunde, No. 117.

—— (ed.) (1987) *The Indonesian City*. Princeton, NJ: Princeton University Press.

—— (1989) 'Town and Countryside in Indonesia: A Sceptic's View'. *Sojourn. Journal of Social Issues in Southeast Asia*, vol. 4, pp. 20–33.

—— (1992) 'Jakarta, City Full of Symbols: An Essay in Symbolic Ecology'. *Sojourn. Journal of Social Issues in Southeast Asia*, vol. 7, pp. 175–207.

—— (1993) *Urban Symbolism*. Brill: Leiden.

—— (ed.) (1998) 'Globalization, Localization and Indonesia'. *Bijdragen tot de Taal-, Land- en Volkenkunde*, special issue, vol. 154, pp. 181–364.

Nas, Peter J.M. and Welmoet Boender (2002) 'The Indonesian City in Urban Theory'. In Peter J.M.Nas (ed.), *The Indonesian Town Revisited*. Münster: Lit Verlag and Singapore: Institute of Southeast Asian Studies, pp. 3–16.

Nash, Manning (1964) 'Social Prerequisites to Economic Growth in Latin America and Southeast Asia'. *Economic Development and Cultural Change*, vol. 12, pp. 225–242.

—— (1965) *The Golden Road to Modernity. Village Life in Contemporary Burma*. New York, London, Sydney: John Wiley and Sons.

—— (1980) 'South-East Asian Society: Dual or Multiple (with comments by Benjamin Higgins and Lucian W. Pye)'. In Evers (1980b), pp. 76–84.

Nathan, Andrew J. (1977) 'A Factionalism Model for CCP Politics'. In Schmidt, et al. (1977), pp. 382–401.

Neher, Clark D. (1981) *Politics in Southeast Asia*. Cambridge: Schenkman Publishing, second edition.

—— (1984) 'The Social Sciences'. In Ronald A. Morse (ed.), *Southeast Asian Studies: Options for the Future*. Lanham, New York and London: University Press of America, The Wilson Center, pp. 129–36.

Neher, Clark D. and Budsayamat Bunjaipet (1989) 'Political Interaction in Northern Thailand'. *Southeast Asian Journal of Social Science*, vol. 17, pp. 53–69.

Nghiem Lien Huong (2004) 'Female Garment Workers: The New Young Volunteers in Vietnam's Modernization'. In Taylor (2004a), pp. 297–324.

Nguyen, Phuong An (2002) 'Looking beyond *Bien Che*: The Considerations of Young Vietnamese Graduates When Seeking Employment in the *Doi Moi* Era'. *Sojourn: Journal of Social Issues in Southeast Asia*, vol. 17, pp. 221–248.

—— (2003) *Between 'Still Society' and 'Moving Society': Life Choices and Value Orientations of Hanoi University Graduates in Post-reform Vietnam*. University of Hull, Unpublished PhD thesis.

—— (2006) *Youth and the State in Contemporary Vietnam*. Lund University: Centre for East and South-East Asian Studies, Working Papers in Contemporary Asian Studies, No. 17.

Nicholas, Ralph W. (1977) 'Factions. A Comparative Analysis'. In Schmidt, et al. (1977), pp. 55–73.

Nye, J.S. (1967) 'Corruption and Political Development: A Cost-benefit Analysis'. *American Political Science Review*, vol. 61, pp. 417–427.

O'Brien, Leslie (1982) 'Class, Gender and Ethnicity: The Neglect of an Integrated Framework'. *Southeast Asian Journal of Social Science*, vol. 2, pp. 1–12.

—— (1983) 'Four Paces Behind: Women's Work in Peninsular Malaysia. In Manderson (1983a), pp. 193–215.

—— (1988) 'Capitalist Penetration and Segmentation of the Malaysian Labour Force'. In Chandler, Sullivan and Branson (1988), pp. 41–62.

O'Connor, Richard A. (1983) *A Theory of Indigenous Southeast Asian Urbanism*. Singapore: Institute of Southeast Asian Studies, Research Notes and Discussions Paper No. 38.

—— (1995) 'Indigenous Urbanism: Class, City and Society in Southeast Asia'. *Journal of Southeast Asian Studies*, vol. 26, pp. 30–45.

Ockey, James (2001) 'On the Expressway and under it: Representations of the Middle Class, the Poor, and Democracy in Thailand'. In Yao (2001b), pp. 313–337.

—— (2004) 'State, Bureaucracy and Polity in Modern Thai Politics'. *Journal of Contemporary Asia*, vol. 34, pp. 143–162.

Öjendal, Joakim (2005a) 'Democratization amidst Globalization in Southeast Asia. Empirical Findings and Theoretical Reflections'. In Loh and Öjendal (2005b), pp. 345–372.

—— (2005b) 'A New Local State in Cambodia? Decentralization as a Political Commodity'. In Loh and Öjendal (2005b), pp. 287–315.

Ong Aihwa (1987) *Spirits of Resistance and Capitalist Discipline: Factory Women in Malaysia*. Albany: SUNY Press.

—— (1988) 'The Production of Possession: Spirits and the Multinational Corporation in Malaysia'. *American Ethnologist*, vol. 1, pp. 28–42.

—— (1990) 'Japanese Factories, Malay Workers: Class and Sexual Metaphors in West Malaysia'. In Atkinson and Errington (1990), pp. 385–422.

—— (1995) 'State Versus Islam: Malay Families, Women's Bodies, and the Body Politic in Malaysia'. In Ong and Peletz (1995b), pp. 159–194.

—— (1999) 'Clash of Civilizations or Asian Liberalism? An Anthropology of the State and Citizenship'. In Henrietta Moore (ed.), *Anthropological Theory Today*. Cambridge, Mass.: Polity Press, pp. 48–72.

Ong Aihwa and Michael G. Peletz (1995a) 'Introduction'. In Ong and Peletz (1995b), pp. 1–18.

—— (eds) (1995b) *Bewitching Women, Pious Men. Gender and Body Politics in Southeast Asia*. Berkeley, Los Angeles, London: University of California Press.

Ong Jin Hui, Tong Chee Kiong and Tan Ern Ser (1997a) 'Overview'. In Ong et al. (1997b), pp. vii–xxi.

—— (eds) (1997b) *Understanding Singapore Society*. Singapore: Times Academic Press.

Ooi Giok Ling, Sharon Siddique and Soh Kay Cheng (1993) *The Management of Ethnic Relations in Public Housing Estates*. Singapore: Times Academic Press, The Institute of Policy Studies.

Ortner, Sherry B. (1974) 'Is Female to Male as Nature is to Culture?' In Michelle Z. Rosaldo and Louise Lamphere (eds), *Woman, Culture and Society*, Stanford: Stanford University Press, pp. 56–87.

Osborne, Milton (2004) *Southeast Asia. An Introductory History*. Crows Nest: Allen and Unwin, ninth edition, first published 1979.

Ossowski, S. (1963) *Class Structure in the Social Consciousness*. London: Routledge and Kegan Paul.

—— (1969) 'Old Notions and New Problems: Interpretations of Social Structure in Modern Society'. In Béteille (1969b), pp. 79–89.

Owen, Norman G. (1971a) 'Introduction: Philippine Society and American Colonial-ism'. In Owen (1971c), pp. 1–12.

—— (1971b) 'Philippine Economic Development and American Policy: A Reappraisal'. In Owen (1971c), pp. 103–128.

—— (ed.) (1971c) *Compadre Colonialism. Studies on the Philippines under American Rule.* Ann Arbor, Michigan: The University of Michigan, Centre for South and Southeast Asian Studies, Michigan Papers on South and Southeast Asia No. 3.

—— (ed.) (and contributors David Chandler, William R. Roff, David Joel Steinberg, Jean Gelman Taylor, Robert H. Taylor, Alexander Woodside, David K. Wyatt) (2005) *The Emergence of Modern Southeast Asia. A New History.* Honolulu: University of Hawai'i Press.

Oxaal, Ivar, Tony Barnett and David Booth (eds) (1975) *Beyond the Sociology of Development: Ecponomy and Society in Latin America and Africa.* London and Boston: Routledge and Kegan Paul.

Palmier, L.H. (Leslie) (1960) *Social Status and Power in Java.* London: The Athlone Press, LSE Monographs on Social Anthropology, 20.

—— (1985) *The Control of Bureaucratic Corruption. Case Studies in Asia.* New Delhi: Allied Publishers Private Limited.

—— (2003) 'Corruption in Context'. In Kidd and Richter (2003b), pp. 73–89.

—— (2006) 'Indonesia: Corruption, Ethnicity and the "Pax Americana"'. *Asian Affairs*, vol. 37, pp. 147–160.

Panopia, Isabel S., Felicidad V. Cordero-MacDonald and Adelisa A. Raymundo (1995) *General Sociology: Focus on the Philippines.* Manila: Popular Book Store, abridged paperback edition.

Paritta Chalermpow Koanantakool (2002) 'Thai Middle-class Practice and Consumption of Traditional Dance: "Thai-ness" and High Art'. In Wee (2002c), pp. 217–241.

Parkinson, Brien K. (1967) 'Non-economic Factors in the Economic Retardation of the Rural Malays'. *Modern Asian Studies*, vol. 1, pp. 31–46.

—— (1968) 'The Economic Retardation of the Malays – a Rejoinder'. *Modern Asian Studies*, vol. 2, pp. 267–272.

Parsons, Talcott (1951) *The Social System.* London: Routledge.

—— (1960) *Structure and Process in Modern Societies.* Glencoe: Free Press.

Pasuk Phongpaichit (1982) *From Peasant Girls to Bangkok Masseuses.* Geneva: International Labour Office.

Pasuk Phongpaichit and and Chris Baker (1995) *Thailand: Economy and Politics.* Kuala Lumpur: Oxford University Press.

—— (1997) 'Thailand in the 1990s'. In Hewison (1997b), pp. 21–41.

—— (2004) *Thaksin: The Business of Politics in Thailand.* Chiang Mai: Silkworm Books and Copenhagen: NIAS Press.

Pasuk Phongpaichitand and Sungsidh Piriyarangsan (1996) *Corruption and Democracy in Thailand.* Chiang Mai: Silkworm Books, second edition.

Peacock, James L. (1978) *Muslim Puritans: Reformist Psychology in Southeast Asian Islam.* Berkeley: University of California Press.

Peletz, Michael G. (1987) 'The Exchange of Men in 19th-Century Negeri Sembilan (Malaya)'. *American Ethnologist*, vol. 14, pp. 449–469.

—— (1995a) *Reason and Passion: Representations of Gender in a Malay Society*. Berkeley and Los Angeles: University of California Press.

—— (1995b) 'Neither Reasonable nor Responsible: Contrasting Representations of Masculinity in a Malay Society'. In Ong and Peletz (1995b), pp. 76–123.

Pels, Peter and Oscar Salemink (eds) (1999) *Colonial Subjects: Essays on the Practical History of Anthropology*. Ann Arbor: University of Michigan Press.

Pham, Julie (2004) 'Ghost-Hunting in Colonial Burma. Nostalgia, Paternalism and the Thoughts of J.S. Furnivall. *South East Asia Research*, vol. 12, pp. 237–268.

—— (2005) 'J.S.Furnivall and Fabianism: Reinterpreting the "Plural Society" in Burma'. *Modern Asian Studies*, vol. 39, pp. 321–348.

Phelan, John Leddy (1959) *The Hispanization of the Philippines. Spanish Aims and Filipino Responses, 1565–1700*. Madison: The University of Wisconsin Press.

Phillips, D.R. and A.G.O. Yeh (eds) (1987) *New Towns in East and South-east Asia: Planning and Development*. Hong Kong: Oxford University Press.

Phillips, Herbert P. (1973) 'Some Premises of American Scholarship on Thailand'. In Fischer (1973), pp. 64–81.

Pholsena, Vatthana (2006) *Post-war Laos. The Politics of Culture, History and Identity*. Ithaca, New York: Cornell University Press, and Copenhagen: NIAS Press.

Pinches, Michael (1996) 'The Philippines' New Rich. Capitalist Transformation amidst Economic Gloom'. In Robison and Goodman (1996b), pp. 103–133.

Pineda-Ofreneo, Rosalinda (1988) 'Subcontracting in Export-oriented Industries: Impact on Filipino Working Women'. In Chandler, Sullivan and Branson (1988), pp. 17–40.

Popkin, Samuel L. (1979) *The Rational Peasant: The Political Economy of Rural Society in Vietnam*. Berkeley and Los Angeles: University of California Press.

Powers, John C. (1997) 'Human Rights and Cultural Values: The Political Philosophies of the Dalai Lama and the People's Republic of China'. *Pacific Rim Report*, No.2, pp. 1–20.

Preston, Peter W. (1987) *Rethinking Development. Essays on Development and Southeast Asia*. London and New York: Routledge and Kegan Paul.

Price, Susanna (1983) 'Rich Woman, Poor Woman: Occupation Differences in a Textile Producing Village in Central Java'. In Manderson (1983a), pp. 97–110.

Provencher, Ronald (1971) *Two Malay Worlds: Interaction in Rural and Urban Settings*. Berkeley: University of California Press, Center for South and Southeast Asian Studies, Monograph No. 4.

Prudhisan Jumbala and Chantana Banpasirichote (2001) 'Thai Middle Classes: Between Class Ambiguity and Democratic Propensity'. In Hsiao (2001), pp. 381–413.

PuruShotam, Nirmala (1997) 'Women and Knowledge/Power: Notes on the Singa-porean Dilemma'. In Ong et al. (1997b), pp. 535–561.

—— (1998a) 'Disciplining Difference. Race in Singapore'. In Kahn (1998b), pp. 51–94.

—— (1998b) 'Between Compliance and Resistance: Women and the Middle-Class Way of Life in Singapore'. In Sen and Stivens (1998), pp. 127–166.

Pye, Lucian W. (1962) *Politics, Personality, and Nation Building. Burma's Search for Identity*. New Haven and London: Yale University Press.

—— (1967) *Southeast Asia's Political Systems*. Englewood Cliffs, New Jersey: Prentice-Hall, Comparative Asian Governments Series.

—— (2001) 'Civility, Social Capital and Civil Society: Three Powerful Concepts for Exploring

Asia'. In Robert Rotberg (ed.), *Patterns of Social Capital, Stability and Change in Historical Perspective*. New York: Cambridge University Press, pp. 386–387.

Quah, Jon S.T. (1982) 'Bureaucratic Corruption in the ASEAN Countries: A Comparative Analysis of their Anti-corruption Strategies. *Journal of Southeast Asian Studies*, vol. 13, pp. 153–177.

—— (1983) 'Public Bureaucracy, Social Change and National Development'. In Peter S.J. Chen (ed.), *Singapore. Development Policies and Trends*. Singapore: Oxford University Press, pp. 197–223.

—— (1985) 'Public Housing'. In Jon S.T. Quah, Chan Heng Chee and Seah Chee Meow (eds), *Government and Politics of Singapore*. Singapore: Oxford Uni-versity Press, pp. 233–259.

Quilty, Mary Catherine (1998) *Textual Empires. A Reading of Early British Histories of Southeast Asia*. Clayton, Monash University: Monash Asia Institute.

Quinones, Enery (2003) 'The OECD Convention in Asia'. In Kidd and Richter (2003b), pp. 27–45.

Raffles, Thomas Stamford (1965) *History of Java*. Kuala Lumpur: Oxford University Press, reprint, first published 1817, London: Black, Parbury and Allen, 2 vols.

Rasiah, Rajah (1995) *Foreign Capital and Industrialisation in Malaysia*. London: Macmillan.

—— (1997) 'Class, Ethnicity and Economic Development in Malaysia'. In Rodan, Hewison and Robison (1997), pp. 121–147.

Reid, Anthony (1980) 'The Structure of Cities in Southeast Asia'. *Journal of Southeast Asian Studies*, vol. 11, pp. 235–250.

—— (1988) *Southeast Asia in the Age of Commerce: 1400–1680*, Vol. 1, *The Land Below the Winds*. New Haven: Yale University Press.

—— (1993) *Southeast Asia in the Age of Commerce: 1400–1680*, Vol. 2, *Expansion and Crisis*. New Haven: Yale University Press.

—— (1999) 'A Saucer Model of Southeast Asian Identity'. *Southeast Asian Journal of Social Science*, Special Focus, *Reconceptualizing Southeast Asia*, Amitav Acharya and Ananda Rajah (eds), vol. 27, pp. 7–23.

Resnick, Stephen A. (1970) 'The Decline of Rural Industry under Export Expansion: A Comparison among Burma, Philippines, and Thailand, 1870–1938'. *Journal of Economic History*, vol. 30, pp. 51–73.

Reynolds, Craig, J. (1995) 'A New Look at Old Southeast Asia'. *The Journal of Asian Studies*, vol. 54, pp. 419–446.

—— (1998) 'Globalization and Cultural Nationalism in Modern Thailand'. In Kahn (1998b), pp. 115–145.

—— (2001) 'Globalisers and Communitarians: Public Intellectuals Debate Thailand's Futures'. *Singapore Journal of Tropical Geography*, vol. 22, pp. 252–269.

—— (ed.) (2002) *National Identity and Its Defenders: Thailand Today*. Chiang Mai: Silkworm Books, second revised edition.

Reynolds, Craig, J. and Hong Lysa (1983) 'Marxism in Thai Historical Studies'. *The Journal of Asian Studies*, vol. 43, pp. 77–104.

Ricklefs, M.C. (1981) *A History of Modern Indonesia, c.1300 to the Present*. London and Basingstoke: Macmillan, Macmillan Asian Histories Series.

Rigg, Jonathan (1997) *Southeast Asia: The Human Landscape of Modernization and Development*. London: Routledge, second revised edition, 2003.

—— (2001) *More than the Soil. Rural Change in Southeast Asia*. Harlow: Pearson Education Limited.

Riggs, Fred W. (1961) 'A Model for the Study of Thai Society'. *Thai Journal of Public Administration*, vol. 1, pp. 87–91.

—— (1964) *Administration in Developing Countries: The Theory of Prismatic Society*. Boston, Mass.: Houghton Mifflin.

—— (1966) *Thailand: The Modernization of a Bureaucratic Polity*. Honolulu: East-West Center Press.

Rivera, Temario (2001) 'Middle Class Politics and Views on Society and Government'. In Hsiao (2001), pp. 209–265.

Rizal Sukuma (2005) 'Ethnic Conflict in Indonesia: Causes and the Quest for Solution'. In Kusuma and Thompson (2005a), pp. 1–41.

Roberts, Bryan (1978) *Cities of Peasants: The Political Economy of Urbanization in the Third World*. London: Edward Arnold.

Roberts, David (2001) *Political Transition in Cambodia, 1991–99*. Richmond: Curzon.

Roberts, K., F.G. Cook, S.C. Clark and E. Semeonoff (1977) *The Fragmentary Class Structure*. London: Heinemann.

Robinson, Kathryn (1983) 'Women and Work in an Indonesian Mining Town'. In Manderson (1983a), pp. 111–127.

—— (1986) *Stepchildren of Progress: The Political Economy of Development in an Indonesian Mining Town*. Albany, New York: SUNY Press.

—— (1998) 'Love and Sex in an Indonesian Mining Town'. In Sen and Stivens (1998), pp. 63–86.

—— (2001) 'Gender, Islam and Culture in Indonesia'. In Susan Blackburn (ed.), *Love, Sex and Power. Women in Southeast Asia*. Clayton: Monash University Press, Monash Asia Institute, pp. 17–30.

Robison, Richard (1978) 'Toward a Class Analysis of the Indonesian Military Bureaucratic State'. *Indonesia*, No. 25, pp. 17–39.

—— (1980) 'Culture, Politics and Economy in the Political History of the New Order'. *Indonesia*, No. 31, pp. 1–29.

—— (1985) 'Class, Capital and the State in New Order Indonesia'. In Higgott and Robison (1985a), pp. 295–335.

—— (1986) *Indonesia: The Rise of Capital*. Sydney: Allen and Unwin.

—— (1987) 'After the Gold Rush: The Politics of Economic Restructuring in Indonesia in the 1980s'. In Robison, Hewison and Higgott (1987a), pp. 16–51.

—— (1988) 'Authoritarian States, Capital-Owning Classes and the Politics of Newly Industrializing Countries'. *World Politics*, vol. 41, pp. 52–74.

—— (1992) 'Industrialization and the Economic and Political Development of Capital: The Case of Indonesia'. In McVey (1992a), pp. 65–88.

—— (1993) 'Indonesia: Tensions in State and Regime'. In Hewison, Robison and Rodan (1993), pp. 41–74.

—— (1996a) 'Ideology and the Politics of Asian Values'. *The Pacific Review*, vol. 9, pp. 309–327.

—— (1996b) 'Looking North: Myths and Strategies'. In Robison (1996c), pp. 3–28.

—— (ed.) (1996c) *Pathways to Asia. The Politics of Engagement*. St. Leonard's, NSW: Allen and Unwin.

—— (1997) 'Politics and Markets in Indonesia's Post-oil Era'. In Rodan, Hewison and Robison (1997), pp. 29–63.

—— (1998) 'The Emergence of the Middle Classes in Southeast Asia and the Indonesian Case'. In Schmidt, Hersh and Fold (1998a), pp. 60–77.

—— (2001) 'Indonesia: Crisis, Oligarchy and Reform'. In Rodan, Hewison and Robison (2001a), pp. 104–137.

—— (2003) 'Looking Back on the Asian Crisis: The Question of Convergence'. *Asian Journal of Social Science*, vol. 31, pp. 162–171.

Robison, Richard and David S.G. Goodman (1996a) 'The New Rich in Asia. Economic Development, Social Status and Political Consciousness'. In Robison and Goodman (1996b), pp. 1–16.

—— (eds) (1996b) *The New Rich in Asia. Mobile Phones, McDonalds and Middle-class Revolution*. London and New York: Routledge.

Robison, Richard and Vedi R. Hadiz (2006) 'Indonesia: Crisis, Oligarchy, and Reform'. In Rodan, Hewison and Robison (2006a), pp. 109–136.

Robison, Richard, Kevin Hewison and Richard Higgott (eds) (1987a) *Southeast Asia in the 1980s: The Politics of Economic Crisis*. Sydney: Allen and Unwin.

Robison, Richard, Richard Higgott and Kevin Hewison (1987b) 'Crisis in Economic Strategy in the 1980s: The Factors at Work'. In Robison, Hewison and Higgott (1987a), pp. 1–15.

Roces, Mina (1998) 'The Gendering of Post-war Philippine Politics'. In Sen and Stivens (1998), pp. 291–316.

—— (2000) 'Kinship Politics in Post-War Philippines: The Lopez Family'. *Modern Asian Studies*, vol. 34, pp. 181–221.

Rochaya Machali (2001) 'Women and the Concept of Power in Indonesia'. In Susan Blackburn (ed.), *Love, Sex and Power. Women in Southeast Asia*. Clayton: Monash University Press, Monash Asia Institute, pp. 1–16.

Rodan, Garry (1985) 'Industrialisation and the Singapore State in the Context of the New International Division of Labour'. In Higgott and Robison (1985a), pp. 172–194.

—— (1989) *The Political Economy of Singapore's Industrialization: National State and International Capital*. London: Macmillan.

—— (1993) 'The Growth of Singapore's Middle Class and its Political Significance'. In Garry Rodan (ed.), *Singapore Changes Guard*. New York: St. Martin's Press, pp. 52–71.

—— (1997) 'Civil Society and other Political Possibilities in Southeast Asia'. *Journal of Contemporary Asia*, vol. 27, pp. 156–178.

—— (2001) 'Singapore: Globalisation and the Politics of Economic Restructuring'. In Rodan, Hewison and Robison (2001a), pp. 138–177.

—— (2004) 'International Capital, Singapore's State Companies, and Security. *Critical Asian Studies*, vol. 36, pp. 479–499.

—— (2006a) 'Singapore: Globalisation, the State, and Politics'. In Rodan, Hewison and Robison (2006a), pp. 137–169.

—— (2006b) 'Singapore in 2005. "Vibrant and Cosmopolitan" without Political Pluralism'. *Asian Survey*, vol. 46, pp. 180–186.

Rodan, Garry and Kevin Hewison (1996) 'A "Clash of Cultures" or the Convergence of Political Ideology?' In Robison (1996c), pp. 29–55.

—— (2004) 'Closing the Circle? Globalization, Conflict, and Political Regimes'. *Critical Asian Studies*, vol. 36, pp. 383–404.

Rodan, Garry, Kevin Hewison and Richard Robison (eds) (1997) *The Political Economy of South-East Asia. An Introduction*. Melbourne: Oxford University Press.

—— (2001a) *The Political Economy of South-East Asia. Conflicts, Crises, and Change*. Melbourne: Oxford University Press, second edition.

—— (2001b) 'Theorising South-East Asia's Boom, Bust, and Recovery'. In Rodan, Hewison and Robison (2001a), pp. 1–41.

—— (eds) (2006a) *The Political Economy of South-East Asia. Markets, Power and Contestation*. Melbourne: Oxford University Press, third edition.

—— (2006b) 'Preface'. In Rodan, Hewison and Robison (2006a), pp. x–xviii.

—— (2006c) 'Theorising Markets in South-East Asia: Power and Contestation'. In Rodan, Hewison and Robison (2006a), pp. 1–38.

Romein, Jan (1962) *The Asian Century*. London: Allen and Unwin.

Rosaldo, Michelle Z. (1974) 'Woman, Culture and Society'. In Michelle Z. Rosaldo and Louise Lamphere (eds), *Woman, Culture and Society*. Stanford: Stanford University Press, pp. 17–42.

Rose, Richard (1964) 'Parties, Factions, and Tendencies in Britain'. *Political Studies*, vol. 12, pp. 33–46.

Rostow, Walt W. (1960) *The Stages of Economic Growth. A Non-Communist Manifesto*. Cambridge: Cambridge University Press.

Roxborough, Ian (1979) *Theories of Underdevelopment*. London: Macmillan.

Runciman, W.G. (1969) 'The Three Dimensions of Social Inequality'. In Béteille (1969b), pp. 45–63.

Rutten, Rosanne (1990) *Artisans and Entrepreneurs in the Rural Philippines: Making a Living and Gaining Wealth in Two Commercialized Crafts*. Amsterdam: VU University Press, CASA Monographs 2.

Said, Edward W. (1985) *Orientalism*. London: Penguin, originally published 1978.

St John, Ronald Bruce (2006) 'The Political Economy of Laos: Poor State or Poor Policy?' *Asian Affairs*, vol. 37, pp. 175–191.

Saliha Hassan and Carolina Lopez (2005) 'Human Rights in Malaysia: Globalization, National Governance and Local Responses'. In Loh and Öjendal (2005b), pp. 110–137.

Samuel, Hanneman (1999) 'The Development of Sociology in Indonesia: The Production of Knowledge, State Formation and Economic Change'. Swinburne University of Technology: unpublished PhD thesis.

Saravanamuttu, Johan (2001a) 'Is There a Politics of the Malaysian Middle Class?' In Abdul Rahman Embong (ed.), *Southeast Asian Middle Classes: Prospects for Social Change and Democratisation*. Bangi: Penerbit Universiti Kebangsaan Malaysia, pp. 103–118.

—— (2001b) 'Malaysian Civil Society-Awakenings?' In Maznah and Wong (2001b), pp. 93–111.

Saravanamuttu, Johan and Francis Loh Kok Wah (2004) 'Development and Democracy in Southeast Asia'. In Abdul Rahman Embong (2004), pp. 352–375.

Sarkisyanz, E. (1965) *Buddhist Backgrounds of the Burmese Revolution*. The Hague: Martinus Nijhoff.

Schiller, Anne and Bambang Garang (2002) 'Religion and Inter-ethnic Violence in Indonesia'. *Journal of Contemporary Asia*, vol. 32, pp. 244–254.

Schmidt, Johannes Dragsbaek, Jacques Hersh and Niels Fold (eds) (1998a) *Social Change in Southeast Asia*. Harlow: Longman.

—— (1998b) 'Introduction. Changing Realities of Social Transition in Southeast Asia'. In Schmidt, Hersh and Fold (1998a), pp. 1–20.

Schmidt, Steffen W., Laura Guasti, Carl H. Landé, and James C. Scott (eds) (1977) *Friends, Followers, and Factions: A Reader in Political Clientelism*. Berkeley, Los Angeles: University of California Press.

Schober, Juliane (2007) 'Buddhism, Violence, and the State in Burma (Myanmar) and Sri Lanka'. In Cady and Simon (2007a), pp. 51–69.

Schrieke, Bertram J.O. (1955–57) *Indonesian Sociological Studies: Selected Writings of B. Schrieke*; 2 Volumes, The Hague: W. van Hoeve (Volume 2 is separately titled *Ruler and Realm in Early Java*).

Schulte Nordholt, Nico and Leontine Visser (eds) (1995) *Social Science in Southeast Asia: From Particularism to Universalism*. Amsterdam: VU University Press, Comparative Asian Studies 17.

Schuurman, Frans J. (ed.) (1993a) *Beyond the Impasse: New Directions in Development Theory*. London and New Jersey: Zed Books.

—— (1993b) 'Introduction: Development Theory in the 1990s'. In Schuurman (1993a), pp. 1–48.

Scott, James C. (1969) 'The Analysis of Corruption in Developing Nations'. *Comparative Studies in Society and History*, vol. 11, pp. 315–341.

—— (1972a) 'Patron–Client Politics and Political Change in Southeast Asia'. *American Political Science Review*, vol. 66, pp. 91–113; republished in Schmidt, et al. (1977), pp. 123–146.

—— (1972b) 'The Erosion of Patron-client Bonds and Social Change in Rural Southeast Asia'. *The Journal of Asian Studies*, vol. 32, pp. 5–37.

—— (1972c) *Comparative Political Corruption*. Englewood Cliffs, New Jersey: Prentice-Hall.

—— (1976) *The Moral Economy of the Peasant: Rebellion and Subsistence in Southeast Asia*. New Haven and London: Yale University Press.

—— (1985) *Weapons of the Weak: Everyday Forms of Peasant Resistance*. New Haven and London: Yale University Press.

—— (1998) *Seeing like a State. How Certain Schemes to Improve the Human Condition Have Failed*. New Haven: Yale University Press.

—— (2001) 'Seeing Like a Social Scientist'. In Jomo (2001), pp. 100–107.

Scott, James C. and Benedict J. Kerkvliet (1977) 'How Traditional Rural Patrons Lose Legitimacy: A Theory with Special Reference to Southeast Asia'. In Schmidt, et al. (1977), pp. 439–458.

Sculli, Domenic (2003) 'Culture and Level of Industrialization as Determinants of Corruption in Asia'. In Kidd and Richter (2003b), pp. 203–219.

Seah Chee Meow (ed.) (1977) *Asian Values and Modernization*. Singapore: Singapore University Press.

Searle, Peter (1996) 'Recalcitrant or *Realpolitik*? The Politics of Culture in Australia's Relations with Malaysia'. In Robison (1996c), pp. 56–84.

—— (1999) *The Riddle of Malaysian Capitalism. Rent-seekers or Real Capitalists?* St Leonards, NSW: Allen and Unwin, Asian Studies Association of Australia.

Sears, Laurie J. (ed.) (1996a) *Fantasizing the Feminine in Indonesia*. Durham and London: Duke University Press.

—— (1996b) 'Introduction: Fragile Identities. Deconstructing Women and Indonesia'. In Sears (1996a), pp. 1–44.

Sebastian, Leonard C. (1999) 'Values and Governance Issues in the Foreign Policy of Singapore'. In Han (1999b), pp. 219–250.

Selochan, Viberto (ed.) (1991) *The Military, the State, and Development in Asia and the Pacific*. Boulder, Colorado: Westview Press.

Selosoemardjan (1962) *Social Changes in Jogjakarta*. Ithaca, New York: Cornell University Press.

Selth, Andrew (2002) *Burma's Armed Forces: Power without Glory*. Norwalk, Conn.: Eastbridge.

Selveratnam, V. (1974) *Decolonisation, the Ruling Elite and Ethnic Relations in Peninsular Malaysia*. University of Sussex: Institute of Development Studies, IDS Discussion Paper No. 44.

Sen, Krishna (1998) 'Indonesian Women at Work: Reframing the Subject'. In Sen and Stivens (1998), pp. 35–62.

Sen, Krishna and Maila Stivens (eds) (1998) *Gender and Power in Affluent Southeast Asia*. London and New York: Routledge.

Sethuraman, S.V. (1974) *Urbanization and Employment in Jakarta*. Geneva: World Employment Programme, ILO.

Shamsul Amri Baharuddin (1989) *Village: The Imposed Social Construct in Malaysia's Developmental Initiatives*. Bielefeld: University of Bielefeld, Sociology of Develop-ment Research Centre, Working Paper No. 115.

—— (1995) 'Malaysia: The Kratonization of Social Science'. In Nico Schulte Nordholt and Leontine Visser (eds), *Social Science in Southeast Asia: From Particularism to Universalism*. Amsterdam: VU University Press, Comparative Asian Studies 17, pp. 87–109.

—— (1998) 'Bureaucratic Management of Identity in a Modern State. "Malayness" in Postwar Malaysia'. In Gladney (1998b), pp. 135–150.

—— (2001) 'A History of an Identity, an Identity of a History: The Idea and Practice of "Malayness" in Malaysia Reconsidered'. *Journal of Southeast Asian Studies*, vol. 32, pp. 355–366.

Siddique, Sharon (1997/1990) 'The Phenomenology of Ethnicity: A Singapore Case Study'. In Ong et al. (1997b), pp. 107–124.

Sieh Lee Mei Ling (1992) 'The Transformation of Malaysian Business Groups'. In McVey (1992a), pp. 103–126.

Siffin, William J. (1966) *The Thai Bureaucracy: Institutional Change and Develop-ment*. Honolulu: East West Center Press.

Silverstein, Joseph (1980) *Burmese Politics: The Dilemma of National Unity*. New Brunswick: Rutgers University Press.

Sinha, Vaneeta (2000) 'Moving Beyond Critique: Practising the Social Sciences in the Context of Globalization, Postmodernity and Postcoloniality'. *Southeast Asian Journal of Social Science*, Special Focus *Alternative Discourses in the Social Sciences*, vol. 28, pp. 67–104.

Skinner, G. William and A. Thomas Kirsch (eds) (1975) *Change and Persistence in Thai Society. Essays in Honor of Lauriston Sharp*. Ithaca and London: Cornell University Press.

Sloan, Stephen (1967) *An Examination of Lucian W. Pye's Theory of Political Development – Through a Case Study of the Indonesian Coup of 1965*. New York University, PhD thesis.

Smith, Martin (1991) *Burma: Insurgency and the Politics of Ethnicity*. London, New York: Zed Books.

—— (2001) 'Burmese Politics after 1988: An Era of New and Uncertain Change'. In Taylor (2001a), pp. 15–40.

Smith, Ralph (1986) 'The Evolution of British Scholarship on South-East Asia 1820–1970: Is There a "British Tradition" in South-East Asian Studies?' In D.K. Bassett and V.T. King (eds), *Britain and South-East Asia*. University of Hull: Centre for South-East Asian Studies, Occasional Paper No. 13, Special issue, pp. 1–28.

Soedjatmoko (1965) 'Cultural Motivations to Progress: The "Exterior" and the "Interior" Views'. In Robert N. Bellah (ed.), *Religion and Progress in Modern Asia*. New York: The Free Press, pp. 1–14.

Spencer, Robert F. (1971) 'Introduction: Religion in Asian Society'. In Robert F. Spencer (ed.), *Religion and Change in Contemporary Asia*. Minneapolis: University of Minnesota Press, pp. 3–13.

Spiro, Melford E. (1967) *Burmese Supernaturalism: A Study in the Explanation and Reduction of Suffering*. Englewood Cliffs, N.J.: Prentice-Hall.

—— (1970) *Buddhism and Society: A Great Tradition and its Burmese Vicissitudes*. New York: Harper and Row.

Spiro, Shimon E. (1977) 'The Relocation of Villagers into Public Housing: Some Suggestive Findings from a Singaporean Study'. *Southeast Asian Journal of Social Science*, vol. 5, pp. 42–54.

Stauffer, Robert B. (1985) 'The Philippine Political Economy: (Dependent) State Capitalism in the Corporatist Mode'. In Higgott and Robison (1985a), pp. 241–265.

Steinberg, David Joel (1990) *The Future of Burma. Crisis and Choice in Myanmar*. Lanham: University Press of America.

Steinberg, David Joel, et al. (1971) *In Search of Southeast Asia. A Modern History*. New York: Praeger Publishers Inc., Holt Rinehart and Winston.

Stenson, M. (1976) 'Class and Race in West Malaysia'. *Bulletin of Concerned Asian Scholars*, vol. 8, pp. 45–54.

—— (1980) *Class, Race and Colonialism in West Malaysia*. St Lucia, Queensland: University of Queensland Press.

Sternstein, Larry (1972) 'Planning the Future of Bangkok'. In Dwyer (1972c), pp. 243–254.

Stivens, Maila K. (1988) 'Sexual Politics in Rembau: Female Autonomy, Matriliny, and Agrarian Change in Negeri Sembilan, Malaysia'. In Chandler, Sullivan and Branson (1988), pp. 79–114.

—— (1991a) 'Why Gender Matters in Southeast Asian Politics'. In Stivens (1991b), pp. 9–24.

—— (ed.) (1991b) *Why Gender Matters in Southeast Asian Politics*. Monash University: Centre of Southeast Asian Studies, Monash Papers on Southeast Asia, No. 23.

—— (1992) 'Perspectives on Gender: Problems in Writing about Women in Malaysia'. In Kahn and Loh (1992), pp. 202–224.

—— (1998a) 'Theorising Gender, Power and Modernity in Affluent Southeast Asia'. In Sen and Stivens (1998), pp. 1–34.

—— (1998b) 'Sex, Gender and the Making of the New Malay Middle Classes'. In Sen and Stivens (1998), pp. 87–126.

Stockwin, J.A.A. (1970) 'A Comparison of Political Factionalism in Japan and India'. *Australian Journal of Politics and History*, 16 December, pp. 361–374.

Stoler, Ann (1975) 'Some Socio-economic Aspects of Rice Harvesting in a Javanese Village' *Masyarakat Indonesia*, vol. 2, pp. 51–87.

—— (1977) 'Class Structure and Female Autonomy in a Javanese Village'. *Signs*, vol. 3, pp. 74–89.

Strange, Heather (1980) 'Some Changing Socioeconomic Roles of Village Women in Malaysia'. In Chipp and Green (1980b), pp. 123–151.

Suchit Bunbongkarn (1991) 'The Thai Military and its Role in Society in the 1990s'. In Selochan (1991), pp. 67–82.

Suehiro, Akira (1989) *Capital Accumulation in Thailand 1855–1985*. Tokyo: Centre for East Asian Cultural Studies.

—— (1992) 'Capitalist Development in Postwar Thailand: Commercial Bankers, Industrial Elite and Agribusiness Groups'. In McVey (1992a), pp. 35–63.

Sukamdi (1996) 'Urbanization and the Structure of Urban Employment in Indonesia'. *Sojourn. Journal of Social Issues in Southeast Asia*, vol. 11, pp. 52–75.

Sukma, Rizal (1999) 'Values, Governance, and Indonesia's Foreign Policy'. In Han (1999b), pp. 115–145.

Sullivan, J. (1992) *Local Government and Community in Java: An Urban Case Study*. Oxford: Oxford University Press.

Sullivan, Norma (1983) 'Indonesian Women in Development: State Theory and Urban Kampung Practice'. In Manderson (1983a), pp. 147–171.

—— (1991) 'Gender and Politics in Indonesia'. In Stivens (1991b), pp. 61–86.

Sungsidh Piriyarangsan (1983) *Thai Bureaucratic Capitalism*. Bangkok: Chulalong-korn University Press.

Sunindyo, Saraswati (1996) 'Murder, Gender, and the Media. Sexualizing Politics and Violence'. In Sears (1996a), pp. 120–139.

Surin Maisrikod and Duncan McCargo (1997) 'Electoral Politics. Commercialisation and Exclusion'. In Hewison (1997b), pp. 132–148.

Suryakusuma, Julia I. (1996) 'The State and Sexuality in New Order Indonesia'. In Sears (1996a), pp. 92–119.

Sutherland, Heather (2005) 'Contingent Devices'. In Kratoska et al. (2005b), pp. 20–59.

Suthy Prasartset (1980) *Thai Business Leaders: Men and Careers in a Developing Economy*. Tokyo: Institute of Developing Economies.

Tai Ching Ling (1988) *Housing Policy and High-Rise Living: A Study of Singapore's Public Housing*. Singapore: Chopmen Publishers.

Tambiah, S.J. (1973) 'Buddhism and This-Worldly Activity'. *Modern Asian Studies*, vol. 7, pp. 1–20.

—— (1976) *World Conqueror and World Renouncer: A Study of Buddhism and Polity in Thailand against a Historical Background*. Cambridge and New York: Cambridge University Press.

Tan Ern Ser (2004) *Does Class Matter? Social Stratification and Orientations in Singapore*. Singapore: World Scientific Publishing.

Tanabe, Shigeharu and Charles F. Keyes (eds) (2002) *Cultural Crisis and Social Memory: Modernity and Identity in Thailand and Laos*. Honolulu: University of Hawai'i Press.

Tanter, R. and K.R. Young (eds) (1992) *The Politics of Middle Class Indonesia*. Centre of Southeast Asian Studies: Monash University.

Taufik Abdullah (n.d.) 'Something about Something: Asian Studies in Southeast Asian Perspective'. Leiden: International Institute of Asian Studies, http://www.iias.nl/iiasn/iiasn2/somethi.txt.

Tay Kheng Soon and Robbie B.H. Goh (2003) 'Reading the Southeast Asian City in the Context of Rapid Economic Growth'. In Goh and Yeoh (2003b), pp. 13–27.

Taylor, John G. (1979) *From Modernization to Modes of Production.* London and New York: Macmillan.

Taylor, John G. and Andrew Turton (eds) (1988a) *Southeast Asia.* 'Sociology of Developing Societies' series, Basingstoke and London: Macmillan.

—— (1988b) 'Introduction'. In John G. Taylor and Andrew Turton (eds), *Southeast Asia.* 'Sociology of Developing Societies' series, Basingstoke and London: Macmillan, pp. 1–13.

Taylor, Philip (ed.) (2004a) *Social Inequality in Vietnam and the Challenges to Reform.* Singapore: Institute of Southeast Asian Studies.

—— (2004b) 'Introduction: Social Inequality in a Socialist State'. In Taylor (2004a), pp. 1–40.

Taylor, Robert H. (1982) 'Perceptions of Ethnicity in the Politics of Burma'. *Southeast Asian Journal of Social Science,* vol. 10, pp. 7–22.

—— (1987) *The State in Burma.* London: C. Hurst and Co.

—— (1995) 'Disaster or Release? J.S. Furnivall and the Bankruptcy of Burma'. *Modern Asian Studies,* vol. 29, pp. 45–63.

—— (ed.) (2001a) *Burma. Political Economy under Military Rule.* London: C. Hurst and Co.

—— (2001b) 'Stifling Change: The Army Remains in Command'. In Taylor (2001a), pp. 5–14.

Tham Seong Chee (ed.) (1972) *Modernization in Singapore.* Singapore: University Education Press.

—— (1977) *Malays and Modernization. A Sociological Interpretation.* Singapore: Singapore University Press.

—— (1980) 'Values and Modernization in Southeast Asia'. *Southeast Asian Journal of Social Science,* vol. 8, pp. 1–11.

Thomson, George G. (1978) 'The Political Elite in Singapore'. In Chen and Evers (1978b), pp. 61–72.

Thongchai Winichakul (1994) *Siam Mapped: A History of the Geo-body of a Nation.* Honolulu: University of Hawai'i Press.

—— (2005) 'Trying to Locate Southeast Asia from Its Navel: Where is Southeast Asian Studies in Thailand?' In Kratoska et al. (2005b), pp. 113–132.

Tinker, Hugh (1969) 'Continuity and Change in Asian Societies'. *Modern Asian Studies,* vol. 3, pp. 97–116.

Tin Maung Maung Than (2004) 'The Essential Tension. Democratization and the Unitary State in Myanmar (Burma)'. *South East Asia Research,* vol. 12, pp. 187–212.

—— (2005) 'Dreams and Nightmares: State Building and Ethnic Conflict in Myanmar (Burma)'. In Kusuma and Thompson (2005a), pp. 65–108.

Trager, Lillian (1988) *The City Connection: Migration and Family Interdependence in the Philippines.* Ann Arbor, MI: University of Michigan Press.

Tremewan, Christopher (1996) *The Political Economy of Social Control in Singapore.* Houndmills: Macmillan Press, and New York: St. Martin's Press, St. Antony's Series.

Trocki, Carl A. (1981) 'Power and Paradigms. Review Essay: Thailand'. *Bulletin of Concerned Asian Scholars*, vol. 13, pp. 64–73.

Turner, Byran S. (1974) *Weber and Islam: A Critical Study*. London: Routledge and Kegan Paul.

Turner, M.M. (1978) 'Interpretations of Class and Status in the Philippines: A Critical Evaluation'. *Cultures et développement*, vol. 10, pp. 265–296.

Turton, Andrew (1989) 'Local Powers and Rural Differentiation'. In Gillian Hart, Andrew Turton and Benjamin White (eds), *Agrarian Transformations in South-east Asia: The State and Local Processes of Accumulation*. Berkeley, Los Angeles, and Oxford: University of California Press, pp. 70–97.

Unger, Danny (1998) *Building Social Capital in Thailand: Fibers, Finance, and Infrastructure*. Cambridge: Cambridge University Press.

United Nations (2006) 'UN World Population Prospects. The 2004 Revision'. Department of Economic and Social Affairs, Population Division, http://esa.un.org/unpp/index/.

Van den Muijzenberg, Otto D. (1980) 'Involution or Evolution in the Philippines'. In Evers (1980b), pp. 209–219.

Van den Muijzenberg, Otto D. and Willem Wolters (1988) *Conceptualizing Development. The Historical-Sociological Tradition in Dutch Non-Western Sociology*. Dordrecht and Providence, RI: Foris Publications, Centre for Asian Studies Amsterdam, Comparative Asian Studies, 1.

Van der Kroef, Justus (1953) 'Entrepreneur and Middle Class in Indonesia'. *Economic Development and Cultural Change*, vol. 2, pp. 297–325.

Van Dijk, Meine Pieter (1986) 'Formalization and Informalization Processes in a Small Town in Central Java'. In Peter J.M. Nas (ed.), *The Indonesian City. Studies in Urban Development and Planning*. Dordrecht and Cinnaminson: Foris, Verhandelingen van het Koninklijk Instituut voor Taal-, Land- en Volkenkunde, No. 117, pp. 237–249.

Van Esterik, John (1996) 'Women Meditation Teachers in Thailand'. In Penny van Esterik (ed.), *Women of Southeast Asia*. Northern Illinois University: Center for Southeast Asian Studies, Monograph Series on Southeast Asia, Occasional Paper No. 17, pp. 33–41.

Van Esterik, Penny (1995) 'Rewriting Gender and Development in Southeast Asia'. In Karim (1995b), pp. 247–259.

—— (1996) 'Introduction'. In Penny van Esterik (ed.), *Women of Southeast Asia*. Northern Illinois University: Center for Southeast Asian Studies, Monograph Series on Southeast Asia, Occasional Paper No. 17, pp. 1–12.

Van Leur, Jacob (1955) *Indonesian Trade and Society: Essays in Asian Social and Economic History*. The Hague: W. van Hoeve.

Van Niel, Robert (1992) *Java under the Cultivation System. Collected Writings*. Leiden: KITLV Press, Verhandelingen van het Koninklijk Instituut voor Taal-, Land- en Volkenkunde, No. 150.

Van Schaik, Arthur (1986) *Colonial Control and Peasant Resources in Java: Agricultural Involution Reconsidered*. Amsterdam: University of Amsterdam Institute for Social Geography, Netherlands Geographical Studies 14.

Vickers, Adrian (2004) 'The Country and the Cities'. *Journal of Contemporary Asia*, vol. 34, pp. 304–317.

Von der Mehden, Fred R. (1968) *Religion and Nationalism in Southeast Asia. Burma, Indonesia and the Philippines*. Madison, Milwaukee and London: University of Wisconsin Press.

References

—— (1986) *Religion and Modernization in Southeast Asia.* Syracuse, N.Y.: Syracuse University Press.

Vo Van Ai (2000) 'Human Rights and Asian Values in Vietnam'. In Jacobsen and Bruun (2000b), pp. 92–110.

Wallerstein, Immanuel (1974) *The Modern World System.* New York: Academic Press.

—— (1979) *The Capitalist World Economy.* Cambridge: Cambridge University Press.

Wang Gungwu (2005) 'Two Perspectives of Southeast Asian Studies: Singapore and China'. In Kratoska et al. (2005b), pp. 60–81.

Wang, L.H. (1987) 'Residential New Town Development in Singapore: Background, Planning, and Design. In D.R. Phillips and A.G.O. Yeh (eds), *New Towns in East and South-east Asia: Planning and Development.* Hong Kong: Oxford University Press, pp. 23–40.

Ward, Barbara, E. (ed.) (1963) *Women in the New Asia: The Changing Roles of Men and Women in South and Southeast Asia.* Paris: UNESCO.

Warren, Bill (1980) *Imperialism, Pioneer of Capitalism.* London: Verso Books.

Warren, Carol (1985) 'Class and Change in Rural Southeast Asia'. In Higgott and Robison (1985a), pp. 128–45.

Weber, Max (1947) *The Theory of Social and Economic Organisation.* trans., New York: Free Press.

—— (1951) *The Religion of China: Confucianism and Taoism.* Glencoe: The Free Press.

—— (1958) *The Religion of India: The Sociology of Hinduism and Buddhism.* Glencoe: The Free Press.

—— (1963) *The Sociology of Religion.* Boston: Beacon Press.

—— (1971) *The Protestant Ethic and the Spirit of Capitalism.* Trans. London: Unwin, originally published in German in 1905.

Webster, Andrew (1990) *Introduction to the Sociology of Development.* Basingstoke: Macmillan, second edition.

Wedel Yuangrat (1981) *Modern Thai Radical Thought: The Siamization of Marxism and its Theoretical Problems.* University of Michigan, PhD thesis.

—— (1982) 'Current Radical Thai Ideology: The Returnees from the Jungle'. *Contemporary Southeast Asia*, vol. 4, pp. 1–18.

Wee, C.J.W-L (1996) 'The "Clash" of Civilizations or an Emerging East Asian Modernity'. *Sojourn. Journal of South-East Asian Social Issues*, vol. 11, pp. 211–230.

—— (2001) 'Representing the Singapore Modern: Dick Lee, Pop Music and the "New" Asia'. In Yao (2001b), pp. 243–269.

—— (2002a) 'Introduction: Local Cultures, Economic Development, and Southeast Asia'. In Wee (2002c), pp. 1–27.

—— (2002b) 'From Universal to Local Culture: The State, Ethnic Identity, and Capitalism in Singapore'. In Wee (2002c), pp. 129–157.

—— (ed.) (2002c) *Local Cultures and the 'New Asia': The State, Culture, and Capitalism in Southeast Asia.* Singapore: Institute of Southeast Asian Studies.

Wee, Vivienne and Chan Yuk Wah (2006) 'Ethnicity and Capital: Changing Relations between China and Southeast Asia'. *Journal of Contemporary Asia*, vol. 36, pp. 328–349.

Weekley, Kathleen (2004) 'Saving Pennies for the State. A New Role for Filipino Migrant Workers?' *Journal of Contemporary Asia*, vol. 34, pp. 349–363.

Weggel, Oskar (2005) 'Cambodia in 2005. Year of Renaissance'. *Asian Survey*, vol. 46. pp. 155–161.

Weightman, George (1975) 'Sociology in the Philippines'. *Solidarity*, vol. 9, pp. 43–58.

—— (1978) 'Comments' [on the Chapter on Sociology, in Chester L. Hunt and Dylan Dizon]. In Donn V. Hart (ed.), *Philippine Studies: History, Sociology, Mass Media and Bibliography*. Northern Illinois: Northern Illinois University, Centre for Southeast Asian Studies, Occasional Paper 6, pp. 178–179.

Wertheim, W.F. (Wim) (1959) *Indonesian Society in Transition: A Study of Social Change*. The Hague: Van Hoeve, second revised edition, first published 1956.

—— (1964a) *East–West Parallels: Sociological Approaches to Modern Asia*. The Hague: Van Hoeve.

—— (1964b) 'Peasants, Peddlers and Princes in Indonesia. A Review Article'. *Pacific Affairs*, vol. 37, pp. 307–311.

—— (1969) 'From Aliran towards Class Struggle in the Countryside of Java'. *Pacific Viewpoint*, vol. 10, pp. 1–17.

—— (1973a) *Dawning of an Asian Dream. Selected Articles on Modernization and Emancipation*. Amsterdam: Universiteit van Amsterdam, Antropologisch/Sociologisch Centrum, Afdeling Zuid- en Zuidoost Azië, Publication 20.

—— (1973b) 'Resistance to Change – From Whom?' In Evers (1973b), pp. 97–107.

—— (1974) *Evolution and Revolution. The Rising Waves of Emancipation*. Harmondsworth: Penguin Books.

—— (1980a) 'Changing South-East Asian Societies: An Overview'. In Evers (1980b), pp. 8–23.

—— (1980b) 'The Trading Minorities in South-East Asia'. In Evers (1980b), pp. 104–120.

—— (1993) *Comparative Essays on Asia and the West*. Amsterdam: VU University Press, Comparative Asian Studies 12.

Westcott, Clay (2003) 'Combating Corruption in Southeast Asia'. In Kidd and Richter (2003b), pp. 237–269.

White, Benjamin (1983a) *Agricultural Involution and Its Critics: Twenty Years after Clifford Geertz*. The Hague: Institute of Social Studies, Working Paper 6.

—— (1983b) '"Agricultural Involution" and Its Critics: Twenty Years After'. *Bulletin of Concerned Asian Scholars*, vol. 15, pp. 18–31.

White, Nicholas J. (2004) 'The Beginnings of Crony Capitalism: Business, Politics and Economic Development in Malaysia, c.1955–1970'. *Modern Asian Studies*, vol. 38, pp. 389–417.

Wilder, William D. (1968) 'Islam. Other Factors and Malay Backwardness: Comments on an Argument'. *Modern Asian Studies*, vol. 2, pp. 155–164.

Willner, Ann Ruth (1980) 'Expanding Women's Horizons in Indonesia: Toward Maximum Equality with Minimum Conflict'. In Chipp and Green (1980b), pp. 182–190.

Wilson, D.A. (1962) *Politics in Thailand*. Ithaca: Cornell University Press.

Wilson, Ian Douglas (2006) 'Continuity and Change.The Changing Contours of Organized Violence in Post-New Order Indonesia'. *Critical Asian Studies*, vol. 38, pp. 265–297.

Winzeler, Robert L. (1997) 'Introduction'. In Robert L. Winzeler (ed.), *Indigenous Peoples and the State: Politics, Land, and Ethnicity in the Malayan Peninsula and Borneo*. New Haven, CT: Yale University Press, pp. 1–29.

References

Wisseman Christie, Jan (1985) *Theatre States and Oriental Despotisms: Early Southeast Asia in the Eyes of the West.* University of Hull: Centre for South-East Asian Studies, Occasional Paper No. 10.

Wittfogel, Karl A. (1957) *Oriental Despotism: A Comparative Study of Total Power.* New Haven: Yale University Press.

Wolf, Diane Lauren (1990) 'Daughters, Decisions and Domination: An Empirical and Conceptual Critique of Household Strategies'. *Development and Change*, vol. 21, pp. 43–74.

—— (1992) *Factory Daughters: Gender, Household Dynamics and Rural Industrial-ization in Java.* Berkeley and Los Angeles: University of California Press.

—— (1993) 'Women and Industrialization in Indonesia'. In Jan-Paul Dirkse, Frans Hüsken and Mario Rutten (eds), *Development and Social Welfare: Indonesia's Experiences under the New Order.* Leiden: KITLV Press, Verhandelingen van het Koninklijk Instituut voor Taal-, Land- en Volkenkunde No. 156, pp. 134–151.

—— (1996) 'Javanese Factory Daughters. Gender, the State, and Industrial Capitalism'. In Sears (1996a), pp. 140–162.

Wolf, Eric R. (1966) 'Kinship, Friendship and Patron–Client Relations in Complex Societies'. In M. Banton (ed.), *The Social Anthropology of Complex Societies.* London: Tavistock Publications, ASA Monographs in Social Anthropology, pp. 1–22.

Wolters, O.W. (1999) *History, Culture and Region in Southeast Asian Perspectives.* Ithaca, New York: Cornell University, Southeast Asia Program Publications, Studies on Southeast Asia, No. 26; revised edition in cooperation with the Institute of Southeast Asian Studies, Singapore; originally published by the Institute of Southeast Asian Studies, Singapore, 1982.

Wolters, William (1983) *Politics, Patronage and Class Conflict in Central Luzon.* The Hague: Institute of Social Studies, Research Report Series No. 14.

Wong, Aline K. and Stephen H.K. Yeh (eds) (1985) *Housing a Nation: 25 Years of Public Housing in Singapore.* Singapore: Housing and Development Board.

Wong, Diana (2004) 'Globalisation and the End of Empire?' In Abdul Rahman Embong (2004), pp. 52–61.

Woodcroft-Lee, Carlien Patricia (1983) 'Separate but Equal: Indonesian Muslim Perceptions of the Roles of Women'. In Manderson (1983a), pp. 173–192.

Woodward, Mark (2007) 'Religious Conflict and the Globalization of Knowledge in Indonesian History'. In Cady and Simon (2007a), pp. 85–104.

World Bank (2006) *World Development Indicators.* http: //web.worldbank.org, and http:// devdata.worldbank.org/external/.

Yao Souchou (2001a) 'Introduction'. In Yao (2001b), pp. 1–23.

—— (ed.) (2001b) *House of Glass. Culture, Modernity, and the State in Southeast Asia.* Singapore: Institute of Southeast Asian Studies.

—— (2001c) 'Modernity and Mahathir's Rage: Theorizing State Discourse of Mass Media in Southeast Asia'. In Yao (2001b), pp. 46–69.

Yengoyan, Aram A. and Perla Q. Makil (eds) (1984) *Philippine Society and the Individual. Selected Essays of Frank Lynch, 1949–1976.* University of Michigan, Center for South and Southeast Asian Studies, Michigan Papers on South and Southeast Asia, No. 24.

Yeoh Seng Guan (2001) 'Creolized Utopias: Squatter Colonies and the Post-colonial City in Malaysia'. *Sojourn. Journal of Social Issues in Southeast Asia*, vol. 16, pp. 102–124.

Yeung, Yue-man (1973) *National Development Policy and Urban Transformation in Singapore: A Study of Public Housing and the Marketing System*. Chicago: University of Chicago Press.

Yoshihara, Kunio (1988) *The Rise of Ersatz Capitalism in South-East Asia*. Singapore: Oxford University Press.

—— (2004) 'The Problem of Globalisation for Southeast Asian Countries. The Case of Malaysia'. In Abdul Rahman Embong (2004), pp. 83–102.

Young, Ken (2004) 'Globalisation and the Changing Management of Migrating Service Workers in the Asia Pacific'. *Journal of Contemporary Asia*, vol. 34, pp. 287–303.

Yun Hing Ai (1984) 'Women and Work in West Malaysia'. *Journal of Contemporary Asia*, vol. 14. pp. 204–218.

Zakaria, F. (1994) 'Culture is Destiny: A Conversation with Lee Kuan Yew'. *Foreign Affairs*, vol. 73, pp. 109–126.

Zakaria Haji Ahmad and Suzaina Kadir (2005) 'Ethnic Conflict, Prevention and Management: The Malaysian Case'. In Kusuma and Thompson (2005a), pp. 42–64.

Zamora, Mario D., Donald J. Baxter and Robert Lawless (eds) (1982) *Social Change in Modern Philippines. Perspectives, Problems and Prospects*. Manila: Rex Book Store for St. Mary's College of Bayombang, 2 vols.

Zariski, Raphael (1960) 'Party, Factions and Comparative Politics: Some Preliminary Observations'. *Midwest Journal of Political Science*, vol. 4, pp. 27–51.

Author/Name Index

(Page numbers in **bold** = extended coverage)

Abdul Rahman Embong, 100, 102, 104, **270**
Abdullah Ahmad Badawi, *Datuk Seri*, 144
Abrams, P.H., 20
Adas, M., 74
Aguinaldo, E., 86
Alatas, S.H., 2, 38, 178, 186, 194, 247
Ananda, King, 121
Anderson, B.R., 4, 5, 14–15, 19, 122, 249, **271–2**
Anwar Ibrahim, *Dato' Seri*, 183
Appadurai, A., 150
Apter, D., 38, 56
Aquino, C., **118–19**, 182
Arghiros, D., **158**, **174–6**
Armstrong, W., 232
Askew, M., 232
Atkinson, J.M., 205
Aung-Thwin, M., 67–8
Ayal, E.B., 44

Bagyidaw, King, 144
Baker, C., 176
Banharn Silpa-archa, 173
Baran, P., 54, 56, 58, **60–1**
Batan, C., 24, 29
Bautista, C., 23, **273**
Bauzon-Bautista, Ma.C.R., 21
Bell, P.F., 67, 200, 215
Bellah, R.N., 195
Bellwood, P., 16
Bendix, R., 38
Benjamin, G., 129
Berger, M.T., 110
Bit, S., 49
Blackwood, E., 208
Bodawpaya, King, 144
Boeke, J.H., **7–8**, 23–4, **41–3**, 53, 74, 78, 232–3, 248

Boender, W., 231
Bonifacio, A., 86
Bottomore, T.B., 91, 97
Branson, J., 207, 223
Brennan, M., 99, 135, **138–40**, 143
Brewer, A., 56, 60
Brooks, A., 190
Brown, David, 129, 130, 134, 138, **142–4**, **146–50**, **151–2**
Brown, D.E., 31
Brummelhuis, H. ten, 176
Bruun, O., 182, 188, 191
Bukharin, N.I., 35, 58
Bunnell, T., 238
Burger, D.H., 54
Burling, R., 15–16

Cady, L.E., 132
Callahan, M.P., 46
Catley, B., 63, 64
Chai-anan, S., 48, 126
Cham, B.N., 248
Chan Kwok Bun, xi
Chan Yuk Wah, 130
Chatichai Choonhavan, 125
Chatthip, N., 67
Chen, M., 187
Chen, P.S.J., xi, 21, 22, 31, 38, 47, 99, **183–6**, **277–8**
Chong, T., x, 37
Chua Beng Huat, 101, 182, 189, **240–1**, 251, **278–9**
Chuan Leekpai, 125, 173
Chulalongkorn, King, 6, 121
Clad, J., 168
Clammer, J., 183, 188, 242, 247, **279**
Cohen, E., 48, 50, 67, 216, 255, **279**
Cook, N., 217

Cordero, F.V., 28
Coyle, S., 200
Crawfurd, J., 7
Crouch, H., 140, 142, **280**
Cushner, N.P., 82

Daendels, H.W., 76
Darwin, C.R., 38
de Legazpi, M.L., 82
del Pilar, M.H., 86
Dhakidae, D., 23, 29, 101, **102–3**
Diamond, L., 49
Dick, H., 101
Dizon, D., **28–9**
Doner, R.F., 23, 156
Dore, R.P., **52–3**
Durkheim, E., 2, 21, 28, **40**, 92

Earl, C., 100, 103, 199
Eisenstadt, S.N., **49–51**, 155, **281–2**
Elson, R., 77, 78
Emmerson, D.K., 52, 165
Errington, S., 205
Estrada, J., 103, **119–20**
Evans, G., 35, 91, 105, 106, 134
Evers, H-D., xi, xv, 2, 21–3, 26, 31–2, 34, 47,
    49, **51–3**, 91, 92, **98–100**, 102, 107, 109,
    112, 127, 141, 234, 247, **283**

Fahey, S., 199
Farish A. Noor, 178
Fasseur, C., 77, 78
Fenichel, A., 70
Fisher, C., 13
Fold, N., 24, 25
Forbes, D.K., 233
Forbes, Dean, 225
Frank, A.G., 54, **56–65**, 106, **284–5**
Fukuyama, F., 187
Furnivall, J.S., **7–8**, 13, 23–4, 54, 70, 71,
    132–3, 248, **285**

Geertz, C., xvi, 26, 27, **46–7**, **53–4**, 76,
    78–80, 81, 111, 131, **232–3**, 247, **286**
Geertz, H., 27
George, K.M., 192
Gerke, S., 21
Girling, J.L.S., 48
Gladney, D.C., 129
Glassman, J., **126**

Goh, R.B.H., 234, 237, 240, 244
Goh Beng Lan, 154, 231, 237, **238**, **239**
Goh Chok Tong, 181
Goh Keng Swee, Dr, 183–4, 186
Gomez, E.T., 169
Goodman, D.S.G., 100, 101, 103–4

Hadiz, V.R., 23, 29, 166
Hall, I.P., 185
Hamilton, A., 216
Han Sung-Joo, 186, 190–1
Hanks, L.M., 156, **172–3**
Hannerz, U., 228
Hantrakul, S., 205
Harsja Bachtiar, 29
Hart, G., 217
Hasan, Bob, 167
Hashim Hussin Yaacob, 138
Hassan, R., 242, 243
Hawes, G., 62
Healey, L., **220–1**
Hedman, E-L.E., 104
Hefner, R.W., 249
Helliwell, C., 197, 198
Heng Pek Koon, 100
Hersh, J., 24, [25]
Heryanto, A., 23
Hettne, B., 56–7
Hewison, K.J., x, 25, 35, 48, 67, 101, **120–7**,
    172, 177, 178, 189, 220, **289–90**, **313–15**
Heyzer, N., **199–200**, 212, 216, 217, 224
Higgins, B., 42–3
Higgott, R., 24, 26, 32, 99, 106, 107, 109, 155,
    313–14
Hilferding, R., 58
Hirschman, C., 2
Hitchcock, D., 186
Ho Chi Minh, 37
Ho Kong Chong, xi
Ho Wing Meng, 185, 186
Hong, L., 23, 57, 67
Hoogvelt, A.M.M., 57
Hoselitz, Bert F., 41, **43–4**
Hsiao Hsin-Huang, M., **100–4**
Huff, G., 70
Hughes, C., 49, **158–9**
Hull, V.J., 207
Hulme, D., 32
Hunt, C.L., **28–9**
Huntington, S.P., 50–1, 52, 178, **180**, 181, 189

Hutchinson, J., 101, 119, 162
Huxley, T., xi, xvi

Jackson, K.D., 155
Jacobs, N., 195
Jacobsen, M., 182, 188, 191
Jamieson, N., 199
Jaspan, M., xv
Jay, R., 27
Jayasuriya, S.K., 118, 179, 189
Jellinek, L., 233, 235
Jesudason, J.V., 169–70
Jocano, F.L., 234
Jomo K.S., 156, 169

Kahin, G.McT., 27
Kahn, J.S., 110, 129, 135, **248–9**, 253, **295**

Karim, W.J., 198, 204, 212
Kasian, T., 250
Kemp, J., **296**
Kemp, J.H., 176
Keng, W.M.L., 200
Keyes, C.F., 205, 249
Khan, M.H., 156
Khin Nyunt, 252
Khondker, H.H., xi, 31
King, V.T., **vii-xiii**, xvi, 21, 24, 46, 103, 157, 291, **297–8**
Kirsch, A.T., 44, 205
Konbaung dynasty, 144
Korff, R., 232, 234, 235
Kratoska, P.H., 16, 298
Kriangsak Chomanan, General, 123
Kwong, J., 200

Laclau, E., 61
Landé, C.H., 155
Larkin, J.A., 81, **85–6**
Law, L., 216
Lawson, S., 187, 189, 190
Leaver, R., 62
Lebra, J., 198
Leclerc, J., 237
Lee Hock Guan, 251
Lee Kuan Yew, 23, 151, 181, 182, 184, 189, 190
Lee Sheng Yi, 99
Lenin, V.I., 58–9
Liddle, R.W., 165, **300**
Lie, M., **210–12**

Liem Sioe Liong, 166–7
Lim Mah Hui, 138, 248
Lingle, C., 190
Loh Kok Wah, F., 250–1
Luckham, R., 156
Lund, R., **210–12**
Luxemburg, R., 35, 58–9
Lynch, F., 28

Macapagal-Arroyo, G., 176, 252
Macaraig, S.D., 28
McCargo, D., 127
McCarthy, S. 46
McGee, T., 225, 231–2
McVey, R.T., 1, 14, 20–1, 30, 31, 32, **48**, 62, 100, 110, 193, 195, 246, 253
Magdoff, H., 63
Magsaysay, R., 88
Mahathir bin Mohamad, *Datuk Seri* Dr, 103, 143, 170, 171, 178, 180–1, 183, 185–6, 187, 189, 191
Maleenond family, 177
Manderson, L., 200, **303**
Marcos, F.E., 23, 52, 89, 97, 103, **116–18**, 119, 156, **161–2**, 182
Marcos family, 117
Marr, D.G., 25
Marsden, W., 7
Marx, K.H., 2, **10–11**, 12, 21, 35, 40, 57–8, 60, 61, 92, **95–7**, 98, 181
Mauzy, D.K., 182
Maznah Mohamad, 249, 251, 252
Mee, W., 250
Miller, D., 207, 223
Mills, C.W., 99
Moelia, T.S.G., 28
Mohamed Halib, xi, xvi
Mongkut, King, 6
Montri, C., 67
Moore, W.E., 37, 41
Morell, D., 48, 126
Morin, A.J., **43**
Mortimer, R., 107
Mountbatten, Lord, 14
Mozart, J.C.W.A., 178
Mulder, N., 98, 100, 105, 255, **305**
Myint, M., 69, 70

Nagata, J.A., **141**, 240, **306**
Narong Kittikachorn, 173

Nas, P.J.M., 231, 237, **306**
Nash, M., **44–5**, 50
Ne Win, General, 72, 73, **148–9**
Neher, C.D., 22–3
Nghiem Lien Huong, 199
Nguyen Huu Minh, 103
Nguyen Phuong An, 103
Nixon, R.M., 30
Nu, U, 72, 146
Nye, J.S., 162

O'Brien, L., 209, 212
O'Connor, R.A., 225
Ockey, J., 48, 103, **126–7**, 251
Öjendal, J., 250–1
Ong Aihwa, 201, 205, 206, **212–16**
Ong Jin Hui, xi, 23, 31, 254, 308
Ortner, S.B., 198
Osborne, M., 4, **9**, 16, 59, 93, 129
Owen, N.G., 1, 88

Palmier, L.H., xvi, **163**, 165, 168
Panopio, I.S., 28
Parkinson, B.K., **192–3**
Parnwell, M., xvi, 257, 291
Parsons, T., **40–1**, 56
Pasuk Phongpaichit, 173, 176, **309–10**
Paulson, J., 198
Peacock, J.L., 47
Peletz, M.G., 201, 205, 214
Pelzer, K., 15
Phao Sriyanon, Police General, 177
Phelan, J.L., 56, 83–4
Phibun Songkhram, Field Marshal, 94, **121–2**
Pholsena, V., 134
Pinches, M., 101, 104
Pol Pot, viii
Powers, J.C., 187
Prajadhipok, King, 121
Prapass Charusathiarana, 173, 177
Prasert Rujirawongse, General, 177
Prem Tinsulanond, General, 123
Preston, P.W., 23–4
Price, S., 221
Pye, L.W., **45–7**, 49, 155

Quilty, M.C., 7

Raben, R., 298

Raffles, Sir Thomas Stamford, xv–xvi, 7, 75, 76
Rajaratnam, 183
Ramos, F., **119**, 120, 182
Ramsay, A., 156
Regan, D., 47, 99
Reinsma, R., 54
Reynolds, C.J., 23, 57, 67, 250, **312**
Ricardo, D., 58, 61
Ricklefs, M.C., 75, 78, 79
Rigg, J., xii, **230–1**
Riggs, F.W., 48, 50–1, **122**, 155, 156, 172
Rivera, T., 104–5
Rizal, J., 86
Roberts, D., 49
Robinson, K., **218–19**
Robison, R., x, xv, 24–6, 32, 35, 62, 99–104, 106, 107, 109–11, **112–14**, 155, 161, **164–8**, 180, 251, **289–90**, **313–15**
Roces, M., 204
Rochayah Machali, 207
Rodan, G., x, 25, 35, 108, 153, 178, 189, 251, **290**, **314–15**
Romein, J., 33, 49
Roniger, L., 155
Rosaldo, M.Z., 198
Rostow, W.W., 39, 41, 49
Roxborough, I., 57
Rutten, R., **222–3**

Said, E.W., 7
St John, R.B., 159
Samuel, H., 23
Saravanamuttu, J., 104
Sarit Thanarat, General, 122, 124, 173
Saw Maung, General, 73
Saya San, 71, 146
Schmidt, J.D., 24, 25
Schrieke, B.J.O., 2, 10, 12, 33–4
Schulte Nordholt, H., 298
Schulte Nordholt, N., 23
Scott, J.C., xiii, 34, 105, 106, 107, **157–64**, **317**
Searle, P., **168–71**
Sears, L.J., 201
Selosoemardjan, 29
Selveratnam, V., 138
Sen, K., 202
Shamsul Amri Baharuddin, 23, 249
Sharp, L., 27
Siddique, S., 153

Sieh Lee Mei Ling, 62
Smith, Adam, 58, 61
Smith, M., 145
Soedjatmoko, 41
Sophonpanich family, 177
Spencer, R.F., 178
Spiro, M.E., 46, 194
Stauffer, R.B., 118
Stenson, M., 138
Steward, J., 54
Stivens, M.K., 100, 199, 201, **320**
Suchinda Krapayoon, General, 103, 125
Suehiro, A., 62, 124
Suharto, General, ix, 52, 80, 81, 94, 100, 103, **110–15**, 116, 165, **166–8**, 182–3, 207, 237, 252
Suharto family, 114, 167–8
Sukarno, 14, 37, 80, 81, 94, 103, 111, 165, 167, 207, **237–8**
Sullivan, N., 207
Sunardi Sudarmadi, 29
Sungsidh Piriyarangsan, 173
Sutherland, H., 17
Suthy, P., 67

Tambiah, S.J., 44, 194
Tan Ern Ser, xi, 101, 254, 308
Tan Giok-Lan (Mely G. Tan), 29
Tanabe, S., 249
Taufik Abdullah, 27, 247
Tay Kheng Soon, 240
Taylor, J.G., 22, 32, 57
Taylor, P., 97, 103
Taylor, R.H., 70, 73, 74
Tejapaibul family, 177
Thaksin Shinawatra, 126, 176
Shinawatra family, 177
Tham Seong Chee, 26, 195
Thanin Kraivixien, General, 123
Thanom Kittikachorn, 103, 173
Thibaw, King, 144
Thompson, W.S., 132
Tin Maung Maung Than, 150
Tinker, H.R., 39–40
Tong Chee Kiong, xi, 254, 308
Tremewan, C., 244
Turner, M., 32
Turton, A., 22, 32

Umar Khayam, 29
Unger, D., 55

Vajiravudh, King, 121
van den Bosch, J., 75
van den Muijzenberg, O.D., 20, 32, 33
van der Kroef, J., 42, 44
van Dijk, M.P., 233
van Esterik, J., 205
van Esterik, P., 197, 202, 203, 205, 209, 216, 217
van Leur, J.C., 2, 10, 11, 12, 34
van Niel, R., 53, 77, 81
Vickers, A., 231
Visser, L., 23
Vo Van Ai, 187–8
von der Mehden, F.R., **191–4**, 195
von Heine-Geldern, R., 15

Wang Hong-Zen, 101
Ward, B., 201
Warren, B., 58
Weber, M., 2, 10, 21, 32, 40, 42, 47, 56, 92, 97, 109, 157, 163, 178, 181–2, **195–6**, **324**
Webster, A., 57, 107
Wee, C.J.W-L., 110, 150, **152–4**, 249–50, **325**
Wee, V., 130
Weightman, G., **28–9**
Wertheim, W.F., vii,x, xv, xvi, 2, 8, 11–12, 14, 20, 21, 22, 32, **33–5**, 47, 49, 52, 66, 105, 131, 155, **195–6**, 248, **325–6**
Wilder, W.D., xvi, 157, **192–3**
Willford, A.C., 192
Wilson, D.A., 48, 155, 172
Wittfogel, K.A., 10
Wolf, D.L., 210, 214
Wolf, E.R., 155
Wolters, W., 20, 33
Wong Soak Koon, 249, 251, 252

Yao Souchou, 110, 183, 249
Yeoh, B.S.A., 234, 237
Yeoh Seng Guan, 228, **236**
Yoshihara, K., 168
Young, K., 220
Yudhoyono, S.B., 114

Zakaria Haji Ahmad, 184, 190

Subject Index

(Page numbers in **bold**=extended coverage

abaca, 85, 88
Aceh/Acehnese, 132, 137
administrator-scholars, 23, 30
Africa, 2, 15, 22, 56, 64
agency (human), 16, 20, 201, 224
Agrarian Law (1870), 76
agricultural involution (Geertz), xvi, 47, **53–4**, 78, 81, 247
agriculture, xi, 22, 64, 73, 74, 83, 85, 87, 90, 115, 119, 122, 123, 138, 174, 197, 199, 200, 202, 204, 210, 212, **217–21**, 222, 226, 230, 245
aid, 41, 46, 52, 112, 113, 116, 122, 168
AIDS/HIV, 217
alcaldes mayores (provincial governors), 84
alipin (slaves), 83
alliances, 111–15, 120, 125, 167
Amsterdam, 77
Angkor, 9, 227
Anglo-Burmese wars, 67, 144
anthropology, 31, 33, 54, 246, 247, 248
Anti-Fascist People's Freedom League (AFPFL), 146
Arakan/Arakanese, 67, 72, 145, 146
Aristocracy/nobility, 11, 77, 78, 99, 120, 135, 138, 141, 143, 148, 177
armed forces, 46, 48, 72, 97, 111, 116, 121, 148, 165, 171, 172
articulation (Marxian concept), 61
Asia, 2, 56, 58, 60, 62, 63, 64, 116, 178, **179–80**, 186
Asian financial crisis (1997–8), viii, xi, 55, 105, 114, 125, 167–8. 154, 191, 223, 252
Asian Survey, 176
Asian values, x, xi, 18, 31, 38, 44, 110, 152, 154, 177, **178–96**, 243, 249, 251
see also family: values; Western values

Asiatic mode of production (Marx), 10
Association of Southeast Asian Nations (ASEAN), viii, 4, 18, 26, 31, 118, 253, 254
Ateneo de Manila, 28
Australia, 14, 24, 35, 106
Austroasiatic language family, 16
Austronesian language family, 16
authoritarianism, 26, 49, 50, 52, 103, 104, 109, 114, 117, 122, 125, 134, 140, 151, 160, 167, 174, 181, 186, 190, 191, 249, 251, 252
Ava, 67

balance of payments, 115–16
Bali, ix, 11, 17, 47, 79, 223
Balikpapan, 79
Bangkok, 13, 102, 176, 206, 216, 226, 227, 228, 230, 232, 235,
Bangkok Bank, 177
Bangkok Metropolitan Area, 226
Bangladesh, 16
Bank of Ayudhya, 177
Bank Negara (Malaysian Central Bank), 170
banking, 113, 117, 120, 121, 123, 177
barangay (local communities/villages, Philippines), 12, 83, 84
barrio (village, district, ward, Philippines), 83
barrio teniente (executive/leadership of village, Philippines), 83
batik, 113, **221–2**
behaviouralism, 24, 28
Belgium, 75
Bengal/Bengalis, 137, 144, 150
Bombay, 137
Borneo/Kalimantan, 5, 13, 14, 79, 80, 90, 132, 137
boundaries, **131–2**, 144, 145, 163, 169

bourgeoisie, 58, 73, 89, 95, 97, 98, 99, 101, 104, 107, 111, 112, 113, 114, 117, 120–4, 126–8, 130, 139, 142, 169
  see also middle class
Bowring Treaty (1855), 120
bribery, 162–3, 174, 175
Britain, *see* United Kingdom
British Commonwealth, 133
Brunei/Negara Brunei Darussalam, xii, xv, xvii–xix, 3, 4, 5, 16, 25, 30, 31, 93, 254
Buddhism, 29, 40, 48, 71, 72, 74, 93, 132, 134–5, 144–8, 179, 187–8, 192, **205**, 217
  Hinayana/Theravada, 10–12, 17, 44, 178, 179, 194, 228
  Mahayana, 9–12, 17, 178
Buddhist kingdoms, 97
Buddhist monks, 193–4
Bulletin of Concerned Asian Scholars (1968–), 30, 106, 248
bumiputra (sons of soil, Malaysia), 134, 139
bupati (Javanese regents), 76
bureaucracy/bureaucrats, 2, 12, 48, 51, 52, 77–8, 87, 98, 99, 100, 111, 112, 116, 117, 127, 128, 139, 141, 142, 144, 151, 155, 156, 160–77 *passim*, 182, 195, 196, 218, 227, 232, 233, 253
bureaucratic bourgeoisie (Brown), 109, 138, 143, 169
  ~ capitalism (Dutch), 74
  ~ capitalist class (Brown), 143
  ~ polity (Riggs), 48, 122, 126, 156, 176
  ~ state, 116
Burma, xii, xviii, 3, 5, 9, 10, 13, 14, 25, 43, 44, **45–7**, 50, 66, **67–74**, 76, 80, 83, 89, 93, 133, 134–5, **144–50**, 151, 192, 193, 197, 244, 247
  ~ Army (regular), 71; colonial army, 145, 148
  ~ Communist Party (BCP), 149
  ~ Delta/Irrawaddy (River/Delta), 5, 67–9, 72, 74, 144
  ~ Immigration Act (1947), 72
  ~ Independence Army, 71
  ~ Socialist Programme Party (BSPP), 72, 73, 148
  Myanmar, ix, xviii, 4, 25, 97, 132, 154, 156, 163–4, 176, 217, 221, 244, 252, 254
Burmans (Buddhist), 45, 71, 72, 145, 146–7, 148, 151
Burmese Way to Socialism (Ne Win), 73, 93, 148
businessmen-politicians, 174–5, 176

cabecera (parish, Philippines), 82
cabeza de barangay (chief/leader of village or parish, Philippines), 83–4, 85
caciquism (rule of local chiefs or bosses), 84, 88
Cambodia, viii, xii, xvii, xviii, 3–5, 9, 10, 14–16, 25, 49, 93, 134, **158–9**, 163–4, 176, 217, 252, 254
Canada, 42
Cantonese people, 137, 150
capital, 8, 41, 59, 60, 74, 76, 100, 107, 108, 109, 111, 112, 114, 115, 118, 120, 122, 123, 136, 138, 142, 143, 144, 157, 166, 177, 182, 210, 215, 238
capital accumulation, 42, 47, 61, 64, 111, 112, 125, 167, 168, 169, 223
capital cities, 9, 133, 226, 227, 228, 229, 236–7
  see also cities
capitalism, viii, 2, 22, 24, 26, 35, 38, 39, 40, 42, 49–63 *passim*, **64–5**, 66, 70, 71, 74, 77, 89, 93, 99, 106, 107, 116, 120, 135, 152, 153, 167, 168–9, 171, 179, 181, 189, 190, 195, 210, 214, 228, 240, 249–51, 253
  capitalist class, **122–3**, 125, 127, 140, 177
  ~ relations of production, 109, 174, 192
  capitalists, 62, 113, 123, 126, 136, 138, 139, 144, 166, 169
  crony capitalism, **117–20**, 128, 161, 168–9, 176, 252
capitán municipal (chief/governor of colonial administrative district, Philippines), 84
capitation tax, 68
casamajan (sharecropping), 85
cash crops, 12, 75–6, 78, 85, 87–8
caste, 95, 127, 178
censuses, 131, 137
central business districts, 227, 228
central government, 132, 147–8
central planning, 72, 93
Central Provident Fund (CPF), 243
centre/periphery, 9, 12, 52, 60, 62, 250
  metropolis/satellite, 56, 57, 60, 250
  'semi-periphery', 60
Ceylon/Sri Lanka, 10, 14
Champa, 9
Chams, 5
Chaozhouhua, 137
cheap labour, 59, 68, 108–9, 122, 139, 200, 209–10, 211, 212, 213, 218, 241
Chettiars, 69, 70
child-care, 208, 217

child-rearing, 197, 206, 220
children, 125, 185, 201, 210, 211, 217, 219, 244
Chin (people), 71, 145, 147–8
China, viii, xviii–xix, 3, 4, 5, **8–12**, 13, 14, 15,
    16, 17, 18, 26, 58, 63, 65, 71, 79, 81, 82, 147,
    149, 180, 182, 184, 187, 190, 193, 197, 255,
Chinatowns, 123, 227, 234
Chinese (overseas), 7, 13, 17, 31, 48, 70, 77,
    80–1, 89, 99, 111–12, 114, 115, 119, 120,
    122–5, 127, 128, 133, 135–43, 146, 148,
    150, 156, 169, 171, 173, 177, 188–9, 192–3,
    198, 240, 241
    see also immigrants; Indians (overseas)
Chinese, Malay, Indian, and Other (CMIO,
    Singapore), 153
Christianity/Roman Catholicism, 6, 12, 17,
    40, 47, 59, 63, 71, 81, 82, 83, 118, 132, 145,
    148, 180, 182, 186, 187, 195, 239
Chulias, 137
cities, 66, **227–9**, 236–7, 245
    see also urban areas
cityscapes, 236, 237, 238, 240, 263
civil society, 97, 104, 108, 164, 174, 242, 250–3
    see also vested interests
clash of civilizations (Huntington), **180**, 189
class/social class, xi, 1, 2, 12, 48, 52, 58, 65,
    70–1, 83, 90, 92, 95–6, **98–100**, 105,
    106, 109–10, 118, **120–7**, 128, **130**, 133,
    135, 139, 143, 154, 156, 158, 160, 164–5,
    172, 173, 176, 199, 201, 223, 224, 231,
    234, 236, 242, 244, 247, 249, 251, 253
    ~ conflict, 54, 140, 142, 181
    ~ consciousness, 92, 96, **105–6**, 141, 214
    ~ formation, 254
    ~ fractions, 99, 109, 115, 118, 127, 138,
        140–2, 232
    ~, the state and political economy, xi, xii,
        20, 34, 49, 89, 90, **91–128**, 130, 140–1,
        155, 164, 171, 176, 249, 250
    ~ structure, 94, 96, 104, **105–6**, 109, 127,
        141, 166, 167, 170, 177
clientelism, 158, 160, 172, 173, 174
    see also patron–client relations
cliques, 155, 157, **160–1**, 165, 168, 172
clusters, **159–60**
coalitions, 160–1
coconuts, 79, 88, 117, 222
coffee, 75, 76, 77, 78, 79, 85
Cold War, 14, 106
colonial era, 109, 131, 133
colonial legacy, viii, 45, **74**, 80, 88, 89, 92–3,
    97–8, 104, 110, 111

colonialism, 4, 5–6, **7–8**, 11, 12, 13, 33, 34,
    43, 53, 54, 56, **57–8**, 59, 63, 64, 65, 66,
    67–89, 91, 92, 93, 110, 127, 131–2, 133,
    134, 135, 136, 137, 142, 144, 145, 150, 153,
    158, 164, 193, 207, 218, 227, 237, 247, 248
command economy, 148
commercial houses, 85
commercial treaties, 63
commercialization, 8, 230
Committee of Concerned Asian Scholars, 30
commoditization, 157, 230
commodity prices, 117, 119, 123
communalism, 141, 142
communism, 15, 24–5, 39, 41, 49, 66, 80, 88,
    118, 122, 148, 176, 190, 252
    communist insurrection, 14, 136
    Communist Party of Indonesia (PKI), 14,
        81, 111, 112, 165
    Communist Party of Philippines, 116
community/community spirit, 181, 184, 185,
    190, 207, 242, 244, 247
compadrazgo/*compadrinazgo* (godparent/
    ritual co-parenthood), 159
companies, 111, 112, 139, 166, 169, 170, 172,
    173, 207, 210, **211–12**
    see also joint ventures
comparative advantage, 108
comparative method, 2, 105, **254–5**
compradors, 67, 90, 99, 107, 110, 121, 124,
    128, 138, 140
concessions, 168, 177
conflicting value systems (Wertheim), 12, 34
Confucianism, 9, 12, 18, 40, 152, 178–80,
    181–2, 186–8, **188–9**, 194
conglomerates, 113, 114, 123, 125, 143, 167, 171
Congress (Philippines), 118
Congress of the Labor Organization
    (Philippines), 88
construction, 124, 167, 241
consumer goods, 94, 121, 230
consumerism/consumption, 100, 103, 179,
    199, 214, 233, 239, 250, 253, 255
contexts, **20–36**, **43–9**, 101, 110, **160**, **161–4**,
    195, **226–9**, 248, 251
corporate plantation system (Geertz), 76
corporatism (Singapore), 151
corregidor (magistrate, chief officer,
    Philippines), 84
corregimientos (colonial administrative
    district, Philippines), 84
corruption, xi, 52, 75, 89, 94, 103, 113, 115, 119,
    120, 126, 128, 144, 148, **155–77**, 191, 204, 253

credit, 167, 218
creolization (Wertheim), 131
Critical Asian Studies (2001–), 106
Cuba, 86
Cultivation System (*Cultuurstelsel*), 67, **74–8**, 81
Cultural Motivations to Progress in South and Southeast Asia (conference, Manila, 1963), 41
culture, 8, 9, 12–13, 15–16, 38, 42, 43, 46, 49, 54, 61, 72, 81, **130–1**, 134, 138, 146, 151, 152, 154, 179, 181, **185–7**, 190, 193, 198, 232, 246, 248, 249, 250, 252, 253, 254, 255
cultural conflict (Huntington), 178
~ ecology, 54
culturalist argument (Jayasuriya), 179
currency, 116, 123, 125
custom, *see* tradition
Cyberjaya, 238

data deficiencies, xvii, **25–6**
datu (chiefly class), 83, 84
Dayak, 137
de-industrialization (Frank), 65
de-urbanization (Frank), 65
debt/indebtedness, 89, 123, 167
debt peonage, 83, 85
decentralization, 250
decision-making, 152, 153, 170, 179, 185, 199, 201, 205, 223, 252
decolonization, viii, 14, 27, 33, **37**, 63, 66, 133, 136, 151, 225
deference, 176, 177
Deli, 79
democracy, 26, 39, 45, 49, 50, 51, 66, 71, 97, 103, 116, 125, 134, 148, 160, 164, 173, 176, 180–2, 187, 188, 190, 252, 254
democratization, 33, 114, 168, 250, 251
demography, 226, 244–5
dependency, 22, 32, 60–1, 91, 155, 158, 231
see also underdevelopment
desakota (village-town), 231
developed countries, 167
developing countries, 36, 43, 44, 49, 50, 52, 58, 60, 62, 91, 99, 109, 163, 185, 200, 207
Third World, 14, 32, 57
development, 23, 32, 38, 39, 67, 94, 108, 112, 149, 175, 206, 209, 216, 230, 231
~ plans, 44, 123, 138, 139, 207
developmental state, 94–5, 191
Dharma Wanita (Indonesia), 207
dialectical evolutionism, 33

dialectics of progress (Romein), 33, 49
dictatorship, 23, 80, 97, 103, 161, 173, 181
discipline, **180–1**, 186, 189, 220
discourse/s, 27, 248, 250, 251
see also narratives
divide and rule, 145
division of labour, 40, 44, 58, 60, 62, 94, 95, 133, 136, 140, 150, 197, 207, 210, 211, 217, 219, 233, 250
domestic work, 197, **201–3**, 219, 220, 221
domino theory, 15
dry zone (Upper Burma), 68
dualism (socio-economic), 7, **41–3**, 53, 74, 248
dyads, 155, 157, 159
dynasties, 10, 11

East Asia, 18, 102, 103, 107, 255
East India Company (British), 144
East India Company (VOC), 63, 75, 76
East Timor (Timor Lorosa'e/Timor Leste), xvii, xix, 4, 6
economic
castes (Furnivall), 8, 133
development, 29, 41, 42–3, 156, 185, 238, 252, 254
diversification, 118, 138, 211–12
growth, 31–3, 38, 43, 46, 57, 73, 94–5, 108, 112, 116, 123, 125, 128, 138, 139, 178, 182, 186, 192, 239–41
policy, **93**
pragmatism (Singapore), 240, 251
Economic Development and Cultural Change (journal, 1952–), **43–4**
Economic Intelligence Unit, 176
Economic Planning Unit (Malaysia), 170
economics, 20, 108
economy, 89, **106–10**, 135, 136, 164, 192, **204–5**, 251, 252
education, 6, 78, 85, 92, 101–3, 133, 135, 141, 146, 152, 184, 186, 201, 206, 218, 230, 233, 255
educational attainment, 98, 100, 181
egalitarianism, 10, 12, 92
elections, 87, 88, 119, 126, 138, 158, 173–4, 175, 251
electronics, 108, 138, 139, 209
elite/s, 7, 11, 31, 41, 45, 48, 50, 52, 67, 73, 78, 87, 92, 93, 95, 97, 98, 99, 105, 109, 117, 123, 127, 133, 145, 146, 149–51, 158, 159, 162, 170, 172, 173, 174, 207, 218, 222, 227, 232
emancipation period (Wertheim), 14

empiricism, vii, 19, 22, 24, 29, 31, 33, **45–6**, 54, 60

employment, 53, 142, 163, 197, 200, 202, 203, 206, 208, **209–15**, 224, 229, 230, 232, 233, 235, 240, 241, 245

encomenderos (colonial grantee/landlord over labour and tribute, Philippines), 84

encomiendas (colonial grant system, Philippines), 84

entrepreneurs/entrepreneurship, 41–5, 57, 70, 74, 80–1, 98, 111, 112, 130, 139, 156, 171, 223, 254

ethnicity, ix, xi, 1, 8, 11, **12–13**, 31, 46, 49, 65, 71, 74, 98, 104, 110, 127, 128, **129–55**, 156, 163, 165, 169, 234, 235, 244, 249, 251

ethnic conflict, 37, 69, **70–1, 132**

~ groups, 45, 71, 168, 241, 252, 253

~ self-determination, 149

ethno-class (Wee and Chan), 130

ethnocentricity, 48, 51

ethnocratic state (Brown), 147

Eurasians, 138, 151, 239

Eurocentrism, 195

Europe, 4, 14, 39, 41, 47, 58, 59, 63, 64, 65, 163, 188, 189, 246, 248

evil, **184**, 190

evolution/evolutionism, 7, 26, 34, 39–40, 48–51, 54

exploitation, 77, 91, **157**, 159, 161, **199–200**, 205, 210, 232

export-processing zones, 209

exports, 80, 89, 123, 222–3

factions/factionalism, 148, 159, **160–1**, 165, 168, 172

factories
manufacturing, 76, 80, 210, 222, 230
trading stations, 63

factory employment, 197, 202, 212, 224, 232

factory women, 205, **209–15**

false consciousness, 106, 130

family, xi, 9, 42, 112, 123, 124, 126, 152, 156, 162, 165, 166, 168, 177, 181, 184, 189–90, 199, 201, 203, 207, 224, 241, 243

planning, 206, 208, 253

values, 102, 184, 185, 189; *see also* values

Far Eastern Economic Review, 176

Far Eastern Tropics, 5

fear of dearth (Scott), 157

Federal Land Development Authority (FELDA), 211

Federal Party (Philippines), 87

flats/apartment blocks, 240–1, 243, 244

food, 93, 94, 135, 209

foreign exchange, 221, 236

forestry/forests, 11, 167

France, 6, 25

France d'outremer, 5

free-trade zones, 209

friendship, 162, 163, 165, 184, 185, 235

Frontier Areas (Burma), 145

Fujian, 137

functionalism, 28, 253

gas, 112, 113, 138

gender, xi, 1, 15, 96, 100, 139, 190, **197–224**, 233, 249, 253, 254, 255

General Council of Burmese Associations (GCBA, 1917–), 146

Germany, 6

global economy/world economy, 24, 60, 73, 74, 87, 144, 154, 179, 182, 247

globalization, ix, xii, 1, 18, 130, 180, 186, 191–2, 199, 224, 230, 232, 238, 245, **248–53**, 254

gobernadorcillo (chief/governor of colonial administrative district, Philippines), 84

godparent/ritual co-parenthood (*compadrazgo/compadrinazgo*), 159

gold, 13, 64

Golkar, 112, 166

governance, 186, 190

governments, 60, 235–6

Great Depression (late 1920s, early 1930s), 69, 79, 146

Greater East Asia Co-Prosperity Sphere, 13–14

gross domestic product (GDP), 115, 122, 123, 173

gross national income (GNI), xvii

gross national product (GNP), xvii

Guangdong, 137

Guangfuhua, 137

Guided Democracy/Economy, 81, 111

Gujaratis, 137

Guomindang troops, 147

Hailamese, 137

haj (pilgrimage), 192, 194

Hakka, 137

handicrafts, 202, 210, 217, 221, 222–3

Hanoi, 13, 226, 228

Institute of Sociology, 253

harbour principalities (van Leur), 11, 12, 227

head tax, 84
Hegelian view, 35
heritage, **238–40**
hierarchy, 10, 12, 34, 49, 91, 172, 176, 181
high-rise living, 31, 234, 239, **240–4**
hill peoples, 15, 16, 81
Hinduism, 10, 12, 17, 40, 178
  Hinduism–Buddhism, 5, 9, 12
  linggam/yoni, male/female, 238
historical materialism, 61
historical-sociological approach, x, 8, 10, 20, 89, 247, 253
history, x, xii, 1, 2, 20, 21, 34, 54, 251, 255
Ho Chi Minh City, 226, 228
  Saigon-Cholon, 8, 13, 227
  (Southern) Institute of Social Sciences, 254
Hokkien, 137, 150
Hong Kong, 14, 18, 62, 102, 182, 220
household management, 204, 223
housing, 31, 152, 229, 234–5, 236, 239, 242
Housing and Development Board (HDB), **240–4**
Hukbalahap (Huks), 88
human rights, 7, 104, 149, 180, 181, 187, 188

ideal types (Weberian), 34, 40, 54
identity, 46, 129, 131, **132**, 137, 144, 145, 147, 148, 150, 152, 159, 191, 206, 240, 244, 248, 249, 252
  see also national identity
ideology, 103, 106, 132, 136, 139, 140, 142, 143, 154, 158, 161, 172, 174, 177, 180, 181, 185, 187, 188–90, 196, 200, 201, 203, 208, 240, 247, 251
ilustrados (enlightened ones, Filipino educated elite), 85–6, 87
images, 31, 199, 250, 257–69
imaginaries (Healey), **220–1**
imagined communities (Anderson), 19, **133–5**, 249
immigrants/immigration, 5, 8, **12–13**, 68–9, 70, 82, 89, 90, 129, 133, 135–7, 139, 144, 150, 193, 229,
  see also Chinese (overseas); Indians (overseas)
imperialism, 27, 35, 51, 54, 56, **58–60**, 59, **62–6**, 180, 191
imports, 11, 69–70, 123, 228
Independent Party (Philippines), 87
India, 3, 4, 5, **8–12**, 13–18, 58, 63–5, 68–71, 144, 197, 226–7
Indian Ocean, 5, 13–14, 18

Indianized states, 9–10
Indians (overseas), 7–8, 12–13, 17, 68–9, 70, 89, 89, 135, 136, 137–8, 141, 144, 146, 150, 227, 229, 241
  see also Chinese (overseas); immigrants
indigenous people, 8, **12–13**, 129, 134, 135, 136
indigo, 75, 76, 85
indirect rule, 87, 90, 145
individualism, 181, 184, 187, 189, 190
Indochina, 5, 24–5, 26, 66, 67, 106, 248
Indonesia, viii, ix, xii, xv, xvii, xviii–xix, 2, 4, 16, 23, 25, 26, **29**, 31, 33–4, 37, 42, 44, 47–53 *passim*, 63, 80, 81, 92, 93–5, 97, 99–104, **110–15**, 116, 118, 128, 132, 150, 151, 156, 161, **164–8**, 171–2, 176, 182, 192, 197, 200, 202, 204, 206, **207–9**, 210, 217, 219, 221, 226, **232–3**, **237–8**, 240, 247, 252
  Netherlands/Dutch East Indies, 3, 5, 14, 27–8, 41, 67, **74–81**,
Indonesian Archipelago, 137
Indonesian Central Bank, 114
Indonesian Institute for Sciences, 254
industrial estates, 240, 241
industrial revolution/s, 64, 65
industrialization, viii, x, 32, 37, 38, 49, 58, 66, 70, 88, 91, 92, 106, 123–6, 186, 210, 221, 227–8, 229
  export-oriented (EOI), 55, 62, **94–5**, 107–8, 109, 114, 116, 123, 125, 138, 182, 209, 212, 241
  import-substitution (ISI), **93–5**, 102, 107–8, 111, 113, 115, 119, 122, 124, 138, 209, 229
inequality, viii, ix, 1, 49, 54, 88, 89, 94, 140, 141, **156–7**, 158, 160, 253
informal sector, 229, 232, 233, 234, 235
infrastructure, 93, 116, 122, 143, 229, 230, 245
inheritance, 205, 208
Institute of Malaysia and International Studies, 254
institutions, 35, 51
insurrection/insurgency, 80, 147–8, 149, 150, 154, 159
intelligentsia/intellectuals, 98, 112, 115, 118, 125, 136
intermarriage, 13, 131, 138, 145
international financial markets, 167
International Labour Organization (ILO), 94, 232–3
International Monetary Fund (IMF), 94, 116
international terrorism, 252
investment, 60, 70, 73, 79, 81, 88, 94, 111, 114, 116, 119, 122, 169, 185
Ireland, 58

Irian Jaya (West Papua, Western New Guinea), xix, 5, 17, 30, 80, 132
irrigation, 10, 11, 54, 67–8, 78, 227
Islam/Muslims, 4, 6, 10–12, 40, 79, 82, 97, 111, 114, 132, 134, 137, 138, 143, 150, 151, 180, 189, 192–4, **205–6**, 207, 214, 218, 233, 238, 240
    Islamic law, 178–9, 208
    Muslim-Malay Monarchy (NBD), 31, 93
Islamic Youth Movement of Malaysia, 206

Jakarta/Batavia, 8, 28, 114, 226, 227, 230, 233, 235, 236, **237–8**
    National Monument, Independence Square, 238
    West Irian monument, 237–8
jao pho (godfather), 175
Japan, 4, 8, 14, 15, 18, 41, 53, 62, 66, 71, 81, 152, 180, 184, 209, 255
Japanese Occupation, 4, 37, 71, 79, 88, 122, 146
Java, 7, 9–10, 12, 27, 43, 47, **53–4**, 63, 66, 67, **74–81**, 83, 89, 100, 111, 210, 214, 221, 227, 231, **232–3**
    Java War, 75
    Javanese, 137, 150
Johor, 211
joint ventures, 111, 116, 123, 124, 210, 239
Journal of Contemporary Asia (1971–), 106, 248

Kachin/s, 71, 72, 145, 146
    ~ Independence Army (KIA), 149
    ~ Independence Organisation (KIO), 148
Karen (Kayin), 71, 72, 145, 146, 147–8, 149
    ~ National Association (KNA, 1881), 147
    ~ National Defence Organization (KNDO), 148
    ~ National Liberation Army (KNLA), 149
    ~ National Union (KNU), 147, 149
Karenni (Kayah), 71, 145, 146, 148, 149
    ~ National Progressive Party (KNPP), 149
    ~ states, 146
Kejiahua, 137
Khmer Rouge, viii
Khmers, 227
kinship, 156, 158, 159, 163, 165, 184, 201, 204, 235
Klang Valley, 104, 226, 235
knowledge dependency, 21–2
Kokang (people), 149
KOMTAR project, 239
Korea, 18, 26, 62, 102, 181, 255
Kuala Langat, 213

Kuala Lumpur, 31, 142, 226, 235, 236, **238–9**
    International Airport, 238
    Petronas Towers, 238

labour, 8, 10, 65, 67, 68, 74, 78, 79, 80, 87, 116, 135, 136, 159, 184, 185, 219, 227, 243
    ~ force/workforce, 202, 214, 229, 230
    ~ services, 83, 84, 85, 157; corvée, 75, 76, 78
    see also wage labour
Lahu Nationalist United Party (LNUP), 149
land, 8, 11, 54, 58, 65, 66–70, 72, 75–8, 80, 81, 83, 85, 86, 93, 117–18, 121, 124, 135, 159, 205, 213, 228, 236, 240–2
    ~ reform, 80, 88, 111, 112
    ~ rent system (Java), 75–6, 77, 78
Land Alienation Act (Burma, 1941), 69
landed class/es/landowners, 111, 113, 115, 117–20, 164, 166, 230
landlessness, 53, 77, 78, 84, 85, 88–90, 92, 143, 156, 157, 166, 175, 218, 230
landlords/landlordism, 87, 138, 158, 166
language, 6, **16–17**, 33, 82, 89, 129, 131, 133, 135, 137, 141, 146, 152, 182, 202
Laos (Lao People's Democratic Republic), viii, ix, xii, xv, xvii, xviii, 3–5, 10, 14–16, 25, 49, 67, 93, **134**, 159, 163–4, 176, 217, 252, 254
late development effect (Dore), **52–3**
Latin America, 2, 3, 15, 18, 22–3, 39, 44, 56, 60, 61, 64
law, 9, 76, 142, 219, 174, 178–9, 180, 203, 208, 219
    ~ and order, 83, 102, 104, 117
Liberal Period (Netherlands East Indies), 76
liberalization, 26, 159, 167, 171, 238, 250
licences, 113, 139, 164, 167
life expectancy, xvii
lifestyle, 129, 155, 199, 224, 230, 242, 253, 255
literacy, xvii, 218
literature, xv, 2–3, 91, 253, 255
living standards, viii, 94, 96, 235
loans, 111, 112, 113, 118, 122
local government, 83, 84
Lombok, 79
loyalty/disloyalty, 158, 159, 165, 172
lumpenbourgeoisie (Frank), 60
Luzon, 82, 86, 88

Madagascar, 16, 17
Madura, 80
    Madurese, 137

Makassar/Ujung Pandang, 233, *268*
Malabar, 138
Malacca/Melaka, 3, 6, 138, 227, 239
   Chittys, 138
   sultanate, 10, 11, 12, 227
Malay-Indonesian world, 10
Malaya, 3, 13, 14, 67, 92, 135, 137
   Malay states, 5
   Malayan Emergency, 14, 30, 136
   ~ Peninsula, 13, 66, 135
   ~ Union, 136
Malayalees, 137–8, 150
Malays, 31, 129–30, 135, 136, 137, 138, 139,
   140, 141–3, 144, 150, 169, 170, 171,
   192–3, 227, 235, 239, 241, 249
Malaysia, viii, ix, xii, xv, xvii, xviii–xix, 3, 4, 13,
   14, 16, 23, 25, 27, **31**, 38, 48, 55, 92–5, 99,
   102–4, 108, **135–44**, 150, 151, 156, **168–71**,
   175, 176, 180, 182, 186, 192, 193–4, 200, 202,
   204, **206–7**, 209, 212, 214, 218, 220–1, 226,
   235, 236, **238–40**, 244, 247, 249, 252
   Ministry of Finance, 170
   Ministry of Trade and Industry, 170
Malay(si)an Chinese Association (MCA), 138
Malay(si)an Indian Congress (MIC), 138
male–female equality, **203–9**
Malilipot (Bicol region, Luzon), **222–3**
Malolos Constitution (1899), 86
Maluku, 132
Mandalay, 67, 71, 144
Manila, 27, 41, 82, 84–8, 102–3, 164, 210,
   226, 227, 230, 234, 235, 236
manufacturing, viii, 53, 64, 74, 89, 94,
   110–11, 113, 118, 119, 122, 123, 124, 136,
   138, 139, 209–11, 218, 233, 235
marketing, 204, 218
market/s, 58, 59, 66–7, 69, 75, 76, 120, 122,
   123, 210,
   market, the, 8, 51, 65, 158, 225, 231, 233, 250
   ~ capacity (Weberian notions), 101
   ~ economy/~ forces, 77, 93, 134, 167, 189,
   213
   ~ -trading, 202, **223**
marriage, 211, **214**, 219, 221
Marriage Act (Indonesia, 1974), 207
martial law (Philippines, 1972–81), 52, 117–18
Marxism, xii, 6, 8, 23, 27, 54, 56, 59, 61, 106,
   248
Marxism-Leninism, 187
Massachusetts Institute of Technology, 27
Mataram, 9, 63
materialism, 184, 194

matrilocal post-marital residence, 204–5
means of production, 65, 95, 96, 101, 109,
   127, 140
media, 26, 132, 133, 150, 182, 184, 208, 221,
   226, 230, 250, 253, 255
mercantilism, 11, 60, **63–4**, 74
merit, 48, 172, 179
meritocracy, 152, 251
mestizos, 81, 85, 86, 88–9, 90, 115, 119
   mestizo cultures (Wertheim), 131
Mexico, 82
middle class, 44, 52, 72, 76, 81, 96–9, **102–3**,
   105, 108, 114–22, 124–7, 133, 139–42,
   170, 182, 199, 201, 206–9, 217, 219, 224,
   232, 233, 239, 243, 250, 253
   see also new middle class
Middle East, 2, 3, 4, 10, 12, 17, 116
middle forces (Pinches), 104
migration, 201, **217–21**, 254
   see also rural–urban migration
military
   coups, 44, 50, 72, 124, 126, 148, 173, 252
   officers, 99, 166, 252
   rule/dictatorship, ix, 23, 73, 80, 173, 109
Minahasan (Sulawesi), 223
Minangkabau, 137, 208
Mindanao, ix, xix
minerals, 88, 112
mines, 66, 135, 136
minorities, 131, 147
mode of production, 57–8, 61, 106
Modern Indonesia Project (Cornell), 27
modern patrimonialism (Eisenstadt), 51
modernism, 232
   reactionary, **189–91**
modernity, xi, 110, 238, 239, **189–91**, **246–55**
modernization/ modernization theory,
   viii, x–xi, 1, 7, 8, 14, 17–18, 20, 24, 26–8,
   30–3, 35, **37–55**, 56, 57, 58, 60, 81, 93, 94,
   99–100, 106, 108, 121, 122, 130, 142, 157,
   161, 163, 178–80, **181–6**, 191, 192, 194, 201,
   206, 207, 224, 233, 237, 244, **246–7**, 248
Modjokuto (Java), 47
Moluccas, 76
monarchy, 67–8, 120, 121, 134, 141, 144, 150,
   172, 177, 237
   Muslim-Malay (NBD), 31, 93
money economy, 219
money laundering, 163–4
money politics, 115, 168
money-lenders, 13, 69, 77

monopoly, 59, 110, 113, 114, 119, 122, 143, 166, 167, 168
~ capitalism, 63, **65–6**
Mons, 16, 145, 146, 148, 149
Monsoon Asia, 5
moral economy (Scott), xii, 105
patron–client relations, **157–9**
morals, 181, 188, 189
Moro Islamic Liberation Front, ix
mosque/s, 237
Muda Irrigation Scheme (Kedah), **217–18**
multi-disciplinary perspective, **20–1**, 248, 253
multi-racialism, 240
Multimedia Super Corridor (Kuala Lumpur), 238
multinational corporations, 63, 108–9, 170, 209, 212, 213
multiple modernities (Eisenstadt), 50
multiple society (Nash), 45
multiracialism, 151–2, 242
Myanmar, *see* Burma

Nabas (Panay), **222–3**
Nam Viet/Nan Yueh, 3, 8
Nan-Hai (Southern Sea), 8
Nan-Yang ('southern' region reached by sea), 8
nanyo/nampo (Japanese), 8
narratives, 135, 136, 139, 248
see also discourse
nation-bearing segment (Nash), 45
nation-building/nation state 4, 14, 16, 18, 29, 30, 31, 33, 35, 45, 46, 50, 51, 62, 93, 129, 133, 134, 150, 154, 164, 183, 193, 225, 228, 240, 244, 246, 247–8
National Alliance/National Front (Malaysia), 138
national culturalism (Wee), 150, 153–4
national identity, 110, **133–5**, 151, 182–3, **220–1**, 225, 238, 240, 244, 245, 249, 250, 252
see also identity
National Progress Party (Philippines), 87
national security, 124, 240
national symbolism, 133, 153–4, 237
nationalism, 41, 66, 74, 89, 93, 96, 115, 122, 126, 133, 134, 146, 149, 166, 185, 191, 192, 207, 225
Nationalist Union (Philippines), 87
nationalization, 72, 73, 80, 93, 148
nature/culture dichotomy, **198–9**
Nederlandsche Handel-Maatschappij (NHM), 75

neo-colonialism, 57, 89
neo-liberalism, 154
neo-Marxism, x, 32, 33, 29–30, 35–6, **56–7**, 130, 135
Neolithic revolution, 16–17
nepotism, 126, 163, 167, 170, 191
Netherlands, x, 74, 75, 77, 89, 248
Department of Colonies, 76
Dutch East Indies, *see* Indonesia
Parliament, 76
see also W.F. Wertheim
networks, 155, 156, 164, 165, 166–7, 169, 172, 175, 176, 235, 241
patron–client relations, **159–60**
New Economic Policy (Malaysia, 1970–90), 138–9, 143, 169, 170, 171, 235
new middle bourgeoisie (Anderson), 122
new middle class, **100–5**, 117, 250
see also proletariat
new oligarchs (Stauffer), 118
New People's Army, 116
new rich, ix, 17, 100, 101
new social forces, 125
New Society (Marcos), 118
new society (Singapore), 242
New York: Population Council, 253
newly-industrializing countries, 55, 62, 107, 254
nickel mining, 218–19
Nicobar Islands, 16
non-farm activities, **217–21**, 230
non-governmental organizations (NGOs), 126, 127, 140
norms, 161, 162

Occidentalism, 179
oil, 15, 72, 79, 81, 108, 111, 112, 113, 114, 117, 138, 166, 167
oil palm, 79
oligarchy, 162, 167
oligopoly, 143, 171
Orang Asli/Malayan Aborigines, 16, 137
organic statism, 181
organized labour, 114, 125, 126, 127
Oriental despotism (Marx), 10
orientalism, 7, 24, 31, 33, 179
othering process, 31, 129, 131, 147, 153, 190
Outer Islands (Indonesia), 66, 77, 78, 79, 80, 89–90
outworking, 210, 212

Pacific Asia, 156
Pacific Ocean, 3, 6, 13–14, 16, 17
pacto de retrovendendo (cash crop contract), 85
Padang (Sumatra), *259, 267*
Pagan, 9, 67
Palaung, 145
Palembang-Jambi, 79
Pancasila, 182–3
Pao, 148
Pao Nationalist Movement (PNM), 149
pariah entrepreneurs (Riggs), 156, 169, 170
parliaments, 76, 86, 87, 126, 175
paternalism, 158, 174
patih (regents), 78
patriarchy, 189, 205–6, 207, 217, 220
patrimonial bureaucracies (van Leur)/patri-
    monialism (Weber), 10, 12, 63, 115, 121,
    157, 163, 165, 169, 170, 176
patron–client relations/dyads, xi, 28, 29, 92,
    113, 121, 141, 154, 155, , **156–61**, 165–7,
    171, 172–3, 175, 176
    see also clientelism
patronage, xi, 1, 46, 49, 51, 62, 77, 111, 112, 119,
    124, 127, 128, 140, 144, 145, **155–77**, 252
pattern variables (Parsons), 41
peasantry/peasants, xii, 11, 12, 33, 42, 45, 52,
    53, 58, 69–71, 73, 75–80, 86, 88, 89, 99,
    100, 105, 112, 118, 139, 157, 159, 166, 230,
    231, 232
Pegu, 67
Pekengede (Bali), 223
Penang/Pinang, 3, **239–40**
Penang Eurasian Association (PEA), 239
people power, 103, 120, 252
People's Action Party (PAP), 23, 151, **240–4**,
    251
pepper, 76, 79
permanent transition (Geertz), 47
permissiveness, 183–4
Pertamina, 166
Philippine Commission, 87
Philippine Revolution (1898–9), 86
Philippine Sociological Review, 24, 28
Philippines, ix, xii, xv, xvii, xix, 3, 4, 6, 10–17
    passim, 25–7, **28–9**, 48, 49, 52, 66, 67,
    81–9, 90, 92–4, 95, 97, 100–5, 108, **115–20**,
    128, 132, 147, 156, 159, **161–2**, 164, 176, 182,
    192, 197, 204, 209, 210, 212, 215, 216, 217,
    220, 221, **222–3**, 226, 244, 247, 252
Phnom Penh, 13, 226
plantations, 78, 79, 80, 87, 135, 139
Plassey (1757), 64

plural society/pluralism (Furnivall), xii,
    7–**8**, 13, 31, 71, 73, 74, 129, **132–3**, 134,
    135, 137, 151, 182, 227, 229, 240, 248
pluralism, xi, 227, 229
población (small town), 83
political economy/economists, xi, xii, 18, 23,
    24, 25, 26, 27, 32, 33, 35, 48, 51, 54, 57,
    58, 61–2, 73, 87, **91–128**, 130, 167, 168,
    170, 177, 231, 247–51, 253, 255
political parties, 159, 160, 164, 168, 172, 174,
    175, 182
political stability, 122, 182–3
politicians, 162, 164, 166, 169, 173, 196
politico-bureaucrats, 100, 113, 114, 165–8
politics, 20, 47–8, 140, 142, 164, 165, 168,
    174, 175, **186–7**, 190, 197, 198, 204, 205,
    208, 248, 249, 250, 252, 253
'politics of representation', 249
polo (draft labour), 84
population, viii, xvii, 8, 40, 69, 79, 89, 229
    ~ growth, 68, 78, 185, 241
ports, 12, 13, 66, 85, 228
Portugal, 6
positivism, 24, 28, 184
post-colonial/independence era, 37, 72, 92,
    109, 112, 130, 135, 136, 138, 139, 145, 148,
    169, 201, 222, 227, **229**
post-modernity/modernism, xii, 130, **248–53**
post-war era (1945–), 2, 10, 14, 17, 25, 27,
    29, 30, 32, 33, 35, , **37–55**, 60, 72, 79, 80,
    92–3, 106, 115, 117, 122, 123, 133, 155, 171,
    225, 228, 246, 248
poverty, viii, 49, 73, 78, 88, 93, 118, 136, 161,
    229, 254
power, 1, 35, 52, 91, 109, 110, 112, 139, 143,
    144, 155, 157, 158, 160, 161, 163, 165, 166,
    167, 172, 176, **203–4**, 208, 229, 231
power elite, 95, 99, 100, 127
Presidential Assistance (Indonesia), 166
Presidential Instruction (Indonesia), 166
prestige, **97**, 175, 229
priests, 81, 82, 83, 84, 86
primary products, viii, 120, 135, 138
primordialism (Geertz), 131
principalia (elite/nobility, Philippines), 84–8
private property, 65, 102, 117, 127
private versus public spheres, 197, **198–9**,
    201–3
private sector, 76, 123, 139, 162, 236
privatization, 119, 143, 171, 250, 252
priyayi (Javanese elite/nobility), 78
production, 144, 179, 197, 198

profit/s, 42, 47, 60, 70, 82
proletariat, 58, 95, 97, 99, 139, 166
  see also working class
property, 101, 203, 238
prostitution, **215–17**, 229
protest, 34, 50, 71, 80, 85–6, 88, 105, 114,
  120, 125, 126, 158, 206
Protestant ethic, 40, 186, 187, 195
pseudo-urbanization, 229
psychology, **45–6**, 49
public sector, 162, 167, 229
pueblo (municipal township), 83, 84
Putrajaya, 238

quasi-groups (Evers), **98**, 159

race, 16, 17, 65, 131, 135, 199
racism, 161
rationalism, 179
rationality, 37
raw materials, 57, 59, 64, 65, 66, 88, 210,
  222, 228
reciprocity, **157**, 158, 174, 235
Red River (Songkoi) Delta, 8
reformasi (reformation [movement]), 103
'regnant paradigm' (McVey), 31, 32, 246
religion, 31, 42, 44, 81–3, 112, 129, 131, 132,
  137, 142, 146, 178, 179, **191–5**, 198, **205–6**,
  251, 253, 255
remittances, 70, 235
rent, 243
Rent Control Act (Penang) (1948), 239–40
rent-seeking, 113, 114, 120, 159, 164, 167,
  168–9, 171
rentier state, 31
repression, ix, 125, 126, 135, 156, 191
resettlement, 139, 242–3
  transmigration, 8
retailing, 13, 119, 136, 139, 230, 233, 238,
Revolutionary Council (Burma), 148
rice, 10, 13, 54, 66, **67–8**, 70–2, 78, 80, 82,
  85, 120, 175, 217, 218, 222, 227
rioting/riots, 71, 114, 138–9, 142, 143, 146
risk, 42, 43
robber baron capitalism (Robison), 167
Rome, 237
Royal Dutch/Shell, 79
rubber, 13, 15, 66, 67, 79, 135, 136
ruling class, 96, 97, 99, 128, 140, 143, 156
rumah kilat (lit. 'lightning house', rapidly
  erected, makeshift house), 236

rural areas, xi, 43, 69, 98, 112, 118, 121, 122,
  126, 135, 141, 206, 218, 224, 232, 254
rural–urban migration, 142, 217, 218, 225–7,
  229–31, 234, 244, 245

Sabah/North Borneo, 3, 5, 30
sakdina (social rank system, Thailand), 67,
  120, 121, 172
Salatiga (Java), 233
sanctions, 163, 165, 190
sangha (Buddhist monkhood), 144–5
santri ('student'/'follower', pious Muslims,
  Java), 47
Sarawak, 3, 5, 30
Sarekat Islam, 80
sawbwas (Shan leaders), 148
scholars (indigenous), **21–9**
secessionism, 72, 132, 148
service sector, 96, 113, 218, 229, 233, 235, 236
sex tourism, **215–17**
sexuality, 199, 206–7, 212, 224, 253
Shan States, 16, 146
  Shan Hills, 147
  Shan State Independence Army (SSIA,
    1958–), 148, 149
  Shans, 71, 72, 145, 148, 149
sharecroppers/sharecropping, 78, 85, 230
Siem Reap, *258*
silver, 64, 82
Singapore, ix, xi, xii, xv, 2–4, 8, 13, 14, 16,
  18, 21, 23, 25, 30, **31**, **38**, 48, 49, 55, 92,
  93, 94, 99, 101, 103, 107, 108, 134, 135,
  150–4, 181, 182, **183**, 186, 188, 190, 200,
  212, 225–7, 236, **240–4**, 247, 251, 254
  Institute of Southeast Asian Studies, 254
Sino-Tibetan language family, 16
slavery, 64, 83
slums, 232, 234, 236, 241
small-scale production and trade (women),
  221–3
small-holders/smallholdings, 66, 78, 79, 84,
  89, 118
social
  action: Asian values, **178–96**
  change, 2, 8, 28, 29, 32, 34, **37–55**, 182
  class, *see* class
  conflict, 35, 50
  engineering, 169, 244
  mobility, 96, 97, 223, 230
  organization, 2, 35
  structure, 20, 34, 38, 43, 64, 70–1, 91, 92,
    95, 101, 110

socialism, 6, 14, 26, 39, 41, 49, 58, 62, 66, 73, 134, 190, 199
Socialist Front (Singapore), 241
Socialist Republic of Union of Burma, 72
socialization, 46, 100, 208, 213, 221
society, viii, 12, 33–4, 39, 40–1, 42, 45, 50, 54, 60, 74–5, 76, 81, 85, 86–7, 91, **129–54**, 157, 166, 208, 247
socio-culture, **15–17**
sociological context, x, xi, 12, **20–36**
sociology, ~ of Southeast Asia, vii, x, xi, xvi, **1–3, 21–4**, 40, **43–9, 67–89**, 110–27, **135–54**, 155, **164–76**, 181, 246, 247, 248, **253–5**,
solidarity (mechanical/organic) (Durkheim), 40
Soroako (Sulawesi), **218–19**
South Asia, 2, 3, 15, 18, 22
South China Sea, 13, 18
Southeast Asia, viii, ix, xvii, **1–36, 92–5**, **98–110**, 198, 225, 226, 227,
Southeast Asia (journal, Southern Illinois University), 30
Southeast Asia Command, 14
Southeast Asian Studies, 14
Spain, 6, 66, 82, 85, 89
spices, 12, 59, 64, 82
spirit of capitalism (Weber), 42
spirit possession, 215, 212
squatters, 232, 234, 235, 236, 241
Sri Lanka, 17
Srivijaya, 9, 11, 63, 227
stages of economic growth (Rostow), 39, 41
state, the/state power 10, 22, 35, 48, 62, 64, **65**, 67, 70, 84, **91–128**, 112–13, 125, 131, **133–5**, 138, 139, 140, 142, 151, 154, 155, 158–60, **163–5**, 166, 167–70, 173, 181, 195, 208, 226–7, 231, 238, 248–52 254
State Law and Order Restoration Council (SLORC), 73, 149
State Peace and Development Council (1997–), 73
state-led development, **206–9**
status, 1, 97, 103, 109, 141, 149, 172, 175, 201, **203–9**, 204, 219, 220, 224, 231, 234, 238
status groups, 95, 127
stereotypes, 137, 185, 190, 221
Straits of Malacca, 12
Straits Settlements, 5, 137
strategic groups (Evers), 34, 52, **98–100**, 102, 102, 109, 112, 127, 141, 232
stratification, **95**, 97, 141, 155

structural adjustment, **108–9**, 123
structural functionalism, 24, 26–8, 34, 48, 51, 95
structuralism, 33, 248
subjective pluralism (Nagata), 141
subsidies, 166, 169
subsistence, 85, 157–8, 223
~ agriculture, 67, 76, 78
Südostasien, 15
sugar, 64, 75–9, 81, 85, 87, 88, 94, 110, 117, 120
Sugar Law (1870), 76
Suharto regime, **110–15**
suicide, 242
Sulawesi, xix, 80, 90, 132, 223, 233
sultanates/sultans, 97, 135, 150
Sumatra, 5, 7, 9, 79, 80, 90

Tabanan (Bali), 47
Tai-Kadai language family, 16
Taiwan, 16, 17, 18, 62, 102, 182, 220, 221, 255
Tamils, 136, 137, 150
Taoism, 40
tariffs, 65, 88, 167
Tatmadaw (military government, Myanmar), 73
tax concessions, 109, 122
taxation, 67, 75–7, 83–6, 131, 173
tea, 75, 76, 79
tenants/tenantry, 78, 85, 87–9, 118, 157, 166, 230
Tenasserim, 67
Teochiu (ethnic group), 137, 150
terms of trade, 119, 223
territorial control/fixed borders, 66, 144
textiles, 64, 93, 94, 108, 113, 122, 138, 139, 209, 210, 233
Thai Rak Thai Party, 126
Thailand, viii, ix, xv, xvii, xviii, 2, 3, 4, 6, 10, 13, 16, 23, 25–7, **29–30**, 31, 48–9, 55, 57, 62, 66, 67, 71, 92, 93–5, 99, 100, 102–4, 108, **120–7**, 128, 132, 147, 149, 156, 158, 163–4, **171–6**, 193–4, 200, 202, **205**, **215–17**, 228, 245, 247, 249, 250, 252, 254
theory, vii, xii, 20, 26, 38, 60
timagua/timawa (freemen), 83
timber, 15, 72, 81, 85, 112, 120, 138
tin, 13, 15, 66, 135, 139, 136
tobacco, 64, 75, 76, 79, 85, 88, 93
tourism, 124, 230, 236, 238, 239, 240
trade, 8, 9–10, 11, 12, 59, 85, 227, 233
traders, 13, 70, 223

tradition/custom, 28, 42, 31, 57, 137, 179, 181
trafficking, 163–4
Training Schools, 78
transport, 65, 229, 230
tribal areas (Burma), 145
tribal peoples, 11, 33

underdevelopment/dependency, viii, x–xi,
 8, 12, 18, 20, 23, 24, 27, 29–30, 32, 35, 43,
 47, 49–50, 52–5, **56–90**, 91, 106–7, 109,
 110, 111, 115, 130, 133, 144, 155, 164, 250
underemployment, 212, 219, 234
unemployment, 114, 116, 124, 219, 234
unequal exchange, 65
United Kingdom, 6, 14, 21, 74, 89, 95, 144
United Malays National Organisation
 (UMNO), 136–44, 169, 170
United Nations, 6, 200
United States, vii, xv, 4, 6, 14, 15, 23, **24–32**, 33,
 39, 41, 43, 60, 62, 66, **86–8**, 89, 99, 106,
 122, 124, 178, 185, 190, 209, 248, 254, 257
 House of Representatives, 87
 Information Agency, 186
 Senate, 86
upper class, 85, 86, 88, 105, 115, 116, 118–20,
 133, 140, 141, 143, 158
urban areas/worlds, xi, xii, 13, 31, 70, 78,
 121, 133, 136, 145, 190, 206, 223, 224,
 225–45, 249, 251
 see also capital cities
urbanization, viii, x, xi, xvii, 1, 2, 31, 38, 206,
 226, 229, **231–4**, 244, 245, 247
usury, 178

values, 34, 35, 40, 41, 43, 46, 51, 91, 161, 162,
 178–96, 207, 214, 244, 246, 247
 see also Asian values; family: values;
 Western values
vandala (compulsory sale), 84–5
vested interests/interest groups, 127, 163, 238
 see also civil society
Vietnam, viii, ix, xii, xv, xvii, xviii, 3, 4, 5, 9,
 10, 11, 15, 16, 37, 49, 103, 126, 176, 187–8,
 190, 199, 210, 217, 245, 247, 252, 253, 254
Vietnam, 26, 93, 228
Vietnam War, 14, 25, 30
Vietnamization policy (Nixon), 30
village/s, 10, 40, 58, 75–6, 77, 78, 83, 84, 145,
 147, 202, 211, 225, 231, 241
village headmen, 78, 170
violence, ix, 115, 125, 132, 134, 150, 168, 204,
 252, 253

visita (visits by non-resident clergy), 82
vote-buying, 159, 160, 175, 176

Wa, 145, 149
Wa National Army (WNA), 149
wage labour, 58, 61, 66, 76, 77, 79, 80, 92, 98,
 112, 124, 127, 135, 202, 230
 see also workers
wages, 125, 202, 203, 222–3
Wanita UMNO, 204
Wat Thaalaat, 260
wealth, 141, 165, 172, 229
weapons of weak, xii
Weberian approach, xii, 2, 8, 11, 34, 101
wedana (district heads), 78
West, the, 15, 42, 43, 44, 49, 57, 60, 62, 63,
 64, 66, 93, 96, 97, 108, 130, 153, 161, 178,
 183, 184, 190, 210, 228, 250, 252
Western values, 38, 39, 151, 152, 156, 173, 179,
 180, 183, 187, 188
 see also Asian values; family: values
Westernization, 186, 214, 232
westoxification, x
women, xi, 100, 103, 125, 137–9, 153, 179,
 190, **197–224**, 235, 243, 244
 women in development paradigm, **200–1**
workers/labourers, 86, 118, 159, 230
 see also cheap labour; proletariat
working class, 118, 125, 133, 139, 243
 lower classes, 140, 142
 see also bourgeois
workplace, 184, 185
World Bank, 94, 116, 200
world system/s, 22, 63, 250
World War I, 15, 66
 inter-war era, 137, 189
World War II (Pacific War), 13–14, 71, 88
 see also post-war era
worldviews, 6, 40, 252, 253

xenophobia, 148, 221

Yangon, 5, 226
 Rangoon, 8, 68, 71, 144, 146, 227
Young Men's Buddhist Association (1906),
 145–6, 147
youth, 253, 254, 255

zakat and *fitrah* (tithe or alms and virtue in
 humanity in Islam), 194